Listening Perspectives
in Psychotherapy

A SERIES OF BOOKS
EDITED BY ROBERT LANGS, M.D.

THE FIRST ENCOUNTER: THE BEGINNINGS IN PSYCHOTHERAPY
William A. Console, M.D., Richard D. Simons, M.D., and
Mark Rubinstein, M.D.

PSYCHOANALYSIS OF CHARACTER DISORDERS
Peter L. Giovacchini, M.D.

TREATMENT OF PRIMITIVE MENTAL STATES
Peter L. Giovacchini, M.D.

A CLINICIAN'S GUIDE TO READING FREUD
Peter L. Giovacchini, M.D.

TECHNICAL FACTORS IN THE TREATMENT OF THE SEVERELY DISTURBED
PATIENT
Edited by Peter L. Giovacchini, M.D. and L. Bryce Boyer, M.D.

BETWEEN REALITY AND FANTASY: TRANSITIONAL OBJECTS AND
PHENOMENA
Edited by Simon Grolnick, M.D., and Leonard Barkin, M.D.,
with Werner Muensterberger, Ph.D.

SPLITTING AND PROJECTIVE IDENTIFICATION
James S. Grotstein, M.D.

EARLY DEVELOPMENT AND EDUCATION OF THE CHILD
Willi Hoffer, M.D.

STRESS RESPONSE SYNDROMES
Mardi J. Horowitz, M.D.

HYSTERICAL PERSONALITY
Edited by Mardi J. Horowitz, M.D.

BORDERLINE CONDITIONS AND PATHOLOGICAL NARCISSISM
Otto Kernberg, M.D.

OBJECT-RELATIONS THEORY AND CLINICAL PSYCHOANALYSIS
Otto Kernberg, M.D.

INTERNAL WORLD AND EXTERNAL REALITY
Otto Kernberg, M.D.

CHILDREN AND PARENTS: PSYCHOANALYTIC STUDIES IN DEVELOPMENT
Judith Kestenberg, M.D.

DIFFICULTIES IN THE ANALYTIC ENCOUNTER
John Klauber, M.D.

THE TECHNIQUE OF PSYCHOANALYTIC PSYCHOTHERAPY VOLS. I AND II
Robert Langs, M.D.

THE THERAPEUTIC INTERACTION 2 VOLS.
Robert Langs, M.D.

THE BIPERSONAL FIELD
Robert Langs, M.D.

THE THERAPEUTIC INTERACTION: A SYNTHESIS
Robert Langs, M.D.

TECHNIQUE IN TRANSITION
Robert Langs, M.D.

THE LISTENING PROCESS
Robert Langs, M.D.

Listening Perspectives
in Psychotherapy

Lawrence E. Hedges, Ph.D.

New York   **Jason Aronson**   *London*

Notes

Chapter 6 was first presented as a lecture to the Hoag Hospital Department of Psychiatry in 1973, revised for presentation to the Orange County Psychological Association in 1978, further revised for in-service training at Kaiser Permanente Department of Psychiatry in 1979, and first presented in this form at the Newport Center for Psychoanalytic Studies, November 1, 1980 (Hedges 1980b).

Chapter 7 was presented in a modified form at the Newport Center for Psychoanalytic Studies, November 1, 1980. The last section of this chapter (pages 93–98) was first presented at the Kohut Memorial Lecture sponsored by the Newport Center for Psychoanalytic Studies in Newport Beach, California, January 15, 1982.

Chapter 8 was first presented at the California Graduate Institute, April 25, 1980 and is dedicated to Mary E. Walker for her continued appreciation and enthusiasm in the development of these ideas.

Chapter 10 was first presented to the Southern California Kaiser-Permanente Medical Group, Department of Psychiatry, April 2, 1981.

Copyright © 1983 by Jason Aronson, Inc.

10 9 8 7 6 5 4 3 2 1

Library of Congress Cataloging in Publication Data

Hedges, Lawrence E.
  Listening perspectives in psychotherapy.

  Bibliography: p. 309
  Includes index.
  1. Psychoanalysis 2. Psychotherapy. 3. Listening.
I. Title. [DNLM: 1. Psychoanalysis—Methods. 2. Psycho-
analytic therapy—Methods. 3. Communication. WM 460
H453L]
RC504.H33   1982   616.89'17   82-13877
ISBN 0-87668-618-8

To Breta

*Whose love and understanding has created
the time, space, and freedom for my
continuing work.*

Contents

Foreword

It is with pleasure and some curiosity that I read Dr. Hedges' manuscript, *Listening Perspectives*, and accepted his invitation to write the foreword for this most interesting volume. My curiosity, at first perhaps more self-loving than it should be, centered around the question as to how much I, one of his teachers some years ago, contributed to his current views on psychoanalysis and psychotherapy. Of course, I thought I knew him well during that phase of his psychotherapeutic education, but in reading his book I discovered that we have much more in common. I suddenly discovered common roots of a kind that I never suspected. If one would only know one's students better!

Hedges was once a student of the philosopher Gustav Bergman at the University of Iowa. Bergman and I, he a little earlier than I, were students in Vienna and exposed to the *Wiener Kreis*, the school of philosophy that included such men as Moritz Schlick, Rudolf Carnap, and Herbert Feigl, all of whom were deeply influenced by Ludwig Wittgenstein. This school of philosophy was deeply concerned with *Meaning*. Its contributors such as Gustav Bergman investigated the meaning of philosophical and scientific theories and were concerned also with the *Meaning of Meaning*, the theme of many of the contributions of Bergman.

Wittgenstein and Freud shared the same cultural atmosphere in Vienna at the turn of the century, and in some way one might well say that both were concerned with meaning. This, of course, is the main task of the psychotherapist as he tries to understand the meaning of his patient's communications, may they be expressed in language, action, acting out, play, or even the language of silence.

The therapist must listen in order to capture the meaning of what the disturbed person is trying to convey to him. His task is to get the psychotherapeutic dialogue going. The author of this book is concerned with the different ways that one can listen to a patient. He speaks about the Listening Perspectives of the different therapeutic schools, and thus he is concerned not only with the system of communication of the patient but with the system of responding on the part of the psychotherapist; systems which sometimes hinder understanding and which sometimes make understanding possible.

I spoke once about the Tower of Babel in psychotherapy and psychology, referring to the different psychotherapeutic schools which have developed different languages and theories in order to make it possible for the therapist to listen and to understand. These theories are then the Listening Perspectives of the therapist, and each of these groups believes, of course, that its way of listening and therefore of responding and interpreting, is—if I may use a phrase of Freud's—"the royal road to the unconscious" of the patient. In this book, Dr. Hedges shows us how he has tried to identify himself with the Listening Perspectives of different schools—those that dominate Western psychotherapy—and shows the advantages of each Listening Perspective as well as its limitations. That pursuit, I believe, has only been possible for him because he once had Gustav Bergman as his teacher. Our philosophical education perhaps keeps us free of dogma and makes it possible for us only to temporarily overidentify with our psychotherapy teachers, and thus to learn from different schools without, one hopes, becoming eclectic.

My fantasy of a sequel to this book would be one concerned with the *Talking Perspectives* of the patients, their way of free association. It is my belief that each symptom, each emotional or mental illness, is in some way a Talking Perspective, a way of communicating, albeit a pathological way.

It follows then that the Listening Perspective would have to be one that was not completely bound by theory (which is no more than a disguised *method* of treatment), and some elasticity would have to be developed in order to match the therapist's Listening Perspective with the patient's Talking Perspective. This is not to overlook that the patient too has a Listening Perspective.

Elsewhere I have spoken about a battle whose goal is not to heal but to destroy—two different kinds of victory. I think of the gladiators in the Roman Colosseum who had to fight each other to the bitter end, unlike therapist and patient who struggle with each other until the task of healing, for which both are responsible, is accomplished. One of the gladiators fights with a short sword and a small shield, while the other gladiator uses a net and a trident. Each has a different method for attack and defense. Each must also know the other fighter's method of attack and defense. Such is psychotherapy: each Listening Perspective requires a special Interpreting Perspective. And this is true for both the patient and the therapist. Often therapy is experienced as a battle, full of transference and countertransference implications. Dr. Hedges, in studying the Listening Perspectives of therapists, has identified himself with the idea that one must sometimes change the Listening Perspective and also the interpreting, responding perspective.

The colleagues and students who read this volume will find that their ways of listening will deepen and their ways of responding will be improved, and thus they will find new value in building a bridge between psychoanalytic and psycholinguistic thinking.

Rudolf Ekstein, Ph.D.

Preface

The decade of the 1970's saw traditional psychoanalytic thought emancipated from its somewhat restricted adherence to powerful but narrow principles. Traditional clinical theory evolved out of the work of Freud, Jung, Rank, Adler, Klein and their colleagues or represented various branchings of the Ego Psychology of Anna Freud, Hartmann, Rapaport, Gill, and Schafer. The basic clinical teachings of others such as Rogers, Perls, Berne, and Moreno also relied heavily on the metapsychological and dynamic assumptions first enunciated by Freud.

This book is a result of a series of lectures which I developed over several years and represents a personal attempt to keep up with the rapid expansion of innovative ideas recently generated in the psychoanalytic community but not available elsewhere. The original lectures, somewhat modified here, were designed to familiarize practicing clinicians with the major trends and important thinkers of our time.

Any introductory survey of extensive subject matter necessarily suffers from the flaw of simplification. It has been my purpose to provide an overview of contemporary contributions. It has not been possible to attend systematically to the differentiated richness of the psychoanalytic tradition. As the book evolved, a number of my own ideas became included, with the result that the text alternates from survey material to sometimes difficult or complex original contributions.

A problem arose regarding how to *illustrate* the broad sweeps of contemporary psychoanalytic theory. Several choices had to be made. The time-honored method of illustration has been the comprehensive case study, of which I have included a few.

Another approach to illustrating theory has been to relate brief "vignettes" which are selected and synthesized for the purpose of illustration, and I have indeed used this method in several places. However, present purposes suggested another illustrative method. Advanced students and practicing clinicians for whom these lectures were originally prepared generally have an interest and curiosity about "how other people do it." One does not have to be very far into the practice of psychotherapy before one realizes that therapy and analysis are processes which reflect the highly individualized nature of spontaneous interaction between two living human beings. The human participants are endowed with special and unique personalities which inevitably influence the specifics of the clinical interaction. The problem in a consideration of the nature of therapeutic interaction becomes how to honor and include the unique stylistic aspects of the people involved while simultaneously extracting generalizable aspects of the interaction.

In responding to the illustrative challenge of this book, I have chosen to highlight therapeutic principles by presenting interactions of therapists and patients as recorded (from memory) by the therapists themselves, usually for purposes of consultation or case review. I then undertake a brief discussion of each clinical interaction for the purpose of applying theoretical considerations to the clinical encounter. The disadvantages of this approach are clearly: (1) the reader is exposed to information extraneous to the point under consideration, (2) the reader will have his/her own interpretations of the interaction which may be neglected in the discussion, and (3) theoretical remarks offered may do violence to the various meanings of the actual interaction, either by misplacing the focus as experienced by the patient or the therapist, or by misunderstanding or misstating the major trends of the actual therapeutic process for the purpose of didactic focus. Nevertheless, the clinical advantages of providing "raw" data from "live" interchanges seem to outweigh the problems, so this method of illustration predominates. No attempt has been made to "prove" or "validate" the illustrations. They stand simply as attempts to apply theory.

I hope that the *Listening Perspectives* approach serves to clarify a scientific and philosophical position which has long been developing in psychoanalysis. The "self and other" developmental schema offered here provides one important way of organizing ourselves for the crucial task of clinical listening.

Contributors

Deep appreciation is expressed to the friends and colleagues who have permitted their clinical and literary work to be incorporated into this book. Privacy, discretion, and literary license make it inappropriate to properly credit where credit is due. I have indicated in the text each time a contribution appears that was prepared by one of the writers below.

Mary Cook   Arlene Dorius   Jeanna Riley
Susan Courtney   David Garland   Mary E. Walker
Charles Coverdale Charles Margach

Acknowledgments

This book is a survey of contemporary psychoanalytic thought applied to a variety of clinical problems. The organizing concepts have been worked out over several years in conjunction with many others: students in classes, private seminars, and field placements; professional colleagues in consultation; and the people who come to the consulting room to tell about themselves. To these I owe a debt of gratitude and wish to express my thanks.

My undergraduate experience at Austin College taught me the value of the integration of ideas developed in diverse fields. My experience at the University of Iowa with Gustav Bergman, Leonard Eron, and Jane Anderson forms the backdrop of this book. My professional training was further moved along at the Institute of Living in Hartford, especially by David Hill, Adelaide Dollin, and Marvin Reznikoff. Barbara Carr, Rudolf Ekstein, Esther Lampl, Mortimer Meyer, Rocco Motto, and W. Marshall Wheeler provided the core of my training at the Reiss-Davis Child Study Center in Los Angeles. To these friends I am especially grateful. Also, thanks to John Moffat for his ongoing concern and contribution to my training experience.

A special word of recognition is due to David Eisenman and his staff at the Mardan Center for Educational Therapy in Costa Mesa, California. For ten years we have arranged ongoing consultation seminars, and many of the ideas put forward here have emerged from my discussions with the teachers and therapists at Mardan.

Special appreciation goes to Hedda Bolger, Barbara Carr, Rudolf Ekstein, James Grotstein, Burton Lasker, and Lars Lofgren, who graciously consented to review various portions of the manuscript and were most helpful in offering suggestions and raising crucial questions. It was Michael Russell whose tutoring in philosophy helped me rethink and reformulate my ideas in a more coherent and sensible form.

The person who more than any other is to be credited with the ideas and human understanding which made this book possible is Mary E. Walker, a counselor and play therapist at the Mardan Center.

Marvin Koven, Jordan Packer, and Ethel Deitshman at the California Graduate Institute have provided continuing interest and support. Most of the material from this book was first presented in a lecture series delivered at the California Graduate Institute in the spring of 1981.

Thanks goes to those who have, at times on an almost daily basis, shared the work of preparing and assembling the manuscript from assorted bits of paper, restaurant napkins, cassette tapes, and various other scribblings: Carolyn Milhem, Susan Venable, Lynn Van Sweden, Annette Packer, and Joani Haws.

Thanks also to Nomi Morelli, Ray Calabrese, Robert Van Sweden, Christopher Murphy, and Milton Olsen for help in preparing the final manuscript. Joan Langs, Robert Langs, and Jason Aronson have provided the enthusiasm for putting my ideas into final book form.

Introduction

Sophisticated listening involves the attainment of a subjective grasp of the private experience of another person based on careful and empathic observation of that person's words and actions. Psychotherapists cultivate the art of listening because people feel they benefit from having their words and actions understood. Serious attempts to comprehend the private experience of others have given rise to many different ideas about the mind and its workings. Psychological theories are usually framed to focus attention on what become defined as mental events, processes, structures, transactions and so forth. What often becomes obscured is an awareness of the extent to which the subjective frame of reference of the listener determines what is to be heard. That is, we hear that which we are prepared and able to hear.

In the century since Freud and Breuer first opened their own listening processes to complex, private experience in *Studies on Hysteria*, many styles and devices for increasing one's listening potency have been developed. The resulting "schools" of psychology and psychoanalysis can be defined effectively in terms of what features of private experience are considered consistently discernable and worthly of attention. The existence of many well-conceived but contrasting schools of thought suggest that the various psychological theories serve primarily as Listening Perspectives through which one person can approach a grasp of the private experience of another.

The clinical usefulness of psychological theories as listening devices is uncontested, but *which* theories, approaches, assumptions, or perspectives are considered most useful has become highly controversial. The thesis of this book rests on the idea that each school of thought has successfully defined crucial features of private experience. Each school has delineated concepts and techniques which encourage the elaboration of personal meanings along various subjectively helpful lines. Uncritical ecclecticism destroys the unique and powerful contribution which each style of listening has to offer. The emerging problem has become one of how to integrate the crucial contributions of many into a comprehensive and consistent framework while avoiding the pitfall of dilution through eclecticism.

The unifying idea to be presented in this book is that when considering a *listening context,* various psychological approaches possess differential effectiveness in bringing into focus different aspects of the human developmental

1

experience. The major psychological schools can thus be viewed as Listening Perspectives for grasping unique and private experience which is, to a greater or lesser extent, characteristic of various levels or stages of development of the human relatedness potential. This book will illustrate four distinctly different styles of listening that have emerged in psychoanalysis. It will survey the contributions of many and explore the possibilities of each Listening Perspective as a separate *mode* of psychoanalytic inquiry.

PART

I

Listening Perspectives as Clinical Frames of Reference

1

"Self and Other" Psychology

> The aspects of things that are most important for us are hidden because of their simplicity and familiarity. (One is unable to notice something— because it is always before one's eyes.) The real foundations of his inquiry do not strike a man at all. Unless *that* fact has at some time struck him. And this means: we fail to be struck by what, once seen, is most striking and most powerful.
>
> Ludwig Wittgenstein
> *Philosophical Investigations* I:129

Freud's studies of neurosis and dreams opened the 20th century with a startling new concept of man. Bridging the gap in the longstanding nature-nurture controversy, Freud took a somewhat balanced position in asserting the preeminence of a third force, the developing inner world. Freud held that crucial dimensions of man's inner world were developed and crystalized in the first few years of life. Basic attitudes and expectations established during these early years were thought to determine various significant aspects of later emotional life.

It is no mere historical accident that the psychoanalytic movement owes its origin to the general atmosphere in turn-of-the-century Vienna. The cultural and intellectual climate made possible Freud's amalgamation of a Talmudic tradition of scholarship, discipline, and meditation with an emerging Germanic metaphysical, philosophical, and scientific outlook which was deeply rooted in Socratic principles and the healing tradition of Hippocrates.

Following Freud's beginnings, psychoanalytic thought witnessed a major florescence between the European wars. This was interrupted by the diaspora forced by the Hitler regime, the death of Freud, and the waning interest in an exclusively Id Psychology based on Freud's early doctrine of wish fulfillment.

A postwar Anglo-American revival provided a second florescence of psychoanalytic thinking led chiefly by Anna Freud, Ernst Kris, Edith Jacobson, Erik Erikson, and Heinz Hartmann. The focus was shifted to a study of ego-superego concerns. Ego Psychology, as it was called, was not envisioned as replacing Id Psychology but rather as subsuming the earlier work within a broader theoretical framework and more encompassing clinical technique. Virtually all modern psychotherapies have been derived in one way or another from a combination of interests in the id and ego aspects of personality and how these can be elaborated in order to expand the fabric of personality in relation to the world.

The clear emergence of a new wave of psychoanalytic thinking marked the decade of the 1970s, though many of its conceptual origins date from much earlier. The third paradigm of psychoanalysis stems from more contemporary philosophical and metapsychological positions and represents an elaboration of concepts related to the differentiation and individuation aspects of early human development. This new wave of psychoanalysis moves toward a more careful use of language and a more thorough study of the adaptive context of the psychotherapeutic situation. The new studies focus on:

1. The origins, transformations, and organizational functions of experiences of self.
2. The gradual emergence of contrasting experiences of others.
3. The differentiations and integration of the affective aspects of self and other experiences as they relate to features of the real world.
4. Ultimately, the decisive influence very early development exerts on the later emergence and waning of the oedipal situation.

This new wave or third paradigm of psychoanalysis encompasses a wide range of theoretical concepts and a diversity of innovative treatment techniques. The new approaches center around an awareness of expectable developmental sequences in which the early experiences of self shift in relation to an expanding awareness of others. The self-other experiential base or patterning, once achieved, is thought to influence subsequent interpersonal relationships through an endless repetition or a search for some form of emotional experience which replicates (in the world) the internal patterning laid down by early self-other experience. The "Self and Other" approach to psychoanalysis holds forth new possibilities for treating more seriously disorganized persons than has been believed possible with previously available concepts and techniques. "Self and Other" Psychology has far-reaching implications for issues of child rearing, marriage, and family life, and most other forms of significant human interactions. The "Self and Other" approach promises perhaps for the first time, systematic therapeutic access to the most archaic aspects of the human personality and offers an expanded vision of man and his interpersonal relationships.

EXPERIENTIAL PSYCHOANALYSIS

Psychotherapy and psychoanalysis represent specific ways persons come to know one another and themselves. Psychoanalytic interaction is generally undertaken for the purpose of promoting growth and development. As with most forms of human growth, a person wishing to expand his or her knowledge calls upon another whose experience and knowledge in the area is presumed greater. Although, as every teacher knows, it is by one's pupils one must be taught! Psychoanalysis differs from other forms of human education in that there is no prescribed body of knowledge or experience to be gained. Rather, the subject of one's study is the unique way in which one experiences life.

Psychoanalysts, beginning with Freud, have attempted to concretize and schematize not only the nature of the psychoanalytic process but also, from the study of this process, the nature of man. Each school of psychoanalysis and psychotherapy has grasped special aspects of human experience common to many. Each has schematized those experiences either in terms of the nature of man and his interactions or in terms of the nature of the psycho-therapeutic task itself. Not only does each schema seem to reflect certain aspects of human experience, but schemas and theories also reflect the point of view or perspective of the theorist and therapist. For example, Freud's theory and technique of psychoanalysis was heavily influenced by a philo-sophical and scientific outlook which emerged with prestige and clarity toward the last part of the 19th century. Freud's ideas about psychoanalysis naturally reflected the somewhat mechanistic and materialistic point of view then in vogue. By way of contrast, Sartre expressed his views in a vocabulary and social bent popularized in an atmosphere of social despair which flourished in European thought following the Second World War. Sartre's psychoanalysis advocated a search for *personal* meaning in one's own intents and projects, an attitude that evolved in the wake of a general disillusionment with social structures and socially derived meanings.

Following these two examples, it could be shown that each existing school or approach to psychoanalysis and psychotherapy can be characterized in terms of the specific point of view which it has to offer on the nature of man and/or the nature of man's experience. Modern psychoanalytic thinking has come to place special emphasis upon the way in which the human mind *develops*. A developmental point of view of psychoanalysis and psycho-therapy requires that much of what has already been said be reformulated in a developmental vocabulary and also forces a focus on various types of developmental *experience.*

An experiential approach to developmental psychoanalysis is built around the presupposition that different stages or phases can be defined in the development of the human mind. It places special interest and emphasis upon understanding any particular person in terms of his or her special developmental experiences. Experiential psychoanalysis also acknowledges there are many ways in which the listener may hear and respond to the person who comes to the analyst expecting a growth experience. Thus, the analyst's own experience also becomes a focus of the study. The develop-mental or experiential psychoanalyst already has at his or her disposal a rich tradition of ideas about the stages or phases of emotional growth which are likely to be brought to the consulting room.

The purpose of this book is to review the four major phases of emotional growth that have been described in the psychoanalytic literature. Each of these phases of human psychological experience is characterized by certain features. Empathic contact with different phases of human development requires different Listening Perspectives or styles of responding. "Listening" is meant in the broadest sense of the word to include all forms of information received by the analyst and any responses by the analyst that indicate his or her receipt of that information. Clearly, one's ears represent only one means of listening. The four kinds of developmental experience, along with their corresponding Listening Perspectives, are based on developmental, experiential, and logical considerations. While the developmental phases as well as the Listening Perspectives frequently overlap, they are offered as an overall organizing and integrating framework for clinical theory and practice.

EXPERIENCES OF SELF AND OTHER

Human growth and development can be thought of as representing changes or shifts in the way a person differentiates experiences relating to a sense of self from experiences relating to a sense of others.[1] The specific way in which a person's subjective world may be thought of as organized may be grasped through a careful understanding of the unique subjective patternings of self and other experiences. These patternings are conceptualized as evolving through four broad phases or nodal points.

The earliest experiences of self and others have generally been thought to occur in an inconstant "oceanic" context or an inconstant "self-other matrix." Earliest organizational experiences seem to occur in terms of part-others (breasts, faces) and part-selves (hands, mouth) interacting in more or less mechanical, automated, or mysterious ways often beyond the sense of control of the organizing infant or adult. For persons functioning in a mode typical of this earliest phase, the corresponding Listening Perspective would focus upon organizational experiences of part-objects and part-selves acting and interacting in a more or less mystical, mechanical, chaotic, inconstant, or uncontrollable context which lacks meaningful and reliable reality and/or affect controls.

The next phase of human development has been characterized by the experience of a sense of merger or oneness between experiences of the self and the other widely referred to as "symbiotic." The corresponding Listening

[1]For the purposes of exposition in this book, the traditional term "object" is used synonymously with the term "other" to refer to important persons to whom the child, and later the adult, becomes attached.

Perspective would focus on the ways in which or the interactions through which the person experiences the merger or symbiotic other.

Subsequently the sense of self has been thought to separate and individuate from the symbiotic merger. The other comes to be recognized as an other but still responded to as though the other were still a part of (or were serving various functions of) the self. This has come to be called the experience of the "selfobject" It is at this level of development that the growing child, aware of the other, turns toward or derives from the other a sense of affirmation, confirmation, and comfort, which serves to *consolidate* the sense of self. The other is looked to as a source of comfort and relief from tension. As such, the other either is responded to as a part of a grandiose experience of self (some sort of a psychological reflection or twin) or becomes idealized for the purposes of completing or augmenting the sense of self. The corresponding Listening Perspective focuses on the way a person experiences tension relieving "selfobjects."

As human growth continues, others are thought to be slowly recognized as more or less separate centers of initiative with needs and motives independent of the sense of self. This latter achievement of human growth has been referred to as a period of self and object "constancy" in which the other is recognized as possessing, and tolerated for having, separate and different motivations and experience from the self. This level of human development emerges from the period widely referred to as "oedipal" which is characterized by the child's growing wish for special involvement with important others as well as his or her awareness of erotic and aggressive complications in triadic relationships. The corresponding Listening Perspective focuses on conflictual experiences of (oedipal, differentiated, separate) constant others. These four developmental phases accompany the evolution of human consciousness and nonconsciousness. As will be shown, nonconscious experience is differently understood and conceptualized at each developing phase of self and other differentiation.

These four phases of human experience correspond roughly to the four broad but familiar traditional diagnostic classifications: psychotic, borderline, narcissistic, and neurotic. The necessarily different psychotherapeutic approaches for each diagnostic classification might be conceptualized in a manner roughly analogous to the progressive unfolding processes of parenting or parental response in child development. One implication of this line of thinking would be that parent or therapist might commit a grave error in empathy if he or she were to respond to a child or other person who experiences the world in terms of part-objects or merger objects as though the child or person experienced the world in terms of separate objects. To understand the world of the infant or toddler in adult terms is, simply, to misunderstand. That children and patients turn away from parents and therapists who misunderstand them seems natural, appropriate and expectable. For a therapist to listen to a person in such a way as to assume that the person experiences the world at the developmental stage of object constancy might lead to various interpretations of internal conflict or resistance when the patient is attempting to express much more basic or earlier developmental experiences or needs. Differential response afforded by complementary Listening Perspectives holds forth a possibility for establishing and maintaining optimal empathic contact with persons presenting or expressing very different developmental phases of patternings of self and other experience.

INTROSPECTION AND INTERACTION

Within the psychoanalytic situation, it is generally assumed that persons express experiences of the world to the analyst or therapist. An adolescent or adult may use words while a child may use play. A therapeutic study of these expressions has often been referred to as the study of introspection through empathy (Kohut 1959). However, in persons presenting experiences of part-objects and merger objects, verbal and playful introspections are seldom the most effective forms of communication. Instead, actual interactions or enactments with the therapist are often more telling. In general, the higher the developmental phase attained, the more likely experiences will be expressed in verbal introspections or symbolic play. Conversely, the lower the developmental phase being expressed, the more likely experience will be communicated through interactions with or enactments involving the therapist. The most empathic therapists are open and available for various personal experiences to be communicated differentially through both introspective and interactive modes.

Careful listening also requires attention to the manifest as well as to the potentially latent content of all introspections and interactions, particularly with regard to the adaptive context of the psychotherapeutic relationship. The relative importance of latent and manifest content differs markedly depending upon the phase of developmental experience which the person brings to the consulting room. When the person expresses higher level conflicts and defense, the importance of understanding latent content will be heightened; whereas the expression of earlier developmental (e.g., merger) needs seldom requires so much or so complicated a manifest disguise.

The various clinical theories to be reviewed in this book will be considered in the context of Listening Perspectives for understanding and empathically responding to persons whose experiences of the world and response to life is limited to or unduly dominated by a particular developmental phase of self and other experience. Persons whose growth is arrested at earlier phases lack the freedom and richness which comes through considering and accepting the psychological separateness of others. On the other hand, personalities repressively organized in later phases of conflictual oedipal experience systematically deprive themselves of the richness, and spontaniety of the earlier, deeper, or less differentiated aspects of human experience. The therapist or therapeutic milieu capable of listening and responding in the broadest possible context provides the greatest potential for promoting emotional flexibility and expanding the domain of personality. This experiential approach to psychoanalysis sheds fresh light on old issues and raises new questions about current clinical theory and practice.

HISTORICAL OVERVIEW OF SELF AND OTHER PSYCHOLOGY

In 1950, Heinz Hartmann fostered a revolution within psychoanalysis by conceptually distinguishing between ego and self. The ego, having been traditionally conceptualized as an agency or structure of the psyche or as a set of functions within the mind, was seen by Hartmann to contrast with the self conceptualized as the evolving and integrating (subjective) center of the personality.

Sandler and Rosenblatt (1962), in studying the development of superego qualities in young children, traced the influence of others back to early memory traces and mental images. These "mental representations" of self and love objects along with their relations to each other came to be known as "the representational world."

In 1964 Edith Jacobson followed Hartmann's distinction with an elaboration of the integrating experiences of the self *in contrast* to evolving experiences of the world of love objects. Jacobson placed "the world of the self and the object" against the traditional framework of psychoanalysis, which had been built upon the idea of instinctual drives conflicting with other developing aspects of the personality (ego and superego) and reality.[2]

Margaret Mahler in 1968 formulated a theory, derived from her careful study of psychotic children which was later extended to a study of normal children and their mothers (Mahler, Pine, and Bergman 1975). This landmark theory of human symbiosis has provided a crucially different child development framework than had previously been available. Although her developmental schema was derived from a setting of child observation, Mahler explicitly formulated her theory as a set of *intrapsychic* experiences involved in human growth and development.

This emphasis on self and object experiences and on the separation-individuation of self experience from object experience has long been a subject of study by the "object relations" school of psychoanalysis led by

---

[2]Gedo (1979) points out that "self" is used by Hartmann and Jacobson in the sense of being opposed to the "not-me," a non-psychological definition, but that "self representation" refers to a system of memories. Gedo prefers "self organization" (p. 177f).

Melanie Klein. Otto Kernberg (1975, 1976, 1980) has drawn upon the ideas of ego psychology in order to make extensive elaboration on object relations theory within the framework of classical psychoanalysis. Kernberg follows Mahler in the separation-individuation sequencing and indeed revises her theory slightly to suit his own purposes. However, he still retains the metapsychological outlook of Freud, based upon the theory of instinctual drives in conflict with "higher" aspects of personality. Despite Kernberg's stated interest in the ideas of Jacobson, Sandler, and Mahler, his incisive theoretical contributions as well as his treatment approaches to borderline personality organization still rest heavily on the traditional Freudian metapsychological perspective. Heinz Kohut (1971, 1977, in press) has elaborated extensively what he calls the "Psychology of the Self." He has focused securely upon that stage of self and object differentiation in which the object is experienced as a part of the self for purposes of tension relief and the establishment of a sense of self cohesiveness.

This book will follow Jacobson's departure from Freudian metapsychology to develop a treatment approach and a line of intervention and interpretation based on Margaret Mahler's theory of symbiosis and the separation-individuation process of human development. The "self and other" approach to be offered is consistent with, but somewhat different in overall conceptualization from, object relations and classical psychoanalysis as well as the approaches of Kohut and Kernberg. Its general underpinning reflects the "self and other" revisionistic attitude espoused recently by Robert Stolorow, Frank Lachman, George Atwood, Jerome Oremland, John Gedo, and many others. It stems from the "revolution from within" started by Hartmann and developed by Jacobson, Sandler, and Mahler. This altered theoretical and clinical approach has evolved out of a much broader context which must now be specified.

THE TREATMENT APPROACH OF
SELF AND OTHER PSYCHOLOGY

A separation-individuation motif in psychotherapy and psychoanalysis requires first and foremost an emphasis on phenomenology. While Jacobson (1964) speaks of self and object "representations," she is quick to point out (p. 6) the term "representation" is *not* experiential but metapsychological—far removed from human experience.[3] A treatment approach for observing the contrasting and emerging *experiences* of self with various experiences of others requires a subjective phenomenological frame of reference. The term

[3]Michael Russell (personal communication) points out that the concepts of "self and object representations" might serve well to refer to organizing themes in one's life. However, to avoid the "divided mind" and Privileged Access pitfalls, one must use "self representation" more in the sense of a stance or attitude and less like something which can be an object of consciousness.

(mental) "representation" tends to obscure this emphasis. The phenomenological approach to be advocated here is based on considerations offered by Ryle (1949) and Wittgenstein (1953) as well as Sartre's contribution (1956) on the search for one's "original project" and Fingarette's emphasis (1969) on "spelling out" the nature of one's "engagement with the world."

The next general context of a treatment approach based on Mahler's theory would be a revised philosophy of science. Psychoanalysts from Freud forward have attempted to place psychoanalysis in various positions relative to the natural sciences. The use of the natural science model for psychoanalytic investigation has gradually given way to thinking of psychoanalysis in the context of an interpretive discipline involving the systematic study of introspective and interactional experience. What has lacked clarification so far is a crucial notion stemming from Mahler's developmental approach: *that each person coming for treatment lives a unique patterning of self and other experience characteristic of a certain phase of emotional development.* People in treatment might be thought of as having reached various plateaus of self and other differentiation or as having experienced arrests in the sequencing of the pre-symbiosis to separation-individuation experience. Persons who come for therapy with different developmental stages, or ways of experiencing self and others, necessarily experience the psychotherapeutic situation and the therapist in very different ways. Persons emotionally stuck or arrested at earlier levels will experience their therapist and communicate to their therapist in ways strikingly different from persons who have developed to later phases of self and object differentiation.[4]

The broadest context for conceptualizing psychoanalytic psychotherapy thus becomes a study of the way in which a therapist *listens* to the self and object experiences presented through the introspections and interactions of the person in treatment. A historical review of psychoanalysis suggests that four Listening Perspectives have evolved which represent distinctly different ways therapists have come to respond to or listen to persons who express different phases or nodal points of self and object differentiation.

An important nuance of this self and other developmental line of thinking is not only that these "phases" overlap but that consolidations at the earlier

---

[4]The manner of speaking of "developmental arrests" employed in this book permits a departure from previous conceptions based on medical notions of "pathology." However, the idea of developmental limitation or arrest runs the risk of introducing the equally undesirable notion of "immaturity." Loewald (1980) points out that psychoanalysis and psychotherapy are conducted in a format (even with children) which requires the participation, cooperation, and commitment of the mature aspects of patients' minds, regardless of how regressed or infantile other *aspects* of their personalities may be. The frequent distinction made between cognitive and intellectual maturity versus emotional maturity is oversimplified and misleading in that developmental arrests can and do occur in any and all areas of potential functioning. Perhaps Loewald's example should be followed in speaking of various "aspects" of the personality which have retained the character of a certain developmental phase.

levels determine or are embedded in the character of later self and other relatedness patterns and potentials. Thus, for example, an individuals' experiences of self and object constancy will encompass previously attained modes of self to selfobject resonance and include certain merger or symbiotic yearnings as well as crucial part-self and part-object aspects. Diagnostically, one listens for the *dominant level of integration of experience* while being heedful of the ways in which and the occasions during which various higher and lower levels may be apparent.

This book will begin by specifying the general considerations which make a separation-individuation conceptualization of psychotherapy and psychoanalysis possible. The four Listening Perspectives of psychoanalysis will then be presented within the context of the therapeutic task of listening. Empathic listening focused on different developmental phases is thought to foster the differentiation and expansion of self and other experience. The book moves toward a survey of the "new wave" in psychoanalysis, an integrative summary of the challenges to thinking afforded by the breakthroughs in conceptualization by Hartmann, Jacobson, Sandler, Mahler, Kernberg, Kohut and many others. It concludes with a consideration of the nature of the therapeutic action in psychoanalysis and psychotherapy.

2 The Backdrop: Listening Perspectives as Clinical Frames of Reference

"The general form of propositions is: This is how things are."—That is the kind of proposition that one repeats to oneself countless times. One thinks that one is tracing the outline of the thing's nature over and over again, and *one is merely tracing round the frame through which we look at it*. (Italics added.)

Ludwig Wittgenstein
Philosophical Investigations I:114

Imagine yourself at high noon in a large square of a great city. Thousands have gathered from all over the world for the grand unveiling of Picasso's last great sculpture. For months the square has been filled with scaffolding and drapery. A great shroud of secrecy has cloaked the artist's masterpiece until today. The mayor and town councilmen are giving speeches honoring the artist and the citizens whose devotion and donations made the commission possible. On the portico of the courthouse sits a group of courtroom artists, sketchpads in hand. A photographic society has members strategically stationed at all angles in hopes of publishing a portfolio of the event. Critics from a dozen magazines carry recorders while television cameras scan the crowd. People jam the windows and the balconies all around. Many will be writing letters to friends or home to Mom. Many came solely for personal experience—to feel sheer joy or inspiration in the presence of great artistic creation.

The dedication ceremony ends and a hush falls over the crowd as the rush of many fountains and splashing water begins. The scaffolds are quickly drawn away, the great canvas drops, and a silent chill passes through the crowd at the first glimpse of this momentous creative achievement.

What one sees, of course, depends on *who* one is, *where* one stands and *what* one wants to look for. As the sun passes its zenith, shadows entirely change the visage. In the evening, lights illuminate the dancing waters, adding a magical quality of mystery to the angles and convolutions. When the city has gone to bed the moon transforms the stone and steel into a nocturnal spectacle.

In applying this metaphor to the problems inherent in observing and communicating observations about the human mind, three problems are immediately brought into focus:

1. What is seen and experienced when considering any complex phenomenon is, to a large extent, a function of the observer, and the observer's interests and background.

2. What a person sees is also a function of whatever points of view or perspectives one assumes in time and space.

3. *Communication* about what one sees or how one thinks is a function of the medium and the "purpose" of that communication. Meaningful communication, furthermore, implies some common set of terms based on shared experience and a system of symbols.

In other words, psychological theories are necessarily going to reflect *who* one is, *what perspective* one takes and *what purpose* one has in forming theories.

Edgar Allan Poe in his essay "The Poetic Principle" (1850) studied this set of issues in the context of the poetic experience. Poe pointed out that the poet has a primary experience of something such as a landscape. The poet's task is to render in words and form a comprehension of the experience in his reader. The reader's primary experience remains the poem and only secondarily, the landscape. In considering the complex problems of perception and communication, Poe alludes to Plato's cave image to indicate that the poem may be the only reality the reader knows but that the poem is only a "shadow" on the cave wall compared to the rich experience of the poet.

PERSPECTIVES IN SCIENCE

In this same regard psychological theories, like all scientific theories, are necessarily limited when compared to the richness and complexity of the human phenomena the theory purports to describe or account for. Freud's own theorizing was based on a Newtonian model of scientific inquiry and a philosophical commitment to the Hegelian dialectic. He never tired in his effort to make psychology a logical extension of biology.

A more modern perspective highlights the paradigmatic nature of theorizing. It marks a post-Einsteinian cultural movement away from "belief" in constructions to an awareness of the use of various models, often seemingly contradictory ones, as mere vehicles for thought, i.e., arbitrary conceptions to be cast aside when their usefulness is past. A popular analogy is the "wave" versus "particle" theories of light which are thought to be contradictory and yet various observations involving light can be understood only on the basis of one or the other of the theories.

Modern theorizing is also based on a view of epistemology which holds that inquiry into the nature of "reality" may best be thought of less as "discovery" and more as "creativity." A simple but illuminating statement of this approach is contained in Chilton Pearce's small volume, *The Crack in the Cosmic Egg* (1971). Pearce envisions humanity as living in the midst of a dark and endless forest, gradually carving out of the wilderness a world and a reality largely of human invention and design.

A scientific theory might be thought of first as *a logical and internally consistent system of thought.* Scientific theory is an abstraction, a set of ideas, assumptions, and postulates which are on the one hand presumably derived from data, but on the other hand serve as a framework for limiting, collecting, and organizing data. A theory need not be thought of as "correct" or "true." A theory neither stands nor falls on the basis of data or facts. Recall the example of the two theories of light, both of which remain useful, but each of which is contradicted by certain facts. The contradictory or unique event has no direct sway over theory. The unique event remains of interest only insofar as it may give rise to hypothesis formation, hunches, or intuitive leaps, which further aid theory formation. Traditionally considered, the theory which tends to be most useful is the one which makes the fewest number of assumptions, provides the most parsimonious explanations, is successful at making predictions, is refutable, and has heuristic value, i.e., is rich enough in its terms and postulates to continue to generate thought and further investigative hypotheses. A theory must also come to grips in some way with the problem of the observer. Usually mechanized and standardized methods of observation are sought. In analytic psychology the tool for observation is human, and controls remain difficult to establish.

In what ways might a theory fail to serve adequately or might lead one astray?

1. The prestige value of a theory may cause uncritical acceptance of many of its postulates.

2. A theory is logical and continuous while one forgets that phenomena in nature are not.

3. A theory by definition seeks to limit and guide perceptions and thoughts into certain patterns so that one indeed continues to see data which support the point of view to be explored, i.e., a theory tends to be self-confirming, especially psychological theories. The confirmed hypothesis depends upon the terms in which it was cast.

4. Psychological theories "used" in a clinical setting often destroy (by changing) the very phenomena to be observed, i.e., the spontaneous verbalizations or interactions of the clinical encounters.

5. The theory may cause one to "see" or to "infer" what is not there, just because in similar instances one might infer such things.

6. Uncritical extension of theory from one set of data to another is unjustifiable.

7. Failure to separate theory from observation is common. The example here is the statement that "white light is composed of all different colors." Is this a theory or an observation?

With these thoughts in mind one can approach the study of psychoanalysis more thoughtfully seeking to grasp what Freud was originally interested in, where other writers have gone, where their ideas may be useful and which ways ideas have carelessly been extended into areas far afield from the basic data.

A recent difficulty in psychoanalytic theorizing, to be discussed extensively in this book, stems from the frequent attempt to integrate incompatible conceptualizations, (e.g., the old with the new) thus making the error of utilizing concepts and terms from one universe of discourse in another universe where they do not apply.

Another attitude which remains prevalent in psychoanalytic theorizing stems from a 19th-century approach to science and philosophy in which theoretical advances are seen as "discoveries." Thoughts are developed and observations are then collected with the hope of finding out "what's really there" or "how things really are." In contrast, modern epistemology is generally based on the assumption that reality and truth are elusive, generally unknown and unknowable, but that there are a variety of ways of interacting with what might be termed truth or reality by inventing or creating ideas about how things are. This point of view holds that "realities" continue to expand as long as there are inventive and creative minds set to the task. While many psychoanalytic writers would be quick to endorse this modern epistemological approach, psychoanalytic conceptualizations and formulations still continue predominantly to reflect an earlier philosophic perspective. Current scientific thinking tends toward viewing theories as inventions or pictures to help organize thinking and clarify vision. There is less concern now with discovering what "really is" and more interest in defining and creating "perspectives" or "visions" of reality. Modern theories are understood as created "points of view" or "conceptual lenses" which momentarily bring into focus something one wants to look at.

This book seeks to provide an application of these contemporary scientific and epistemological attitudes to traditional areas of psychoanalytic study and to focus on psychoanalysis as it pertains to the listening process in clinical practice. It will be the task here to find and to trace the thin cord of Ariadne—clinical utility—through the labyrinth of psychoanalytic thought.

THE PROBLEM OF METAPSYCHOLOGY

At every juncture in his theory formation Freud sought to link his clinical theories with those of the natural sciences in a body of work which has come to be known as "metapsychology." The familiar notions of the unconscious mind, the id, ego, superego structures, the transmutations of psychic energy, the psychosexual stages of development and the psychological theory of instincts all bear the earmarks of Freud's contradictory attempts, on the one hand, to maintain the Cartesian (mind-body) split while on the other hand to resolve the split with bridging concepts.

Ryle (1949) has shown the Cartesian myth to be an historical curiosity in the form of a category error. According to Ryle, Galileo's framing the universe in a vocabulary of mechanics led quite unnecessarily to a "Ghost in the Machine" conception of man. Propositions regarding mental causes, states, and processes were cast into an analogous mechanistic and deterministic vocabulary. Ryle examines the historical, logical, and grammatical considerations which erroneously led to considering mind and body as concepts within the same universe of discourse. He demonstrates the unfortunate consequences which the perpetuation of the Cartesian manner of speaking has had on the subsequent development of clinical and theoretical propositions in psychology.

George Klein's bold proclamation (1970, 1973) that now, once and for all, the complications of psychoanalytic metapsychology could be set aside in favor of a strictly clinical theory of psychoanalysis came as welcome relief to many. According to Klein, what Freud and later Hartmann called metapsychology might indeed claim legitimacy as a branch of natural science but metapsychology serves no discernible *clinical* purpose. Klein declared, "The central objective of psychoanalytic clinical explanation is the *reading of intentionality*; behavior, experience, testimony are studied for meaning in this sense" (p. 10).[1] Klein has pointed out that the salient common feature of *clinical* statements in psychoanalysis is that they concern purpose, intention, significance, and meaning. An ambiguity of this approach which Klein overlooks resides in the various meanings of "meaning." For example, Klein does not clarify in the instance of something said to have "unconscious meaning" (as in a slip of the tongue or a dream), when this meaning is properly attributed to the individual acting or dreaming and when this meaning is properly assigned solely to the interpreter! This failure to distinguish systematically between the meanings, intents and purposes of the person in analysis from various meanings, intents, and purposes of the analyst has been a longstanding problem in psychoanalytic theorizing. Nowhere is this more clearly evident than in the interface between clinical theory and metapsychology.

Rubenstein (1976) takes sharp issue with Klein, pointing out that a key function of metapsychology has always been to *justify* the presuppositions

---

[1]Klein fails to note that an emphasis on intentionality certainly entails a metapsychological commitment.

which the general clinical hypotheses represent. In an extended argument against the possibility of there ever being a strictly clinical theory of psychoanalysis, Rubenstein maintains that while "person" and "organism" are not synonymous, the separate studies of "meanings" and "causes" are *not* mutually exclusive. He likens the relationship between a person and the corresponding organism (which the person also is) to the relationship between the color red and electromagnetic waves with a wavelength of 7×10^{-5} cm. The two attributes can be seen as functions of two *different modes of observation*. It would make no sense to say that one is more real than another or that knowledge about one fact might not shed light on the other. Rubenstein argues that the search for metapsychological theory is legitimate in its own right and that it derives its force mainly from a refusal to accept as final the existing simple clinical theory. He contrasts several of the more future oriented (but admittedly somewhat incomplete, dry and factual) metapsychological models (Klein 1967; Peterfreund 1971; Peterfreund and Franceschini 1973; and Rubenstein 1974) with the more appealing ones "shrouded in the nostalgically old-fashioned, somewhat fanciful garb of current metapsychology" (p. 262).

Rubenstein points out that one necessarily "takes the first step" toward description in the mode of natural sciences as soon as one eliminates references to the person from statements and instead speaks about such things as wishes, feelings, and thoughts. One might also add "representations." However, he does not feel (as perhaps does Schafer, 1976) that this first step commits one to take a further step in that direction. In fact, this step may be unavoidable if one wishes to understand *more fully* what it means to say a person does certain things. He cites many writers who, for the sake of exposition, freely take the first step, soon shifting the focus back to the person. With Hartmann he believes the first step is unequivocally one toward a "depersonalized" metapsychological description in the mode of natural science. Rubenstein suggests that one way out of the dilemma would be to adopt what he calls a "critical point of view" with an "extension of ordinary language." This is in contrast to a more common-sense point of view using ordinary language for describing the unobservable activity attributed to a person as Schafer seems to advocate (1976). Rubenstein's "critical view" still considers the *person* the subject of an activity, for example thinking, without implying anything about the precise *nature* of the relationship between the thinker and thinking. While the critical view highlights the unknown or mysterious nature of the relationship between the person and his/her unobservable activities, it only points to the general problem but stops short of offering a solution. In this particular instance— thinking—the riddle might at times be solved, according to Rubenstein, by acknowledging the thinker's *conviction* that he or she is the subject of the activity (thinking) and that this "sense of being" is most likely derived from what Rubenstein refers to as a "sense-of-being-a-person-thinking." Thinking could then, in a general way, be characterized as an *"unobservable activity associated with experiences of particular kinds"* (p. 244). Wishing, doubting, loving, etc. might have similar formulations. Rubenstein acknowledges the common-sense view pervades literature, history, and everyday life, but he maintains that it must be given up for the "critical" view if one is to understand the clinical theory of psychoanalysis. Rubenstein's solution may sound unduly complex at first hearing but his "critical" point of view does have the advantage of "taking the first step" toward a natural-science mode of expression while still retaining the focus on the person as actor.[2]

An entirely different angle on the problem of metapsychology is afforded by the philosopher Wittgenstein (1953). In regarding this triangle:

he points out that it can be seen as a three-sided hole, a solid, a line drawing, as standing on its base or hanging from its apex; as a mountain, a wedge, a pointer, an overturned object, half a parallelogram, etcetera (II:xi, p. 200). He then asks how it is possible to *see* an object according to its *interpretation*. In considering how to speak about many things including mental processes and mental states, Wittgenstein refers to defining statements as "pictures." One problem with pictures (such as metapsychological propositions) is that "a picture is conjured up which seems to fix the sense so *unambiguously*. The actual use, compared with that suggested by the picture, seems like something muddied." (I:426, p. 127). He points out another problem with pictures:

> The evolution of the higher animals and of man, and the awakening of consciousness at a particular level. The picture is something like this: Though the ether is filled with vibrations the world is dark. But one day man opens his seeing eye, and there is light.

---

[2]Michael Russell (personal communication) suggests that this entire argument which psychoanalysts engage in under the rubric of "clinical *vs.* metapsychological" and "causality *vs.* intentionally" is philosophically unnecessary. Each of the many arguments might be thought of as another interesting "language game" engaged in for the purpose of clarifying and elaborating various ways of conceptualizing the world and our relationship to it. It is not that one or the other view is more correct or true but rather that language and concept games continue to provide us with valuable extensions and elaborations of our sensory and mental processes, thus permitting more elaborate and interesting exchanges with our personal environment. The importance of such discussions lies not in the controversy *per se*, or its outcome, but rather in the gaming processes themselves.

What this language primarily describes is a picture, what is to be done with the picture, how it is to be used, is still obscure. Quite clearly, however, it must be explored if we want to understand the sense of what we are saying. *But the picture seems to spare us this work: it already points to a particular use. This is how it takes us in.*(II:vii, p. 184, italics added)

But one might protest that mental states and processes have a certain reality, mainly that they "happen in me."

Certainly all these things happen in you—and now all I ask is to understand the expression we use—the picture is there. And I am not disputing its validity in any particular case.—Only I also want to understand the application of the picture.

The picture is *there*; and I do not dispute its *correctness*. But *what* is its application? Think of the picture of blindness as a darkness in the soul or in the head of the blind man. (I:423 and 424, p. 126)

Wittgenstein's position is not against using any picture metapsychological or otherwise but he argues that "It is necessary to get down to the *application*, and then the concept finds a different place, one which, so to speak, one never dreamed of" (II:xi, p. 201, italics added). ". . . the best I can propose is that we should yield to the temptation to use the picture, but then investigate how the *application* of the picture goes " (I:374, p. 116).

Thus while Rubenstein advocates the necessity of "taking the first step" toward a natural science mode of expression, he stipulates the focus of emphasis must ultimately remain on the subject or actor. In contrast, Wittgenstein wouldn't care "how many steps" one took so long as one was aware that the pictures one creates generally contain an implicit interpretive element which determines what and how things are to be viewed, i.e., the applications. Furthermore, applications which "take us in" tend to be embedded almost imperceptibly in whatever pictures one forms. Wittgenstein argues one should use whatever pictures (theories, concepts) one is tempted to and then get down seriously to the *applications* where one may find some interesting surprises.

The concept of Listening Perspectives as general frames of reference for the consulting room arises from these crucial considerations put forward by Ryle, Rubenstein and Wittgenstein. That is, the various branches or schools of psychoanalytic study have created a series of pictures which have more or less cogent and potent applications for listening to persons who have achieved differential developmental phases in the human engagement referred to as the progressive differentiation of "self and other" experiences.

In the chapters which follow each Listening Perspective will be treated primarily as a set of pictures in clinical theory and will then be systematically linked to the underpinning metapsychological assumptions which form pictures of a different order and must be regarded as coming from a different universe of discourse, i.e., clear statements about the organism in the mode of natural science rather than the more clinical statements about personal intents, meanings, and experiences.[3]

MOTIVATIONAL CONSIDERATIONS

With the waning interest in energy concepts and drive theories, Gedo (1979b) points out that psychoanalysis is in danger of being without a viable theory of motivation. Klein (1976), apparently modifying his earlier position on there being no need for metapsychological propositions, postulates a (biological) propensity for humans actively to seek repetition of the *patterns* of their earlier experiences, whatever the qualities of those patterns may have been. Similarly, Winnicott (1960) had previously spoken of early memories of object relationships serving as a primary source of motivation. Gedo (1979b) postulates a motivational principle operating in his concept of "self-organization" which he defines as "the sum of personal goals stemming from the need to reproduce the patterned qualities of earlier experiences." Kohut (1971, 1977) speaks of the need to express the pattern of the nuclear self in relationships with important others and particularly within the psychotherapeutic situation. These and many other evolving hypotheses in the literature point toward a new theoretical option apart from drive theory. This alternative theory of motivation presumably derived from the principle of the "repetition compulsion" would be founded on the notion of "patterns of earliest experience and the biological necessity for their repetition in the active mode" (Gedo 1979).

In another search for a motivational principle in the context of developing a metapsychological definition of self, Lichtenstein (1965) draws similarities between Sandler's (1960) concept of an organizing activity beginning early in life, Erikson's (1950) epigenetic principle, Spitz's (1959) "organizers of the psyche," Spiegel's (1959) frame of reference for internal perception and his own motivational concept of 'primary identity' (1964). Lichtenstein views Hartmann's general approach to the problems of adaptation as an anticipation of what he calls the "psychology of the whole person." Using Hartmann's

---

[3]This general argument for a revitalized metapsychology may appear unfair to the many clarifying points of George Klein and others. He was a leader in recognizing the severe limitations of using strictly Freudian metapsychology (see Chapter 5). He spoke for the adoption of principles closer to everyday clinical practice. However, as the developmental perspective has gained prestige in psychoanalysis, it has become possible to restore Freud's original "points of view" to their rightful place in the study of psychoneuroses and to elaborate different specific metapsychological principles for studying various phases of pre-oedipal (pre-neurotic) development. (For full details see Chapter 5, and the sections on metapsychology in Chapters 6, 8, and 12.)

concept of an autonomous or inborn third force (complementary to the drives and the demands of reality), Lichtenstein conceptualizes a third independent variable in human development which he says profoundly affects the early experiences (or mental representations) of self and others. He proposes that it is the operation of this third autonomous motivational force which "transmutes man's adaptation to reality into the activity of his historical existence. . . ."

In a similar vein Stolorow and Atwood (1981b) conceptualize the world of self and objects as a set of distinctive configurations which shape and organize a person's subsequent experience. Their studies of "the representational world of self and objects" have led them to a phenomenological position with a focus on a series of personal aims. They propose a general motivational principle: *a striving or need to maintain the organization of early self and object experience in the later patterning of human action.* An interesting sidelight to their approach is that dreams come to be viewed as an affirmation and solidification of the nuclear organizing structures of the dreamer's life. Dreams are seen as "guardians of psychological structure." Some (oedipal phase) dreams serve this purpose by way of concrete symbolization which "actualizes particular configurations of experience" while other (preoedipal) dreams serve "to maintain the psychological organization of the representational world *per se.*"

This general shift from a drive oriented motivational principle to an orientation which highlights the human need or tendency to repeat specific patterns or configurations of early self and other experience means a corresponding shift in emphasis from a biologically based to a psychologically based theory of motivation which would be welcome to many. Kernberg (1980b) in criticizing Kohut on this very kind of shift, sees as a consequence the necessity of postulating a "growth drive" or at least developing a theory specifying what mechanisms or processes are involved in repetition as well as change (i.e., growth). Gedo (1979b) while generally agreeing with this motivational trend points out that those who would use self and object (i.e., object relations) concepts as theories of motivation have yet to systematize their hypotheses or to specify the *manner* in which early object relations become transformed into a source of later motivations.

Using Listening Perspectives as clinical frames of reference will be shown to obviate the need for deciding definitively the basis for human motivation. In listening to the more advanced (oedipal) phases of the continuum of experiences of self and object differentiation, drives and conflicts still seem to appear with *subjective* (phenomenological) clarity as motivators. In contrast, at the earlier phases of this line of development the push for some type of experience of merger of the self with the other has the stronger claim to motivational urgency. The therapist prepared to listen and to formulate clinical material in a variety of different ways according to the level or developmental phase of "self and object" experience being expressed may well have the leap on the game. This skill would presumably derive from a careful study of developmental sequencing and from the same kind of personality flexibility that permits a parent to respond differently to children of different ages and to change responses as each child grows.

CONCLUSIONS

One necessarily starts with Freud because it was, after all, Freud's concern with understanding himself and the people who came to him that gave psychoanalysis its momentous beginning. Fortunately, there have been enough well conceived recent developments so that hindsight about where and how *clinical* psychoanalysis originated and the subsequent course of its development are now much clearer than when Freud opened the 20th century with his startling ideas about dreaming and the unconscious.

Referring back to the metaphor of the unveiling of Picasso's last sculpture, one quickly surmises a series of problems that confront any effort to organize one's thoughts or make sense of complex human experience:

1. How does one *define and limit what*, in the universe of psychoanalytic ideas, one *wants* to look at?

2. Within the confines of that decision, *what perspectives offer the best vantage points* for one's particular study?

3. In talking with one another, what *vocabulary or way of speaking gives the greatest clarity* to one's purposes?

There must be many ways one could respond to these questions about psychoanalysis. This book will attend to the issues from the point of view of clinical listening of the psychotherapist or psychoanalyst who frequently wishes he/she had a better grasp on theory when attempting to understand the specific experiences of people who come for help.

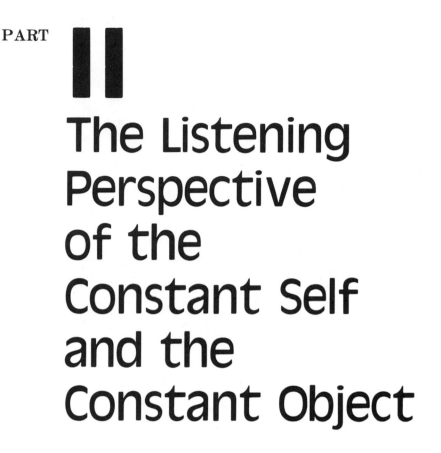

PART

II

The Listening Perspective of the Constant Self and the Constant Object

3 Constancy: The Waning of the Oedipus Complex

> Where does the dialogue begin? In his first partnership outside the womb, the infant is filled up with the bliss of unconditional love—the bliss of oneness with his mother. This is the basic dialogue of human love. The next series of mother-infant dialogues concerns the way the infant separates from the state of oneness with the mother. As he separates he will learn the conditions of actual love and acquire the sense that he is himself and nobody else. *All later human love and dialogue is a striving to reconcile our longings to restore the lost bliss of oneness with our equally intense need for separateness and individual selfhood. These reconciliations are called constancy.* (Italics added.)
>
> Louise J. Kaplan
> *Oneness and Separateness* (1978, p. 27)

While Freud succeeded in providing a broad outline for the entire field of psychoanalysis and human development, his studies reached greatest potency in their detailed attention to that constellation of emotional events just preceding movement to the experience of constancy, the (phallic) phase he called the Oedipus complex. In his well-known 1924 paper, "The Dissolution of the Oedipus Complex," Freud outlined the emotional complexities faced by the young child in continuing (separation-individuation) into the arena of triadic family relationships. Further, he specified the processes through which destruction or abolition of oedipal attitudes is optimally accomplished. However, Freud maintained that if conflictual strivings are too intense oedipal issues may not dissolve or pass but instead undergo repression in various (defensive) forms. Strivings thus repressed represent an evasion of the emancipatory "murder" of the parents and constitute an arrest at the phase of experiencing parricidal and incestual oedipal relations, a phase which would normally occupy only an intermediate place between preoedipal merger experiences and postoedipal experiences of constancy. The necessary developmental ingredients (parricide and incest) must be experienced, borne and passed beyond if a stultifying neurosis based on preservation (via repression) of the Oedipus complex is to be averted. Freud's familiar formulations refer to "relinquishment of oedipal object cathexes" and their "substitutions by identification" with parental authority (the formation of the superego) and the subsequent "transformations" (via sublimations) of oedipal strivings into tenderness and mutuality.

As modern psychoanalysis has focused increasingly on preoedipal issues of symbiosis and separation-individuation and as the proportion of "pure" neurotics seen in clinical practice has declined over the years, the general interest in the Oedipus complex has likewise declined. However, now that a significant measure of conceptual clarity has emerged with regard to the development of preoedipal object relationships, the myth of Oedipus can be retold with some interesting and new variations.

Loewald (1979) speaks of the "Waning of the Oedipus Complex" to refer simultaneously to the repeated resurgence of oedipal issues throughout life and to their ever diminishing effects through the repeated impact of novel love relationships. In a similar vein he speaks of the lifelong waning but also the persistence of a "sense of and quest for irrational nondifferentiation of subject and object" which owes its impact to the power of preoedipal object relations. Loewald's reworking of oedipal concerns from the standpoint of Self and Object Psychology continues the traditional focus on the mythic aspects of parricide and incest. Assuming responsibility for one's own life and its conduct (the separation–individuation task itself) is psychically equivalent to murdering one's parents, i.e., renouncing their authority and usurping their power, competence and responsibility and taking it unto the self. The parricidal crime is the violation of the sacred (preoedipal nurturing) bond between parent and child. The result is guilt for the attainment of independent selfhood.[1] He points out that the identificatory organization of the superego represents a narcissistic transformation of object relations. The organization of self comes to possess or live various aspects or features characteristic of early interpersonal experiences. As such, superego formation is an atonement for (makes up for and restitutes) as well as a metamorphosis of object relations (through a live re-creation or internalization). According to Loewald, it is through the *bearing* of oedipal guilt (with the help of a "holding environment") that hasty forms of repression and/or punishment (castration) are avoided. Gradually self and object constancy is achieved which represents a reconciliation of the conflictual strivings for loving merger with the parent and the simultaneous push toward emancipation and self responsibility. Self responsibility is thus the parricide crime and paradoxically at the same time the atonement for the crime (because independent selfhood is also seen as virtue). Without the guilty deed there can develop no autonomous self. The implication is that *guilt need not be looked upon* as some troublesome affect to be eliminated but rather *as one of the continuous driving forces in the organization of the self.* Loewald maintains that a favorable outcome of child development and also of analysis might be

---

[1]Sartre's play *The Flies* captures the essence of the existential crime of parricide through winning a sense of selfhood through personal commitment.

thought to be the increasing attainment of a sense of equality and mutuality between autonomous, constant selves.

Loewald further indicates that the necessary oedipal move toward incestually tinged object relationships is also a crime in that the sacred innocence of preoedipal unity and family bond is violated. Just as parricide may be pursued passionately, incest may be pursued with a vengeance directed either jealously toward a third party or enviously at the love object for receiving third party attention. Midway on the necessary developmental path from experiences of merger and selfobject relationships to experiences of constant, separate and novel love relationships is the oedipal love (incestuous) object who is neither a full fledged separate object nor an unequivocal merger object. The maintenance of oedipal-incestual ties, either through actual incest or massive repression of the Oedipus complex, interferes with development by fostering continued dependency upon compulsively repeated experiences of less than separate and constant objects. The perpetuation of the oedipal-parricidal or oedipal-incestual experience of objects via repression (or related defense maneuvers) constitutes the core of neurosis. Loewald thinks of the Oedipus complex as an ambiguous (intermediate) phase on the lifelong road in the direction of (self and) object constancy. Through repeated experiences of constancy, i.e., reconciliations between "our longing to restore the lost bliss of oneness with our equally intense need for separateness and individual selfhood" (Kaplan 1978), the gradual dissolution or waning of the Oedipus complex is continuously carried out.

The progressive elaboration of neurotically repressed experiences of oedipal objects was, and remains, the goal of Freud's psychoanalytic technique and the focus of extensive theorizing. Even today the treatment of oedipal neurosis remains in many regards the most complex treatment task despite the fact that the number of neurotics requesting treatment may be diminishing in comparative incidence. A knowledge of the dynamics of oedipal neurosis remains a crucial tool in the treatment armamentarium of *every* therapist. Kohut (1971), Gedo (1979a), Stolorow and Lachman (1980) as well as others continue to make the point that more or less full fledged oedipal constellations can be regularly expected to appear toward the end of all successful analytic work with preoedipal personality organizations. This is generally seen as the gradual emergence of a new possibility in object relations which becomes opened up by the separation-individuation experiences of the therapy. These oedipal, parricidal-incestual episodes which emerge toward the end of preoedipal analytic work are also thought to be intermediate on the way to constancy. They are often experienced directly with the person of the analyst as patients show an increased interest in the various relationships which the analyst (like the oedipal parent) has with friends or family. It is still, then, worthwhile for all clinicians to possess a good foundation in oedipal-neurotic dynamics and to know how treatment of oedipal issues differs from therapy with preoedipal arrests. For this, one must turn to the earliest underpinnings of psychoanalysis laid out by Freud in his theory on the formation and treatment of neurosis.

4 The Legacy of Freud: Neurotic Personality Organization

One way of ascertaining what is important in psychoanalysis would be to trace the historical development of psychoanalytic thought. Freud's own ideas evolved over a number of years, as he sought to develop ways of helping his patients. The various changes in Freud's thoughts represented primarily shifts in emphasis and focus. His thinking never underwent any abrupt or complete changes in orientation.

In reviewing the development of Freud's ideas, it is important to remember that his theories were primarily elaborated in connection with free association (introspective) experiences of *neurotic adults* in a clinical setting. Like all theories, the concepts and inferences of psychoanalysis are more likely to retain their usefulness in settings similar to those from which they were derived. Theory evolves based on certain types of observational data, here, *listening* to the free associations of adults on the couch. The area of greatest applicability of the theory is likely to remain a similar one. Uncritical extension or generalization of psychoanalytic theory to sociology, anthropology, history, and other areas may be interesting and of use to researchers in those fields, but narrowly defined *classical psychoanalysis remains a clinical theory for the treatment of neurosis in adults.* Generalizing Freud's ideas to children appears in many instances to have worked well, probably because every adult on the couch was once a child. However, generalizations of Freud's ideas to preoedipal arrests in development have not always worked out so well.

FREUD'S TECHNICAL PROCEDURES

It has been possible to trace Freud's earliest interest in psychiatric cases at least as far back as 1882, when he heard the case of *Anna O.* (1893–1895) from Breuer. Freud was apparently fascinated with the spontaneous trances which Anna O. developed with Breuer in which she relived traumatic past events and subsequently experienced relief. Freud spent the Winter months

---

In this chapter I am indebted to the extensively quoted and paraphrased ideas of Ralph Greenson as put forth in his book, *The Technique and Practice of Psychoanalysis* (1967). Many of the ideas here were developed in connection with supervisory and seminar experiences with W. Marshall Wheeler, at the Reiss-Davis Child Study Center in Los Angeles.

of 1885–1886 in Paris studying hypnosis with Charcot. However, in his own work, he continued to employ the conventional techniques of his time: electrical stimulation, hydrotherapy and massage in the treatment of "mental disorders." By 1887 Freud began using hypnotic trances in an effort to suppress symptoms (Greenson, 1967, p. 8). By 1889, Freud reports, in the case of *Emmy von N.* (1893–1895) his first use of hypnosis for the purpose of theraputic catharsis. Freud induced a hypnotic trance and forced the patient to talk about the origin of each of her symptoms. He asked what frightened her, what made her vomit, when it started and what else could she tell him? Emmy von N. responded by providing memories which were charged with strong affect.

By 1892, Freud had written the case of *Elisabeth von R.* (1893–1895) as the first case completely treated with "waking suggestion." Freud had discovered many of the limitations of the hypnotic technique and understood that, in many cases, either the patient was unhypnotizable or that his own ability to hypnotize that patient was limited. The choice which Freud had was to abandon the cathartic method of therapy or to continue the catharsis approach without the hypnotic state. Freud's attitude was clearly that his patients "knew" everything of significance in the formation of the neurosis, and that it was his task to "force" them to communicate it to him (Breuer and Freud, 1893–1895, p. 108). Using the authority of a healing physician, he ordered his patients to lie down, to shut their eyes and to concentrate on remembering. As was the custom in those days, he frequently applied pressure with his thumbs on the foreheads of his patients, insisting the upsetting memory would appear (Breuer and Freud, 1893–1895, p. 270).

Freud's *The Interpretation of Dreams* (1900) was largely completed by 1896, so by that date it seems clear Freud had abandoned hypnosis altogether as a therapeutic tool. Freud had developed a good understanding of the structure and meaning of dreams and symptom formation so that he was no longer reliant on the patient's cooperation in reporting traumatic memories. Freud's work on dreams enabled him to use construction and interpretation to arrive at the repressed memories. Many years later, Freud still felt that *The Interpretation of Dreams* was his most important book: "Insight such as this falls to one's lot but once in a lifetime" (Freud's preface to the third English edition, 1931).

The technique of "free association" apparently developed sometime prior to 1896 and was gradually refined from the use of hypnosis, suggestion and the technique of thumb-pressing and questioning. In the case of *Emmy von N.* (1889) Freud reports he was pressing his thumbs and questioning her when she reproached him for "interrupting" her thoughts. Taking his cue from her, Freud began to feel free association was a good substitute for hypnosis (Jones 1953, pp. 242–244).

Freud's technique of free association consisted basically of refraining as much as possible from exerting any influence over the patient. He advised the physician to invite the patient to lie down on the sofa, keeping out of the line of vision without asking the patient to close his/her eyes and avoiding all physical contact. The physician was to engage the patient in an ordinary conversation in which one rambles on quite disconnectedly and at random except that one person is spared every muscular exertion and distracting sensory impression which would divert his/her attention from his/her own mental activity (Freud 1904, pp. 250–251). The technique of free association came to be considered the "basic rule" of psychoanalysis (Freud 1912a, p. 107). It may be more appropriate to think of free association as the main technical procedure of psychoanalytic investigation. "Interpretation" was viewed as the ultimate instrument or therapeutic tool of the analyst. Other kinds of communication occur in the course of any particular psychoanalytic study, but free association and interpretation have generally been thought to be *typical* of psychoanalysis (Greenson 1967, p. 10).

A side note on the use of the couch in a psychoanalytic or psycho-therapeutic setting is perhaps appropriate, particularly because of the humor and hostility which has been directed at the analytic couch. Certain analysts, for many reasons, abandoned the use of the couch, preferring a sitting arrangement frequently at 90 degrees to the patient (e.g., Sullivan 1953). The principle remains the same. In ordinary conversation, there are many social rituals and interpersonal exchanges such as knowing glances, noddings of the head or mutual scrutiny of body movements and facial musculature. While these and other forms of body language may be crucial forms of social communication, they are seldom helpful in the psychoanalytic task. Psy-choanalysis remains an interpretive discipline (Schafer 1976) or an intro-spective process (Kohut 1957) which has been compared by many to medita-tion. The social interactions which characterize ordinary conversation tend to detract from the main course of psychoanalytic work.

In contrast, by encouraging a state of (regressed) relaxation and self-observation, the analyst encourages a working-together on "a creative ex-ploration of the way one's mind works" (Giovacchini 1979a) quite apart from the social interaction and the ritualistic distractions of ordinary inter-personal communication. Beyond this basic reason for using the couch, Freud was himself the first of many analysts to indicate the strain which one experiences in having to maintain intense interpersonal contact and concentration through the course of a long day. Psychotherapists and psychoanalysts who use the couch with many of their patients generally report the relief which they experience during "couch hours." Their own capacities to concentrate and to follow effectively the introspective work seem considerably enhanced. From the patient's viewpoint, there may be initial embarrassment, discomfort, and dynamic resistance to this highly unconventional way of spending important time with another person. However, once one has moved past the initial discomfort of using the couch, people typically express great appreciation at not having to be constantly monitoring the therapist. They feel considerable relief from the burden of interpersonal rituals so they can focus on the business at hand, i.e., studying one's own introspective process.

Especially fascinating are those persons who, from time to time, move back and forth from a sitting position to a couch position.[1] A traditional psychoanalytic stance might tend to discourage this behavior, but a more contemporary approach focuses on the various meanings of the wish for "face-to-face" versus "couch" work in the ongoing development of the therapeutic process.

For beginning therapists or clinicians already in practice, the hesitancy to invite the people they work with to use the couch has many sources, central of which may be the therapist's personal (conscious or unconscious) reluctance to engage in intense introspective investigation. In this country some years ago as psychoanalysis gave way to the popularization of dynamic psychiatry and behavioral psychology, widespread use of the couch was abandoned. Only recently, as contemporary psychoanalysis makes itself heard in the therapeutic community, are many clinicians again finding the couch useful for encouraging an introspective process which is minimally influenced by the therapist.

FREUD'S THEORY OF THERAPY

Freud continued throughout his lifetime the struggle to discern what aspects of psychoanalysis were *essential* to the therapeutic process. In Freud's early *Studies on Hysteria* (Breuer and Freud 1893–1895), he put forth certain ideas which formed the basis for the psychoanalytic theory of psychotherapy. Greenson (1967, pp. 10–11) points out that it was characteristic of Freud that he began by defining obstacles and struggling to overcome them, only later to come to the understanding that these obstacles to his approach were crucial dimensions for understanding the patient and the psychoanalytic process.

In *Studies on Hysteria*, Freud put forth what might be called a "cathartic" theory of therapy. Psychiatric symptoms were viewed as stemming directly from traumatic experiences in the past which had become absent from normal memory processes. Through hypnosis, the disturbing memories and their accompanying affects could be recalled and described in detail and words. Following Aristotle's ancient idea, abreaction or catharsis

[1]See the case of George in Part III.

was conceptualized as an "emotional discharge" which, in turn, was viewed as depriving the memory of its power with the result being the disappearance or easing of the psychiatric symptom. The catharsis theory was consistent with previous observations in the *Anna O.* case (1882) in which the patient developed spontaneous trances with Breuer, relived traumatic past events, and subsequently felt relieved, calling the therapy a "talking cure" (p. 30).

In the case of *Elisabeth von R.* (written in 1892), Freud reported the "first great obstacle" to psychoanalysis. He was unable to hypnotize her and she "refused to communicate certain of her thoughts despite persistent urging" (p. 154). The inner force which opposed treatment Freud called "resistance." He conceptualized it as the same force which held troubling ideas and memories from the past out of consciousness. "Not knowing" was assumed to be "not wanting to know" (pp. 269-270). Freud's earliest attitude was that the task of the therapist was to "overcome the resistance." The analyst, as a physician and authority figure should exert personal influence in this regard and offer himself as elucidator, teacher, and, if necessary, Father Confessor (p. 282).

In the subsequent work of Freud and in its elaboration by many others, the force of "resistance" has come to be viewed in many ways. As a technical term, "resistance" is used almost invariably to refer to *resistance to the content and the process of the therapy.* The central and universal resistance has generally been thought to be a reluctance to experience and to introspectively explore the attitudes, beliefs, opinions and feelings which one attaches to the therapist and to the therapeutic situation, i.e., the so-called "transference" (Chertok 1968). Over the years, resistance forces have come to be recognized as the bearers of vital information. Resistance opposes the elaboration of content and process, opposes the establishment of transference attitudes and opposes introspective elaboration in such a way that *resistance has come to be thought of as a form of memory, inevitable—and vital—to the therapeutic process.* Analysis of resistance has become one of the most fascinating aspects of psychoanalysis and almost inevitably leads to an understanding of the earliest experiences of fears and wishes. Freud was the first to realize that resistance need not be thought of as a negative force opposing psychoanalysis. He came to believe resistance could be conceptualized as an expectable phenomenon, which serves to make available for analytic understanding crucial forms of (usually preverbal or nonverbal) emotional experience from the deepest recesses of human personality (Freud 1916-1917, Ch. XXVIII).

Shortly after defining "resistance," Freud (1905) reported that the "greatest obstacle" to psychoanalysis occurred when the doctor-patient relationship became disturbed. He felt a disturbance in this relationship could occur when the patient either feels neglected or becomes overly dependent, thus transferring to the physician distressing ideas from the content of the analysis. This obstacle was labeled "transference" and Freud advised dealing with transference by tracing it back to the moment in treatment when it had first arisen.

Thus, Freud's early work helped him define the forces or processes of resistance and transference; but in his early writings he still viewed them as obstacles to what he believed to be the main objective of treatment, i.e., achieving an affective abreaction or catharsis in the course of recovering a traumatic memory. Only later did it become possible for Freud to view resistance and transference as bearers of vital information about the patient's repressed history. Viewing resistance and transference as forms of memory became possible only as Freud refined his theory of therapy.

In *Studies on Hysteria* (1893–1895), Freud and Breuer documented their approach of tracing each distressing symptom to its ideational content under the influence of a hypnotic trance. By 1901, Freud had completed the writing of the *Dora* case (1905), in which he declared psychoanalytic technique revolutionized from the earlier symptom treatment. In *Dora*, Freud advocated *allowing the patient* to choose the subject matter of each session and to work on whatever surface of the unconscious appeared during that hour. Following his work on dreams in which construction and interpretation became possible, Freud realized that a symptom-by-symptom approach was inadequate for viewing the complex picture of a neurosis. Freud had recognized the principle of overdetermination in mental functioning and realized symptoms were the result of many causes (Greenson 1967). By 1904, his paper on psychoanalytic procedure boldly asserted that hypnosis and suggestion "conceal the resistances," and, as such, must be considered incomplete therapeutic techniques. Freud's attitude in the 1904 paper was that the therapist must "overcome resistances" and "undo repressions."

Several shifts in Freud's early thinking become apparent. The main technical shift was from an active, authoritarian role on the part of the therapist to a more passive, receptive role. The goal shifted from the promotion of emotional catharsis to the overcoming of amnesia. Catharsis was still seen to provide temporary relief but was no longer viewed as the primary aim of psychoanalysis. The primary aim had become "making the unconscious conscious." The art of construction and interpretation was used to overcome the resistances. Transference (*Dora*, 1905) came to be seen as the "most powerful ally if its presence could be detected in time and explained to the patient."

By 1912, Freud focused again on the "Dynamics of Transference" (1912a). He described the ambivalence involved in transference, and the so-called "positive" and "negative" transference. Later that year (1912b), Freud warned against transference gratification. By that he meant the tendency on the part of the therapist to go along with the transference need and to provide a gratification of the need rather than an analysis of it. He suggested that the analyst instead remain as an "opaque mirror," retaining an optimal degree of anonymity. He further described the "acting out" of the transference and connected it with the principle of the repitition compulsion (1912b). Freud labeled what happened during the course of psychoanalysis as "the establishment of a transference neurosis." In making the observation that the course of psychoanalysis typically involved relinquishing the psychoneurosis in favor of a "transference neurosis," Freud was taking a position on the essential nature of psychoanalytic "cure" in neurosis. This is one of Freud's most elegant and misunderstood ideas and requires elaboration.

Freud had become aware of the crucial importance of what he called the oedipal period of development in the formation of neurosis. The oedipal drama represents the child's understanding of the emotional realities of his/her early family environment. The oedipal child has matured enough to study emotional triangulations (Abelin 1980) involving ambivalent, incestual and parricidal feelings such as love, hate, envy and fear.

The "infantile neurosis" is said to have formed when certain solutions or attitudes stemming from the oedipal dilemma become adopted by the child and embedded in the personality. Inevitably, solutions based on experience with family members fail to generalize to other interpersonal situations in many regards. To the extent that the child's early family (parricidal-incestual) attitudes remain inappropriate in other settings, the attitudes might be thought of as "neurotic." In the course of psychoanalysis these neurotic attitudes typically appear in relationship to the psychoanalyst or the psychotherapist (the transference). By maintaining a reflecting position with some degree of anonymity, the therapist maintains a position in which he/she is able to reflect inappropriate or faulty assessments of the therapeutic relationship which have stemmed from entrenched incestual and parricidal attitudes derived from early childhood.

Central to a psychoanalytic concept of "cure" is the emergence of unconscious and preconscious (oedipal) incestual and parricidal attitudes and conflicts into the psychoanalytic situation so that they can be seen for what they are: narrow emotional attitudes developed by a young child in response to his early environment. These attitudes tend to become "automatically activated" in later intense emotional relationships. Stated differently, the emotional issues which once confronted the mind of the young child and were solved by the development of specific attitudes and reactions toward emotional relationships are reactivated in the therapeutic relationship. They can now be considered and reworked (consciously and unconsciously) by the mind of an adult. The task of the analyst has traditionally been seen as interpreting the defensive and resistive forces which have kept the infantile attitudes from emerging into the full light of day for so many years. Once these so-called "transference attitudes" have emerged with clarity in relationship to the therapist, they are generally assumed to lose the power which they have held for so long in the emotional life of the individual.

How does the adult *resolve* long-buried emotional issues of dependence, attraction, envy, fear or hatred in relationship to the analyst? This is, of course, of no immediate concern to the analyst; the therapist's task ends when the resistances to the unburying of the early and limiting emotional conflicts have been laid aside and the emotional forces have emerged in full force within the contemporary analytic relationship. The patient may choose to do many things with his newly liberated energies, forces and attitudes. Typically, a set of attitudes and beliefs develops about the analyst, some of which are accurate and many of which are inaccurate but which may reflect with some degree of accuracy the analyst's performance and availability during the analytic hours. As such, the patient is seen to form a "transference neurosis." *It is the (conscious, ego) ability developed and evident in the formation of the transference neurosis which constitutes the psychoanalytic meaning of "cure."* Whatever else the patient does beyond establish transference attitudes in full realization (usually conscious) with the analyst is beyond the scope of psychoanalysis. The *mere establishment* of the transference neurosis is considered to be sufficient cure in psychoanalysis. The repeated *experiencing* of (i.e., working through) the impact of infantile conflicts in the contemporary emotional relationship *leads to the gradual dissolution of the infantile neurosis.* The early unconscious solutions to the oedipal drama no longer hold sway. All other ideas are extraneous and superfluous to this central psychoanalytic meaning of "cure" in relation to psychoneurosis.

Even as early as 1912 (a, b), Freud was aware that it was the (more or less conscious) re-experiencing of childhood emotional conflicts which characterized forward movement of the psychoanalytic process. For this reason, hypnosis and suggestion were totally abandoned as partial or incomplete methods for the treatment of neurosis. They bypassed the functioning of the conscious ego and neglected the analysis of the resistant forces (memories) and the elaboration of the complex transference potentials.

By 1923, in *The Ego and the Id*, Freud had added one other ingredient to his theory of therapy—*growth*. He understood that when unconscious, incestual conflicts were re-experienced in the analytic situation and were understood (analyzed), an alteration of ego occurred. Accordingly, his former goal of making the unconscious conscious gave way to the idea of expanding the dominance of the ego in his famous dictum, "Where id was, there ego shall be."

By way of review, one can see that as Freud began to distill from many experiences what he felt was therapeutic about therapy, hypnosis as a tool was abandoned, but all other elements had been retained with varying emphases. Suggestion was no longer used for obtaining memories, but was considered a temporary supportive measure, the need for which ultimately had to be understood. Catharsis or emotional abreaction had been abandoned as the main goal of psychoanalysis but was still seen as temporarily valuable in the relief of tension, which might make other tensions easier to see and understand. The analyst was still seen as attempting to get beyond the barriers of consciousness and able, through the use of the free association technique, to employ dream analysis, reconstruction, and interpretation. *The major field for psychoanalytic work had come to be viewed as the understanding (analysis of) resistance and transference phenomena* (Greenson 1967). The expectation evolved that many unconscious impressions would become conscious, but the ultimate goal of psychoanalysis involves a *growth* process, i.e., the increase of the relative strength of the ego in relationship to the superego, the id, and the experience of the external world. Within the analytic hour it became *the aim of the analyst simply to understand the patient*, and to limit his/her influence as much as possible. On the other hand, *the aim of the patient is generally to "get better"* in one way or another, which might be thought of as a wish to increase one's abilities, or, in technical terms, to increase the capacities of the ego.

CONCLUSIONS

Despite the many ways in which Freud's essential ideas have been reworked, modified, transformed, and applied, and despite the enormous social and theoretical superstructures which have evolved around the field of psychoanalysis, the legacy of Sigmund Freud remains an attitude or Listening Perspective *primarily* appropriate for the understanding (analysis) of neurotic personality organization. Freud startled the world with his ideas on infantile sexuality (incest). He also opened to view the astounding emotional complexities with which children between the ages of four and eight struggle to understand the world which surrounds them. This oedipal period of emotional development is characterized by conflicting fears, feelings, attitudes, and beliefs about the important persons in the child's immediate family life. The outcome or the resolution of the child's researches into the parricidal-incestual situation of early childhood has been referred to as the Oedipus complex. It can be viewed as resulting in the development of enduring attitudes, beliefs, feelings, fears, inhibitions and structural conflicts (between id, ego, and superego) which constitute the "infantile neurosis."

Analytic and psychiatric literature has continued to contrast "normal" with "neurotic" for historical, literary, and rhetorical purposes, but the general understanding remains that the normal, expectable course of human development entails the formation of an infantile neurosis which may or may not develop in such a way that psychoanalytic attention might ever be sought. That is, in sophisticated psychoanalytic thought the outcome of normal or fortunate development is assumed to be neurotic personality organization to a greater or lesser extent.

"Neurosis" simply indicates an expectable developmental experience or *achievement* in which the oedipal (parricidal-incestual) objects acquire an enduring impact on the personality attitudes and structure of the growing child. The subsequent waning of the Oedipus complex is a lifetime experience (Loewald 1979).

The basic therapeutic notions of Freud as applied to the study of neurosis have remained largely intact through time. They are as relevant to the practice of psychotherapy and psychoanalysis today as they were when first enunciated by Freud so many years ago. This book begins with the Listening Perspective Freud provided that has served the test of time in following the introspective experiences of persons entering psychoanalysis who have attained what might be described as neurotic personality organization. The remainder of the book will survey three subsequent Listening Perspectives which have developed to augment Freud's studies on psychoneurosis.

That Freud extended his ideas about the Oedipus complex somewhat uncritically and that he may have overgeneralized the importance of parricidal-incestuous constellations has no bearing on the importance and the validity of what he did observe and the way in which he did learn to *listen* to neurotic patients. Freud extended his ideas into the study of psychosis with (by his own admission) quite limited success. He was also unable to refrain from the temptation of extending his ideas about neurosis to literature, cultural anthropology and the history of the Jewish people. Freud's uncritical extension of his ideas to areas of limited applicability can be understood (1) on the basis of the excitement which he as a person must have felt upon entering for the first time the world of "internalized objects;" (2) on the grounds that his own "narcissistic grandiosity" was unanalyzable at the time due to limited knowledge and technique (Kohut 1977); and (3) on grounds of Freud being a human who was subjectively immeshed in the problems of the Jewish people, being himself forced to flee his homeland by harsh and hostile social and political forces. Contemporary interest need not be to vindicate Freud from the criticisms that many of his ideas are subject to, but rather to be appreciative of his powerful pioneering work and the Listening Perspective which he was first able to assume.

5

Freud's Metapsychology

Students and practicing clinicians usually have enough familiarity with psychoanalytic literature to know that there is such a thing as "metapsychology" and to sense that discussions of metapsychology tend to be complex and elusive but are important. In keeping with the survey spirit of this book, an attempt will be made to provide a summary or an overview of exactly what is meant by "metapsychology" and what understandings of metapsychology are likely to be interesting and helpful in the clinical task of listening. A general understanding of metapsychological principles clarifies and puts into order many bits and pieces of things one has heard all along but not known quite how to organize. Rather than a long section on metapsychology or many brief cryptic allusions spread throughout, the approach chosen for this book is to begin by introducing an overview of Freud's metapsychology and subsequently to provide brief sections called "metapsychological considerations" showing contemporary alterations in metapsychological outlook.

What exactly is meant by metapsychology? "Metapsychology," literally meaning "beyond" or "above" psychology, refers to *basic assumptions* which psychologists make which are *not* open to psychological investigation; the psychologist's "articles of faith," so to speak. "Freud's metapsychology" refers specifically to the set of assumptions which Freud's theorizing required.[1] His assumptions were few and can be clearly and explicitly stated.

FREUD'S "GENERAL METAPSYCHOLOGY"

Freud borrowed five assumptions from the other sciences which have come to be called "the metapsychological principles."

1. THE PLEASURE PRINCIPLE (or pleasure-pain principle) rests on the assumption that all living matter tends to be attracted toward "pleasure" and to avoid "unpleasure" or "pain." What is pleasurable and unpleasurable, of course, varies along the phylogenetic scale.

[1]David Rapaport (1967) is, perhaps more than any other, to be credited with clarifying the metapsychological positions in psychoanalysis.

2. THE REALITY PRINCIPLE is assumed to modify the pleasure-pain response in accordance with other features ("reality") in the environment, giving rise to such things as delay of gratification and complex "foraging" or "hunting" behaviors.

3. THE HOMEOSTASIS PRINCIPLE (constancy or nirvana principle) assumes a tendency for organisms to seek a steady state, an internal balance or a homeostasis quite apart from "pleasure-pain" or "reality" considerations.

4. THE PRINCIPLE OF REPETITION COMPULSION assumes a tendency for an organism to repeat what has been "learned" in the past in consideration of the "pleasure-pain," "reality" or "homeostatic" principles.

5. THE PRINCIPLE OF OVERDETERMINATION (or multiple causality) assumes that for every effect there are multiple causes, i.e., living organisms are so complex that no simple cause and effect equations can be drawn.

All formulations of Psychoanalytic Psychology rest on these five general assumptions borrowed by Freud from the natural and biological sciences.

FREUD'S "SPECIFIC METAPSYCHOLOGY"

Freud somewhat systematically developed five separate "points of view" which are *peculiar to psychoanalysis* and stand as *mutually exclusive* ways of considering clinical material. In principle, one cannot claim full psychoanalytic understanding of any particular neurotic phenomenon until one has analyzed it from *all five* points of view. In practice, of course, this is almost always impossible so understanding, more often than not, has to be considered partial or incomplete. A sixth point of view (adaptation) was openly, specifically and adamantly opposed by Freud but is included because it remains, nevertheless, implicit in psychoanalysis.

1. THE TOPOGRAPHIC POINT OF VIEW represents Freud's earliest model of the mind based on the distinctions between conscious, preconscious and unconscious modes of mental activity. In his "Project for a Scientific Psychology" (1895) and Chapter 7 of *The Interpretation of Dreams* (1900) Freud discusses different modes which characterize conscious and unconscious functioning in his distinction between primary and secondary processes. Freud defined "primary process" functioning as almost exclusively unconscious and lacking a firm sense of time, order, space and logic. Contradictions and inconsistencies may co-exist in primary process without nullifying each other. Condensation and displacement in dreams illustrate the primary process. "Secondary process" thinking is conscious, logical,

cause and effect oriented and sensitive to discrepancy, contradiction and inconsistency.

2. THE STRUCTURAL POINT OF VIEW was outlined in Freud's 1923 book *The Ego and The Id*. Designed originally as a replacement for the topographic model, this later came to be viewed as simply a different way of looking at things. The structural view is based on the idea that it is useful to define enduring mental qualities, "agencies," or "structures." These persisting functional units were named by Freud "id" (the more primitive, animalistic, instinctual) "ego" (a more reality oriented set of functions for affect and reality control including perception, memory, judgment and motility) and "superego" (the subset of socially determined values referred to as "conscience" and "ego ideal"). These "structures" are assumed to be partly conscious and partly unconscious. They give rise to what is referred to as "structural" or "intrapsychic conflict." The continued *emphasis* on the structural point of view is what has tended to set classical psychoanalysis apart from many other psychoanalytic approaches.

3. THE DYNAMIC POINT OF VIEW assumes that mental phenomena result from an *interplay of forces operating in time* as illustrated by parapraxes such as slips of the tongue. Various mental "forces" may be working concurrently in harmony or discord to produce such things as interests, conflicts, symptoms and ambivalence.

4. THE ECONOMIC POINT OF VIEW relates to concepts regarding the distribution, transformation, and expenditure of "psychic energy." Such terms as "cathexis," "decathexis," "binding," "neutralization," "sexualization," "aggressivization," and "sublimation" are rooted in this point of view. It might be said that through time the economic point of view has tended to be the least useful and interesting to clinicians. However, Heinz Kohut (1971) has recently put forward the "psychoeconomic point of view" to describe the ebb and flow of early tension states. This view is somewhat different from Freud's and will be discussed in a later chapter.

5. THE GENETIC POINT OF VIEW relates to the origin and development (cause and effect) of mental phenomena. The genetic approach studies the ways the past is contained in the present and why certain solutions were developed in response to certain conflicts. The well known sequencing of libidinal development (oral, anal, urethral, phallic, genital) employs the genetic approach.

6. THE ADAPTIVE POINT OF VIEW encompasses all statements and implicit assumptions which pertain *to the organism's relationship (adaptation) to the environment*. (Love) object relations statements belong here. Freud, however, in the formulation of psychoanalytic theory specifically advised against all formulations which related to adaptation to the environment. Freud believed that in listening to free associations of neurotic in-

dividuals, symptoms can only be understood (analyzed) by attention to *intra*psychic "structural" conflict. Freud remained adamant in his conviction that the only appropriate listening stance for analytic work with neurosis was from an *internal* point of view. Freud firmly maintained that neurotic symptoms *do not arise* from adaptational problems or interpersonal conflict but are a product of internal conflict.

Freud's adherence to an *internal* Listening Perspective for the study of (oedipal, incestual, or structural) neurotic conflict may be his most enduring contribution to the field. However, the adaptational point of view has been particularly useful in the field of Ego Psychology which has traced the development of many ego functions to transactions with the environment. Object relations analysts rely heavily on understanding emotional development as an interactional process. Various other developmental psychologists (e.g., Mahler 1968) place heavy emphasis on the adaptational point of view as do the "social" analysts.

These are "the principles" and "the points of view" which have comprised Freudian metapsychology. Needless to say, they have been the subject of much scrutiny and controversy through the years. As the book proceeds, attention will be drawn to various important objections to and extensions of Freud's ideas.

III

The Selfobject
Listening
Perspective

6 Narcissistic Personality Organization

The decade of the 1970's saw the clear emergence of a fresh paradigm or Listening Perspective called the Psychology of the Self. Based on Heinz Hartmann's (1950) conceptual distinction between ego and self; Heinz Kohut, a training analyst at the Chicago Psychoanalytic Institute, has written a series of books and papers presenting a startling new set of ideas for understanding the therapeutic work of persons having what Kohut calls, "Narcissistic disturbances."

In 1975, Gedo declared that Kohut's radical proposals signify "the end of the leading paradigm of psychoanalysis referred to as Ego Psychology" (cited in Ornstein's essay in Kohut 1978). In saying this, Gedo indicated what had been clear for some time: psychoanalysis as originally conceptualized had run its course. Its vitality had been stifled by a growing awareness of the limits of Freud's original ideas which were developed for understanding psychoneuroses.

This chapter will review the historical origins of Kohut's thinking, systematically compare the classical paradigm of psychoanalysis with the paradigm of self psychology, review the metaphor of the "bipolar self" and conclude with comments on his final contributions on the notion of cure.

For those to whom Kohut's ideas are new, several difficulties are likely to arise. The first is with the word "narcissism." It would be as misleading to associate the Psychology of the Self with the myth of Narcissus as it would be to associate the entire study of psychoneurosis with the myth of Oedipus. Narcissus, as portrayed in Greek mythology, was said to have fallen in love with himself (in a homosexual version of the myth) in a reflecting pond. The heterosexual version of the myth holds that it was his twin sister that he fell in love with. "Narcissism," as Kohut uses the term, is *not* concerned with self-love or selfishness in such a limited sense. Kohut has said, "The attitude of certain layers of society toward Narcissism resembles Victorian hypocrisy toward sex. . . . I think that the overcoming of the hypocritical attitude toward Narcissism is as much required today as was the overcoming of sexual hypocrisy a hundred years ago" (1971).

Special thanks to Lars Lofgren for his careful attention to this section and his very useful questions and comments.

49

A second problem relates to another technical use of the word "narcissistic" in the work of many writers, including Otto Kernberg (1975) and James Masterson (1981). They conceptualize narcissism and narcissistic disorders in entirely different terms from Kohut and from each other.

The third problem with understanding the Psychology of the Self is that one does hear more readily that which is familiar than that which is unfamiliar. Kohut's ideas are innovative. His conceptualizations are not merely elaborations or extensions of traditional psychoanalytic ideas so one must be careful not to attempt to integrate Kohut's approach too quickly with what one already knows. Perhaps one would do best to heed the words of Samuel Taylor Coleridge to "willfully suspend disbelief" in order to listen to Kohut on a journey "in search of the self."

HISTORICAL DEVELOPMENT OF KOHUT'S IDEAS[1]

In 1950, Kohut wrote "On the Enjoyment of Listening to Music" in connection with a musicologist (Levarie). The paper concerned the subject of what makes music interesting. Kohut talked about the ebb and flow of consonance and dissonance. As dissonance increases, interest and tension increases, which give way to a sense of calm relief when the dissonant factors begin to merge in some form of consonance. The concept of *rising and falling tension states* which first attains clarity in this paper, remains Kohut's basic model for the increase and decrease of narcissistic tensions. This tension model will be crucial later to understanding the importance of Kohut's definition of the "selfobject."

In 1957, Kohut wrote another paper crucial to the development of his ideas, "*Death in Venice*; a Story about the Disintegration of Artistic Sublimation." This paper is a psychological analysis of Thomas Mann's novel, about an aging artist, Gustave Aschenbach, whose writing and personality integration were deteriorating, and who journeyed to Venice in hopes of finding fresh literary and personal inspiration. As he enters the city, various images of death confront the reader. Soon a plague begins to surround the aging artist in the city. Physical illness encroaches. What develops is a gradual disintegration of the man rather than the hoped for inspiration and sublimation in creative writing. As his sense of creative artistic sublimation begins to diminish, the artist's sense of self begins to fragment and (to use Kohut's terminology) the "by-products of the disintegration of the self" become evident in various hostilely-tinged intrigues at the hotel and in the city, and in the crude homosexual interests which he displays toward the young boy, Tadzio. One of the themes that Thomas Mann plays on in *Death*

---

[1]The reader is referred to Paul Ornstein's survey of the complete development of Kohut's ideas in *The Search for the Self* (Kohut 1978).

in Venice is the deterioration of male-to-male tenderness in the wake of the disintegration of the self. The fragmented aspects of the self then appear in crude, sexualized forms.

This particular theme, cohesiveness of the self giving rise to creative sublimation and the disintegration of self-cohesiveness producing by-products of a crude sexual or aggressive nature, remains the second great theme of Kohut's work.

By 1959, Kohut's paper, "Introspection, Empathy, and Psychoanalysis: an Examination of the Relationship between Mode of Observation and Theory," stated clearly his metapsychological perspective on the nature of psychoanalysis. Kohut asserts, "Each branch of science has its natural limits, determined approximately by the limits of its basic tools of observation. . . . Each science thus arrives at a small, optimal number of basic concepts. The limits of psychoanalysis are given by the limits of potential introspection and empathy. . . . Introspective science must come, however, to acknowledge the limits beyond which the observational tool does not reach and must accept the fact that certain experience cannot at present be further resolved by the method at its disposal" (in Kohut 1978, p. 231).

Kohut (1959) discusses the psychoanalytic term "drive," and indicates that it is "derived from the introspective investigation of inner experience. Experiences may have the quality of drivenness (of wanting, wishing, or striving) to various degrees. A drive, then, is an abstraction from innumerable inner experiences; it connotes a psychological quality that cannot be further analyzed by introspection; it is the common denominator of sexual and aggressive strivings" (in Kohut 1978, p. 227). Kohut (1971, 1977) maintains that an introspective study of drive remains appropriate in the psychoneuroses where structural conflict is the focus for study. However, in the study of pre-oedipal, pre-structural narcissistic fixations drives are *not* the central experience but rather the cohesiveness (or lack of such) of the self.[2]

Kohut thus conceives of psychoanalysis as essentially a study of introspection via the observational mode of vicarious introspection, which he terms "empathy."[3] Kohut has come to hold that empathy is "as much a tool or faculty for human observation as are the basic senses of sight, hearing and touch" (1971). He states that empathy refers to the human capacity to

[2]Kohut (in press) modifies this focus somewhat in his last work.

[3]The terms "introspection" and "vicarious introspection" (empathy) used throughout this book are derived from Kohut's 1959 paper. Kohut's terms are powerful and evocative in expressing the rich exchange of human understanding in psychoanalysis. However, for the sake of clear dialogue, the term "introspection" must ultimately be abandoned because it is philosophically misleading.

The image of "my mind doing something" while at the same time another part of my mind (as behind a TV camera) "watching me do what I am doing" represents excess baggage in psychological theory. Gilbert Ryle (1949) argues that "findings of introspection," like so-called

vicariously introspect such that one has a sense of knowing something about the inner life of another human being.

In the second basic period of Kohut's writing, he studied problems of applied psychoanalysis. He was particularly interested in looking "Beyond the Bounds of the Basic Rule" (1960). Taking a look at history, anthropology, art and philosophy, he concluded that *psychoanalysis remains basically a science of introspection* but that psychoanalytic psychology certainly has many other interesting applications than on the couch.

Following ten years of teaching Freudian literature at the Chicago Psychoanalytic Institute, Kohut prepared a paper with Seitz, "Concepts and Theories of Psychoanalysis" (1963). In this paper, they rework classical theory considerably, particularly with reference to the deficiencies of the classical point of view in understanding borderline patients.

Kohut's third period of writing dates from the mid-1960s to the present and might be viewed as the major florescence of his work. The monograph, which has by now become a classic in the field, is *The Analysis of the Self* (1971). In this monograph Kohut abandons the idea of aggression as an instinct and traces libido in two separate forms, narcissistic libido and object libido. (This view on which he does not later elaborate is illustrated in Figure 1.) *The Analysis of the Self* met wide criticism on the basis of its being extremely difficult to read and unduly complex. In retrospect, it appears that the major difficulty in the initial reading is partly a function of the reader's reactions to an entire set of unfamiliar formulations. Once the Psychology of the Self is understood in its essence, the monograph turns out to be a lucid statement of Kohut's ideas. The beginning reader might do well, however, to start with Kohut's later book, *The Restoration of the Self* (1977). The serious student of Kohut would certainly want to review the entire set of published papers now available in two volumes entitled *The Search for the Self* (1978). Those interested in clinical applications are directed to a volume which contains six fascinating case studies by Kohut's colleagues, *The Psychology of the Self; A Case Book* (Goldberg 1978). The best introductory overview of

---

"deliverances of consciousness," constitute Priviledged Accesses to a second status world and as such perpetuate the "ghost in the machine" view of reality inherent in the Cartesian myth.

Ryle (1949) favors use of the term "retrospection" when speaking autobiographically (pp. 66-67) as one normally does in psychoanalysis. Retrospection, prompt or delayed, is not a process troubled by the hidden assumption of divided attention nor by the assumption that even violent agitations can be the objects of cool, contemporary scrutiny (Hume's argument against introspection). Ryle holds that "the official theories of consciousness and introspection are logical muddles" (p. 155).

The free association of psychoanalysis can be thought of as a living diarization or historization. Finding or catching oneself doing something can be understood as *retrospection* and empathy thus considered *vicarious retrospection*. Relinquishing the notion of divided attention of the sort implied by use of the word introspection is as important to clear conceptualization in psychoanalysis as the abandonment of the metaphor of internality (proposed by Schafer 1976).

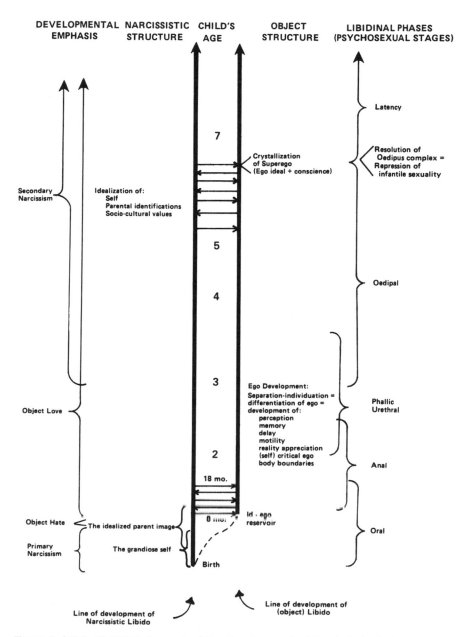

Figure 1 / Kohut's (1971) Concept of the Development of Narcissistic Libido Related to a Classical View of the Development of (Object) Libido

Kohut's work appears in a 100-page essay by Paul Ornstein which is the introduction to the two-volume *The Search for the Self* (1978). New Developments appear in *Advances of Self Psychology* (Goldberg, 1980).[4]

In introducing and exploring new ideas, it is frequently useful to select a series of key points and to provide a comparison of the old and familiar with the new and unfamiliar. The classical Listening Perspective of the "Constant Object" is graphically compared with the new Listening Perspective of the "Selfobject." (The reader is advised to refer to Table 1 now.)

As this book proceeds, the reader will realize that these two models represent the first two of four Listening Perspectives which might also be referred to as four paradigms or four listening styles of psychoanalysis based on four nodal points of development. While the temptation is to view such conceptualizations as "models of the mind" (Gedo and Goldberg 1971) or "paradigms of mental functioning," it appears preferable to conceptualize these developmental progressions in terms of listening stances, listening styles, or Listening Perspectives which provide ways of hearing and organizing the introspective experience of persons who come to the consulting room. That is to say, Freud's original interest in psychoanalysis was to form a science of the mind parallel to the other physical sciences and, in doing so, Freud introduced mechanistic conceptions and the Newtonian model of science into psychoanalysis. More contemporary attitudes toward psychoanalysis *as a clinical science* tend to regard psychoanalysis as either a "science of introspection" (Kohut 1959) or an "interpretive discipline" (Schafer 1976).

THE METAPHOR OF THE BI-POLAR SELF

Many readers have thought it odd that Kohut would start his 1977 book, *The Restoration of the Self*, with a lengthy discussion on termination of treatment. It must be remembered that Kohut addressed primarily an audience of psychoanalytic readers. Criticisms of his work had taken several focal points which are worth noting as they make the organization of the 1977 book more comprehensible. Within the framework of classical psychoanalysis, "successful" analytic work has ultimately been defined by the patient's capacity to give up or relinquish his dependent attachment to the analyst, usually described as the "establishment of the transference neurosis" and the "resolution of the infantile neurosis." Thus, the termination phase of a "successful" analysis was thought to be a process akin to mourning and a process made possible only by advanced capacities on the part of the analysand to emotionally let go of the analyst. Borderline and psychotic

[4]Unpublished at this time are: *The Future of Psychoanalysis*, edited by Arnold Goldberg; Vol. III of *The Search for the Self*, edited by Paul Ornstein and *How Does Psychoanalysis Cure?* by the late Heinz Kohut.

individuals have not traditionally been thought of as possessing this particular capacity because their early object relationships are thought to have been so damaging that a therapy process might "end" but would not "terminate" in the usual sense of letting go of internalized objects from early childhood as well as the analyst.

The group of patients Kohut defines as narcissistic are patients who, heretofore, would have been regarded "borderline." As such, the usual criteria of "successful" analysis would not be met in the termination process. Kohut, in order to satisfy his analytic colleagues that narcissistic disturbances *are analyzable,* had to redefine or reconceptualize the process of termination in psychoanalysis in such a way that it would include the group of narcissistic disturbances which, he maintained, were "analyzable." This may seem a labored way of going about things but this was the line of thinking Kohut apparently needed to address. In doing so, Kohut elaborated the concept of the "bipolar self" in order to account for why he felt it was possible for narcissistic personalities to successfully "terminate" psychoanalysis.

Kohut had previously spoken of two "structures" of the self (1971), the "grandiose self" and the "idealized parent imago". These two aspects of the self later became conceptualized as poles with "a tension arc of talent and skills" existing between them (1977). It is important to understand the grandiose and idealizing aspects of the self and how they appear in clinical material. Furthermore, it is helpful to know the appropriate therapeutic response to the grandiose and idealizing tendencies.

Before looking at a graphic representation of the metaphor of the bipolar self, a few brief words on how Kohut first came upon each of these two major trends in his clinical work.

The "grandiose self" is understood as an internal structure or set of attitudes which knows no bounds or limits, a set of implicit beliefs that in some way one is not subject to the ordinary laws which govern the rest of the universe! The grandiose self functions as a set of convictions regarding feelings of grandeur and supreme self-satisfaction (as if one were Napoleon, Jesus, or Superman/woman). One may experience or act as if he/she were "above it all," invincible, invulnerable, omniscient, and omnipotent. People tend to be regarded as but extensions of one's own mind or body, as if they were a twin or an alter ego, or as if they were but a mirror in which one could merge, see, and admire one's self.

Kohut (1971) tells of Miss F., who was in treatment with him for some time. Miss F. would come to her hours with a great many things to tell Dr. Kohut and for a long period of time he was aware that she seemed to require merely a mirroring or echoing attitude from him. If he would alter or add even the slightest detail to her account of things or the way she experienced them, she would fly into a rage. At one point she even accused him of interrupting, interfering, and "trying to ruin the analysis." In the develop-

Table 1 / A Comparison of "The Constant Object" and "The Selfobject" Listening Perspectives

	The Constant Object	The Selfobject
MAIN AREAS OF CONCERN:	THE TRADITIONAL PSYCHOLOGY OF INTERNAL CONFLICT (Also called Drive Theory, Structural Psychology, Conflict Psychology, Ego Psychology, and Mental Apparatus Psychology.) This psychoanalytically derived tradition has been developed to account for the structural, or conflict, oedipal neuroses in persons with a firmly established ego with clearly defined mind-body boundaries, good reality appreciation and reliable affect regulation.	THE PSYCHOLOGY OF THE SELF (Also called the Psychology of Narcissism or Narcissistic Libido.) This new model has been developed to account for the (more regressive) disorders of the self: ie., the psychoses, borderline states, narcissistic personality disorders, narcissistic behavior disorders, and certain disorders of a schizoid, psychopathic and perverse nature. This model also can be used to account for normal fluctuations of self-esteem. Kohut ultimately extended his ideas to include the "life-long need for selfobjects."
KEY CONCEPTS:	This approach rests on the assumption of some concept of unconscious mental functioning, some prime mover of the mental apparatus, and the existence of states of internal conflict which have been variously described by theorists such as Freud, Jung, Klein, Sullivan, Hartmann, Fromm, Perls, Berne, Kernberg and others.	This approach rests on the assumption of an early developing self defined *not* by mental content or conflict but by the ebb and flow of early tension states which are empathically responded to by the human environment in order to maintain a psychobiological steady state or equilibrium (e.g., the mother soothing her child). The maturing infant only gradually through conditioning and experience acquires the capacity for maintaining its own steady state, ie., only gradually acquires a cohesively functioning self.

Table 1 / A Comparison of "The Constant Object" and "The Selfobject" Listening Perspectives (Continued)

	The Constant Object	The Selfobject
DEFINITIONS OF "PATHOLOGY":	Pathology according to this model results from internal or structural conflict and therapy is oriented at bringing to light whatever conscious or unconscious forces are responsible. The conflicts typically are conceived of between such things as impulses *vs.* defenses or Parent tapes *vs.* the Adult or the Child.	Pathology according to this model results when the cohesive self (the steady state function) has been faultily developed so that the person persists in turning to the outside human environment for help in maintaining the internal state which he has not learned to maintain on his own.
	Stated less precisely, conflict pathology is characterized by symptoms and/or traits which in some way represent an inefficient or ineffective compromise or resolution of the internal conflict, often evident in a lowered capacity for enjoyment of work, sex and personal relationships.	Stated less precisely, self pathology is characterized by a flaw in the regulation of self-esteem which results from a poorly developed self. The chief complaints are usually vague and diffuse with the person feeling unable to derive joy from the persuit of his ambitions or goals as well as a failure to develop talents satisfactorily.
THE "DEVIL IN THE MENTAL APPARATUS":	Conflict psychology of necessity involves some notion of a prime mover of the mental apparatus such as instincts, impulses, drives, wishes or whatever.	The Psychology of the Self is "without original sin." i.e., no notion of a prime mover is required. The regulation of self-esteem (or the functions which develop to regulate a biological-psychological steady state) is nacent or virtually absent at birth. It is only slowly acquired by empathic contact with the nurturing, soothing other who is experienced as a part of the self, i.e, the *selfobject.*

57

Table 1 / A Comparison of "The Constant Object" and "The Selfobject" Listening Perspectives (Continued)

	The Constant Object	The Selfobject
THE "DEVIL IN THE MENTAL APPARATUS" (*Continued*):		According to this model the postulation of psychological instincts is unnecessary. The bottom line here is *disappointment* with the empathic selfobject who makes an early sense of self possible. This disappointment leads to a disintegration or a fragmentation of the self experience with resulting rage, shame or bodily (autoerotic) preoccupations. These disintegration reactions are only later mentally organized into what structural psychology finds useful to call the aggressive and sexual drives.
VISION OF MAN:	According to Kohut conflict psychology conceives of "*Guilty Man*," man living within the pleasure principle attempting to satisfy his pleasure seeking drives, but unable to achieve his goals because of real external obstacles and internal conflicts.	The Psychology of the Self conceives of "*Tragic Man*," who endeavors to *express the pattern of his early self-experience* (his nuclear self). Tragic man persists in searching for soothing functions outside himself in the style or pattern once possible with the original empathic environment. In this effort, his failures overshadow his successes so he is thought of as "Tragic Man."
LOVE OBJECTS AND TRANSFERENCE:	Conflict psychology deals primarily with the psychoneuroses and therefore, with the oedipal (incestuous) objects from the oedipal period of development in which the child *already* has a *firmly* established ego with	Self psychology deals with the empathic love objects of early childhood which were experienced as part of or extensions of the self. The selfobject transferences (or narcissistic transferences) reactivate

Table 1 / A Comparison of "The Constant Object" and "The Selfobject" Listening Perspectives (Continued)

	The Constant Object	The Selfobject
	good boundaries and reality appreciation. He is able to experience others as separate from himself, as independent centers of initiative. The (object) transferences in therapy reactivate the loves and hates of the oedipal objects so that they are experienced in a *repetitive* form in the therapy relationship.	early experiences of tension build-up and release in which the selfobject serves as the empathic regulator of the steady state and self-esteem. The therapist then assumes the role of the soothing selfobject.
CONCEPT OF CURE:	The working through of the oedipal transferences provides an expansion of consciousness. Psychological health is established through working out a contemporary solution to internal conflict as opposed to the inadequate solutions arrived at in early childhood. The therapeutic progression is viewed as a *repetition* of early childhood conflict which can then be resolved on a more mature or adult level.	The working through of the selfobject transference is achieved through the reestablishment of empathic closeness to the responsive selfobject therapist. Psychological health is established through the transformation of a formerly fragmented self into a cohesive self. The therapeutic progression is *not* seen as mere repetition of childhood conflict but *a new edition of selfobject experience.* The "optimally failing empathy" of the therapist permits the acquisition of tension regulating functions and the restoration of the self. Stated differently, the person learns (by working through repeated experiences of disappointment with the therapist's empathy) to be "empathic with himself" and to regulate his own self-esteem.

Table 1 / A Comparison of "The Constant Object" and "The Selfobject" Listening Perspectives (Continued)

	The Constant Object	The Selfobject
THERAPEUTIC TECHNIQUE:	Assuming that neurosis is an endless repetition of an unsatisfactory resolution of childhood conflict, the therapist typically encourages the expression of ideas and feelings while interpreting the resistances and transference manifestations which block the flow. Crudely stated, the therapist says, "I hear these feelings that you are developing toward me and wonder if perhaps they haven't come up before in some other context. What can you remember? Where did these feelings come from?"	Assuming that an empathic situation will recreate the early selfobject atmosphere, but that perfect empathy is never possible, the therapist tunes into the patient and waits for signs of his own empathic failures. Depending on the developmental level of the original failures, the therapist learns how to listen for signs of empathic failure as the steady state or self-esteem take a dive. The therapist then attempts to locate the exact point at which his/her empathic responses failed. Crudely stated, the therapist then says something like, "No wonder you've been upset and nervous. When you told me what you did, you expected me to share your enthusiasm, but from my response you felt I wasn't interested. It sounds like I let you down, you were greatly disappointed." Kohut describes other types of inadequate or incomplete therapist responses which can lead to fragmentation such as incomplete interpretations or interruptions or changes in the continuity or rhythm of therapeutic contact. Interpretation always involves a recognition of some shortcoming in the therapeutic contact and the person's response to that shortcoming.

Table 1 / A Comparison of "The Constant Object" and "The Selfobject" Listening Perspectives (Continued)

	The Constant Object	The Selfobject
THEORY OF THERAPY:	Interpretations remove defenses, primitive wishes or drives intrude into consciousness and under the repeated impact of the primitive wishes new structures are formed in the ego which are able to modulate and transform archaic strivings through such processes as delay, neutralization, aim inhibition, substitute gratification, absorption through fantasy formation, etc. The working through involves countless internalizations. New ego structure is built to handle the pressure of the drives.	The re-establishment of the empathic environment of the original selfobject through the empathic responses of the therapist sets the stage for empathy failures. The effects of the failures can be investigated in terms of exactly when and how the therapist provided the disappointment. Through repeated experiences of tension build-up and release due to failure and re-establishment of empathy of the selfobject therapist, "transmuting internalizations" lead to the acquisition of a cohesive self or at least a functionally rehabilitated self with ambitions, goals and talents.
INTERNALIZATION AND TRANSMUTING INTERNALIZATION:	The classical formulations have typically called upon the spatial metaphor of "internalization" to describe the process (or observation) of enduring ego attitudes. It has become common to talk of such things as an "internalized mother," "internalized superego prohibitions" or "internalized conflict." Kohut, building on Freud's (1923) famed formulation, "the ego is the precipitate of abandoned object cathexis," describes "transmuting internalizations" as a process akin to mourning. There must be (1) a readiness for an introject, (2) the willingness to relinquish the person (object) upon whom a specific function once depended, and (3) an internalization and depersonification of that function. It is this process of transmuting internalization through which narcissistic selfobject fixations are thought to be relinquished so that the person possesses his/her own tension relieving and self-soothing abilities.	

61

ment of this "mirror-transference" the patient required primarily empathic approving, echoing and confirming responses; she became indignant if Kohut attempted to express himself beyond those dimensions.

In contrast, the "idealized parent imago" functions as a set of beliefs and attitudes one step removed from the total self-experience of the grandiose self. Acknowledgement of persons or imagoes outside or beyond one's own mental sphere exists, although these imagoes possess an existence yet abstract and unreal or idealized. For example, the mother who always gives milk when one needs it, the spouse or friend who is always available, through thick and thin, or the perfected self capable of impeccable functioning regardless of circumstances. Thus, although these imagoes may rely on stimuli from outside, they are organized according to an internal narcissistic investment, placing oneself at the center of the universe and these idealized imagoes at one's beck and call. In discussing the origin of the concept of the idealized parent imago, Kohut (1971) tells the story of Miss L., a woman in analysis with a colleague who came to him for consultation. The analysis had come to a stalemate and the analyst was distressed. In reviewing some of the early material, it came out that at one point Miss L., raised a Roman Catholic, had spoken idealistically of a priest from her youth. The analyst had responded with a comment to the effect that he was not Roman Catholic. From subsequent interactions it could be inferred that Miss L. heard the analyst's comment as a rebuff as if he had said, "I cannot, nor will I ever be, the idealized version of yourself which you wish." This rebuff led to diminishing analytic work until through consultation the analyst was able to recognize the narcissistic injury which he had inadvertently provided for Miss L. so that her need to idealize the analyst could continue.

Thus the idealizing and the mirroring needs of the self have come to be conceptualized by Kohut as two poles in the structure of the self. As mentioned earlier, the concept of the bipolar self has come to serve Kohut's theorizing by making it possible to speak meaningfully of termination. His idea is that many persons with selfobject fixations or limitations in development during the selfobject period have sustained "damage" to one or the other poles of the self. If the damage sustained is not too extensive, then restoration of the self by working through the selfobject transference via repeated disappointments will be possible. However, in some instances, damage to one pole or the other of the self is extreme. For these instances, Kohut conceptualizes the other pole of the self may develop compensatory features so that the result of analysis and termination would be a "functionally restored cohesive self." The other possibility is that one pole or the other of the self would develop defensive functions to cover up the defect in the self. In either event, Kohut acknowledges persons with narcissistic disorders may have difficulty with the self extensive enough so that a full restoration of both poles of the self is not likely or possible. For clarification Kohut says in growing up an individual has "two chances" of developing a cohesive self. He suggests the admiring and mirroring functions required for a cohesive grandiose self might be thought of as deriving from what has traditionally been thought of as "mothering" while accepting the idealizations seems to develop out of what is often thought of as "fathering." The bipolar concept has the advantage of acknowledging the on-going defects while conceptualizing a "restoration of self" through defensive covering or compensation in one pole by the other pole of the self. The bipolar self metaphor is perhaps best presented in graphic form as in Table 2.

FINAL CONFERENCE: ADVANCES IN SELF PSYCHOLOGY

At Kohut's last professional appearance in Berkeley shortly before his death in October 1981, his most recent manuscripts were reviewed by Paul Ornstein, Mardi Horowitz, Morton Shane and Ernest Wolfe with sum-marizing reflections by Kohut himself. Since the implications of Kohut's final contributions are so far reaching, a brief synopsis will be attempted. The general tone of the conference had shifted from the "*we* of Self Psychology and *they* of the classical Freudian persuasion" of previous years, to an attitude highlighting "the contributions of Self Psychology to Mainstream Psychoanalysis" (which appeared to include all the various schools of psychoanalysis).

The question which occupied Kohut's last theorizing was, *How Does Psychoanalysis Cure?*, the title of his final book. In a penetrating study of the notion of health and illness in psychoanalysis, Kohut concluded that we never outgrow our need for selfobjects. As we grow, the type of selfobjects we need and the ways in which we experience our selfobjects do change. Mental health then becomes definable as the opening up of pathways or channels for permanent self to selfobject resonance, and freedom from the bondage of the archaic self searching for archaic selfobjects. In an effort to understand how analysis cures—not only Self Psychologically informed analysis but all analysis, Kohut reanalyzed Freud's "Rat Man" case. He demonstrated that the oedipal experiences of drive and structural conflict are firmly built on a foundation of self cohesiveness and vulnerability and that psychoneuroses can also be understood with the conceptual tools of Self Psychology. He emphasized that empathic immersion in the life and con-cerns of the patient provides the impetus toward cure, regardless of the theoretical terms in which that empathy is cast.

Kohut's concluding remarks focused on introspection and empathy as the definers of the field of psychoanalysis. He spoke of different kinds of empathy for different levels of selfobject relatedness and even told how some years ago in desperation he had initiated fleeting physical contact with

Table 2 / Metaphor of the Bipolar Self: The Tension Arc of Talents and Skills

POLE OF THE *GRANDIOSE SELF*

Driven by Ambitions in regulating ones' own tension and experiencing the soothing qualities as coming from oneself.

Mature Emotional Qualities: Enthusiasm over ones' own goals and purposes with joy and self-confidence.

Types of Mirror Transference (the broad sense)
1. *Mirror Transference* (the narrow sense): A push toward approving, echoing, confirming responses from the other, often manifest in grandiose fantasies and behavior with a strong need to be looked at and admired.
2. *Alter Ego or Twinship Transference*: The narcissistic twin and the twinship transference were elevated in some of Kohut's (yet unpublished) last papers apparently to the same status as the Grandiose Self and the Idealized Parent Imago. A push toward responses which suggest or confirm sameness (twinship) with oneself (e.g., "We share the same opinions").
3. *Merger Transference*: A push toward experiencing the other as merged with or as an extension of the self.

The Anxiety: A dread of loss of contact with reality or permanent abandonment and isolation from the selfobject.

Clinical Qualities: Vague irritations and complaints accompanied by exhibitionistic fantasies and activities, hypochondriasis, cold or haughty imperiousness, affectations and at bottom reaching paranoid grandiosity with delusional restitution.

POLE OF THE *IDEALIZED PARENT IMAGO*

Pulled by Ideals of perfectionism in tension regulation with the soothing effect being derived from the admiration of idealized others or variously defined ideas of perfection.

Mature Emotional Qualities: Idealization of important others and pleasure in one's own moral and social standards.

Levels of Idealizing Transference
1. A pull toward the idealized external figure from whom strength and perfection are derived.
2. A pull toward mystical feelings of awe and ecstatic excitement associated with contact with the idealized other.
3. A pull toward relinquishing one's sense of power and perfection to the admired, omnipotent object.

The Anxiety: A dread of loss of self through an ecstatic merger with the omnipotent selfobject.

Clinical Qualities: Diffuse narcissistic vulnerability, unrealistic demands for perfectionism, idealization of powerful figures, quasi-religious hypomania, addictions, depression and at bottom massive mood swings with experiences of "The Powerful Persecutor" or "The Influencing Machine" with psychotic restitution.

MATURE COHESIVE SELF THROUGH FRAGMENTATION TO ARCHAIC SELF

Adapted from Heinz Kohut 1977.

a very vulnerable woman as a fitting and workable empathic gesture. In keeping with his emphasis on a developmental line of selfobject relatedness and a corresponding awareness of the different types of empathy required to respond to various types of selfobject needs, Kohut alluded to considering also a developmental line of interpretation since different forms of environmental responsiveness (empathy) are required for different levels of self to selfobject resonance.[5]

The conference was adjourned prematurely due to Kohut's illness. He closed by announcing this would be the last Self Psychology Conference he would be able to attend but he wanted to keep his promise to appear. He told his audience "good-bye" four days before he died.

SUMMARY

The first five chapters have focused concern on the contemporary clinical situation in psychoanalysis and psychotherapy. While psychoanalysis has come to mean many things to many people, the chief legacy of Freud to the practicing clinician is the development of a Listening Perspective which has been useful in understanding that level of psychic organization characterized by a capacity to experience oedipal (incestuous, triangular) emotional relationships. The complex picture of the psychoneuroses is characterized by psychic structures, the availability of repression, the operation of ego defenses, and the experience of emotional ambivalence. These advanced mental features give rise to the introspective experiences of drive and conflict which characterize all forms of neurosis. Freud's classical Listening Perspective has made it possible to follow the introspective experiences of those individuals who have attained a neurotic level of personality functioning.

The second Listening Perspective has its conceptual origin in Hartmann's (1950) distinction between the Ego and the Self and in Heinz Kohut's comprehensive development of the Psychology of the Self (1971, 1977). This chapter has introduced the Psychology of the Self in terms of its main areas of concern as contrasted with the traditional psychology of internal conflict. Definitions of pathology, the "tragic" view of man, the concept of "selfobject transferences," and the metaphor of the bipolar self have all been discussed as crucial aspects of the Listening Perspective of the selfobject.

In the next chapter, clinical interactions will be reported which illustrate this Listening Perspective from a diagnostic and therapeutic standpoint demonstrating the usefulness of understanding the developmental experiences elaborated by Kohut and his colleagues. Subsequent chapters will

---

[5]The developmental lines of empathy and interpretation will be illustrated in the next chapter.

contrast these two Listening Perspectives with two additional Listening Perspectives designed for understanding the introspective efforts of persons whose developmental arrests are at yet earlier periods.

A final note would include the comment that many persons come to the consulting room bringing a predominant relationship style of *being* or *acting the part* of the selfobject. That is, many persons become aware of constantly serving as a selfobject for others. Kohut's work is conspicuously lacking systematic attention to this phenomenon. In some instances the "selfobject role" may be performed masochistically and repetitively. In other instances it seems to be either an imitation or the defense, "identification with the aggressor" (A. Freud 1936). Both of these instances seem likely to stem from basically neurotic personality organization. However, when the compulsion to *be* a selfobject represents a fending off or defending against the wishes to *have* a selfobject, the behavior likely stems from the narcissistic fabric of the personality. It will be interesting to see how future writers treat this phenomenon.

METAPSYCHOLOGICAL CONSIDERATIONS

Metapsychology refers to the assumptions required for a particular psychological (clinical) theory. In the previous discussion of Freud's metapsychology, assumptions were divided into *general metapsychology*, "the principles," and *specific metapsychology*, "the points of view." The *general* metapsychology (i.e., the pleasure principle, the reality principle, the homeostasis principle, the principle of repetition compulsion and the principle of overdetermination) remains throughout psychoanalysis, and was borrowed from the other sciences originally by Freud.

However, in viewing the theories of Heinz Kohut, there is one change of focus. In the study of psychoneuroses, the idea of object, incestual transferences being a *repetition* of early emotional childhood relationships relies on the principle of repetition compulsion. In the Psychology of the Self the principle of repetition compulsion still *accounts* for the tendency of narcissistic personalities to repeat in the therapeutic relationship their need for selfobject mirroring and idealization. But the working through of the selfobject transferences is thought by Kohut to be "a new edition" of selfobject experience (1971, 1977). That is, while the selfobject transference is *formed* on the basis of repetition compulsion, the therapeutic work or the *working through* of selfobject transference involves "picking up where the original selfobject left off." Classical working through is not considered a new edition but rather is thought to involve the attainment of insight through interpretation.

Moving to a consideration of Freud's *specific* metapsychology, it is useful to reconsider the "points of view."

1. *The topographic point of view*, which Freud elaborated in his study of dreams (1900), highlights the importance of conceptualizing mental functioning in terms of conscious, preconscious and unconscious modes. While Kohut did not abandon references to conscious and unconscious functioning, he emphasizes the idea of a "vertical split" as complementary to the "horizontal split" implied in Freud's dichotomy between conscious and unconscious (Kohut 1971). That is, Kohut speaks of narcissistic grandiosity and idealization as being "split off," "walled off," dissociated or "disavowed" by the mainstream of the personality. These grandiose and idealistic trends may be largely absent from consciousness, but according to this formulation are *not* thought to be unconscious in the usual dynamic repressed sense. Thus, Kohut alternates back and forth between thinking of the mind as split between conscious and unconscious (i.e., the horizontal split) and between thinking of the main personality and the walled off or disavowed narcissistic sectors (i.e., the vertical split). The history of the psychoanalytic concept of splitting cannot be traced here but a number of writers have spoken differently of the process of splitting. Kohut specifically speaks of splitting the narcissistic selfobject trends off from the main personality such that they appear spontaneously, sporadically and consciously from time to time.

2. *The structural point of view*, first outlined by Freud in *The Ego and the Id* (1923), sought to define enduring mental qualities, agencies, or structures. Freud's structures were, of course, the id, the ego, and the superego. While Kohut finds the traditional structures useful in considering the psychoneuroses, he feels that preoedipal, *preneurotic* structure is characterized by the development of the supraordinant center of personality, the self. The self is variously thought of by Kohut in the sense of the *content* of the mind, and also as a *structure* of the mind which is evident *prior to the point at which id, ego and superego can be said to have fully differentiated* or are available to introspective experience. The self is conceptualized to be bipolar in nature with the grandiose self and the idealizing imago being its component parts. His later work (unpublished) also acknowledges the alter-ego twin component.

3. *The dynamic point of view* assumes mental phenomena result from an interplay of forces operating *in time* and is still held by the Psychology of the Self.

4. *The economic point of view*, as Freud conceptualized it, related to shifts, movement, displacement and investment of psychic energy. While Kohut seldom makes explicit reference to the economic point of view in terms of psychic energy, he frequently refers to the "psychoeconomic point of view" by which he means the rise and fall of tension states. While tension states certainly might be said to have behavioral referents, *the way Kohut uses "tension states" relative to selfobject needs remains a metapsychological assumption* akin to Freud's idea of psychic energy.

5. *The genetic point of view* which relates to the origin and the develop-

ment of mental phenomena was developed extensively in Kohut's monograph (1971) and largely neglected in Kohut's later writings. The genetic point of view in Freudian theory highlights the development of mental functions and focuses particularly on the development of libidinal and aggressive drives. Kohut rejects the concept of the aggressive drive as being a useful one in the Psychology of the Self and in the 1971 monograph speaks of two kinds of libido. The so-called "object libido" is that libidinal investment which Freud described as the various psychosexual drives and which relates to love objects in the study of neurosis. Kohut postulates a separate line of development for "narcissistic libido" in which grandiose mirroring slowly gives way to idealization. While Kohut does not revise or disavow this metapsychological thinking in his later writings, in his effort to define the bipolar self and to refine treatment techniques, he does not further elaborate his views on two kinds of libido.

6. *The adaptive point of view* which pertains to the organism's relationship or adaptation to the environment was implicit in Freud's writings although he consistently preferred an internal point of view which did not take into account the so-called "reality" of the developing organism. While Kohut would appear to agree with Freud's insistence on maintaining an *internal* point of view; in the course of explaining selfobject needs and accounting for arrests in selfobject development, Kohut talks repeatedly about "the optimally failing mother" and "the optimally failing therapist." That is, Kohut, like Freud, acknowledges that psychic development is influenced by parenting forces and attempts to specify, via the concept of empathy, exactly what parenting process fosters the internalization of the tension-reducing or self-soothing functions. That is, (optimal) frustrations permitted or created by the parent allow the development of an ability to relieve tension and to soothe the self. Psychotherapy and psychoanalysis follow a similar course. Failures of empathy from the therapist serve to provide optimal frustration so that the person develops "empathy" with the needs of the self so that the tension-relieving, self-soothing functions become "internalized." Thus, although on the surface Kohut's thinking seems to reflect the adaptive point of view, *Kohut, like Freud, maintains an internal point of view*. An understanding of selfobject transferences does not rely on explicit or crucial references to the adaptive point of view but rather on metaphorical references to it.

In summary, the metapsychology of Freud and Kohut differ primarily in Kohut's abandonment of drive theory to account for disturbances in the development of selfobject functions. He does not deny the importance of Freud's metapsychology in understanding neurosis but states that the psychic structures (id, ego and superego) and the concept of drive leading to structural conflict are simply unnecessary to postulate when attempting to understand narcissistic disorders. Kohut minimizes the importance of the conscious-unconscious (horizontal) split characterized by the topographic point of view and highlights the notion of (vertical) splitting or disavowal of narcissism. Of importance also is Kohut's notion that the working through process with narcissistic disorders is a *new* edition of experience rather than experience which is only compulsively repeated.

CONCLUSION: THE SELFOBJECT LISTENING PERSPECTIVE

Kohut's later work emphasizes the clinical phenomena which he refers to as the fragmentation and cohesion of self as related to the quality of contact with the (selfobject) therapist. This feature of Kohut's work is perhaps the most crucial from the standpoint of forming a Listening Perspective. That is, if one listens to someone arrested at the selfobject phase of development as though that person actively experiences drives and structural conflict, one would likely fail to grasp the full impact of the way in which that person experiences the world. Instead, to be able with such persons to listen to the ebb and flow of tension states related to selfobject empathy puts one in a position to grasp the alternating states of fragmented and cohesive experience and to relate to the developmentally necessary experiences of "optimal frustration." The therapist's empathy is bound to have its shortcomings, and Kohut's perspective for listening to narcissistic personality organization fixes upon the fragmented experiences which follow in the wake of empathic failure.

The widespread enthusiasm for this Listening Perspective has almost turned Kohut's Psychology of the Self into a "cult of empathy." The uncritical generalization of this style of listening to persons experiencing other phases of developmental arrest has been a questionable side effect of the general popularity of Kohut's approach. Furthermore, Kohut himself in his last writings (unpublished) extended his selfobject approach to a re-analysis of Freud's early work on neurosis. Kohut's final position, first stated in a footnote (1977), holds that people need selfobjects from birth to death. While the position is tenable, it draws attention away from the developmental period in which selfobject need occupies center stage, i.e., the peak period of narcissistic vulnerability which Kohut has so aptly described. Kohut's later expansive position also detracts from the highly potent usage of the Selfobject Listening Perspective in analyzing Narcissistic Personality Organization and overlooks the likelihood that attention to different kinds of self and other experience may provide greater listening potency for other forms of personality organization which arise from different types of developmental arrest.

7 Illustrations of the Selfobject Listening Perspective

The process of learning to be a psychotherapist understandably causes one to become more or less entrenched in certain ways of listening and responding to clinical interactions. To those who have not yet discovered through actual clinical use the extreme relevance of Kohut's Selfobject Listening Perspective with the narcissistic personality organization, the whole preceding chapter may have seemed flat or overintellectualized without case illustrations. In this chapter accounts of four clinical interactions will be presented to illustrate (1) the appearance of *the bipolar self during the diagnostic phase* (George); (2) the use of the Selfobject Listening Perspective in *the early phases of psychotherapy* (Gary); (3) the *working through of selfobject transferences* in extended psychoanalytic psychotherapy (Lou); and (4) the developmental lines of empathy and interpretation.

But before moving to applications of the Selfobject Perspective in actual clinical settings, listening for the appearance of Kohut's selfobject configurations will be introduced by way of looking at an ancient tale retold by Hans Christian Anderson and analyzed by one of my colleagues, Mary Cook.

A KOHUTIAN ANALYSIS OF "THE NIGHTINGALE"

(This section contributed by Mary Cook.)

This is an analysis from a Kohutian perspective of the story "The Nightingale," by Hans Christian Andersen. This is the fictional tale of an Emperor in China who might be said to have a narcissistic selfobject fixation.[1]

The story begins with a description of the Emperor's palace and its grounds. The palace is filled with beautiful and costly things that are so fragile that one must be cautious when touching them. The grounds are so enormous that it is difficult to tell where they end. This might be thought of as a description of the Emperor's internal state, expressing his reliance on external things to attract attention and perhaps to provoke envy,

---

[1]Otto Kernberg (1975, p. 259f.) tells of a moving incident in which one of his patients vividly recalled this story from childhood. The reader is referred to Kernberg's chapters on the Narcissistic Personality for a somewhat different perspective than the one offered here.

i.e., his grandiose self and the concomitant fragility of his ego. The grandiosity and lack of boundaries is also evident in the spaciousness of the grounds. These features might be thought of as a result of a defect in the self.

Outside the grounds, however, was the most spectacular thing in the whole kingdom. Free and available to everyone, was a nightingale, who caught the attention of visitors as well as the people who lived outside the palace grounds. This bird was reputed to be superior to anything in the kingdom because of its most beautiful song. Upon hearing this, the Emperor's envy was aroused and he knew he had to possess this creature.

It is interesting to note that no one in the Emperor's court knew anything about the bird except for the kitchen maid who would pass it in the forest when visiting her sick mother. She explained the nightingale's song as having the same effect as a kiss from her mother. The Emperor's courtiers appeared to represent alter-ego's of the Emperor, and they, like the Emperor, had lost the capacity to recognize the good and giving object. After thinking the nightingale's song was a frog's croak and a cow's bellow, the kitchen maid finally pointed out the nightingale to them. Upon seeing it, they were disappointed that it was just a plain, brown bird.

The nightingale said she would be glad to sing for the Emperor and she followed the courtiers back to court. Upon hearing the bird's song, the Emperor was moved to tears. This represents the establishment of empathy and, in treatment terms, the readiness for a specific introject. The bird represents an outside object experienced as a part of the grandiose self, and as such, its absence cannot be tolerated. The Emperor imprisons the bird in his castle so that he could be near it and proudly exhibit it to others when he desired.

One day someone sent a gift to the Emperor. It was an artificial nightingale and it was adorned with precious stones. It sang one of the songs that the real nightingale sang. Everyone at the court agreed that it sang just as well as the real bird and was much prettier to look at. While thus comparing the two birds, the real nightingale flew out of an open window.

The explanation for the mechanical bird being better than the real one was that, "in the real nightingale you never know what you will hear, but in the artificial one everything is decided beforehand. . . ." You can account for things, you can open it, and show the human ingenuity in arranging the waltzes, how they go, and how one note follows another." The Emperor and his court seem to be describing the proper elements for a successful narcissistic merger, i.e., an object which can be possessed, one whose function is predictable, and is a product of man's omnipotence. One might postulate that the Emperor had suffered minor narcissistic injuries from the lack of these qualities in the real bird and was thus unable to experience a successfully satisfying merger. This prompts the Emperor's regression to a more archaic selfobject, and one that is more representative of his outward grandiosity and inner lifelessness. The description of the artificial bird is reminiscent of the description of the palace and one wonders if this show of external beauty and costliness betrays internal weakness.

The real nightingale was declared an ungrateful escapee and was banished from the kingdom, thus the devaluation of an object which cannot be controlled and which has lost its usefulness via replacement with a more conforming selfobject. Only the people outside the palace grounds are aware that something is missing in this artificial bird, although they don't know what. Could the missing quality be the higher level of empathy which the real bird possessed and was capable of imparting, but which the Emperor was unable to fully appreciate and respond to? The nightingale's banishment is foreboding, perhaps symbolic of the failure to establish empathy, thereby marking the beginning of further disintegration.

Kohut defines empathy in three ways: ". . . the recognition of the self in the other, . . . the expansion of the self to include the other, . . . and accepting, confirming and understanding the echo evoked by the self" (Ornstein, in Kohut 1978, p. 84). The regression to the merger with the more archaic selfobject provides tension relief without recognition of the object's function, without recognition of self and other, and without acknowledging the content of the soothing quality, i.e., the empathy.

The new bird was always with the Emperor and he hung jewels and symbolic representations of ownership upon it. Its song could be mastered and learned by heart and this was an important reason for its usefulness. Kohut's discussion of music sheds light on this function. Music serves to discharge primitive impulses. It affords the opportunity to gain relief from tensions through the exercise of changing dissonance to consonance, and the organization of music allows compliance to rules, thus providing structure to the self. Perhaps the most important aspect of music is that it encourages a specific type of regression. Kohut writes, ". . . controlled temporary regressions tend to prevent or counter uncontrolled, chronic ones" (Kohut 1978, p. 253).

One of the results of a disturbance of the infant's early attempts to merge with the idealized parent imago as a part of the grandiose self, is that the self's narcissistic balance is unstable, and there is little protection from traumatic overstimulation and diffuse narcissistic vulnerability (Kohut 1978, pp. 60–61). As ego strength is invested in archaic images, the unstable self has difficulty in limiting and defining stimulation, thus the attraction to the self-soothing effect of music.

One evening, while the Emperor was listening to the bird, a spring burst and the music stopped. Physicians were sent for but they were unable to help, so they sent for a watchmaker. It's interesting to note how the Emperor thinks of the object as part of himself, and thus calls for physicians as if to heal an illness of the body, rather than thinking in terms of repairing a mechanical device. The watchmaker saves the bird, however he cautions that it is worn out and that the tune may not be the same. Furthermore, it should only be played once a year.

A few years passed and the Emperor grew very ill and was not expected to live. He was pale and cold and could hardly breathe. This seems to be a result of the loss of the selfobject manifesting in a body-mind fragmentation with hypochondriacal preoccupations. Feeling a heavy weight upon him, the Emperor opens his eyes to find Death sitting on his chest, wearing his crown and holding his sword and banner. All around the Emperor were faces which represented the Emperor's good and bad deeds. He grew very frightened and wanted to drown out their voices with music but he was not strong enough to wind up the bird.

Death seems to represent a killing of the defenses and as they break down, the Emperor begins to experience affective splitting as evidenced by his good and bad deeds. This may be looked at as the point of optimal frustration. The Emperor is defenseless in face of numerous traumas. His self-soothing object has failed him, he is aware of a lack of cohesion (his self defect), and he is having to acknowledge confused affect states. His infantile needs are intense, activated and conscious. They are not being gratified, rather the opposite.

Just at this point of optimal frustration, the living nightingale returned and began to sing. As she sang, the faces became fainter and the color returned to the Emperor's skin. Death asked the nightingale to continue and the nightingale said, "Yes, if Death would return the Emperor's crown, sword and banner." Death returned these objects and was so moved by a song about mourning and the mourner's tears bringing new growth, that he slipped away. This reference to mourning might be thought of as part of the process Kohut calls "transmuting internalizations," i.e., the "decathexis" of the external object prior to its depersonification and internalization.

The Emperor expressed his gratefulness to the bird for saving his life and he told her that he was surprised she would do this for him when he had banished her from his kingdom. The nightingale reminds him that he had responded with tears to her first song and that this had created a bond between them. The bird seems to be saying that this readiness for an introject as manifest in his original empathic response is what makes "restoration of the self" possible. The Emperor then said that he would destroy the artificial bird, and the nightingale tells him not to, that the mechanical bird did the best it could, and that it can be appreciated. The idealization of the artificial bird had led to selfobject merger and the response upon it's failing is to destructively abandon it totally.

The Emperor makes an attempt to keep the nightingale with him, but this time, recognizing the object as separate from himself, offers a compromise. He asks if she would be willing to stay with him and only sing when she wanted. The bird declines, reassuring the Emperor that she will come and sing for him frequently but that she prefers to live in the forest and to travel freely. She also introduces a new element. She tells him that not only will she sing songs of joy, but of suffering too, songs of both good and evil. She is thus supporting the emergence of object constancy and ambivalence with her empathy and presence.

Kohut discusses a case which bears a marked resemblance to this story (Kohut 1978, p. 247). He notes three distinct phases which the patient moves through. In the first stage, the patient is soothed by the sound of the analyst's voice and thereby obtains direct tension relief. He pays no attention, perhaps doesn't even recognize that there is a content. In the second phase, the patient is able to listen to the content of the analyst's voice and becomes aware of specific tensions and defects within himself. In the third stage, he is able to acknowledge and gain insight from both the content and the emotions, along with establishing diverse and rewarding social contacts with others. This is accomplished through the recognition of separateness and ambivalence through the support of an empathic analyst.

Kohut's concept of "transmuting internalization" has three phases (Ornstein, in Kohut 1978, p. 64). There must exist *first* a readiness for specific introjects. This lays the groundwork for the process of structure formation. The *second* stage occurs at the point of "optimal frustration," the time for optimal learning. Frustration and disappointment occur repeatedly as infantile needs are activated and not gratified, although empathically contained by the selfobject. In therapy the aim is to recognize the need for the selfobject in terms of its *functions* so that disappointments can be experienced with increasingly less trauma. This permits the partial withdrawal of cathexis or investment in the selfobject, akin to what happens in the process of mourning.

> The ego acquires increasing tolerance for the analyst's absence and for his occasional failure to achieve a correct empathic understanding. The patient learns that the idealizing libido need not be immediately withdrawn from the idealized imago and that the painful and dangerous regressive shifts of the narcissistic cathexes can be prevented. Concomitant with the increase of the ability to maintain a part of the idealizing investment despite the separation, there is also an enhancement of internalization, i.e., the analysand's psychic organization acquires the capacity to perform some of the functions previously performed by the idealized object. (Kohut 1978, pp. 488-489)

The *third* phase (depersonalization) represents a shift from the archaic need for the selfobject, to recognizing the object as separate from the self, to gradually relying on the self when these functions temporarily fail to come from the object; thereby making possible a depersonalization and internalization of the functions by integrating them into the self structure.

This process can be followed in the story from the beginning where the Emperor is surrounded by alter egos and treats the nightingale as a self-object. When this object cannot provide a successful merger, it is given up for a more archaic selfobject. This object failing, the Emperor suffers from fragmentation, becoming surrounded by good and bad deeds (sexual and aggressive by-products of fragmentation?).

When the real nightingale empathically returns, the Emperor is ready for a new kind of relationship. By the final interchange there has been a transformation in the quality of relationship with the object. The Emperor can now tolerate separateness from the bird, having learned increased frustration tolerance through a partial internalization of the *functions* which the object served. The nightingale is willing to continue providing empathic understanding as the Emperor continues to recognize her separateness.

A COMMENCEMENT OF THERAPY SELECTED TO ILLUSTRATE THE BI-POLAR NATURE OF THE SELF (George)

As early as the first visit, George began to idealize me. He had been referred by a psychoanalytic colleague, through a former girlfriend. He was immediately and thoroughly impressed by my manner, intelligence, and capacity "to understand him" and "to explain what therapy was all about."

George presented the appearance of a very bright, ambitious, and highly successful businessman in his mid 30's. His complaints were mostly vague and ill-defined, relating to not having as much zest and enthusiasm for his work as he would like, and not allowing himself more time and energy to enjoy his life, especially with women. He reported working up to 60 hours a week but not being able to figure out why he felt so driven to work since his business is well established and stable. George reported liking his work okay but that he has simply failed to derive as much enjoyment and satisfaction out of it as he feels he should be able to. There were several specific concerns he was able to express relating to fears of impotency, a search for "understanding" women, and a dislike of compulsive masturbation (frequently done in front of a mirror).

He spent several sessions discussing his need for therapy then agreed to embark on what we both understood as long term therapy, meeting twice weekly. Clinicians generally place great emphasis on the importance of the first hour after such a commitment to treatment has been made.

Notes from the Initial Treatment Hour

George entered and moved directly to the couch, reporting a feeling of great exhilaration over getting something going for himself at last! He had decided to give a thumbnail history of his life today.

In a thorough and historical manner, he began back in high school and proceeded to the present, telling about various activities he had participated in, offices he held, international travel adventures, and a string of various other successes. If it had not already been obvious that this was a man of extraordinary accomplishment and talent, it certainly would have been from the facts he thus provided. The most striking aspect of George's story was his hurried and matter-of-fact manner. The modesty was overwhelming.

George then told of a discrepancy which he has felt for a long time, between what he termed his "real self" and his "ideal self." George knows his accomplishments are well above average, although he isn't impressed by them. There are two areas of ambition in his life he wished he could realize: first, to become a concert pianist, and second, to become a professional pilot.

George explained he came from a musical family and that, as a child, he can remember long hours of sitting quietly or lying underneath the grand piano listening to his mother play. He dwelt on the pleasure and the soothing quality of the melodies which his mother used to play for him. When he was quite young, there had been an attempt to give him music lessons, but for some reason, he didn't respond well to the lessons. He simply couldn't learn to read music. As he grew older, he began to sit down and play. George assured me he has a fabulous ear and that that's how he learned to play the piano. He has perfect pitch and has learned through the years to play quite complicated pieces of classical music entirely by ear. He acknowledges this is a rare and extraordinary accomplishment, though he doesn't consider himself an accomplished musician. Fine musicianship is a goal which George feels he could realistically attain. He described the many hours spent quite pleasurably sitting at the piano, emphasizing the self-soothing effect which the music provides for him, clearly connecting it with the pleasure of his early childhood with mother.

George then shifted to his second great ambition of becoming a professional pilot. On weekends, he goes flying and he described in detail the intense sensations that he gets in being able to move away from the earth, soaring quietly above everything and everybody—often noiselessly with the engine shut off—all alone, soaring through the sky, not attached to anything or anyone. Chagrined, he confessed there was only one problem: he has chronic flight sickness, caused by an inner ear sensitivity with nausea and vomiting; a fact which he has concealed carefully even through years of military flight training!

Time was running out. I told George I did want to make one observation today. In his two major life ambitions, one was made possible by a good ear and the other spoiled by a bad ear. George was visibly startled by my comment. He laughed, expressed amazement, and wondered why he had never thought of that before. Instantly he declared that I had to be a genius to make a connection like that!

Subsequent Developments

At the beginning of the next session, George asked if I had any reaction to the previous hour since we had run out of time. I mentioned his reticence to discuss more frankly his good qualities and his many achievements. He at first denied wanting to impress me; I commented that we were, after all, not here for a social gathering, but an honest appraisal of who he was. The main focus of my interpretation was on how difficult it was for him to experience joy and pride in his accomplishments and to relay that sense of enthusiasm to me directly. In subsequent sessions, he brought many similar observations of himself from his business and relationships with women in which he really did want to show off a little, to "toot his horn" about himself, but instead had become matter of fact, hurried, or evasive and embarrassed.

Several months later, there was a holiday interruption of two weeks. George summarized his dreams while I was away as relating to a "quest for power." One fragment pictured him flying on top of a long cylindrical balloon. He also reported more active sexual activity with his girlfriend than he had experienced for a long time. My chief comment, that hour, was to point out how hard it was for him to express his wishes and impulses for power. I spoke of his dreams as statements of *feelings* of grandiosity and expansiveness, inquiring if they might in any way be related to the holiday break? He was fascinated by this idea, but most of all pleased, that I was interested in hearing his "asocial" wishes for power and prestige and, that I didn't consider them unseemly. He left saying this was his "most productive" session. The following hour he brought this dream:

I was going to have an appendectomy in the White House surgical center. Harry Truman was there, and the surgeon was Gerald Ford, but it didn't seem like a Truman or a Ford White House.[2] I was standing in line waiting with John Wayne,[3] since it seemed like he was going to have something done first, maybe the same thing. I could see and recognize the White House, but where I was going was to a brownstone building on the left. I know there's no brownstone building on the left, but there was in the dream.

[2]Truman was the first president he remembered as a child. Ford was the current president.
[3]Many of my patients encountered John Wayne at that time in the elevator and hallway going to his physician. My office would be to the left. He reports being especially fond of brownstone buildings.

Our discussion of the dream highlighted his reluctance to acknowledge his grandiose wish, "to step into the shoes of the president." This reluctance manifested itself as his "having to undergo surgery" along with the movie star, John Wayne. This dream appeared to represent a kind of "telescoping" (Kohut 1971) of the castration concern built upon the grandiose wish and his reluctance in the area of male exhibitionism. My acceptance of his grandiose feelings led to a subsequent flowering of dreams of international scope wherein George was hobnobbing with a cast of the all-time "greats." He laughed in thorough enjoyment at all these dreams as coming from himself—he has always preferred to consider himself a modest man.

A prominent feature of our early hours together was how frequently he would arrive feeling burdened, reporting having had a bad day and knowing that the tension was somehow related to his therapy. In the course of describing things to me, the sense of tension, intense excitement, and bodily preoccupations would completely vanish during the hour, so that he often left very relieved and began to ascribe to the sessions a "magical effect."

The features of George's early therapy hours which are of interest from the standpoint of the study of the self are:

1. The early emergence of the idealizing tendency manifest primarily in his modest devaluation of himself and his simultaneous overestimation of myself, as well as the magical effect derived from an empathic relationship with me.

2. The search for the reestablishment of the original selfobject relationship with mother via music. While music may yet offer George an avenue for creative sublimation, the early piano lessons failed so whatever musical ability that was to develop *had to come from within*; that is, the pattern of the nuclear self that has continued to be expressed demanded that the pleasurable qualities must be experienced, as coming from himself, from his own ear, *not* from music outside.

3. The struggle to liberate himself from (mother) earth *via* the soothing effect of flying, something which he can do on his own, has remained haunted by a pull of a prohibition coming from his inner ear producing nausea and vomiting.

4. The phallic quality of airplanes in general, and his dream of being precariously perched atop a long cylindrical flying balloon may relate to his longstanding fear of impotence. How might "keeping his balloon up" relate to the inner ear prohibition over leaving mother earth, and to the problem of transcending or moving away from the original selfobject pull?

5. Both of George's ambitions carried the idea of natural talent plus "social confirmation" qualities, i.e., a *concert* pianist and a *professional* pilot. George's father, with whom he was close, disappeared before three years of

age (a flight?). Subsequent to these hours, he probed into the family secret he was "never to hear," and found that his father had left for a long prison sentence, never to return.

THE GORILLA'S ARM DREAM: A "SELF STATE" DREAM[4] ILLUSTRATING THE WORKING THROUGH OF THE SELFOBJECT TRANSFERENCE

(Follow-up on George after two years of twice weekly psychotherapy.)

In the initial phase of George's therapy he elaborated on what he called his long-standing trait of "suggestibility." In his hours he has always been ready to consider any thoughts or ideas which I have had. In a most compliant and suggestible manner George would pursue his associations in the direction which he felt *my* comments were pointing. He has at times worried about this suggestible quality in terms of his fear that he is an extremely "dependent" person.

In contrast to this theme of suggestibility and dependency is his very independent, creative and competent professional work. He enjoys his work though he has found himself working up to 60 hours a week and wearing himself out. This overwork is a trait of long-standing nature. He has considered his tendency to overwork in light of possible "self-destructive trends," "masochistic needs," and "demands for perfection." None of these ideas seemed particularly helpful in understanding his dedication or the enjoyment which he receives from long hours of solitary, concentrated and creative work. George has considered the possibility that he is escaping from interpersonal relationships by diving into work, although this has been examined in detail without results. The most useful ideas emerged when I was able to point out to him the sense of joy and firm sense of self-consolidation which he has while working and to point out that these firm, cohesive, self experiences stand in contrast to feelings of helplessness, vulnerability and anxiety which characterize many other aspects of his life, particularly his personal relationships. The problem of overwork has been a persistent one, and after considerable discussion he finally concluded that he had no way to control or limit his work pattern and that even reorganizing his office and setting up more efficient means of getting work done were ineffective in relieving him of the compulsion to take on a heavy load and to get it out impeccably on time. He does not need this work to insure an adequate income. His business is firmly established so he could not use that as a reason either. In many ways he tried to get me to be a limiting force by

[4]Kohut has discussed "self state" dreams in contrast to dreams depicting internal conflict (unpublished).

wanting me to accuse him of being such things as self-destructive, maso-chistic, and so forth. He spoke of his helplessness to do anything about it and his belief that ultimately it probably will be something external to himself like a medical problem which will limit him, i.e., "doctor's orders."

George has maintained a cardiac concern for many years without cause. Although his grandfather died from cardiac complications, he was advanced in age and there is no other history of heart or circulation problems in the family. George is young and has always enjoyed exceptionally good health and a good heart, but nonetheless has continued to worry for fear that some form of cardiac problem will arise. He has been to several doctors but is always reassured that his heart is in excellent condition. He realizes now that his concern is psychological but he doesn't know how to put it into perspective.

The next recurring theme bearing on the dream goes back almost to the beginning of therapy in which George has attempted to conceptualize exactly what the nature of psychotherapy is, what his job is and what my role in the process is. At the outset he had a series of questions and seemed extraordinarily pleased and impressed that I was able to give him satisfactory answers so that we could start the therapy on a basis which he found "intelligent and sensible." On other occasions when he has noticed some aspect of the psychotherapy process he has brought it up and insisted on discussing it, trying to get my opinion on the process and how it's working. This set of discussions culminated in some conclusions about what goes on in therapy, idealizing my role considerably and highlighting the importance of the layman-expert professional model in our work. One day for reasons that were not clear to me at the time, I chose to take issue with him on this point. Being very much aware that I did not want to disrupt the growing idealization transference, I nevertheless felt a need to assert the notion that therapy was, after all, basically *his* mind observing, exploring and expanding and that the layman-expert model was inadequate. George was quite un-happy by my challenge and a lively discussion ensued. I was essentially pointing out the wish for the idealized person who would guide him and, in the process, make him feel secure. I continued to highlight the meditational aspect of analytic therapy and to maintain that I did have a role, but that the role was that of a catalyst or an expert listener, not a wizard on the subject of the human mind. He persisted in wanting to assign to me knowledge and a fund of information which, if he could just think of the right questions, I could share with him the answers. On the occasion in which this discussion culminated I had to tell him that I wasn't sure why I was standing so firmly on my point that this was *his* therapy, that *he* was the only expert on his own mind, and that my expertise was in listening and reflecting to him his own thoughts, his own problems, and his own solutions. George became in-creasingly agitated and left the session extremely troubled by this discussion.

The following session had been a planned miss due to a scheduled business trip, but the following two sessions after that were cancelled only hours before on the basis of excessive business demands such that he could not make it to my office. When he did return ten days later, most of the session was spent filling me in on events leading him to feeling totally overwhelmed with work stress to such an extent that now he "had finally done it." Only that day he had begun to have severe pains in his chest and left arm as a result of pushing himself too hard, too long. He was extremely alarmed by the pains and believed a heart attack was imminent. He had scheduled an appointment with his cardiologist for the following morning. I agreed with the importance of a physical examination but I surprised him by adding that, of course, such symptoms might occur as a result of psychological concerns. If there were such concerns I inquired what they might be. He could only deal with my question in terms of excessive stress producing physical symptoms. I urged him to consider the issue further and he spontaneously remembered having told me recently that the only way his excessive work was going to be limited was by an outside source, namely a doctor, urging him to save his health and his heart. He was very surprised with this connection and was very disbelieving that this could have anything to do with the intense pains and discomfort that he had been having all day long. I did have an opportunity to point out how strong his wish for "another" is and how much he wants certain things to come not from himself but rather from the outside and to remind him how upset he'd become at our last session when I was confronting him on just that point, that is, his wish that in some way I would limit, contain, suggest, or provide guidance for him. He didn't like my putting these things together, but he is a sophisticated man and was able to add some associations. George had chosen to sit up for this hour rather than to use the couch.

The following hour George indicated he was going to sit up again today since he "had just eaten a heavy meal"—if that was okay with me? I assured him (as I had done several times before) that it made no difference to me whether or not he used the couch but I was, of course, interested in his ideas about why some days the couch seemed comfortable and other days he preferred to sit face to face and have what he called a "confrontation." He said he had thought about the matter on the way to the session and knew I was going to ask about it. He was hoping not to have to discuss it and thereby gave me the excuse of having had a large meal. He spent some time discussing why he felt so much better about sitting and talking to me directly and how the feedback and the communication between the two of us was so much more "meaningful" to him. I told him I did have a continued interest in his thoughts on the matter.

George missed the next session because of a business trip. He called in the middle of the afternoon on the day of the following appointment to tell me he was considering not coming again as he had a lot of work to do this evening and if he took an hour off in the middle he was afraid he wouldn't get his work done. I expressed how difficult it is to follow him because he is so busy. When he doesn't come in, I do lose track of what's happening in his life. He seemed pleased I was interested in seeing him and wondered if he could leave it open in case he could get away. I told him that was fine, and he wanted to leave it that if he came, fine; if not, I would go ahead and leave, knowing he would not arrive. He knew he was the last patient of the day.

George arrived ten minutes late which is unusual for him since he is a careful and punctual man. In a cheerful and hearty manner he greeted me and told me to unpack my briefcase, that I still had one more session before my weekend! He wanted to sit up again, and our discussion about his use of the couch continued. He had given it thought and the best he could come up with was that for now he was simply more comfortable talking directly with me rather than lying down on the couch and losing track of where I was and not getting the "feedback" that made the sessions so "meaningful." He discussed the couch in terms of passivity and feelings of helplessness in contrast to the more direct personal feelings of "accomplishment" he gets when we are talking face to face. He hastened to add he feels this is only a phase of the therapy he is going through now. He thinks at some later point he will resume work on the couch.

In passing, he mentioned a "nonsensical" dream about a "gorilla's arm." He laughed, knowing I would be interested in the dream, but unfortunately he had forgotten almost all of it though he had been trying all day to recall it. I asked him what part he did recall. He said really only one thing. In this dream he seemed to be moving around, sometimes walking, sometimes driving his car, sometimes carrying other things; but always he was carrying around with him or dragging behind him or carrying in his mouth this gorilla's arm, a big hairy gorilla's arm. He laughed at what a bizarre image it was. He apologized for not being able to remember more of the dream because he was sure it was a good one. I asked him *which* arm? He laughed at the question as if how could such a detail matter. I told him to remember the dream, look at the arm, and tell me which arm. He thought for a few minutes reconstructing the visual imagery, and said it was the left arm. I asked for associations to the arm, to gorillas, to dragging things around, and carrying things in his mouth, but he was unable to associate to any of those things. He reported "no general reaction to the arm and gorilla," but he thought of the arm in particular as "ugly." He elaborated the part about having to drag it around everywhere he went.

As the session went on, George indicated that he had been thinking increasingly about my comment that this was *his* therapy and that *I* could not provide him with answers or solutions. He said that he certainly could understand I was right. I added, "but you don't like it" to which he heartily agreed. He had been able to determine that the main effect which he was conscious of was the one we had discussed many times which is the calming effect the sessions have on him and in particular my "suggestions" and "feedback" to him. In this connection he recalled several similar and parallel instances outside of therapy we had discussed earlier.

One instance had occurred not long ago with his girlfriend. (This might be thought of as bringing the problem of the selfobject transference into a contemporary situation with his girlfriend so that the relationship to the presenting concern of impotency could be seen.) In this example from three or four weekends before, he was planning on spending the evening with his girlfriend. He reported somewhat reluctantly moving toward lovemaking mainly because he felt that *she* wanted it. He was getting into it when he experienced a "sexual failure" and was very frustrated that he lost and could not regain his erection. His girlfriend was "very accepting and understanding" according to his report and they simply found some other ways to enjoy the evening with her taking essentially a "reassuring role." He was pleased and amazed on the following evening that not only was his performance restored but it was at an all-time high. This incident had been discussed at the time in the context of reassurance and his ability to function better when he had the empathy and reassurance of another.

A similar incident he recalled had been reported a week or two later when he decided to take a weekend trip with his ex-wife. He asked her to go on this particular trip as a companion mostly because he felt that she was the only person he knows he could relax and enjoy himself with. After the weekend he reported for the first time in many months being miraculously calm, relaxed and comfortable; feeling very grateful to his ex-wife for being such a fine person, pleasant to be with. He reported that they had enjoyed basically a "platonic weekend" which was pleasant for both of them. The magical quality of the calm and relaxation was what amazed him the most and in our discussion I once again highlighted the importance of external understanding and empathy whether it was from his girlfriend, his ex-wife, or myself. He then recalled the soothing effect of his mother's piano playing when he was a child.

I announced I was ready to interpret his dream! We both laughed in recognition of what an apparently thin thread I would have to be working with because of the paucity of dream imagery and associations. I began by suggesting that the gorilla's arm may be a part of himself, emphasizing the "part of." It took him a few minutes to make the connection with the left arm and the conversion pains that he experienced the week before in his own left arm. No medical evidence had been found which would indicate a physical problem with the arm and his doctor had been confirming of my hunch that the pains were specific and no doubt psychological. The next phase of our understanding of the dream fragment was that the particular part of himself we were looking at was what he considered to be an "ugly" part. Furthermore, it was a part he felt he had to be constantly dragging around with him or carrying in his mouth no matter where he went or what he did. Yet the arm was not *his* arm but a gorrilla's arm. We discussed various aspects of a gorilla: the dangerous, the instinctual, the masculine, the fatherly, but most of all he emphasized the human.

I told him I enjoyed the dream very much and that it was an extremely creative and helpful image. Then with his help I was able to relate it to the problem of his relationship to me and to the image of a blanket that a young child drags along behind him or holds in his mouth giving himself calm and reassurance. I related his need or wish for an outside someone or, in his dream imagery, a part of someone or something which would give him comfort which he could carry around. We related this back to the reassuring qualities of his girlfriend, the calming influence of his ex-wife, and the calming influence of the therapy sessions with my "direct feedback" to him. I suggest further that there was something about this gorilla's arm that represented me, something unpleasant or ugly. He countermanded immediately saying that nothing could be further from the truth. He enjoyed very much our sessions together, particularly when he was able to discuss things directly with me and to get ideas and feedback. At that point he accepted my reflection that these qualities were exactly what he experienced as ugly. He added the word "dependency." I reminded him of the pains in his arm and how they seemed to be a direct consequence of our discussions about the expert-layman model of therapy which had made him angry with me. I also reminded him that the arm symptom occurred as an effort to get some doctor to provide limitations and guidance. He said at first that I was lumping contradictory things together. He indicated the suggestible qualities and the dependency qualities stood in sharp contrast to the calming and soothing qualities which he gains from having another. I told him I thought the dream image was more effective than either he or I had been in condensing the problem into one of comfort *with* a sense of ugliness. By this time George was resonating fully with the dream image, surprised but enjoying the condensations which the image contained.

I commented on his persistent attempts to tell *me* that his mind "refuses to introspect," and for what he had felt were my "unrealistic expectations" that he would be able to move the therapy ahead on his own. How much more eloquently could we expect his feelings to be expressed than they were in the dream? Almost by way of reassurance, I congratulated him on having an unconscious mind quite capable of producing things that were well ahead of all of the words and thoughts he and I together could muster. He realized that, as much as he didn't like to admit it, *his* dream had made a point and had tied together this series of experiences, highlighting his persistent need to have a strong but "ugly" external force accompany him wherever he went in all of his endeavors. He quickly raised the question, "but is this good or bad?" He answered it for himself realizing that the dream had served to simply define what *is*, including his own feelings of ugliness about his persistent need for something or someone to accompany him and to calm him. He was pleased and we both had the feeling that the work of a number of weeks had come to fruition and definition in this very compelling and helpful dream.

INCEST VIEWED AS NARCISSISTIC RAGE (Gary)
The Therapist's Report[5]

Gary was referred by a self-help organization dealing with intra-familial "sexual abuse." He had been placed on probation with therapy recommended. Probation came as a result of a suspended sentence for a single charge of "molesting" his daughter, age 10. He had pleaded guilty; the charges were dropped from a felony to a misdemeanor resulting in no jail time, but rather probation as defined above.

Gary, blond with blue eyes, looks considerably younger than his 39 years, partly because he is just over five feet tall, but mostly because of his boyish face and many child-like expressions. He was raised in a working class family, the middle child with two brothers. He is currently running his own small business, the same type of business as both his brothers now and his father before his death several years ago. Gary was married twice and divorced for the second time several years ago. Gary is currently living with his mother. His 10-year-old daughter and his 8-year-old son live with their mother, his first wife. Gary rarely saw his children, openly stating that he is frightened of the responsibility and never really wanted to be a father. Gary's first wife made friends with his second wife and, during the time of crisis in this second marriage, both women went "out on the town" together and shared problems and stories.

It was during that time that Gary admits having "revenge fantasies" on his first wife by picturing her walking in on him and his daughter ("when she was 18") having a sexual encounter. He said he was consumed with this fantasy. It was shortly after his second wife admitted to an affair, which led to her leaving, that the incest incident occurred. This incident clinically appears to represent an act of Narcissistic Rage. Kohut's theoretical formulations provide an excellent conceptual framework to explain the clinical data in this case.

---

[5]The therapist is a woman. See note on contributors, p. xix.

Narcissism and Narcissistic Rage

In his classification of the primary disturbances of the self, Kohut (1977, pp. 192–193), includes five groups:

(1) psychoses (2) borderline states (3) schizoid and paranoid personalities (4) narcissistic personality disorders, and (5) narcissistic behavior disorders.

In these last two forms of primary disturbances of the self, Kohut believes the self can enter spontaneously into limited transference with the selfobject therapist making therapeutic working through possible. The limited transference is suggested by the process of tension build-up and reduction within the therapy session.

Therapist's Report Continues

Gary enters the sessions in a mild state of agitation. He characteristically tries to deny this by what has come to be called his "John Wayne" role[6] (his favorite current fantasy hero whom he tries to imitate in times of stress). He only presents issues in the first of the session that enhance his macho image, smoking non-stop all the while.

If I listen quite empathically to every word, he seems to calm down within about twenty minutes. He has occasionally mentioned that he usually calms down when he comes to see me, but that it goes away in a day or two. However, if I get confrontive or make an interpretation, he withdraws all emotional investment or gets confused. According to Kohut, one might expect him to react to these unempathic responses with Narcissistic rage: the precariously established self of the child is renewed in the therapy situation and depends on the near-perfect empathy and control over the selfobject's responses for the maintenance of its cohesion (1977, p. 91).

Gary responds to the failure in empathy primarily by distancing himself from (the rage within and) the therapist. He has explained this process of distancing himself from his feelings (which he states he cannot identify) as something he learned to do consciously. He says he starts to feel "out of control" (having feelings is, to Gary, being out of control), so he totally relaxes his body, letting go of all sensations and then puts other thoughts in his head by force, like a John Wayne fantasy until he feels in control again. The anxiety here would be the dread of the loss of his sense of self—the fragmentation of and the estrangement from his body and mind in space, the breakup of the sense of his continuity in time, as he gets overwhelmed and disoriented.

It is not unreasonable to assume that Gary's mother (his first selfobject) was able to provide only limited empathy for him, thus depriving him of experiences of empathic merger at the stage of development which would have

[6]This series was reported before John Wayne's illness and death. This report is from a woman colleague who works in a different location so that the John Wayne content is not related to seeing him in the building as it may have been with George.

preceded a firm establishment of the self. Such evidence is well founded from many early memories, one of which is provided for illustration.

Gary was about 3½ or 4, as he recalls, when he went out to play with his older brother and cousin, proudly wearing his brand new cowboy boots. They had been cautioned many times never to go near the river where there were gypsies who kidnapped and tortured little children if they caught them. Needless to say, Gary followed the other pair down to the river for a big adventure. During their play, Gary got caught in quicksand and became extremely frightened. The harder he scrambled, the more he sank in. The older boys ran away in fear and told him not to yell or scream because the gypsies would hear him and get him. An older boy finally appeared and rescued Gary, but alas, the boots were gone forever. Gary ran home. First he encountered mother who spanked him terribly for disobeying and sent him to bed. He hid there until father came home and further punished him for losing his new boots.

The story was so poignant as told by Gary, who seemed 4 years old at the time of the telling, that I was very touched and said something spontaneously (empathic?). His eyes welled up with tears, and he suddenly became slightly disoriented. It was then necessary to talk to him quietly and gently until he seemed quite calm again.

Gary stated that, never in his life has he really had a conversation about personal issues or feelings with his mother. She has what he describes as a habit of "not hearing." When I inquired further, he seemed a little baffled, but merely stated that all through his life, there would be times when "if you talked to mother she simply did not hear you" which he lightly tossed off as "she only hears what she wants to and there is nothing you can do about it."

Kohut (1977, p. 121) contends that if the phase appropriate need for omnipotent control over the selfobject has been chronically and traumatically frustrated in childhood, then chronic narcissistic rage will be established. Although rage, according to Kohut, may be a disintegration product of traumatic frustration, if the self becomes seriously damaged, the sexual and/or aggressive derivatives may become powerful in their own right. For example, in order to escape from the painful feelings resulting from self-object disappointment, the child may turn from the selfobject to oral, anal, or phallic sensations and/or lapse into silent or vindictive rage. Kohut's view is that the deepest level to be reached in the analysis of narcissistic disorders is not "the drives" but the threat to the cohesive organization of the self. These ideas lay the groundwork for the assumption that Gary is constantly threatened by the emergence of an expression of his chronic narcissistic rage. He defends against this by detachment, isolation, and fantasies; one formulation would be that it was a breakthrough of this chronic narcissistic rage which could no longer be held back by detachment defenses that resulted in the impulsive act of incest with his daughter.

Gary described his fantasies about having sex with his daughter "when she became 18" as "revenge" against his first wife. According to Kohut's formulations, it would not be due to the aggressive impulse breaking through the defenses but rather that his self was undergoing an ominous change. The rage, in other words, would not be seen as a primary "given," but as a specific regressive phenomenon (disintegration by-product) resulting from a deficiency in empathy from the selfobject.

Another effect which a mother's lack of confirming and affirming "mirroring" responses can have on her child is preventing the transformation into a cohesive self of the archaic narcissistic cathexis of the child's body-self. The crude and intense narcissistic cathexis of the grandiose body-self thus remains unaltered, cannot be integrated and thus remains split off from the reality ego (Kohut 1978, p. 629).

Kohut cautions not to underestimate the importance of the visible genital in this context. The narcissistic demand of the phallic period is another developmental demand for immediate mirroring responses. That his penis will grow may be a useless consolation for the little boy (1978, p. 631).

Gary has often referred to himself as the "short, chubby kid" and his feelings of body inferiority have become evident in his attempts to overcome it by taking karate, becoming a good shot with rifles, and his extensive fantasy life in which he is the swashbuckling adventurer or the cool, tough cowboy who is independent of everyone. It might be hypothesized that the grandiose fantasies are split off from the reality ego at the time a sexual demand is placed upon an uncooperative 10-year-old daughter, as it was in this case. Kohut's explanation of this is that the body-self will, from time to time, assert its archaic claims, either by bypassing the repression barrier via the vertical split or by breaking through the brittle defenses of the central sector. It will suddenly flood the reality ego with unneutralized exhibitionistic cathexis and overwhelm the neutralizing powers of the ego, which becomes paralyzed and experiences intense shame and rage (1978, p. 630).

Gary's disturbances seem even more severe in this area because his father was not emotionally available for a selfobject idealizing experience. His father had withdrawn into work for long hours, leaving Gary with his mother. Gary has, however, taken up the same line of work as his father and the same hobby of collecting guns, but he has no sense of being a father or husband except as a provider and spends most of his time at work.

When the early selfobject does not provide the needed Narcissistic sustenance or does not prevent or dispel the child's discomfort, the selfobject is held to be sadistic by the child because it is experienced as all-powerful and all-knowing. Thus, the consequences of its actions and omissions are viewed by the child as having been brought about intentionally (1978, p. 643). Gary, in his "child-like" view of the world, attributes all sorts of reasons for people's behavior which has a paranoid quality: "If people know how you feel they hurt you." Once I had occasion to share a story with Gary about how I had inadvertently hurt my son's feelings and illustrated how it was unintentional, and how sad and pained I was over it. Gary become mildly disoriented by this story.

Narcissistic Rage

According to Kohut, narcissistic rage occurs in many forms but they all share a specific psychological flavor which gives them a distinct position within the wide realm of human aggressions: the need for revenge, for righting a wrong, for undoing a hurt by whatever means, and a deeply anchored, unrelenting compulsion in the pursuit of these aims (1978, p. 638). In its typical forms, there is utter disregard for reasonable limitations and a boundless wish to redress injury and obtain revenge. The irrationality of the vengeful attitude becomes more frightening, says Kohut, in view of the fact that the reasoning capacity, while totally under the domination and in the service of the overriding emotion, is not only intact, but sharpened. The archaic mode of experience explains why those who are in the grip of narcissistic rage show a total lack of empathy toward the offender, and the unforgiving fury that arises when the control over the mirroring selfobject is lost (1978, p. 645).

Therapist's Report Continues

These theoretical formulations on chronic narcissistic rage have much explanatory power in understanding Gary. One can easily surmise how the lack of empathic mirroring on the part of mother, and the further unavailability of father for idealization, may have led to the experience of chronic Narcissistic rage which is strongly defended (by a wall of isolation, detachment, and fantasies of superiority), lest Gary lose his precarious self cohesion. In the molest incident it might be formulated that the defensive structure gave way during the stress of losing his selfobject (second wife) as he had his first wife and mother when the reality ego became flooded and overwhelmed with intense Narcissistic rage.

Can this narcissistic rage be tamed—that is, come under the dominance of the ego? Kohut would say, "Yes, but with qualifications." He states that the transformation of narcissistic rage is not achieved directly, i.e., via appeals to the ego to increase its control over the angry impulses, but is brought about indirectly, secondarily to the gradual transformation of the matrix of Narcissim from which the rage arose. The patient's archaic exhibitionism and grandiosity must be gradually transformed into aim-inhibited self-esteem and realistic ambitions.

The treatment implications for Gary emerged rather clearly. By acting as the empathic mirroring selfobject, his defensive wall begins to give way. The narcissistic rage emerges when the therapist fails to provide perfect empathic response. The principal goal is the gradual transformation of the narcissistic matrix from which the rage arose.

In therapeutic work with Gary as with many patients, the material could be formulated in several different ways. The ultimate test of the usefulness of the Kohut Listening Perspective came in the gradual build up of self esteem and tension regulation which were achieved in a man whose self had been in chronic danger of massive fragmentation. While some instances of incestual enactment may stem from an acting out of oedipal wishes, the compelling pattern of rising and falling tension states within the clinical hour pointed toward listening to experiences of cohesion and fragmentation as a function of the quality of contact with the (selfobject) therapist.

DISAPPOINTMENT IN THE SELFOBJECT TRANSFERENCE (Lou)

Lou is a bright and successful professional man in his mid-30s who is divorced with three children. His selfobject transferences evolved over almost five years. The first episodes to be reported were ushered in by his renewed interest in the longstanding theme of "stopping therapy since he had now learned what his problems were and it remained for him to work them out on his own."

At the outset he had presented what appeared to be a clear-cut picture of an obsessional neurosis. After two years of therapy and following some major breakthroughs in "oedipal" material he took a three-month break in therapy. When he returned he preferred once weekly face-to-face "conversational" style therapy to the previous twice-weekly, free-association on the couch. I had shown interest in this change of style and this, coupled with a complete lack of dreaming, led me to believe that another layer of "witholding resistance" had surely been activated.

On one occasion in connection with material suggesting withholding from his ex-wife and kids, I seized the opportunity to tell him that I had the impression he was limiting our work together by withholding himself. If he expected me to keep up with him and the progression of his thoughts, he simply had to come more often. Since the costs of separate living were high and his ex-wife had just begun her own therapy, I told him I realized increasing our sessions might necessitate lowering the hourly fee. Lou expressed surprise at my comments and said he would seriously consider my suggestion since on previous occasions I had been "right" even though he hadn't understood at the time. For the rest of the hour he returned to the old (distant and obsessive) themes going back and forth between the joys and heartaches offered on the one hand by his ex-wife and on the other by his girlfriend.

The following session Lou arrived in a very bad mood, quite upset. He had been tense and hypomanic since last session. He hadn't even gone to work that day. He hadn't slept well for several nights and had been plagued by fitful dreaming. He couldn't put his finger on just what the trouble was. He talked a while with his associations and emotional tone being somewhat distant and aloof. I asked if perhaps in our previous hour I had said or done something to upset him. No, he couldn't think of anything but he had decided that I was probably right about the twice weekly sessions even though *he* thought it was time to quit altogether. There were some financial things he had to look into over the weekend but he had decided to go ahead and schedule a second session.

Not satisfied I had heard everything, I continued to question until he found himself in tears telling me how it had really hurt, what I said to him last session. He thought he had been doing everything "right" and was almost "cured." I had implied he was just as sick as ever and furthermore that he wasn't cooperating. He didn't mean to withhold if he was. He was trying his best but apparently I couldn't see that. Together we then explored how insulting and disappointing I had been so that no wonder he'd been so agitated and upset ever since. The tension dramatically decreased and he suddenly reported warm feelings toward his family sweeping over him. He tearfully voiced the hope that someday he could find a way to communicate with them "without laying all my trips on them" or "getting so frustrated and uptight that I have to split."

The next narcissistic injury was afforded Lou during the second session of the following week. It seems refinancing a large loan for his business was necessary in just two weeks. The new and unavoidable financial obligation would make it such that even though he wanted and had already scheduled the second hour he could realistically only afford one for now. He expected business would be picking up after the beginning of the year and, discouraged, he said the second hour would have to wait.

Unempathically (in retrospect), I reaffirmed my stress on the importance of our time together. After reviewing exactly what he could pay and why, I offered to cut my fee in half for a month or so in the interest of maintaining the level of our work together.

Lou was surprised and pleased. He accepted my offer after making certain it was genuine. He took immediate delight and pleasure in my interest in him and my commitment to seeing him. However, his thoughts quickly turned to the longstanding obsessional worries about his ex-wife and girlfriend.

The subsequent tension was manifest in insomnia, fantasies of buying a new car (the kind I own), anxiety about buying new clothes, determination to find new girlfriends, wishes toward expanding his business and fantasies of establishing a new (more controlling) relationship with his family. The tension was relieved in the following session when it became clear to both of us that I had once again insulted him with my interest and my good intentioned, but ill-timed willingness to do for him what he felt unable to do for himself. Tears again expressed his relief at the restored empathy as I showed that I understood the insult which I had provided in offering to cut the fee temporarily.

These two disruptions in the selfobject transference led to an increasing focus on his selfobject ties elsewhere and in the hours. Once Lou suddenly became aware of "feeling down on your case for no reason at all." I told him I was sure there was a reason. He associated awhile and then was able to pinpoint the moment when he had shared some really exciting ideas with me and I hadn't shown much enthusiasm. He had gone to other things but soon began to be aware of being "down on your case." I had failed to provide sufficient approving and mirroring response.

Another "empathy failure" of a different type was even more subtle. It had occurred to him earlier in the day that his most vivid childhood memory which he had related to me some time before couldn't possibly be a memory. He remembered being in the emergency room being stitched up and clearly seeing his mother turn and walk away from him. In his visual recollection of her, some background feature like the house or street clearly dated the memory as coming from a time period much later in his life. I didn't get to pursue this "telescoped" memory further because of his immediate distress over having lost a key word associated with the memory. The recall failure was doubly distressing since he had gone through the same thing with his girlfriend only an hour or so before. All he could say was that this memory failure obviously had to do with me in some way, like it was my fault somehow. As the hour went on we established rapport on some other things and the word which "I had prevented" his remembering was restored. The word was "abandonment."

Lou was becoming practically ecstatic over his "new insights" into how "I manipulate others to get what I think I need to calm me down." He enthusiastically stated that this is the "first positive thing I have ever been able to get hold of in therapy and really work on."

In the session following he brought a copy of an article his girlfriend had given him from *Psychology Today*. He was morosely depressed by the article written by some famous psychologist. He was furious because at last he could see what a "shit" he had been all along, what a terrible thing he does to people—making self-centered claims on them just so he gets what *he* wants, "using them only for me and my own selfish purposes." The high tension that day was characterized by intense anger at himself for being so un-reasonable and demanding in his relationships. I pursued his anger. "What exactly does this anger relate to? Wasn't he being harsh on himself? After all, isn't this what love is all about—seeking comfort from one another? Yes, comfort seeking *could* be "bad" and yes, perhaps at times he had "used" his ex-wife, his kids, or his girlfriend but we knew full well these were the people in the world that he most loved and would least intend to "use" or "misuse" in any way." By now my empathy had improved! I only raised the questions, *he* did the work and as he did the tension melted once again into quiet tears as we shared together the mixed nature of his connections, his love.

Using Kohut's schema one might say the crucial event is, that even as Lou permits me through empathy to join him each time as a soothing selfobject in restoring his self-esteem, a "transmuting internalization" occurs which represents an important building block toward the achievement of empathy with himself, a building block toward the ability to maintain his own self-esteem, toward the restoration of his own cohesive sense of self. Lou firmly creased the article from *Psychology Today* and handed it to me for deposit in the trash can on his way out. He could do just fine by himself. He didn't need some psychologist making fancy interpretations!

TWO DEVELOPMENTAL LINES IN SELF PSYCHOLOGY: SELFOBJECT EMPATHY AND INTERPRETATION

(This section contributed by Charles Coverdale.)

While what I present here relates to highly controversial issues, my purpose is neither to settle controversy nor add to it; rather, to put forth the importance of individual experience. I am thankful to Dr. Kohut for his inspiration and for providing a theoretical framework which brought cohesion to this work. The major issue, so vigorously contested, has to do with the role of empathy. Is it a tool for analytic observation and nothing more, or does this human capacity provide elements of a cure? The second issue, somewhat incidental to the first, concerns the gratification versus interpretation debate. Do we love our patients into health or analyze them toward cure?

The vignette to be considered presents arguments for each side of these two much disputed issues. It also demonstrates how not only are we selfobjects for our patients but they too serve as selfobjects for us.

The controversy not only exists between Self Psychologists and other analytically oriented practitioners; but also within Self Psychology. Indeed, the writings of Kohut take one side at one time and stand in contradiction at another. On the one hand he notes that the therapeutic aim is not indulgence but mastery based on insight, achieved in a setting of tolerable abstinence. One need not provide love and kindness, because understanding and interpretation are sufficient. On the contrary, we are advised that an attitude of cautious reserve and overly muted responsiveness will have deleterious consequences; that if the emerging grandiosity and idealization are not dealt with properly, the result will not lead to cohesion of the self but rather to disintegration. We are warned not to interfere with the patient's needs for phase appropriate mirroring and idealizing (Kohut 1977).

Shortly before his death in October 1981 Kohut, speaking at the University of California at Berkeley, stated that empathy is a method of observation which does not cure. In the same talk he later said that analysis cures by giving explanation through interpretation, based on empathic understanding.

Empathy creates the selfobject matrix and selfobjects provide reassuring functions. At times we are to interpret the patient's subjective experience of us as selfobjects. At other times we are to function simply as selfobjects—new editions. Reconciling these divergent views requires a developmental perspective which will now be illustrated with the aid of the following case.

The patient is a single woman in her late 20s. Due to financial considerations she was seen once weekly for 16 months and subsequently twice weekly. Presenting complaints were that relationships became inevitably ruinous; and that although she was accomplished in her field, she felt compelled to hide her accomplishments, in spite of strong wishes to be known. In the worst of times she felt she was dying and was obsessed with mirrors that were cracked, shattered, or warped (which may give a hint as to the type of transference which developed).

Of the 28 months that she had been in therapy, I will present aspects of the last 12. During this time she sometimes used the analytic couch and sometimes sat in a chair facing me.

Before holidays 16 months into therapy, she spontaneously hugged me at the session's end to thank me for helping her prepare for a visit with her family in another state. Returning from her visit, she was very quiet and often silent for almost two months. During this time my hand drifted toward her head on several occasions, as she lay on the couch facing away. I offered numerous interpretations about her need to be touched, held, or to have physical contact, based on my unusual countertransference reaction; and each time without effect. This was a time of real impasse.

Then, one session I watched my hand drift over, almost involuntarily, and come to rest on her head. The impasse ended immediately with a flood of tears and associations. She recalled feeling that her mother did not touch her, did not want her, did not like being pregnant or giving birth. She remembered that as a toddler her mother had teased about not being her mother. She also reported that two months previously, when she had hugged me, her perception was that I had stood with my arms at my side. (In fact, I had reciprocated in kind.)

Pressing her hand to the back of mine as it rested on her head she asked, "Are you comfortable touching me?" I explained that I had been reluctant but that I now understood how my reluctance had worsened her situation.

Where the numerous attempts at verbal interpretation had failed, the physical interpretation based in archaic empathy had succeeded. However, one can imagine a negative effect in similar situations. If, to give only one example, a therapist were to reach out to a patient based in his/her own archaic feelings of helplessness, the patient would sense only the therapist's ineffectual helplessness.

I had been reluctant to touch this patient. I had learned all the good reasons not to touch patients. This well advised tradition which began with Freud in his work with neurotics, remains of value with most patients. Further, with this attractive woman, I had to question my own unconscious motivation thoroughly.

In this instance an interpretation in concrete and physical terms seemed called for and, like any good interpretation, worked. Empathic contact here served as a tool for observation, a way to gather data. The empathy also proved curative. That is, my archaic, empathic response effected a change. From a developmental perspective, one can imagine the ludicrous scene of a mother responding to her desperate infant by commenting from across the room, "I can see how much you need to be held."

A very active period in this patient's analysis followed. Her needs to be loved and touched became understood as did her reactions to a mother who was unable to respond to such clear but silent, empathically communicated messages. The "vague" states of mind which had reportedly troubled her all her life, subsided. I spent one memorable session with her, both of us in silence and quite content. Sitting behind her, I noticed, much to my surprise, that my arms were in position as if I were holding a sleeping child.

Twenty months into treatment as she began to feel more touchable, the issue became one of being seen, looked at, mirrored. She wanted to be seen, but not exposed. When she felt unobserved, she withdrew, felt ghost-like and unsure of her existence. Increasing "sexiness" was accompanied by feelings of embarrassment and shame—in keeping with her early experiences of thwarted exhibitionism, and also contributed to by what she accurately perceived as my discomfort. A session from the twenty-second month of treatment, presented directly from process notes, will illustrate.

Dressed in a very sexy manner she comes in quite happy only to become quickly self-conscious. She says she doesn't know what to say. I put forth the possibility of her wanting a different response from me than what she is getting. She said she felt good about me all week but now was having difficulty with continuity. I noted she was dressed in a way that's really "out there" (a term she used meaning showing herself, putting herself forward, wanting recognition) particularly considering that she had just come from work. She says she's decided to just be "out there" regardless of the response from co-workers but with me she feels self-conscious, noting that she is blushing. I suggest that perhaps she wants to be more "out there" with me. "No." After a time, I say perhaps this is her way of telling us what happened in the past when she put herself forward. "No." She withdraws into silence and after ten minutes appears to withdraw still futher. In touch with my discomfort over the mild attraction stimulated within me, I ask if she feels I'm different than usual. "No." After another period of time I ask if she sees me as a little more reserved, inhibited than usual. "Yes." No longer withdrawn, she says she does not want to review what's gone wrong in her past but to focus on my reserved quality. I tell her I feel a little inhibited in appreciating her body today. She says she can understand my role and really appreciates it, telling me about a friend at work who had an experience with a therapist who was not so clear about his role. But (she emphasizes) she wants me to appreciate her body and like looking at her. I comment that the issue has changed from being touched to being seen. She applies this to all areas of her life and tells me, "It doesn't seem like contact is an important issue today, rather it's being admired and feeling good about myself that's important."

As time passed a firmer sense of who she was and an increased capacity to feel more lovable developed. The next phase of therapy had to do with loving, in the sense of what she had to give or offer. This perceptive patient was aware that my needs to be useful interfered with her needs to experience the value of what *she* had to offer. She was also aware of how my professional limitations interfered with her expressing her love for me.

Nevertheless, she told me that she loved me, and while my overt response sat well with me, I felt too caring toward her. Thus, in response I said, "This seems like an important feeling to feel;" yet internally, the situation seemed erotically tinged.

I soon realized I was still wanting to respond to this patient in archaic and, therefore, concrete ways because I had been in touch with her concrete ways of receiving. She wanted my appreciation and I wished to provide it in a way which I knew she could receive. My interpretive abilities had been formerly undermined because interpretation represents a higher level of empathy than she was ready for. But while the patient required archaic empathy previously, she now needed understanding on a higher level. My continued caring at an archaic level would now be prone to misinterpretation by a patient who could have seen my feelings for her as romantic. Her thinking I was terrific naturally stimulated my own needs to be mirrored. My sense of concern about this hour could now be understood: archaic empathic response was no longer appropriate.

The next session she was angry with me. I commented that recently our relationship seemed to be an impediment to her growth. She confirmed with a flood of associations about how her father's basic message was "to stay, and have everything she wanted; or to go, and die." The question became, could she be "out there" without jeopardizing her relationship with me? A higher form of verbal interpretation was now appropriate. I gave her messages such as, "No one ever backed you up as you moved away."

Twenty-four months into treatment she told me, "Being known by you has grounded parts of my personality." At 25 months she spent a week with her mother—after ten years of little contact. She noted that in her mother's presence she felt unsubstantial. She realized her perceptions had always been sharp, yet had gone without Mother's support and validation. She recognized her mother's gross inability to relate to her, and characterized Mother as "wearing a mask of supernormalcy which served as a cover for craziness." Yet she felt compassion for Mother, for "Mother was the way she was, because she couldn't be any other way."

A week's vacation with Mother brought on a month's regression during which she turned to me for selfobject functions which had been stimulated but unmet by Mother. She expressed increased needs for confirmation of her experience, as well as for archaic forms of mirroring. The form of my empathic contact with her regressed briefly also during this month. For example, more than usual, I enjoyed looking at her. "Do you enjoy looking at me?" she asked. "Yes," I replied.

My enjoyment of her was accompanied by a great sadness for her mother. I said, "What a shame for anyone to miss out on this experience." With that, the regression ended.

I was to experience more sadness with her for her parents as she described how moving forward and away had been accompanied at first by painful feelings between herself and her family, and then by their indifference. On many levels they were deprived of the valuable experience of enjoying her as she was.

What a rewarding, moving, and enjoyable experience it has been for me to provide her with mirroring in different forms in accordance with her different developmental phases. For a mother, father or therapist to be so preoccupied with themselves, their troubles, or the task of doing a good job that they miss this kind of experience seems most regretable for them as well as for their children or patients.

In reviewing, she thanked me for helping her learn that she is touchable, lovable, and that her love and all she has to offer is worthwhile. In turn, I thanked her for all that I had learned and received. She responded, "It was that which made the experience possible."

Opponents of the Psychology of the Self complain that it is a lovey-dovey kind of therapy. In looking at this case one may ask; was this patient cured by love? The answer may be "no, but somewhat." Greenson (1967, 1978) maintains that the analyst's capacity to love is an essential tool of the job. This patient was aware of my love for her; I mirrored her like the daughter I never had and like the mother who might have enjoyed her but did not. I also grew by experiencing myself in the gleam of her eye. It's often a two-way mirror. Not only was I a good selfobject for her but she had become a special kind of selfobject for me.

Her life has changed from relationships that become inevitably ruinous to experiences with men and women that provide an enhancing, valuable, selfobject milieu. Perhaps more significant is a relationship with a particular man which clearly demonstrates the beginnings of object love based on mutual consideration.

How was she helped? First, my understanding of her needs and feelings served to confirm her experience, and at times her existence. Second, by interpretation in genetic, dynamic, and psycho-economic terms. These interpretations, based in empathic understanding progressed from archaic forms to higher forms. She first had to experience herself through the gleam in my eye before she could feel her own pride, value and goodness. Following this, we could share in enjoying her important achievements.

Earlier developmental phases require archaic forms of empathic contact. Later developmental phases require higher levels of empathy. Empathic contact through interpretive activity assumes a level of complex symbolic communication and becomes assimilated (to use Piaget's terms, 1937, 1962) into an already existing schema.

The selfobject is, by Kohut's definition, a developmental agent. Initially, selfobjects provide functions that the self cannot provide. Later, through transmuting internalizations, the individual is increasingly more able to provide functions for him/herself which previously required the participation of selfobjects. Different forms of empathic contact are appropriate for different developmental levels.

With the help of my patient, I have come to understand that empathy serves as a tool for analytic observation as well as sometimes providing certain elements essential to the curative process. With certain patients, or at particular times, empathy serves as a method of observation only and nothing more. But with other patients, or at other times, empathic contact actually contributes toward the cure.

CONCLUSIONS

These clinical illustrations hardly do justice to the richness and complexity of concepts developed by Kohut and others under the rubric of the Psychology of the Self. All that can be done here is to point toward an important developmental phase and a specialized way of listening to persons whose personalities have become locked in an incessant search for a cohesive self through obtaining confirming responses from outside selfobjects. In contrasting the Freudian and Kohutian perspectives at the level of clinical *listening*, one can readily appreciate these listening frames have different applications. In listening to persons with a neurotic personality organization, the subjective experiences of drive, conflict and defense will be foremost. In listening to persons with narcissistic personality organization, the experiences of self cohesion and fragmentation in relation to selfobjects will take center stage. Careful listening to the way each person experiences self and others can prevent massive empathy failures.

Traditionalists accustomed to listening for drive motivations, structural conflict, and defensive disguises express concern that the Kohut selfobject perspective focuses excessively on the manifest content while ignoring the latent causes and resistances. This argument loses its strength when one considers that, by definition, the narcissistic personality organization precedes in development the oedipal period in which the drives become crystalized (or constituted as such in conscious experience) so that (repressive) processes of defense become necessary. If the person arrested at the selfobject phase *experiences* no drives, structural conflict or defenses as such, there is less need for manifest disguise and, therefore, less need for the analyst to be concerned about the manifest/latent distinction as a tool for listening. This point is made especially clear when Kohut (in press) talks about "self state" dreams. Stolorow and Atwood (1981b) make a similar point about preoedipal dreams and there being less need for disguise since structural conflict is *not* an experience of central importance to these people. Yet more convincing here is Langs's (1980, 1981) argument that the *adaptive context* of the psychotherapy situation itself will be experienced and expressed in latent terms (i.e., encoded derivative communications). Adapting Langs's ideas to the present purposes of listening to the way a person experiences Self and Others, one might expect in preoedipal developmental arrests that whatever latent meanings are to be understood will relate *less* to internal conflict and more to the experience of the adaptive interpersonal context of therapy. Langs's ideas on the adaptive context will be elaborated in a later chapter. The main point here is that different people present different listening challenges to the therapist which are based upon their developmental level of Self and Other differentiation. Different experiences appear to require different ways of listening and the Kohut listening model is securely fixed on a certain phase of developmental experience.

IV

The Listening Perspective of the Merger Object

8

Borderline Personality Organization

GENERAL CONSIDERATIONS

Perhaps the most formidable challenge to psychoanalytic listening has come from the many persons who come to the consulting room presenting what has come to be called borderline personality organization. Systematic study of "borderline syndromes," "primitive mental states," and "pre-oedipal conditions" has increased to such a considerable degree in the last few years that clinicians may easily feel overwhelmed and bewildered with the wide range of diagnostic concepts and diverse treatment approaches. One searches for some clear definition of "borderline" and for some unifying orientation which serves to clear up confusions and permits one to organize reading and to enrich one's work with these very difficult patients.

Kernberg (1975) holds that borderlines present "stable ego pathology" with "primitive defenses" which require "a modified psychoanalytic technique." Giovacchini (1979b) speaks of the "helpless patient" while others speak of the "difficult patient" or even the "obnoxious patient." Volkan (1976) and Kernberg (1976) urge a consideration of "primitive object relations." Mahler (1975) points to the developmental phenomena surrounding the early mother-child "symbiosis." Searles (1969) suggests that studies of "countertransference" yield critical information while Spotnitz (1976) highlights "underdeveloped aggression" as a central concept. Masterson (1972, 1976) presents the idea of an "abandonment depression" as the universal experience of borderlines in response to inadequate mothering. Stolorow and Lachman (1980) focus on "prestages of defense" and "developmental arrests." Stone (1980) has proposed a "three dimensional cube approach" based on a study of "constitutional, personality and adaptational factors." Balint (1968) points to the early area of personality development he calls "the basic fault." Margaret Little (1981) speaks of "basic unity" and "primary total undifferentiatedness." Kohut (1971) has isolated one group of pre-oedipal conditions as "narcissistic disorders" but still considers borderline phenomena essentially psychotic in nature.

This extreme diversity of thought attests to the complexity of the phenomena under investigation as well as demonstrates the high interest

---

Special thanks to Dr. Hedda Bolgar for her questions and comments on this chapter.

103

currently being felt by clinicians everywhere. But unifying concepts have not been forthcoming. Someone recently asked, "When even the leading authorities seem to be in such disagreement, how is the practicing clinician to think?"

General agreement does exist among major contemporary writers that the term "borderline" is a spatial metaphor which broadly describes a group of behavioral and dynamic phenomena which are less well developed than those encountered in the so-called (neurotic and narcissistic) transference disorders but not so undeveloped or "primitive" as those found in the psychotic states. Repeated attempts to extend Freud's structural conflict model to a study of borderline phenomena (including many of the so-called "character disorders") have been of limited usefulness in broadening conceptual grasp or expanding clinical technique. The grave limitations of Freud's model based on concepts of drive, conflict, defense and regression have become increasingly apparent as the leading writers in the field use unwieldly terms such as "transference-like formations," "resistance-like phenomena," "primitive transference amalgamations," as well as other words and phrases which betray an attempt to use established conceptual terms in a different universe of discourse where they have but limited application. Ideas about supportive "parameters" (Eissler 1953) and "corrective emotional experience" (Alexander 1961) cast out of Classical analysis long ago are now being revived with a new spirit (Gedo 1979a) and employed with wholly different meanings. Terms related to "countertransference" have also been frequently bandied about and changed from their original definitions in an effort to describe the various forms of personal involvement which appear to be requisite in the treatment of people with borderline personality development.

The complexities encountered in understanding borderline states have necessitated new conceptual approaches primarily due to the general observation that *borderline states are not reliably available to transference analysis nor do they improve significantly through a traditional analytic study of conflict, defense and resistance.* The Psychology of the Self (Kohut 1977) also seems inadequate in offering a viable *treatment* approach to borderline states, although Kohut maintains that the self-fragmentation/cohesion model can be used to *account for* borderline phenomena.

THE THIRD LISTENING PERSPECTIVE
OF PSYCHOANALYSIS

This chapter will provide an overview of some key concepts currently being elaborated by many writers studying the particular kind of psychological development widely and loosely referred to as "borderline." The assertion will be that a third major Listening Perspective is slowly evolving from many sources which stands in a complementary relationship to (1) Sigmund Freud's Listening Perspective of structural conflict and (2) Heinz Kohut's selfobject Listening Perspective.

Freud's original paradigm of intrapsychic or structural conflict retains its usefulness for the therapeutic study of persons having attained a level of personality integration capable of forming (oedipal, or incestuous) transference neuroses.

The second major complementary paradigm of psychoanalysis, the Psychology of Self, stems from Hartmann's (1950) conceptual distinction between the ego and the self and has been elaborated chiefly by Kohut (1971, 1977, 1978). This model distinguishes a developmentally earlier class of analyzable transference phenomena than Freud was able to observe in his studies. These so-called "narcissistic" or "selfobject" transferences relate to the early developing self and to the fact that the vital self functions of tension reduction were once performed by an external nurturing object, the selfobject. The mirror, twin and idealizing transferences as Kohut has defined them, derive from pre-oedipal experiences with the "tension relieving" selfobject. According to Kohut, the analytic working through of the selfobject transferences is accomplished through understanding repeated disappointments in the empathy of the therapist. Analytic technique in the Psychology of the Self model differs from the Classical model mainly in the utilization of the selfobject Listening Perspective and in the expectation that in narcissistic transferences the patient is likely to find the analyst's empathy repeatedly disappointing. Thus, the Psychology of the Self can be viewed as a broadening and deepening of the Classical approach with the added perspective of selfobject transference which is particularly useful in the analytic study of narcissistic personality organization.

The third major listening approach or paradigm evolving in psychoanalysis is the product of many writers and researchers and stands firmly based on a long tradition of Ego Psychology. Listening focuses on the experience of self which is fused or merged imperceptibly with the other— the "merger object." Gertrude and Rubin Blanck (1979) have suggested the term "Psychoanalytic Developmental Psychology" to refer to the various approaches to the study of borderline development. While Freud's and Kohut's paradigms are also "developmental," the paradigms for the therapeutic study of oedipal and selfobject transferences are also "regressive" approaches. In contrast, the observations and conceptualizations regarding borderline development are not "regressive" in the same sense customarily considered in the neurotic and narcissistic disorders. That is, while many developmentally primitive patterns are observable with persons having limitations in early development referred to as "borderline," these borderline manifestations do not characteristically appear as a result of regression of a threatened psyche organized around a well established cohesive self or a firmly rooted Oedipus complex. Primitive ideation (e.g., primary process), and behavior (e.g., "acting out") *are not unconscious* in the usual dynamic, "repressed" sense but readily observed *to be present or absent from consciousness and behavior in varying degrees depending on the person's overall frame of mind, often as related to external circumstances.*

Psychoanalytic developmental psychology as applied to the study of borderline conditions focuses on the experience of a merger object and on defining what functions and integrations have or have not developed, the conditions under which they *are and are not available*, and the *relationships* of the developed and undeveloped functions to each other and to the external world. That is, the interest is in observing and defining various specific and non-specific *limitations in development* and in understanding the many convoluted and/or distorted coping or adjustment attempts which have appeared to obscure or compensate for atypical development in the preoedipal and pre-cohesive self periods of psychological development.

Five Developmental Points of View will be defined here (which differ from Freud's metapsychological points of view) for the purpose of organizing and thinking about borderline personality organization.[1] Most current writers address all of the issues in each of the five overlapping slants or points of view but tend to focus more heavily on one or another.

FIVE DEVELOPMENTAL POINTS OF VIEW[2]

I. Human Symbiosis

Margaret Mahler's statement of theory was derived initially from a careful study of psychotic children and their mothers. Mahler (1968) defines a progression of phases and subphases to account for various levels of development in a child's capacity for object relations. Many leading theorists are now expressing the opinion that Mahler's developmental phases are likely to prove the conceptual key which will liberate theory from outmoded and overused regressive approaches and open a clearer way for the therapeutic observation of borderline developmental conditions.

Mahler's central thesis is that all psychological life may be traced back to the universal symbiotic conditions of infancy which make physical survival possible in the human species. The term "symbiosis" is recognized as a metaphor borrowed from biology to denote the undifferentiated, fused state

---

[1] The developmental points of view are also to be considered metapsychological in that they are assumptions and postulates about the nature of developmental experience. This is discussed more fully in the last section of this chapter.

[2] This section is limited to a definition of the five points of view which are receiving so much attention. Theoretical implications and clinical illustrations of the points of view appear in subsequent sections.

of the early mother-child relationship based on mutual cueing. Despite the sociological source of the idea of symbiosis, Mahler (1968) makes it clear that the term is defined *intrapsychically* and therefore is an inferred state.

The mother-child symbiosis functions to maintain physiological and psychological homeostasis in the infant. Human symbiosis is likened to a gravitational "orbit" pulling two together or to a common membrane which surrounds the harmonious union of mother and child.[3]

Mahler demonstrates that psychotic states are traceable to a failure (for whatever reason) of the mother-child relationship to attain an effective, harmonious symbiotic state capable of affording psychological homeostasis to the infant. The schizophrenias would presumably originate in the failure of the symbiosis to protect the infant from traumatic stimulation emanating from the *outside* environment, thus producing problems in relation to reality. In contrast, when the symbiosis fails to foster adequate controls over manic (elated) and depressive (depleted) *inner* states, the result would be an affect disorder.[4]

The assumption of the symbiotic origin of psychic life implies two other processes which Mahler and her colleagues have studied extensively by carefully collecting long-term observations of a number of normal mother-child combinations (Mahler, Pine, and Bergman, 1975). The first is the process of *separation*, a term that is used "to refer to the *intrapsychic* achievement of a sense of separateness from mother, and through that, from the world at large" (Mahler, et al., 1975, pp. 7f). The second process, of *individuation*, refers to "those achievements marking the child's assumption of his own individual characteristics" (1975, p. 4). Separation and individuation are conceptualized as "intertwined, but not identical, developmental processes; they may proceed divergently, with a developmental lag or precocity in one or the other" (1975, p. 4). Mahler's studies to date have not attempted a systematic separation of these two basic processes and thus concern the *"separation-individuation process"* which is seen as one part of a progression of overlapping developmental "phases" based on the centrality of the concept of symbiosis.

By way of overview, Mahler describes the first phase of "Normal Infantile Autism" as spanning the first three or four weeks of life in which:

---

[3]Margaret Little (1981) describes "basic unity" which represents the personality feature of borderlines in much this same way. Little prefers her idea to Mahler's because symbiosis is a two body term and the experience of the borderline is one of unity. Both therapists agree that the sense of union with the mother/other is the central feature of the early development of borderline conditions.

[4]This differentiating diagnostic formulation does not imply *why* the symbiosis partially failed to form but only that it did. That is, physical, biochemical and genetic variations are not excluded. The distinction drawn here between the thought disorders and affect disorders is only implied by Mahler but not stated.

. . . the infant spends most of his day in half-sleeping, half-waking state: he wakes principally when hunger or other need tensions . . . cause him to cry, and sinks or falls into sleep again when he is satisfied, that is, relieved of surplus tensions. Physiological rather than psychological processes are dominant, and the function of this period is best seen in physiological terms. (1975, p. 41)

The second phase Mahler defines as "Symbiosis" which is clearly recognizable by the third month. By the "second half of the first year, the symbiotic partner is no longer interchangeable . . . the immature organism cannot achieve homeostasis on its own . . . the mothering partner is called on to contribute a particularly large portion of symbiotic help . . ." (1968), pp. 13f). It is the very special nature of this symbiotic phase which will become so important in discussing borderline development.

Mahler's third phase encompasses the "Separation-Individuation" process which affords the child an avenue out of the symbiotic state. Mahler has divided separation-individuation into four Subphases. The first subphase is called "differentiation" or "hatching" and appears by four to five months. Mahler says:

The "hatching process" is a gradual ontogenetic evolution of the sensorium—the perceptual-conscious system—which enables the infant to have a more *permanently alert* sensorium whenever he is awake . . . the infant's attention, which . . . was in large part *inwardly* directed, or focused in a coenesthetic vague way *within the symbiotic orbit*, gradually expands through . . . outwardly directed perceptual activity during the child's increasing periods of wakefulness. That attention is combined in a growing store of memories of mother's comings and goings, of "good" and "bad" experiences; the latter were altogether unrelievable by the self, but could be "confidently expected" to be relieved by mother's ministrations. (1975, pp. 53f.)

Transitional objects and transitional phenomena (described by Winnicott, 1953) attest the need for contact with mother's body. The "checking back" visual pattern serves as a sign of somatopsychic differentiation. This biphasic visual pattern was first termed "customs inspection" by Brody and Axelrod (1966). The infant is visually interested in mother and "seems to compare her with 'other,' the unfamiliar with the familiar, feature by feature" (1975, p. 56).

By the eighth month, Mahler notes the beginning of the second subphase, "practicing" which is characterized by "the elated investment in the exercise of the autonomous functions, especially mobility, to the near exclusion of apparent interest in the mother" (1975, p. 69).

On all fours, the child begins exploration at some physical distance from mother and soon assumes the upright position which affords a fresh view of the world. Despite apparent disinterest in mother, as the child wilts and fatigues he/she returns to "home base" for "emotional refueling," perks up and goes on about his/her exploring again. (1975, p. 69)

The sixteen-to-eighteen month level seems to be a nodal point of development. The toddler is then at the height of . . . "the ideal state of the self" (so named by Joffee and Sandler, 1965). This is . . . the complex affective representation of the symbiotic dual unity, with its inflated sense of omnipotence—now augmented by the toddler's feeling of his own magic power. . . . (1968, p. 22)

Upright locomotion leads to the toddler's "love affair with the world," with the world being indeed his "oyster" (1975, pp. 70f). Elation as a mood prevails.

However, this "ideal state of the self" developed in the first eighteen months "must become divested of its delusional increments" in the second eighteen months in the subphase Mahler calls "rapprochement."

As the toddler's *awareness* of separateness grows—stimulated by his maturationally acquired ability to move away from mother and by his cognitive growth—he seems to have an increased need, a wish for mother to share with him every one of his new skills and experiences, as well as a great need for (mother's) love. (1975, p. 77)

The "refueling" bodily approach is replaced by a deliberate search for mother ("shadowing") or an avoidance of intimate physical contact ("darting-away" with the expectation of being chased and swept back into mother's arms). Both behaviors seem to indicate the infant's "wish for reunion with the love object and his fear of re-engulfment by it" (1975, p. 77). This alternating and sometimes simultaneous movement toward and away from the object is referred to as an "ambitendency," the precursor to ambivalence. This period is the peak of narcissistic vulnerability. "It is a time when the child's self-esteem may suffer abrupt deflation" (1968, p. 23). "The junior toddler gradually realizes that his love objects (his parents) are separate individuals with their own personal interests. He must gradually and painfully give up the delusion of his own grandeur, often by way of dramatic fights with mother . . ." (1975, p. 79).

By the 36th month the toddler should have reached Mahler's fourth subphase which she calls "on the road to object constancy." ". . . the main task of the fourth subphase is twofold: (1) the achievement of a definite, in certain aspects lifelong, individuality, and (2) the attainment of a certain degree of object constancy" (1975, p. 109). The toddler frequently prefers play with peers to trailing after mother and develops the ability to retain and/or to restore self-esteem. Here is expected the inception of (1) the experience of objects as constant (the psychoanalytically defined "internal mother") and (2) a self-image which is unified and based on ego identifications. The success of these experiences lays the foundation for triangular oedipal, or "contingent" emotional experiences in which parents and others are experienced as centers of initiative separate from the self.

Mahler and others in recent papers have begun to elaborate such ideas as "subphase needs" and "subphase requirements" as well as to evoke the concepts of "adequate" or "inadequate subphase experience." It is anticipated that these concepts will be useful in studying the etiology of various borderline and narcissistic states, that is, that a particular limitation in ego or self-development may come to be thought of as stemming from some particular "inadequacy of subphase experience." Kohut (1971, 1977) has elaborated the implications of rapprochement inadequacies for narcissistic states and other writers (e.g., Kernberg 1975; Blanck and Blanck 1979) are exploring the implications of a subphase approach for psychotherapy with borderline states.[5]

II. Differentiation of Affects

This point of view is perhaps best represented by Otto Kernberg. Kernberg's long-term and intensive study of borderline conditions led him to offer massive revisions of classical and ego psychological theory. His revisions (1975, 1976, 1980a) accord a central position to the *early differentiation of affects* which has important implications for listening.

Kernberg's initial observation was that people with borderline development exhibited specific areas of what he called "impulse" disturbance. That is, Kernberg holds that variations in impulsiveness represent:

> . . . an alternating expression of complementary sides of a conflict, such as acting out of the impulse at some times and specific defensive character formation or counterphobic reactions against that impulse at other times. The patients were conscious of the severe contradiction in their behavior; yet they would alternate between opposite strivings with a bland denial of the implications of this contradiction and showed what appeared to be a striking lack of concern over this 'compartmentalization' of their mind. (1976, p. 20)

That is, "there exists what we might call mutual denial of independent sectors of psychic life . . . or independent 'ego states,' . . . repetitive, temporarily ego syntonic, compartmentalized psychic manifestations" (1976, p. 20).

Kernberg's next observation was, "that each of these mutually unacceptable 'split' ego states[6] represented a specific transference paradigm, a highly

---

[5]Louise Kaplan who has collaborated with Mahler for many years has expanded the basic separation-individuation paradigm and extended it to all aspects of life in her delightful and highly readable book *Oneness and Separateness* (1978).

[6]"Split" is an unfortunate term in that it implies there was once something whole which is now divided. Historically, this is how borderline conditions have been viewed, i.e., as regression from a more "normal" state. "Split" now is used more often to refer to a bifurcation of affective experience which represents an expectable early developmental experience. One characteristic of Borderline Personality Organization is that the positive and negative affects have remained unintegrated or "split" as in Mahler's description of ambitendency.

developed regressive transference reaction in which a specific internalized object relationship was activated in the transference" (1976, p. 21).

Kernberg suggests that the "chaotic transference manifestations" borderline patients present might be understood as the oscillatory activation of these mutually unacceptable ego states, representing what he calls "'non-metabolized' internalized object relations" (1976).

In the expectable oedipal sequence the organizing processes of ego and self will be successful in integrating these early contradictory ego states by either establishing true ambivalence, that is, a conscious or unconscious admixture of contradictory attitudes, or the organizing ego will relegate (via repression) part of the conflict to unconsciousness. The implication of this line of thinking is clearly that in borderline conditions the organizing ego in *certain delineated areas* has *failed to develop* to a level of integration in which ambivalence or repression operate to keep contradictory mental states integrated rather than mutually contradictory or "split."

While it seldom takes a skilled clinician more than a few hours with a borderline person to observe various contradictory ego states or attitudes, for a better understanding of the nature of these alternating states of consciousness and their crucial role in the therapeutic process it is necessary to make a brief foray into Kernberg's developmental theory of the affects to see how the development of affects is tied to object relations.

Kernberg (1976) states that the:

> . . . affects represent inborn dispositions to a subjective experience in the dimension of pleasure and unpleasure . . . Differentiation of affect occurs in the context of the differentiation of internalized object relations; . . . affect and cognition at first evolve jointly, only to differentiate much later. . . . Pleasurable and painful affects are the major organizers of the series of "good" and "bad" internalized object relations. . . . (p. 104)

Kernberg thus considers early positive and negative affect states the experiential basis for future development. Following Jacobson (1964) and Mahler (1968), Kernberg conceptualizes the infant's early task as first a differentiation of "self-representations" from "object presentations" followed rapidly by an integration of libidinally determined ("good") and aggressively determined ("bad") self and object representations (1980a, p. 11). Then it becomes possible to speak of "internalized experiences" or "ego states" which are thought to be the building blocks of personality and are assumed by Kernberg to be composed of:

1. a representation of self
2. a representation of an object
3. a positively or negatively weighted affective link

Thus, these contradictory oscillatory, internalizations or "ego states" are comprised variously of *good, bad, self,* and *object* experiences and as such are conceptualized as the normal developmental process called "splitting."[7] By the third year the infant is said to begin integrating the good with the bad, giving rise to a wide *spectrum of affects.* At the same time, through repression, it becomes possible for a constant integrated experience of self to be reliably differentiated from ambivalently held "constant objects."

Kernberg's general position (1976, 1980b) is pointedly consistent with Mahler's developmental theory even to the extent that he offers elaborations and expansions of her basic phase approach (Kernberg 1975).

III. Private World Development

For centuries man has been accustomed to thinking and speaking of mind and mental processes in spatial terms. Angels and devils in many garbs inhabit man's "inner space." Psychoanalytic theorizing has followed this habit partly because people do speak of "internal discomfort," "conflict within," "deep experiences," and other such things as "the mother inside." Common usage of Freudian terms such as the structural concepts "ego," "superego," and "defense mechanism" continues to *imply* an existence of entities somewhere in time and space despite the more formal definitions highlighting functions, processes, and mental contents. Roy Schafer (1976) has perhaps been the most effective in raising questions about "*what* inside" is spoken of and "*where* is it?" In attempting to limit concepts to sensible and manageable proportions, Schafer concludes that one *can* talk clearly about "internalization" in at least three meaningful and clear ways:

1. *Incorporation fantasies* are experiences which are known and can be spoken about, i.e., the *fantasy* of taking someone or some experience "inside" is valid to speak about.

2. *Private experience* refers to "what is not communicated, perhaps not yet formulated or even not unambiguously communicable; it includes what is unconsciously as well as consciously kept secret or passed over" (Schafer 1976, p. 160). Speaking of the "intrapsychic" as a "private world" is not merely a metaphoric difference but "an entirely different way of thinking about mental and other actions" (ibid.).

3. *Identifications* can be spoken of without requiring the spatial vocabulary of internalization. One can speak about identification as a "change in the way one behaves publicly; . . . the change would be modeled on personal and unconsciously elaborated versions of significant figures in real life or imaginative life (e.g., fictional or historical characters)" (ibid., p. 161). Thus,

---

[7]This term is unfortunate since nothing whole is "split." Rather, different aspects of contradictory experience appear in consciousness at different times without a full sense of their contradictory nature.

according to Schafer, one may speak of identifications or identity in the sense of making possible a "high degree of consistency in certain modes of subjective experience and behavior; on the basis of identification, specific acts of desiring, thinking and doing other things, along with specific emotional modes associated with these actions, may be in evidence much more regularly and readily than they would be otherwise" (ibid., p. 162).

Schafer has extended his piercing argument to the concepts of "internal objects" and "internalized object relations," challenging theorists to conceptualize as clearly as possible without further careless use of spatial metaphor. No one has yet provided a linguistically acceptable developmental sequencing of the maturational series *from entity to identity*. Fortunately, Schafer has demonstrated an interim trick! Recently in a paper reviewing the concept of "self," (Schafer 1980) he concluded with the necessity of ultimately doing away entirely with the term "self" in systematic discourse. After thus banishing "self" from respectable scientific usage, Schafer then explained that for the time being he was personally choosing to retain and use the word because of its "inspirational value!" That is, "self" certainly has many meanings which are highly personal and "will have to do" until it becomes possible to specify what is meant more clearly! (At least "inspirational value" is honest and perhaps more easy to get away from than the time honored rationalization, "heuristic value!")

In the spirit of Schafer, it is clear how concepts of "internalization" are linguistically inadequate because they imply spatialization in more than a mere metaphoric sense, but for the present purposes of viewing borderline development, "internal" concepts will be retained for "inspirational value!" In future study of the development of the "private world" perhaps it will be possible to make progress in non-spatial conceptualizations. Here then, is what might be called the progressive development of the "Private World":

1. *Entity* refers to the child's beginning awareness of "beingness." Gradually the experience of entity is thought to become distinguished from other features in the environment.

2. *Incorporation* in a literal sense refers to the act of taking something inside one's body. In a psychological sense the term implies a fantasy (on the part of either the subject or the observer).

3. *Introjection* according to Kernberg (1976) is the:

... reproduction and fixation of an interaction with the environment by means of an organized cluster of memory traces implying at least three components: (1) the image of an object, (2) the image of the self in interaction with that object, and (3) the affective coloring of both the object-image and the self-image under the influence of the drive representative present *at the time of the interaction.* (p. 28)

This conceptualization enables him to speak of such things as "good internal objects," "bad internal objects," and "internalized object relations."

4. *Identification* Kernberg speaks of as a "higher level of introjection which can only take place when the perceptive and cognitive abilities of the child have increased to the point that it can recognize the role aspects of interpersonal interaction" (1976, p. 28). This more complex cluster of memory traces comprises an "advanced" recognition (phallic or oedipal level?) of social roles and a more elaborated and modified affect component which is less intense than the good-bad extremes found in introjection.

5. *Identity* is conceptualized by Erikson (1954) as (a) a consolidation of ego structures connected with a sense of continuity of self, (b) a consistent overall conception of the world of objects, and finally, (c) a recognition of identifiable consistency by the interpersonal environment and the perception by the individual of this recognition (i.e., social "confirmation").

In *listening* to borderline personalities, one becomes struck by the incorporation and introjection levels whereas ego identifications and a well developed sense of identity are conspicuously lacking.

IV. Mother-Child Adaptation

That mother and child "adapt" to one another through "mutual cueing" (Mahler 1968 and Mahler, Pine, and Bergman 1975) is self-evident. What is becoming clearer in the study of borderline development is that *certain mother-child combinations establish a symbiotic tie from which complete separation-individuation has not been fully accomplished*. The problem becomes how to fault the mothering without necessarily faulting the mother since there are many situations and conditions which over-foster the symbiosis and are not always of mother's making. For example, a child with a (nonpsychological) medical problem may require excessive nurturing. Other reality circumstances such as death, divorce, illness, or accident may distress mother causing her to dwell unduly upon or to end abruptly the symbiotic dependence thus creating what James Masterson (1972, 1978) calls an "abandonment depression." To be sure, the symbiotic yearning often spans several generations of mothers, and clinicians have become accustomed to expecting the mother of a borderline person also to be borderline. There is ample experience to support this expectation in clinical practice but many other possibilities exist as well.

In persons who have a borderline personality organization, the therapist rapidly becomes aware of the need to *replicate* many aspects of the symbiosis in the therapeutic relationship, and from this particularly striking clinical experience (i.e., the replication), many ideas have developed. Chapter 10 is devoted to ways of listening to these interpersonal "scenarios" in therapy.

James Masterson's clinical approach (1972, 1976, 1981) relies on the assumption that various personality functions develop as a result of a process of selective cueing; that is, rewarding (R) or withdrawing (W) responses from mother or other sources referred to as (part) object relations units (-ORU). An "abandonment depression" (being or resulting in a collapse or delay of development) is what occurs in the presence of an excessive W-ORU. Crippling dependency occurs in the presence of an excessive R-ORU. Masterson has elaborated a technique for responding to crippling dependency and "abandonment depression." His general theoretical and clinical approach to the borderline phenomena can be seen as primarily stemming from a developmental rather than a regressive approach and can be seen as quite consistent with the Mahler framework.

Donald Winnicott (1949, 1952, 1953, 1958, 1960, 1965) has made contributions to child development highlighting the early exchange between mother and child. Of particular interest in listening to persons with borderline personality organization is his concept of the "false self." Winnicott formulates (1952) that a failure of active adaptation on the part of the environment at the beginning produces (1) a secret inner life in the infant which has little derived from external reality and (2) a false self built on a compliance basis. The false self represents adjustments and accommodations to the nurturing environment. In children and adults the false self may *appear* as the better functioning aspects of the personality. Little (1980) remarks that the well adapted part of the personality is what psychiatrists often consider the "healthy" personality while, in fact, it constitutes the illness. Conversely, Little explains that the so-called "sick," dependent, clinging, regressive aspects represent the basically normal and healthy core of the personality which can be the basis for the development of patient-therapist unity requisite in analysis. Adequate deciphering of circumscribed false self achievements from ego achievements which are integrated within the matrix of symbiotic relatedness has crucial listening implications.

Melanie Klein (1952, 1957, 1975) has developed extensively the concept of "projective identification" which describes a series of developmental phenomena present in the mutual cueing processes which lead to and are involved extensively in the state described by Mahler (1968) as symbiosis and by Little (1981) as basic unity.

Projective identification as a developmental process will be discussed extensively in the chapter on countertransference. This clinically very useful idea relates back to early mother-child exchanges in which the infant experiments by way of "imaginative conjury" (Grotstein 1981a). The infant experiences mother in certain ways, i.e., projects inner (self) states onto images of her or "into" her. To the extent troubling images are satisfactorily "contained and absorbed" (Bion 1962) the infant can then introject or identify with a positive mothering idiom. Inadequate containment and absorption of troubling aspects of self by the (m)other is said to result in the infant experiencing the other as frightening, dangerous or persecutory. In the replicated symbiosis which emerges in the treatment of the borderline personality organization, aspects of the early uncontaining (retaliatory) mother become experienced in the countertransference—i.e., they are said to be *projected into* the therapist. This aspect of mother-child adaptation requires attention since it lies at the root of the transformational process (Grotstein, personal communication).

Bollas' (1978) concept of "the transformational object" makes a fundamental contribution to the understanding of many human endeavors as well as to an understanding of the basic "ecology" of the analytic relationship. Bollas holds that the first experience of (love) objects is identified with *alterations* of the ego's state. The earliest experience of (self) transformation continues to be sought in a curiously ruthless and impersonal way in order to restore an early "idiom of mothering," an "aesthetic of being." Restoration of early object experience is sought, not out of desire for an object *per se*, but for the purpose of "surrender" to a process that has the power to alter ego states. The search of the gambler, the religious or political extremist, the home buyer, or the aesthete may have in common a sense of reverence for the special moment of transformational connection. In applying this notion to the analytic ambience, Bollas points out Freud's (excusable) blindness in not recognizing that psychoanalytic technique elicits and enacts memories of earliest experiences with objects existentially known only through processes of transformation.

In applying Bollas' ideas to the listening task, one would expect the special idiom of early mothering to emerge with clarity in analysis. The exact nature of the early mother-child exchange for each person must be enacted (not merely verbalized) in the therapeutic relationship. How did the patient experience the early transformational ambience, in what ways does the person still search for transformational experience, and in what ways does the patient's expectation receive attention from the analyst?

V. The Organizing Processes of Ego and Self

The fifth point of view relies on an understanding of normal, expectable developmental progressions of ego and self.[8] Anna Freud's (1965) "Developmental Profile" represents one such categorization of developmental proc-

---

[8] Hartmann (1950) is generally credited with distinguishing conceptually between "ego" as an agency of the psychic structure comprised of a set of functions and "self" as the evolving (subjective) integrating center of the personality. His distinction may be clarifying in many regards, but Hedda Bolgar (personal communication) points out that the field is left with many unresolved issues about exactly what is to be considered "ego" and what is to be considered "self." While many would agree to define ego as a set of functions including integration,

esses. Pine's (1974) classification of ten types of borderline children relies similarly on definitions of fluctuations and stabilizations by various ego and self functions.

By understanding and ordering the development of many personality functions, while taking cognizance of the ego and self as "organizing processes," the separation-individuation subphases which give rise to borderline personality development can be better understood. Blanck and Blanck (1979) provide a full discussion of 14 developmental functions and the various considerations which lead to conceptualizing the ego as an "organizing process." (See Fig. 2.)

Questions now open for clinical investigation would relate to *which* ego, and/or self functions originate and develop through each subphase; and in a given person, which phases or subphases show "adequate" or "inadequate" development. For example, the "rapprochement" subphase in which the toddler turns from the omnipotent elation characteristic of the "practicing" subphase back to mother for mirroring and approval, has been singled out by several writers (Lax, et al. 1980) as the peak period of narcissistic vulnerability. According to this line of thinking, a "subphase inadequacy" in rapprochement would limit the consolidating effects of this period, thus partially or completely blocking the "road toward the establishment of object constancy." The gross result would presumably be borderline personality development. Other writers, including the present one, trace many of the arrests and limitations observed in borderline development to *earlier* separation-individuation subphases and even back to vicissitudes of the symbiosis phase.

IMPLICATIONS FOR PSYCHOANALYTIC THEORY

Theoretical remarks will focus on the traditional subjects of transference, resistance, and countertransference in relation to borderline development.

A. Transference

Theorists generally agree *borderline personality development does not yield to transference analysis in the usual sense.* This is thought to be because object (oedipal, parricidal-incestuous) transferences require an advanced level of development in which (object) constancy is established and

---

organizing, and executive functions, at what point does it become useful to distinguish between such ego functions and the self as the "supraordinate center of the personality" (Kohut 1971, 1977)?

The complex problem of definitively distinguishing between ego and self in the area of organizing processes cannot be addressed here. In this section I have frequently included both terms to indicate the overlapping areas in which one might meaningfully choose to employ either term. Perhaps future thinking will shed light on this problem.

SEPARATION-INDIVIDUATION

	AUTISM / SYMBIOSIS	Differentiation	Practicing	Rapprochement	On the way to object constancy
A.	Living in the body				Living in the mind (structure)
B.	Interpersonal interaction				Intersystemic and intrasystemic operations
C.	Primary process thought				Secondary process thought
D.	Undifferentiated self-object				Differentiated self with gender identity
E.	Direct impulse discharge				Ego as mediator
F.	Fear of annihilation	of loss of object	of loss of love	of castration	Superego
G.	Organismic distress	use of external soothing	use of self soothing		Signal anxiety
H.	Defensive capacity not organized				Capacity for defense and resistance
I.	Simple affects "for" and "against"		affect differentiation		Full affective repertory
J.	Ambitendency				Ambivalence
K.	Split self and object images				Whole self and object representations
L.	Need gratification		object love	(fusion)	Self and object constancy
M.	Search for primary object experience (replication)				Capacity for transference
N.	Dyadic relationship		expanded object world		Oedipal object relationships

Figure 2 / The Fulcrum of Development (Source: Blanck and Blanck 1979) where ambivalence is possible. Narcissistic (or selfobject) transferences require a level of development where at least an archaic cohesive self is present. Both of these features (i.e., an Oedipus complex or a cohesive self) are lacking to a greater or lesser extent in borderline personality development. Rather, various functions are assumed not to have been "adequately supported" or "optimally frustrated" by the nurturing environment (Winnicott's "good enough" mother, 1953). Thus, the organizing processes of ego and self have simply not been able reliably to attain either of these more complex levels or nodal points of integration which are required for a meaningful discussion of transference.

The many "transference-like" phenomena so frequently spoken of by writers in the field are perhaps *best conceptualized as "replication needs" or "replication experiences,"* terms suggested by Blanck and Blanck 1979. The concept "replication" refers to the ever present tendency in the borderline personality to form (or to insist upon) some type of "psychological merger" experience with other persons or situations. This *push toward* or *assumption of some form of psychological merger with every "Other"* can be conceptualized as an attempt at restoring (replicating) some highly idiosyncratic form of early symbiotic or postsymbiotic experience. It would appear that a full emotional "replication" within the therapeutic situation is a prerequisite for further personality differentiation by way of the organizing processes of ego and self. The expression of the replication need within the dynamics of the therapeutic relationship seems directed toward securing "adequate response" from the therapist to unmet or unresponded to subphase requirements so that arrested development can proceed toward more complex levels of personality integration. This altered formulation has enormous implications for the way one *listens* to borderline personality organization.

B. Resistance

According to this line of thinking it is possible to consider the often referred to "resistance-like" phenomena not in the usual sense as resistances to the establishment of transference (Freudian and Kohutian models), but rather as instances of "ambitendency," a developmental phenomena which Mahler describes so well. It seems helpful to conceptualize the "to and fro" or rapid approach and avoidant movements of the person in relation to the therapist as manifestations of the developmental phenomena of ambitendency illustrated so vividly when a toddler rushes toward his mother with delight or just as quickly turns from her in anger and scorn.[9] Ambitendency

---

[9]Developmentally it seems that the child first turns away from mother out of interest and curiosity. The angry, stormy turning away seems to develop later in response to mother's failing to appreciate the child's need to be independent and to search out new things.

might be conceptualized further as an instance of undifferentiated or bipolar affect referred to by many as "splitting" (Kernberg 1976, 1980b). For a therapist to attempt to interpret ambitendency as "resistance" would simply be to misunderstand the developmental level of the expression—i.e., to commit an error in listening.

C. Countertransference

Theoretical consideration of so-called "countertransference" cannot be avoided by any writer in this field because of the compelling interpersonal engagement which the borderline personality requires as he/she strives to replicate the idiosyncracies of the symbiotic or postsymbiotic relationship within the context of the therapeutic relationship. Harold Searles (1960, 1979) has been perhaps the most outspoken in this regard advocating the necessity for extensive personal involvement on the part of the therapist in the treatment of borderlines. Little (1981) speaks of the positive aspects of countertransference. Giovacchini dwells extensively and effectively on countertransference reactions (1972, 1975, 1979a,b). Other writers in the field (e.g., in Epstein and Feiner 1979) have a difficult time getting away from some statement that at least in the early phases of treatment "supportive measures" are required.

In considering "countertransference" with borderlines, the crucial finding seems to be that some form of *interpersonal experience* is required which at least descriptively if not dynamically resembles "re-parenting." That is, whatever has specifically been experienced as a subphase inadequacy must have "adequate response" before the organizing processes of ego and self can proceed to integrate at higher levels.[10]

Thus, fresh developmental conceptualizations of transference, resistance, and countertransference point toward reviewing in new light what has already been learned about favorable therapeutic response. The expectation is that future data as well as past data (collected within a *regressive* framework) will be more intelligible when viewed from a *developmental* framework.

IMPLICATIONS FOR PSYCHOTHERAPY
AND PSYCHOANALYSIS
Traditional Approaches

Most writers continue to conceptualize theory with borderlines as "supportive." However, Kernberg points out:

> . . . a supportive approach frequently fails because the characteristic defenses predominating in these patients interfere with building up of a working relation-

[10]Chapter 11 returns to a discussion of the problems of countertransference.

ship, that is, the "therapeutic alliance" (as discussed by Greenson). . . . Instead of the turbulent, repetitive acting out of the transference within the hours, a situation develops in which the therapist attempts to provide support, which the patient seems incapable of integrating. (1975, pp. 71f)

Kernberg does feel that psychoanalysis is the treatment of choice for borderline personality organization, but he has developed a modified technique which seems modified not so much in overall style as in *what is interpreted*. His technique may be summarized briefly as follows:

1. A systematic elaboration of the "negative transference" while deflecting it from the therapeutic interaction via examination of transference manifestations in relation to others.[11]

2. "Confrontation" of defensive operations as they enter the negative transference.

3. Definite structuring of the therapeutic situation to block acting out of the negative transference *within* therapy.

4. Environmental structuring (hospital, foster home, etc.) to block acting out which threatens to stabilize "pathologically" in real life situations.

5. Selective focusing on transference and real life situations which illustrate defensive operations related to ego weaknesses and reality testing.

6. Careful use of *limited* confrontation of defenses which protect the therapeutic alliance.

7. Fostering more appropriate reality expressions for sexual conflicts, thus freeing sexual expression from its entanglements with pregenital aggression (1975, p. 72 f).

In talking about how his "modified technique" works, Kernberg says:

A major consequence of this general technical approach is the gradual integration of mutually dissociated, or generally fragmented aspects of the patient's conflicts into significant units of primitive internalized object relations. Each unit is constituted of a certain self-image, a certain object-image and a major affect disposition linking these. (1975, p. 197)

One might also consider Kernberg's therapeutic approach as affording *in vivo* a new step forward in the separation-individuation process described by Mahler. Stated differently, Kernberg's observations about what happens in therapy resemble a developmental step away from symbiosis proceeding with (1) a differentiation of *affect* away from the "good-bad" polarity while (2) achieving more advanced *reality* controls in the achievement of "self-other" differentiation.

---

[11]This "projective" technique may empathically permit the experience to be *disowned* or *disavowed.*

The remainder of this chapter will seek to demonstrate that it is possible to systematically apply the central psychoanalytic features of introspection and empathy, as described by Kohut (1959) to a therapeutic study of borderline personality development, thereby abrogating the necessity of considering technique as "covering," "supportive," or "modified." The thesis rests on the fact that, until recently there have not been conceptual tools available to be able to consider work with borderlines truly "psychoanalytic." Despite the widespread recognition that therapy with borderlines might best be *described* as "synthetic" rather than "analytic," Kohut (in press) has recently made the point that it is customary in any science to retain the original name of the science, i.e., "psychoanalysis," even when the subject matter or study techniques evolve beyond the original conceptions.

The Listening Perspective of the Merger Object

As therapists learn to listen more carefully to subphase inadequacies and to respond more empathically or adequately to highly individualized replication needs, it is becoming possible to cease thinking of technique as "supportive" or "modified" psychoanalysis. What Freud believed he was doing with neurotic development was well described by the term "psycho*analysis*," that is, "breaking down" complex psychological formations to their barest phenomenological essentials of drive and defense. However, Kohut has pointed out that it is not the "analytic" or breaking down process *per se* which has been the characteristic feature of Psychoanalysis through time, but rather the persistent investigation of personality by means of introspection and vicarious introspection (empathy). The basic ingredients of psychoanalytic investigation, (introspection and empathy) *fostered within a developmental framework*, can also be considered the essential aspects in the treatment of borderline personality organization.

The Vantage Points of Child and Adult Analysts

Almost as an aside, one might recall the old dispute between child and adult analysts regarding who might have the best vantage point for studying and understanding the nature of neurosis (and later, narcissism). It would appear that the observers working with adult free associations and adult transference reconstruction have historically developed the most comprehensive and heuristic ideas because in many ways narcissistic and neurotic structures continue to expand and complexify, often not clearly or fully crystallyzing until a person is in his/her early or mid 20s. Thus, while neurosis originates in the oedipal period and narcissism originates in the preoedipal period of the cohesive self, the complete structuring of features found in oedipal and selfobject transferences is not usually reliably available to child analysts so that their working data is, more often than not, limited or incomplete. In the study of borderline conditions the case may well be reversed. The vicissitudes of subphase inadequacy as well as other developmental variations may be more readily and reliably observable in the analysis of young children where borderline conditions appear increasingly "pure" the closer the observation point approaches the level of the symbiosis and/or the particular subphase inadequacy. The so-called "symptoms" develop later and represent secondary convoluted coping attempts. That is, social demand does not permit expression of the wish for basic unity (Little 1981), so various adjustments are made to hide it from public view (i.e., Winnicott's "false self" forms 1952).

Borderline development appears to differ from earlier development in the degree to which it becomes possible for the child to experience a relatively harmonious and/or reliable symbiosis which permits the development of basic reality testing and affect regulation. Thus, a fourth complimentary Listening Perspective of psychoanalysis, to be discussed in a later chapter, is suggested as useful in accounting for earlier phenomena stemming from a developmental fixation prior to the establishment of a more or less harmonious symbiosis.

THE DEVELOPMENTAL POINTS OF VIEW APPLIED TO PSYCHOTHERAPEUTIC LISTENING

Having reviewed five basic points of view which afford separate but overlapping views of developmental features which are often limited or distorted in persons with "borderline personality development," it now seems useful to acknowledge that in time other points of view may be defined as well and to specify some of the implications which the Listening Perspective of the merger object has for psychotherapy and psychoanalysis.

I. Symbiosis

In borderline development an ever present tendency is observable in relationships to push toward what has been called a merger or "symbiotic tie." Careful scrutiny demonstrates quite regularly that in more or less limited areas, adequate affect and reality controls once established *within* the early symbiotic relationship never had an opportunity to become completely independent from the symbiotic partner. While the person's overall reality and affect controls may appear basically intact, they tend to be limited in certain highly idiosyncratic ways. Kernberg (1975) talks about this clinical phenomenon as "stable ego pathology" and points to the operation of "primary process thinking" (i.e., faulty reality control) and "selective impulsiveness" (i.e., faulty affect control). Only careful clinical scrutiny—frequently clarified by psychological testing—makes it possible to specify the areas of functioning in which the once fluid boundaries of the symbiosis have *remained unstable*. The "push" referred to is toward a replication of *highly in-*

dividualized and specific qualitative characteristics of the merger tie which never underwent adequate "separation-individuation." The reason this clinical picture—so clear, once one knows what to look for—has continued to elude observation, seems to be that as a child grows chronologically, the expressions of symbiotic and postsymbiotic needs become unacceptable to persons in the environment. Through a variety of learning experiences, the basic symbiotic yearnings become transformed into a variety of convoluted and distorted coping efforts. Often even mother whose personality may once have treasured a specific form of merger can no longer endure many of the adaptational features which have developed when chronologically a symbiosis is no longer desirable or possible. Chronic so-called "acting out," or better expressed, "acting up," further obscures from view the specific nature of the basic symbiotic and postsymbiotic yearnings.

A child once expressed the need for symbiotic togetherness in a form worth mentioning. He was thirteen and had been diagnosed variously as having brain damage, developmental defects and functional aphasia. I had been seeing him twice a week for almost three years. In the course of a long series of sessions taking over six months, this boy began playing board games with me, "Chutes and Ladders" and "Candyland" at first; then checkers, backgammon and chess. He began introducing something I couldn't understand. In "Chutes and Ladders," we would start at the beginning, go to the top of the board and then as we would get one space from the top of the board, i.e., the end of the game, we would reverse and return to the *beginning* of the board. This happened again in Candyland and in Checkers. We reversed positions; we started with kings only to lose them! All of the games went in reverse. I couldn't understand what he was doing. Finally, in came the Monopoly set. Not an ordinary Monopoly—it had double sets of money! We went all the way until every dollar bill was taken out of the bank, then the game was reversed. We started putting money back into the bank and started going backwards on the board! It took a long time until we got to the end of that game, but when we started getting toward the end—which was the beginning—I began teasing him. I was ahead. I was losing money faster than he was! He began to get upset and changing the rules so that instead of losing $200 as I went backwards past "Go," I would lose only $20 (he switched to ten percent on me) so that he could lose more money and catch up. It became clearer as we got around to the last backward move that *we had to be together*, right to the very last square we had to be together! He looked up at me very directly and knowingly said, "In this backwards game, if you win you lose, and if you lose, you win." I thought it was an eloquent expression of the problem of turning loose of the symbiosis and its relation to things backwards! A step forward (to win) means a major loss. His need *that we be together* was thus verbalized.

II. Affect Differentiation

To the extent that borderline development has precluded a full differentiation of "good-bad" experience into a full spectrum of affects, one can expect within the therapeutic replication experience repeated instances of *ambitendency* or splitting. The borderline person, to a greater or lesser extent, will be prone to view persons (including the therapist) as especially "good" or "bad" alternately, similar to what one sees when the toddler "shadows" and then "darts away" from mother, expressing the simultaneous wish for union and fear of being engulfed, being swept up in mother's arms once again. Mahler (1975) provides vivid illustrations of children effectively and joyously seducing their mothers into "chasing" them when they have knowingly gone "too far." Every therapist has felt this same seduction!

In therapy with borderlines, the therapist must be prepared for ambitendency, for sudden, massive and untempered swings of love and adoration which quickly may turn to scorn, vitriolic hate and aggressive "acting out." The borderline has not developed object constancy in which ambivalence and repression are fully possible; so it is incumbent upon the therapist to be prepared for these massive and often puzzling changes of mood. The working through process resembles the original developmental sequence in which the therapist patiently understands and accepts the expression of undifferentiated affect and learns to anticipate sudden ambitendent swings. The therapist shows further empathic understanding of these floods of love and storms of hate by firmly "holding" and "limiting" response to those expressions which are "safe" within the interpersonal relationship, thus demonstrating that the therapist's boundaries are strong and firm—something from which one can differentiate.

The therapist must be prepared to offer these "protective" measures, similar to Modell's "holding environment" (1970), in order to acknowledge and thereby to provide "adequate response" to the subphase need to feel contained, limited, or restrained. Kohut (1971, 1977) has pointed out the classic stance of reflective, "evenly hovering attention" was never meant as a sham for rudeness, inattentiveness, or lack of empathy. He maintains that therapists must not fear extending themselves as necessary in order to achieve the empathic contact which is known to promote the introspective process. Empathic contact with symbiotic states can be expected to require a clear recognition of various "subphase needs." "Adequate response" to those yearnings appears to be required before introspection and empathy can proceed.

I am here reminded of an incident reported by a colleague who presents a 10-year-old boy. She tells how the boy comes into the room, sits in the "psychiatrist's chair," makes *her* be the patient and starts suddenly, hostilely and brutally telling her how "bad" she is and harshly criticizing her, telling her how she hasn't done "this" or "that" and how foolish and how silly she is. Then suddenly, the "bad" psychiatrist vanishes. In comes the "good" psychiatrist, who says, "My poor dear, you need someone to take care of you, you must be treated better." I think this child has found an effective way of communicating to her how he experiences undifferentiated affect—sudden, unpredictable, inexplicable changes from good to bad.

Another therapist recently reported how relieved his patient was when he finally showed an understanding of this same point. He reflected how uncomfortable it must be for her when her intensely loving feelings toward her young son and the man she sees suddenly, and "without cause" change into hatred, anger and repulsion (and vice versa). She could not account for her sudden shifts of mood or alternating states of consciousness but she was elated when her therapist showed an understanding of how disruptive and puzzling they were for her.

III. Private World Development

The development and differentiation of the "private world" can be conceptualized as occurring within the context of the symbiosis and the separation-individuation processes. Under the sway of positive and negative affects associated with object relations, the series *from entity to identity* slowly evolves. In studying borderline development, limitations in private world differentiation are almost always observable. The most frequent and obvious indicator is to be found in the persistent search for the merger of a symbiotic tie during the clinical hour in which the boundaries of "self" and "other" are fluid or unstable, suggesting that "incorporation" of the listener continues to occur on a regular basis.

Therapists are familiar with the person who walks into the consulting room and starts seemingly in the middle of a conversation telling with full speed and affect about something; as if the therapist knew the characters, the place, and the situation. One way of viewing this would be "incorporation." Another way would be to think that the symbiotic boundaries have not been sufficiently differentiated. The therapist is assumed to be the other part of the symbiosis, the other part of one's functioning mind.

Another area open to observation is the lack of differentiation of "sexual identity." In this area fusions and confusions abound which attest to a developmental arrest prior to the establishment of a firm sense of maleness or femaleness. Developmental limitations in this regard are often mistakenly thought of as homosexuality or various perversions but can perhaps best be viewed as indications of delayed or limited differentiation of the private world, producing problems in basic identity and the identification processes. The diagnostic finding turns out, for example, *not* to be problems with sexual identification *per se* but rather problems in establishing many types of identifications and in developing a stable and reliable sense of identity of any sort. This difficulty is often noted in the borderline "search for identity" in social or cultural stereotypes such as "housewifery," the drug subculture, Alcoholics Anonymous, mystical religious cults, teenage conformity or rebellion norms, television or science-fiction addictions, corporation "ethics," or adoption of a "gay lifestyle." Common to all of these searches for identity may be the wish for a symbiotic or merger experience with a partner, a "partner group," or a "partner culture."

IV. Mother-Child Adaptation

As the replication of the symbiosis proceeds, as subphase needs are expressed with ever increasing clarity, and as ambitendency is given full reign within the practical limits of the therapeutic relationship, the need for stylized symbiotic contact with the therapist will intensify according to idiosyncratic demands. Increased personal involvement of the therapist will be required. The following chapter classifies these involvements as various kinds of "scenarios."

Masterson (1972, 1976) has provided one set of ideas which may serve as a schema to help in this regard. He asserts that areas of limited borderline development were originally created by a mothering situation in which emotional support was given (Reward) or taken away (Withdrawal) from *certain areas* of potential growth. Part of the push toward replication of the symbiosis may then be expected to mean that in some very special way the therapist is likely to be experienced as rewarding or withdrawing in the specific style of the individual's early mothering experiences. Masterson's idea of "abandonment depression" may help conceptualize the points at which the therapist's personal and professional stance is likely to be experienced as "emotionally rewarding or withdrawing" such that a collapse in ego or self functions threatens or actually occurs. The working through process in this instance would require a recognition that the borderline person experiences the therapist's empathic contact as manipulative (rewarding and withdrawing). "Empathic support" or "adequate response" during periodic collapsed functioning seems a necessary part of establishing a relationship in which separation-individuation can proceed. Kohut's (1971, 1977) idea of the inevitability of "optimally failing empathy" on the part of the therapist may also be useful here in appreciating the many adaptational shifts borderlines typically present to ensure ongoing empathic contact with the therapist.[12] In a similar vein Searles (1969) points out that "guilt and inadequacy" are often experienced by the patient for not being able to

[12]Kohut (1971) talks about "optimally failing empathy" of the mother, and also "optimally failing empathy" of the therapist. This doesn't mean we try to fail, but it means that empathy can never be perfect. When our empathy does fail, according to Kohut, that is the opportunity to begin studying and working through the reaction.

respond to mother (or the therapist) in such a way that the "other" does not fragment or become unavailable. The patient may feel "responsible" for the therapist's unavailability.

An hour was presented recently by a woman who has been treating a highly disturbed 21-year-old borderline girl. The case was brought for consultation at the point in which the patient, after two years of intensive therapy with hospitalizations and all manner of upsetting experiences, was beginning to move to a point where some separation and individuation was being experienced. The case was brought as the process of "rapprochement" was just beginning. The symbiosis with the therapist was very well established by this stormy, acting-out, suicidal girl. The therapist naturally had been overwhelmed by the treatment. She was hoping to find some way of thinking about and discussing the case further and to find ways of encouraging the patient to grow. The patient's mother in response to the progress, took a two week trip to the Caribbean without leaving an itinerary, leaving this girl for the first time in her life alone! The trip was prepared for in therapy and the girl handled it with only several visits to the hospital (dropping in to talk to the nurses or other patients she knew). She had also "hooked into" Alcoholics Anonymous so there was support there. The therapist was pleased (quite appropriately) that the patient was able to maintain her stability throughout this period. In the session following her mother's return, the girl came in and had a fairly well held together hour with the therapist; sharing with her how well she had done, how well she had functioned. Her therapist rejoiced with her that she had "maintained" so well and showed pleasure over what good use she had been able to make of friends to help her through a difficult period. Then suddenly, almost "without warning or cause," the girl threw a temper tantrum, left the hour storming and screaming, threatening that she would not come back, that "goodness knows" she might kill herself soon! The hour was brought to me immediately and we began to realize that while the girl appreciated the separation support, she wanted to be certain her (symbiotic) therapist was still there! The symbiotic replication for two years had been stormy "Yes I will," "No you won't" "You will grow up, be a nice girl," "No I won't." The volatile and oppositional nature of the symbiosis and the wild, stormy acting out in this instance seemed to be her way of saying, "Are you still there?" The therapist had shared her pleasure at her new level of functioning, thus abandoning the established oppositional symbiosis. The patient then needed "emotional refueling" via the tantrum and the therapist's response of dismay to see that her therapist *was still there!*[13]

V. Organizing Processes of Ego and Self

Kernberg (1975) has discussed at length the subject of "ego deficits" in borderline states and Kohut (1978) has addressed the subject of the "archaic" or "noncohesive" self found in borderline development. Ego Psychologists such as Anna Freud (1965), Blanck and Blanck (1979), Hartmann (1939, 1950), Jacobson (1964, 1966), and others have studied extensively the progressive development of basic functions. Blanck and Blanck (1979) emphasized the importance of conceptualizing the ego "as organizing process." Kohut (1971, 1977) makes a similar point when he refers to the self as a "supraordinate center for organizing the personality."

Diagnostic and therapeutic goals with the borderlines would be to develop an empathic grasp of exactly what the particular symbiotic needs are and to permit them expression through ever more clear and direct replications in the therapeutic relationship. A lengthy working through process would then be required strikingly similar to the original separation-individuation process. The result of working through would be to permit the organizing processes of ego and self to integrate symbiotic needs at more differentiated levels of development. In therapy with children as well as with adults, it is regularly observed that as the symbiotic tie is permitted full merger replication experience, remarkable transformations of ego and self functioning occur.

I was fascinated with a child who was presented by a therapist who works in a room full of many toys. This particular child would come to the table where the therapist was "assigned" to sit and would say "Where is this?" "Where is that?" "Where is something else." In this room lined with toys the therapist would say, "It is over there." The child almost instinctively would look in a different direction, in a different place! To the consternation of the therapist, "Why does this child always do the opposite? Why does this child always do the contrary or always go somewhere else other than where she is instructed?" We began to understand the child either mishears or mislooks, almost oppositionally. One can easily understand why this child is in a special learning program because every time it is pointed out where she can look for the needed information, the child cannot look there. We began to understand in the long-term therapy process with this child, mislooking or mishearing is part of replicating the symbiotic tie, the way of maintaining a hold or grasp on the symbiotic mother. Oppositionality and constriction frequently turn out to be forms of symbiotic attachment.

AREAS FOR FUTURE STUDY

Rapprochement versus Symbiosis

The rapprochement period or "crisis" is receiving considerable attention (Mahler et al. 1975; Blanck and Blanck 1979; Lax et al. 1980) currently because writers are becoming aware that in some areas of development

---

[13]This patient is discussed further in the section on countertransference as Ann.

borderlines have not satisfactorily differentiated from the immediacy of dyadic relationships to either mirroring or idealizing relationships or to oedipal relationships. The "parenting" which helps a young child differentiate and consolidate basic ego and self functions in the second 18 months of life is strikingly similar to the process which a borderline undergoes during a course of analytic therapy. Many frankly call the therapy process "reparenting." Blanck and Blanck (1979) and others take issue with this term, preferring to characterize the therapeutic relationship as "catalytic" rather than "parental."[14] In any event, those familiar with watching the rapprochement of young toddlers continue to liken that period to therapeutic work with borderlines.

However, despite the rising popularity of the "rapprochement crisis" idea for *describing therapy* with borderlines, the lack of satisfactory rapprochement experience does *not* account for the origin or range of limitations in development presented by borderlines. Lack of "adequate response" during the original rapprochement subphase may indeed account for a dearth of mirroring, twinning and idealizing experiences which could lead to a lack of cohesion of the self so that selfobjects are incessantly sought out for the relief of various forms of psychic tension. In this regard, Kohut's Psychology of the Self does provide an effective paradigm for studying (via selfobject transferences) the various failures or limitations of the rapprochement experience. But an understanding of borderline developmental arrests necessitates an intensive study of the symbiotic phase and the postsymbiotic subphases of differentiation and practicing. That is, it seems likely that whatever developmental damage or limitation the borderline experienced has occurred *prior to* the rapprochement subphase and serves to limit the capacity to negotiate the rapprochement crisis.

The Merger Experience and the "Merger Object"

What has set apart Freud's theory from other "schools" of psychoanalysis has been his essentially "structural" approach. Despite the linguistic complications which concepts of structuralization introduce, the consistent usefulness of Freud's structural approach has been in pinpointing for study various *enduring* aspects of oedipal personalities, i.e., the id, ego, superego, and the ego defenses. The classical paradigm highlights conflicts between structures and has endured the test of time in studying neurotic personality organization.

---

[14]It strikes me that the best parenting is also essentially catalytic. Whatever important differences might be between parental and therapeutic support through separation-individuation, they have yet to be spelled out clearly. Perhaps it is becoming the deliberate, focused emphasis on the free associative activity within the countertransference (which leads to confrontations or differentiating activities on the part of the therapist) which puts the therapist more in a "therapeutic" or "catalytic" role than a "parenting" role.

Heinz Kohut's Psychology of the Self follows the classical emphasis on *structural* study and defines the mirroring, twinning and idealizing self-objects for studying narcissistic personality organization.

The Listening Perspective of the Merger Object currently evolving for the study of borderline personality organization focuses on a developmental experience of *the "merger object" at a time when it exists fully and exclusively as the presence of the symbiotic partner.* The only sense of separation or differentiation from the merger object occurs *during the actual loss of functioning at the time of the experienced loss of the merger object.* The "quest for the merger object" or the "push toward a symbiotic tie" differs considerably from Kohut's notion of a "merger transference" in that more than mere transfer to the therapist with empathic working through is involved. It appears that *the subjective experience of merging personalities* must be accomplished in the therapeutic replication of symbiotic and/or postsymbiotic areas of arrest before the separation-individuation process can move on to the rapprochement crisis.[15]

Restated, the current thinking on rapprochement fails to take into account sufficiently that the basic arrests in borderlines occur prior to rapprochement. Limited functioning becomes evident only later when it is clear that certain areas once developed in relationship to the merger object *within* the symbiosis failed to develop by undergoing the separation-individuation of the rapprochement period.

Delineation of Ego and Self Functions

Studying borderline personality development raises new questions regarding ego and self functions. Prior studies in Ego Psychology have led to the postulation that many ego functions are "conflict free" or "autonomous" (particularly the work of Hartmann 1950, 1958). Observations of borderline children suggest that many of these functions are developed within the interpersonal environment which Mahler calls the symbiosis, differentiation, and practicing periods. It would seem that the interpersonal environment either does or does not provide the opportunity for the required number of trials which establish various perceptual and motor functions as "conflict-free." But many things can and do go wrong in the development of the so-called "autonomous" ego functions. In child therapy the therapist often finds him/herself working long hours to discern the exact nature of a developmental deficit and then hovering until the child feels encouraged to try and experience success in a new perception or skill. It is not the mother, nor the teacher, nor the therapist, but *the actual experience itself* which does the conditioning! The attainment of many functions and skills seems to require

---

[15]This experience of merger is referred to as "basic unity" by Little (1981) and spoken of as the core personality of the borderline.

merely the *interested presence* of another human being to make trial and success possible. Previous writers have remarked on the effects of "the auxilliary ego."

A most dramatic example of this was a four-year-old boy who had been referred by the director of a nursery school. For a variety of reasons I chose to see this little boy with his mother in the same hour for a period of time. The mother was narcissistically preoccupied with a great many things and could not attend to the needs of this little boy. During the course of the hour I had to continue to restrain him from spilling imaginary tea and coffee on his mother because I knew *that* would end the therapy soon! But I wasn't prepared for what ultimately ended it. The little boy began expressing more and more openly in our sessions together, *how much he needed his mother.* He then began to draw and cut with scissors (it must have been October, because I remember the pumpkins). This little boy succeeded through a series of hours in showing graphically to his mother and communicating to her that when he sat next to her or on her lap, he *could* draw pumpkins and he *could* cut them out. When he sat three feet down the couch or three feet across the room, he *could not.* There are many instances like this in which *in the presence* of the other person, "the auxilliary ego," skills *are present* but without that person the skills *are absent*!

When first working on this chapter, I started beginner tennis lessons. While learning to serve, I became aware that so long as my tennis instructor could *see* me out of the corner of his eye, I could serve well. But the moment he was distracted or a pretty girl turned his head, my serves deteriorated. I came to realize that it wasn't the loss of him to someone else, but the loss of his watchful presence! It seemed related to a difficult physical skill I was having a hard time developing. The question seemed whether or not he *was able to see me.* I took this up with him: I was afraid he would think I was a lunatic for mentioning such a thing. But he immediately responded, "You know how funny that is? About half the people I work with are that way and they report when I am present they can play, and when I am absent they can't. I understand that, but what I *can't* understand is when it's the other way, some people's skills fall apart when I watch. But at tennis matches I have learned exactly whom I am to watch and whom I am not to watch!" The other phenomenon perhaps relates to a study of someone who experiences the game less from a standpoint of mastering a basic body skill and more from the standpoint of competition, rivalry, exhibitionism, and the like.

Teachers frequently report the same thing. A child *can* perform with the teacher standing close but *cannot* when the teacher's attention or availability is diverted.

Of obvious concern here is some delineation of *which* functions evolve out of *what type* of symbiotic or post-symbiotic experience. Mahler (1975) has observed some "danger signals," but these are as yet global and ill-defined and have the additional disadvantage of being observable only "after the fact."

Borderline "States of Confusion"

Writers and clinicians frequently report "states of confusion," "emotional flooding," "massive regression," "shattering," or periodic "falling apart" in persons with borderline personality organization. Such expressions or labels indicate that the experience is being viewed as "maladaptive" or "regressive," but is this the only way these confusions can be viewed?

Pine (1974) points to "signal anxiety" which in neurosis would trigger a defensive reaction but in borderline children precipitates massive panic. Some have suggested a genetic or early developmental influence akin to Freud's notion of the "stimulus barrier" in order to account for failure in effectively or efficiently screening out traumatically overstimulating experience. The concepts of "signal anxiety" and "stimulus barrier" may or may not prove useful in conceptualizing borderline states of confusion, but there are other possibilities.

Many times one observes a borderline person regaining composure or control over "shattered" functioning at an even more integrated level than before, so that an observer is unjustified in evaluating the confused period as merely regressive or maladaptive. One possibility is that various deficits and limitations of functions tend to be integrated or stabilized at different "levels of development." When new "higher" integrations are made, the old, but stable, consolidations are momentarily disrupted and a state of confusion results. Another possibility is that while a normally developed child may be pleased to be able to "do it by myself," self-sufficiency in certain areas of a borderline's functioning may threaten a loss of support, a loss of togetherness, a loss of crucial symbiotic presence. In therapy, dyadic or fusion experiences are relinquished only with reluctance. The fear which is often seen (by an outside observer) as a reluctance or refusal to grow or to try new experiences may not be merely a maladaptive attitude. When new development leads to a new step in independent thought or action, the old familiar forms of interpersonal support as well as the experience of togetherness *are in fact lost!*

I saw this first in working with teachers. I began to realize that when a particular child *did succeed* in the math problem or in the spelling or in whatever area he was having trouble, *he lost his partner.* His teacher would move on to another child. The particular contact (struggle, or whatever) that had been established around not having this skill would thus be *lost* making the learning of such skills even more complicated.

The expectation in therapy with borderlines is that each new level of integration may be ushered in by some form of confusion which often becomes labeled as "regression," "resistance," or "acting out." Instead, it may be possible to consider that some new ego functions have been or are about to be integrated at a new level of success. As the new level begins to make its appearance, the immediacy of a symbiotic mental state is being relinquished and the person suddenly feels "at sea" or "at sixes and sevens." Each growth achievement implies—and may actually entail—a dreaded experience of loss and separation. A further implication of this line of thinking is that periodic states of confusion may be an inevitable part of the therapeutic growth process with borderlines and that in time states of confusion may be subject to more systematic and controlled exploration by therapists.

CONCLUDING REMARKS

Borderline developmental limitations do not lend themselves to categorization by "symptom" or "syndromes" because the array of behavioral and dynamic possibilities is *literally infinite* since the ways a child reacts to mothering are infinite. Attempts to classify so far have led to sterile groupings of surface manifestations while omitting consideration of the less obvious causes and effects. The five developmental points of view outlined here serve as conceptual tools for listening to persons with early arrests in ego and self functions referred to as "borderline." The points of view afford the possibility of listening to the person's basic experiences beneath the more raucous or visible manifestations.

Historically, the term borderline referred to "borderline insanity" or to the border between "sick psychotics" and "maladjusted neurotics." Indeed, awareness of the nature of borderline phenomena has evolved from a study of fairly disturbed individuals. However, as sophistication has increased and borderline personality organization has come to be viewed in a developmental context, it is becoming rapidly apparent that there are many bright, competent, socially well-adjusted persons whose object relations are constellated or organized at pre-rapprochement levels. Since clinical tradition has tended to regard only blatantly "sick" or disturbed persons as borderlines, the basic relatedness needs of many higher functioning persons have gone unresponded to in psychotherapy. That the traditional interpretive approach with such persons has often led to "negative therapeutic reactions" is not surprising when one grasps the very different kinds of experience borderline personalities require in psychotherapy.

Each child has molded him/herself to a specific mothering person or situation in highly specific ways during the early developmental period referred to as "symbiosis." Reluctance to relinquish the immediacy of the dyadic experience in favor of separation and individuation results in highly idiosyncratic developmental arrests which subsequently undergo a series of adaptive convolutions. The specific area(s) of arrested development, depending on how crucial or how pervasive they are, may have only minor consequences for the future development of the child or may have massive implications for development. Since specific areas of symbiotic yearning depend upon the particular emotional quality of the original mothering process, ego or self deficits can show up in *any specific developmental area.* For example, one mother may unwittingly foster a lack of adequate speech, another fail to encourage forms of motor development, another may discourage looking or listening, while the personality of yet another may have demanded certain forms of clinging dependency.

"Symptoms" represent a series of convolutions and distortions developed as the growing child extends interpersonal contacts beyond the primary mothering person. The result may be an obnoxious, withdrawn, overactive, seclusive, dominating, hypersexual, passive, constricted, obese, abused or aggressive child. These various behavioral styles represent the way a child copes with or adapts to an interpersonal environment which does not provide him with particular "subphase requirements" still needed. The borderline adult characteristically disguises his subphase needs in even more distorted or convoluted ways.

Entrenched pessimism about psychoanalytic treatment of borderline personalities is slowly giving way to new possibilities as the inventory of listening tools increases. The need to think of psychoanalytic work with borderlines as merely "supportive" or "modified" diminishes as more is learned about the developmental arrests involved and as therapists are in a better position to extend empathy to the investigation of borderline personalities via the establishment of a persistent introspective and/or interactive process.

In therapy with borderlines it is expected that certain nodal points of personality integration have not been or have only partially been reached, specifically the developmental stages of the cohesive self and of emotional triangulation, the Oedipus complex. In the therapeutic replication, the limitations of ego and self become repeatedly apparent and in the working through process the therapist is required to be empathically tuned in to the countless demands which the limitations of these organizing processes make. Unusual patience and understanding is required to tolerate the many expectable intrusions into the personal and professional life of the therapist.

Patience is also required to realize that the borderline person's timetable for therapeutic development is usually quite different from the therapist's! Often long months of seemingly little progress are required to establish a full expression of the symbiotic yearnings or to establish a sense of safety sufficient for new experiences in life to be tried. The therapist must learn to tolerate these periods without permitting excessive boredom, impatience, or consternation to intrude into the therapy process. In fact, it is often these so-called "countertransference reactions" or perhaps better stated "reactions to the replication" which provide critical clues to the exact nature of the symbiosis or post-symbiotic states being recreated in the therapy.

For clarification, it should be stated that with borderlines therapy is known to be "ego building" but this does not mean that the therapist should or needs to be "building" anything! As in all psychoanalysis, the processes of introspection and empathy can continue in borderlines quite without "support" or "suggestion" in direct or guiding forms from the therapist. The main difference in therapy with borderlines is *not what one does but how one listens and responds.* The listening focuses on the replication of the symbiosis and on reactions to the loss of the "merger object." Anger and aggression are understood *not* so much as destructive impulses but more as efforts to separate or differentiate from the merger experience or the merger object. Silence is often understood *not* as resistance but either as a wish for "wordless being together" or as a need for the feeling of "being separate." Therapist's questions may at times be experienced as unwelcome intrusions into areas of precariously established independence or separateness. "Telling secrets" may turn out to represent subtle or disguised ways of maintaining or hanging onto symbiotic closeness.

Any specific symbiotic replication may be experienced as over- or understimulating to any particular therapist depending on the personality makeup of the therapist. The central problem which the therapist must ultimately face in therapy with borderlines is being constantly cast into the role of a parent without always feeling free to respond with the ordinary spontaneity of a parent by way of offering praise or blame or being able to mete out disciplinary action or other direct guidance activities which a parent might do.

It is particularly instructive to watch child therapists at work. In the beginning they are frequently required to sit very close or even to be in physical contact with the child (as in the symbiosis). In time, the therapist is permitted to move back and to give reign to freer aspects of play (as in the differentiation). Then often for hours or even months the therapist goes apparently unnoticed while the child's interests and occupations roam free, only occasionally stopping for emotional refueling with the therapist (as in practicing). Then slowly creep in the signs of competitiveness in games and play as the child begins to take delight in his accomplishments and competitive endeavors and to share the delight with the therapist (as in rapprochement). Toward the end of a long course in therapy the child begins to engage in all manner of spontaneous free play from puppet shows to drawings and games, including a wide variety of interacting characters. The child has many things to show and to share with the therapist every hour (as in the oedipal achievement of object constancy). Massive affective flooding, states of confusion and periodic collapses of ego functioning which early in the treatment regularly accompany holidays, missed appointments and vacations, crop up again in full force when termination is in sight and the child realizes he is going to miss his visits with his "special person."

Behavior therapy, encounter, transactional or confrontation techniques as well as crisis counselling are all likely to be helpful to a person with borderline personality limitations. These briefer therapies might be viewed as a means of bolstering or supporting the failing or faltering organizing processes of ego and self. Such interventions appear to increase the person's immediate capacity to *adapt* to social situations which have taxed the coping capacities precipitating some sort of family, social or school "crisis."

On the other hand, reconstructive psychoanalysis or psychotherapy is a long-term and often quite demanding process. The utmost patience and energy reserve of the therapist are often called upon to establish empathic contact with those layers of the personality which were arrested at the toddler phase and which have produced a series of puzzling convolutions and distortions of the basic symbiotic yearnings.

There is, however, reason to believe that if the therapist can hold steady for the long months and years required for (I) the replication of the symbiosis, (II) the differentiation of the affects, (III) the development of the "private world," and (IV) the vicissitudes of adaptational attachment that (V) the organizing processes of ego and self will begin to take hold and propel the person forward, restoring and adding or compensating for missing or inadequate functions. The therapy process can be viewed as a movement toward the establishment of a functional cohesive self (Kohut 1977) and toward forms of self and object constancy in which others can be experienced as separate centers of initiative and triangular (oedipal, incestuous) relationships become possible.

Finally, one might even go so far as to note that the essential basis for spontaneity, creativity and indeed the very wellspring of human love and attachment all originate in the layer of personality once engaged in a rich and rewarding symbiotic relationship. While much may have been gained in relinquishing symbiotic aspects of one's personality, much was also lost. The growing child or the borderline adult may need to muster disgust toward dependent trends in order to escape symbiotic bondage. But when one no longer has need to fear regressive experiences of closeness, one may discover admiration or even envy for the creative capacities and the richness of interpersonal experience possessed by people who have ready access to the so-called "borderline" layers of their personality. Perhaps even the condescension frequently expressed toward persons with borderline personality development can be thought of in the context of "yet another witch hunt" stemming historically from a lack of understanding of these heretofore uncharted regions of the human mind.

METAPSYCHOLOGICAL CONSIDERATIONS

Comparison with Freud's "General" Metapsychology

Within the Listening Perspective of the Merger Object, the *general* metapsychology remains the same as Freud's and Kohut's except as with the selfobject paradigm, the *therapeutic* process with borderline persons is generally thought to involve fresh development rather than the opaque mirroring of the oedipal situation as with Freud's therapy for neurosis.

Comparison with Freud's "Specific" Metapsychology

1. Turning to Freud's specific *metapsychology* or the "points to view," it can be seen that within the Listening Perspective of the Merger Object the *topographic point of view* may be largely irrelevant. Freud's distinction between conscious, preconscious and unconscious modes of functioning gives way to earlier developmental considerations. Freud's notion of unconscious modes depended upon the capacity for repression and ambivalence which are only achieved in advanced stages of psychic development. Similar phenomena in borderlines are conceptualized as splitting (Kernberg 1975) and ambitendency (Blanck and Blanck 1979). As such, they are conceptualized as preambivalent and preconscious. Therefore, Freud's concept of "the dynamic unconscious" is largely superfluous in studying the introspective/interactive experience of "borderlines." Rather it seems more interesting to speak of "alternating states of consciousness" or "contradictory ego states" (Kernberg 1975) in which objects are experienced as "good" and "bad" and in which the self is experienced alternatingly as "good" and "bad." These alternations of conscious experience would be termed ambitendency.[16]

2. Freud's *structural point of view* conceptualizes the enduring aspects or agencies of the personality as id, ego and superego. Heinz Kohut in The Psychology of the Self (1971) agrees with Freud that those structural definitions are adequate for the understanding of advanced psychic development seen in the psychoneuroses, but that the concepts of drive and defense are not adequate in considering preoedipal states of development. In place of tripartite conceptualizations, "ego" and "self" are used variously by different authors to denote *dimensions* of psychological experience and psychological organization and as such may be called structures (Kohut 1971) or may better be referred to as "organizing processes" (Blanck and Blanck 1979) in preoedipal personality organizations.

3. *The dynamic point of view* which assumes mental phenomena result from an interplay of forces operating *in time* remains useful in consideration

---

[16]Stolorow and Atwood (1981b) share this general point of view but use the term, "the prereflective unconscious" to refer to nonconscious experience of persons with preoedipal arrests.

of borderline phenomena. Masterson's (1972) idea of "abandonment depression" represents a special contribution to dynamic and genetic thinking.

4. *The economic point of view* which Freud defined regarding the distribution, transformation and expenditure of "psychic energy" appears not to have been developed or considered extensively by writers in the field except in a formalistic attempt to continue applying the metapsychology of Freud to borderline phenomena. The psychoeconomic notion of Kohut in The Psychology of the Self regarding the ebb and flow of psychic tension and the development of the capacity to soothe the self seems of limited usefulness in considering borderline phenomena. It would appear that the psychoeconomic point of view of Kohut's attains importance during what Mahler has called the rapprochement subphase of the separation-individuation process. As the young child has attained a certain degree of separation from mother, the child reapproaches mother expecting joyful mirroring responses from her. Kohut has held that disorders of the self result when tensions which the child feels for mother to share with him, and to mirror or to admire and confirm him go chronically neglected. Prior to rapprochement there seem to be no crucial formulations involving the economic point of view so that thus far it can be set aside in thinking about borderline phenomena.

5. The *genetic point of view* becomes totally reconceptualized in considering the Listening Perspective of the Merger Object. While early representations may be experienced as "good" and "bad," these are viewed as affective components being attached to memories of self and objects which only later, during the oedipal phase of development become integrated into the experiences of libidinal and aggressive drives (Kernberg 1976, 1980b). Thus, the moment of the genetic point of view here relates *not* to the development of instincts or the curbing or civilization of instincts by the "higher" forces of ego and superego. Rather the genetic point of view in considering borderline phenomena refers to the development of a series of ego and self functions and to the ego and to the self as organizing processes (Blanck and Blanck 1979). The theory of human symbiosis and the separation-individuation process (Mahler 1968) largely replaces previous developmental models when listening to introspective experience of persons with borderline personality development.

6. *The adaptive point of view* becomes difficult to apply when dealing with borderline phenomena. Mahler (1968) insists her phases and subphases of development are *intrapsychic* and, therefore, inferred rather than behavioral so she clearly maintains an intrapsychic stance. However, many writers are not so careful and lapse into talking about early development from an "objective" or "social" view.

7. In observing borderline phenomena, an important metapsychological assumption becomes added to those already defined by Freud and Kohut. While Freud highlighted the relationship to the incestual objects, and Kohut

defined the importance of understanding selfobject investments. A study of borderline phenomena highlights the early *development of self and other (mental) representations* such that another "point of view" or another metapsychological assumption needs to be added. Jacobson (1954) was the pioneer in developing this concept and Sandler and Rosenblatt (1962) as well as Stolorow and Atwood (1979) speak extensively of *the evolution of the representational world.*

Hartmann (in a personal communication to Jacobson cited in a footnote, p. 6, 1964) is credited with the realization that the notions "self and object representations" are metapsychological in nature since they cannot be directly validated by psychological observation.

In summary, the metapsychology of Freud is modified markedly by authors studying the experience of the merger object. The traditional emphasis on conscious-unconscious modes of thinking gives way to the concept of ego splitting or alternating states of consciousness. The structural point of view is no longer important in highlighting intrapsychic conflicts but rather the self and the ego are seen as a set of developing functions and as "organizing processes." The traditional focus of the genetic point of view loses its impact as libidinal and aggressive drive concepts are replaced by good and bad affects related to the development and differentiation of self and object representations which is the key metapsychological assumption of those studying borderline phenomena.

Five Additional Developmental or Metapsychological Points of View involving the differentiation of experiences of self and other come into prominence as a consequence of studying the borderline personality organization. These have been defined as: (I) Symbiosis, (II) Affect Differentiation, (III) Private World Development, (IV) Mother-Child Adaptation, and (V) The Ego and Self as Organizing Processes. These points of view will be systematically applied to case illustrations in the next chapter.

The Developmental Points of View Applied to Clinical Interactions

Accurate listening to experiences of merger objects has been one of the most elusive tasks in psychoanalysis. The five developmental points of view discussed in the previous chapter have been effectively applied by many writers in various places but not yet pulled together in a harmonious and systematic fashion. The purpose of this chapter is to point a direction toward systematic utilization of these points of view in clinical practice. Different clinical interactions will be presented with brief discussion meant to stimulate thought and to suggest a method of organizing one's thinking about persons with borderline personality organization. The first illustrates the usefulness of the Listening Perspective of the Merger Object in three diagnostic sessions with an 8-year-old boy. The second interaction focuses particularly on the metapsychological point of view of private world development in an emerging identity formation of a young woman. A fascinating dream series of an 18-year-old musician/composer is presented which illustrates the move toward separation-individuation. Finally, an instance of an inadvertent replication is studied. The following chapter will move more directly to address the psychotherapy experience with borderlines after the basic usefulness of the developmental points of view of the Listening Perspective of the Merger Object has been demonstrated in the following case illustrations.

The format for the comments will be the five developmental points of view which are outlined in the preceding chapter: (I) symbiosis, (II) affect differentiation, (III) private world development, (IV) mother-child adaptation and (V) the ego and self as organizing processes.

TEDDY BEARS' PICNIC (Bobbi)

Introduction

Dora Kalff visits this country periodically from Switzerland showing slides and lecturing on nonverbal creative techniques with a Jungian psychoanalytic orientation. The therapist in the following presentation employs a similar technique and works in a large playroom lined with thousands of toys. There is also a wet and a dry sand tray. What is to be presented are the therapist's notes from the first three (diagnostic) hours with an 8-year-old recently adopted boy, Bobbie. He was abandoned by his mother at 13 months and up until the past year his (largely absent) father moved him from relative to relative and through a series of foster homes.

The Therapist's Report[1]

Opening Comments / For the intake hour, the adopting mother and father found it necessary to bring Bobbie with them. So that we could talk more freely, Bobbie was taken to a nearby room where he could play with toys. During this hour Bobbie interrupted several times but returned to play alone when his parents told him it would be a little longer.

First Session / Mother brought Bobbie, who was anxious to play. He willingly let his mother go shopping while he came down the hall to an unknown room with me. He remembered the room he had played in last week and started in that direction. He found it no problem to go in the opposite direction to the therapy room. When we entered the room he looked around and remarked, "Lots more things here." He went to the dry sand tray where he began shoveling or pushing the sand around. The sandmill and funnel were near—he experimented, fascinated with the way the sand made the mill wheel turn, but he wanted to use wet sand. We experimented and he saw it would not flow through the bin and funnel. He moved across the room—looked the shelves near the window over and found the nerf (foam) balls—chose one, sat on a chair across from me and played toss and catch the ball. He can throw accurately—we both caught a few. Then he threw one that hit me; fell to the floor and rolled across the room. He found the gravitation toy but dropped the heavy metal ball which rolled under the desk. I handed him the yardstick and he fished it out, placed it on the rods of the toy but then shifted and began batting the punching bag—made a half-turn and picked up the (black) dog's head puppet; made its mouth bark and bite—moved on to the pounding board—knocked the pegs all down—noticed the record player and wanted to play a record on it—chose "Peter and the Wolf." Before I could show him how to set the arm of the player he had jerked it free of the player with about a foot of wires exposed. I was not able to get it to play without the record repeating, so we had to give up that activity. He went back to the dry sand tray—used the sand mill with three wheels. He worked out four places to put sand that would make all the wheels turn besides using the bin at the top of the mill.

Seeing the enamel paint we use to paint the dry clay figures children make, he grabbed a can in each hand and asked to paint. I said, "Not *that* paint," and explained how we use that paint and told him where the tempera

[1]The therapist is a woman. See note on contributors, p. **xix**.

for paper painting is kept. Again he grabbed the jars of tempera, brought them to the table where I helped him open them and got set up to paint. He painted one picture, a woman with no legs. Then he had the idea of mixing sand and tempera. (My knowing the paper on the table would not be a good base to mix on, I set a small tub on the table.) He brought several shovels full of dry sand which he put into the tub. Next he began pouring tempera over the sand. He poured from every jar about 1/4 to 1/2 cup of color; in order, black, white, red, orange, green, blue. He stirred it together with a small plastic shovel. When the liquid and sand were mixed to a dull brown color, he looked up at me and asked, "With my hands?" as he clenched and extended his fingers. ("Sure!") He messed and mixed then lifted fistfuls onto the paper (12″ ×18″ construction paper). The consistency was so sloppy that the water ran off the paper onto the table. Before I could stop him, he had grabbed the towels to sop it up, filling the towels with the muddy mess. I had a sponge in my hand and it does a better job. (Aside: This child seems to have little impulse control, but he perceives situations, is capable, and very bright. Although he had this mess of sand and color to his elbows, he got none of it on his clothes—even cautioned me not to get it on me!) When he had heaped about a 4-inch mound on the paper, he wanted to let his "picture" dry on the floor. Together we put it where he wanted it; after which he left the room to dash down the hall to the restroom. I followed and stood near the door. Soon I heard a banging inside so I asked one of my male colleagues to go in to see that all was well. In a few minutes I heard the toilet flush. When he came out I asked about the noise and he told me he found a stick in there. Back in the therapy room there was some mopping up to do and I did it. He asked me if I liked to work. I assured him it was no problem, that I just wanted to help him keep his clothes clean, and I wiped off the chair seat, the edges of the table, etc. He wanted to take his "sand picture" home, but I told him it would have to dry before he could put it in the car. As I walked him down the hall, he asked me if I "had fun."

At one point in our hour, Bobbie threw a nerf ball. It hit my hip when my back was turned. Another time he stooped down, semi-hidden by furniture, jumped out at me and asked, "Are you scared?" or "Did I scare you?"

The First Session: Developmental Points of View / The lack of ego and self development (V. organizing processes) coupled with aggressive trends and fears are readily apparent in this hour. In his picture of the woman without legs, he depicts the therapist's difficulty in keeping up with his rapid pace (hypomanic trend). The order of the colors might be thought to represent the good-bad split (black and white), followed by anger and fear (red), and other differentiations (II. affect differentiation). Inadequate self-other distinctions (I. symbiosis) are evident in his frequent confusion of himself with the therapist and her supplies. The anal theme is frequent in borderline children, reflecting the psychosexual level of the symbiotic arrest. These themes will be seen to develop in subsequent sessions.

The Therapist's Report Continues

Second Session (one week later) / Bobbie had gone to the restroom so I had a few minutes to talk to his mother. She reported that he had had a bad week, been sent home from school twice, but that instead of punishment, a system of tickets for good behavior had been arranged; six good tickets and a reward. When Bobbie returned from the restroom, he pulled the six tickets from his pocket and told me he would have ice cream on the way home.

Bobbie and I walked down the hall to the therapy room. He asked why the door was locked and was impatient to have it opened. Inside the room, he patted the damp sand in the round tray, then moved to the dry sand in the square tray. He took down the toy loading bin, filled it with sand and was puzzled that the sand did not flow through. I showed him how to open the funnel of the bin so the sand would flow into the dump truck when the truck was pushed under the bin. He walked to the table, and he asked about the dish of raw vegetables. He chose a turnip slice and wanted me to eat one also. Then he saw a licorice ball in the chest of drawers by my chair. He took it out and I told him he might have it. Holding it in his hand, he started the record player (it was possible to have it repaired). He moved the arm gently and carefully; chose "Puff the Magic Dragon," played it once, then found "Rock A Bye Baby." "My mommy sings that with me and rocks me." He picked up the Peter Pan doll and twisted its legs; reached for the three nested dolls, separated them and left the pieces scattered on the table, picked up the calculator and showed me the 100 button doesn't work. He played the record again—picked up the mousetrap—didn't seem to know how to set it—wanted help. He sprung the trap with a pencil. "That scared me" as he jumped back. He saw a sheet of animal picture stickers and wanted them. I gave them to him. He ate more turnips. "What are these?" "Turnips," he was told again. He saw my package of Victor cough drops. "Can I take these?" as he made a grab. "No," was my answer. "Or we will be in trouble?" He threw two plastic missiles across the room. One landed on the floor near the door; the other landed in the round sand tray. He went to stand by the round tray facing me, "Don't look," he told me, and when asked why, he said, "A surprise," as he patted the wet sand with a shovel. "Don't look, I don't want you to—going to be a surprise." The record had stopped playing but was still turning. "Turn on the record," he said in a commanding voice. ("Oh you can do that.") He played the "Rock A Bye Baby" record for a third time. He climbed on a chair and chose a game from the shelf. "Will you play 'Pick up

Sticks' with me?" He held the sticks tightly, "Choose one!" he told me. I did, a red one. "The prettiest goes first," as he chose a blue stick, which he declared was the prettiest and so was first. He was not too observant of sticks that moved but finally did give me a turn. While I was taking my turn he jabbed his blue "prettiest stick" into the grapefruit on the table that I hadn't had time to eat at lunch. He counted his sticks and told me he had won. We began a second game. This time I told him when I thought I saw the pile of sticks move. He denied it and went on with his turn. When it became my turn I was careful to observe the rule of moved sticks. He grabbed the grapefruit and with his teeth pulled off a hunk of peel, then said, "If I cheat, *you* cheat," as he gave me an extra stick to add to my pile. At the end of the game, he had won again.

He noticed the dart board for pointed darts and asked, "Where are the darts for that?" When he was shown the basket of darts he exclaimed, "Oh, wow." He threw darts at the board but had no skill; then he threw one at the ceiling. When I said, "No," he replied, "Okay," sat down on a chair near the dart board and continued throwing, but kept checking to see if I was watching every move. Suddenly he stood up, turned quickly, and gestured toward me with a pointed dart. I just as quickly took the dart from his hand, removed all darts and placed them under my chair. I carefully explained the "no hurting" rule we must both observe in the therapy room. "But I get my candy?" When he realized I had no intention of taking his licorice ball, he picked up the ape and pretended to scare me by thrusting it toward me. He went back to the record player and put on "American Pie."

He asked to paint and chose a set of small jars and small brushes. He made a picture of a woman with no legs again. "Know what this is? An angel." (Done with black tempera, a yellow spot on top of her head. A halo?). As I glanced at the record player, I noticed he had stacked two records, but said nothing. He asked for the pictures he had painted last week. I got them for him from the shelf; even the one that had held the pile of sand. Although the sand had been removed the stain on the paper was a reminder. "I gotta go to the bathroom. Can I come back and play?" ("Yes.") When he came back he had a damp wadded up paper towel in his hand. "Guess what's in it?" My guess was, "just paper." He opened it up to show me his licorice ball candy hidden in the paper. He continued his painting—made a dividing line under his angel which placed her in the upper two-thirds of the paper. Below the line he made balls of color—using dribbles of paint from every jar—green, blue, red, black, yellow, white. Then he went to the dry sand tray for a scoop of sand. He asked for the pan, the one he had used last time to mix sand and tempera. I gave him a smaller pan. He shook dry sand onto the blobs of color on his paper. It was time to go—he wanted to take his angel picture with the sand and paint globs home with him. I insisted it had to dry and he could take it next week. He insisted it was dry, the sand had made it dry but he left with the two pictures he did last week.

I walked down the hall where he met his mother. As they went out the door I said I would see him next Friday. "Every Friday?" he asked.

When he left, I saw the round sand tray contained two low cone-shaped shells, points up, three pine trees close together, and five 1″ by 1″ tiles laid in a path-like row connecting them. I don't know when he did this tray. He moves so fast it is not possible for me to catch all he does!

The Second Session: Developmental Points of View / The aggressive intrusions (I. symbiosis) of this child, which occupied most of the next year of therapy, were foreshadowed in this hour. The yearning for symbiosis (I) is clear in the "Rock A Bye Baby," the various commands, the wish for "even cheating" and the connecting path between two cones (breasts?) and three pines. The split affects (II. affect differentiation) are again portrayed in the contradictory "black angel," which is separated by a line from the discrete blobs of pure color, perhaps representing the lack of affect integration. His identity (III. private world development) as a separate person is not yet established, and many skills (V. organizing processes) are lacking, as in darts. He still desires controls from without (especially of aggression) but fears aggressive retaliation (IV. mother-child adaptation). This demand for control turned into a "scenario," reported in the next chapter.[2] Does the black angel represent his own failure to integrate or his experience of the projected contradictory attitudes of objects (II. affect differentiation)?

The Therapist's Report Continues

Third Session (one week later) / I met Bobbie and mother in the hall. He had a bag of six cookies. "Let's go. Let's go," as he pulled at me. He broke from me to embrace and kiss his mother, then dashed down the hall saying, "We have lots of fun today." He went to the table where he opened the cookies and ate one. He insisted that I eat one also. Then he asked about candy. I was ready with a licorice ball under my appointment book. When I gave it to him he asked about more and I told him "Only one." He wanted to explore the three-drawer chest by my chair but I carefully defined that as my area. Today all drawers were closed. He started the record player and changed the records several times. He picked up the mousetrap, asked for help to set it, had to be told where to press to spring it, used a pencil, and when it went off with a snap he jumped. "That scared me," he said. He had nothing more to do with it, did not even remove the pencil. He announced he wanted to paint, rejected the 9″ × 12″ paper which he could get himself and asked for "big paper"

[2]See the "example scenario."

(12″ × 18″), which I had to get for him. His next move was to find a container and to put dry sand in it. When I questioned that he needed as much sand as he had in the quart container, he insisted. He brought it to the table which was now set up for tempera painting. He put a brush into each jar of paint, chose red and printed his name, Bobbie, at the bottom of the sheet, then drew a line which placed his name in the lower third of the paper. He told me it would dry and he would take it home. I said, "No, this picture will go home next week," and showed him that I had last week's picture ready for him to take home. He got off his chair, spotted the jar of clay, "You got clay too?" I answered, "Yes," and *asked if his picture was finished.* (Note: Here the therapist interrupts his flow and he responds.) He sat down, made a *red* woman with long legs, but there were no arms. He sprinkled sand over the wet paint, looked to me for help to remove the loose sand. He wanted to pour the sand into the quart container. Together we held the paper so loose sand would drop as he wanted it to. On the sand that stuck to the wet paint, he dribbled drops of colored tempera from each jar. He added more sand, mixed colors and sand with his brush, then pinched the sand and color, which became muddy looking, into a reasonably firm mass—(mess). He filled his hands and gestured as if to throw it toward the mirror, which reflected his image. Only a little slipped from his hand and fell to the floor; the rest he dropped on the red figure he had drawn with the paintbrush. Then, with the butt of his open palm, he smeared his picture grinding the sand into the paper. Again he wanted to put the loose sand into the quart container, and I helped. Next he put a generous amount of water into the quart container of sand and color where he mixed it well with a brush. He got another 12″ × 18″ paper. The picture of the red lady was on the table, so this time I suggested he spread his paper on the yellow chest. He brought only the quart container with the thin, muddy-looking sand mixture and his brush. He started to pour the liquid, really just dump the contents of the quart onto his paper. Realizing what a mess that would be, and the possibility of tempera staining, I helped him scoop out the most solid part onto his paper, where he spread it with his hands. The sand and liquid did spill over the paper. When he said he was finished, I quickly sponged up what had escaped the paper and asked him to go outside with me to empty the most liquid part of the mess. When we came back into the room, he washed his hands in a bucket of clear water and ate another cookie and some of the carrot sticks on the table. He saw the grapefruit on the chest of drawers by my chair—grabbed it. I said, "No," and he substituted a nerf ball. This he threw in my face, hitting my glasses. Again I said, "No." He said, "I want a drink," and started toward the door. There was a bottle of drinking water in the room and mugs. I had to remove a tea bag from the mug. He wanted tea. We had no hot water so he had to settle for a cup of water. It was a breakable mug. He pretended to drop it and asked if it would break, then what would I do if he broke it? Would he be in trouble; would I tell his mommy? Then I briefly explained the confidentiality of our time together. He went to the record player and put on "Teddy Bears' Picnic," went to the dry sand tray, filled the large white funnel with sand, and let it all flow to the floor. He got a scoop and scooped the sand back into the tray, but the last scoopful he tossed into the air toward me so it scattered 2/3 of the length of the room. It became impossible for me to take notes. There was a continuous flow of activity around the room. I kept near him and participated in many activities. He finally went back to the table and asked for crayons. I pointed to the place near the 9" X 12" paper where they are kept. He brought a paper and the colored felt pens. He made the bust of a figure, said it was George Washington. I asked him about George Washington, and he told me he was president. He pressed so hard with the pens that he broke off two of the tips. "God damn, these always break off," so I explained he pressed so hard they just "had to break." He told me the picture was not finished, but he wanted to take it home. I told him I would put it on the shelf and he could finish it next time. It was time to go. I put last week's picture in his hand and laid the unfinished one on the shelf. As he left the room he grabbed "my drawer" as he went by, jerking it out but not far enough to spill everything. Seeing his intention, rather than let him knock over shelves of toys, I put my hands under his elbows and started him toward the door. He curled his feet up under him, and I found myself carrying his full weight through the door. When I let go he was on his feet. I closed the door and followed him to meet his mother.

Today the cuffs of his long-sleeved shirt were wet and stained with tempera. In fact, he had quite a little on him. I may need a smock for our next hour.

What I have recorded is rather sequential up to the time he threw the sand. At that point I lost the sequence for a while. I remember that at one point he picked up the dragon and pushed it against my forehead. When I asked him to keep it away from my glasses, he threw it the length of the room.

The Third Session: Developmental Points of View / Bobbie indeed sees the prospect of therapy as a "Teddy Bears' Picnic" (anticipation of satisfying symbiosis: I.). The therapist is punished for her wanting him to finish the picture (so she can see it for herself) which *he* wants to abandon (limitation on the symbiosis reacted to aggressively: I). He objects to limits but clearly hopes to establish a symbiosis with controls being shared and comfortable. After three years of therapy, the boy's social, educational, and behavioral skills have markedly improved (V. organizing processes) and rapprochement (I. symbiosis) is beginning as he delights in sharing his accomplishments with his therapist and eagerly engages in competitive play.

"GETTING MYSELF OF ONE MIND (Ms. Q.)"[3]

Introduction

The following hour has been selected for consideration because it seems to be an initial statement by a woman of her growing wish to establish a consistent sense of personal (and subsequently sexual) identity (III. private world development) and the struggle which she experiences in defining her identity apart from overwhelming symbiotic trends.

After several years of once weekly psychotherapy with an experienced, empathic, male therapist, her work was brought to my attention because, according to the therapist's impressions, she was losing her boyfriend, and the therapist was concerned about the consequences of sexual intrusions into the therapy. During the course of therapy, she had been able to achieve a remarkable sense of symbiotic relatedness (I. symbiosis) to her therapist, in which she could experience a strong sense of "togetherness" to the extent that any offerings from him were simply unwelcome because they violated her need to feel "at one" with him. Between sessions she had taken to walking along the beach in the town where she knew he lived to "suck up the atmosphere" which she experienced as replenishment directly from him, from the air he himself breathed.

In social situations she made heavy use of alcohol and drugs, socializing with a "fast crowd" and priding herself on being seductive and "outrageous." Partly because she is an extraordinarily beautiful woman and partly because her style of "outrageousness" is pleasant and enchanting (if not little-girlish) she is generally received warmly wherever she goes. Her therapist enjoyed her very much. Through a series of reported outside episodes as well as incidents which occurred during her hours, her therapist and I came to view this social style as an incessant search for symbiotic closeness and merger with people and situations around her. Her perpetual role as "sexual enchantress" served to bring people (men and women) within her orb, though her invariable wish was to enjoy the "play" and ultimately "to be held."

This symbiotic perspective helped the therapist to relax his concerns somewhat and to stop "fending off" her encroachments into what he experienced as his "personal space" during sessions. He began feeling more free to simply enjoy and appreciate her style as she displayed it to him while simultaneously radiating a reassuring (holding) attitude, indicating that sexual or other personal encounters were simply "not in the cards." This simultaneous loosening of attitude and firming up of personal boundaries on the part of the therapist brought a florescence of ideas, attitudes and behaviors which left no doubt that her growth process and the movement

[3]The therapist is a man. See note on contributors, p. xix.

toward what might be called a "rapprochement crisis" was well under way. Her extensive use of drugs diminished dramatically and abruptly; she stopped letting herself be "tucked into bed, wasted"; she began showing an interest in interpersonal relatedness, primarily with gay men and lesbian women, though she was not interested sexually in either; she made a visit to a distant city to see her idealized father and was able to experience him for the first time as narcissistically preoccupied and very disappointing. At this juncture, she was able to refine her work habits on her job as a "temporary secretary" so that she could afford and could arrange to schedule two sessions each week and was now for the first time willing and able to present with a sense of joy and pride a series of highly creative poems and essays to her therapist for his perusal, reflection, and admiration.

From these brief comments it should be clear that her most secure sense of "self" has tended to be experienced in connection with drugged, symbiotic, and well nurtured states of mind, in which other people and situations could be sought out and cultivated for their "holding" qualities (IV. adaptation). As the "holding function" of the therapeutic relationship became secured (as understood through the therapist's countertransference experience of her being "stuck, unable to move forward, unable to make use of therapeutic interventions"), she gradually became aware that she was "somebody different" to everybody she knew (III. private world development). She experienced many "selves," and her private sense of who she was depended heavily, if not exclusively, on who or what situation she could find to merge with (incorporate?) for the moment. She felt that there was "very little inside" that she could "call her own." In this context, the following session occurred which seems to represent, among other things, the expression of her conflict between her wish to experience identity in diverse "outrageous" merger experiences versus her wish to have her own "inside" sense of identity, to, as she put it, "get myself of one mind."

The Therapist's Report

Ms. Q. enters wearing a leotard, tights, and wrapped skirt. She takes off the skirt and announces, "I'm trying to make the inside look as good as the outside." She told of how an old friend called her, saying, "Hello, Beverly, I hear your apartment is being converted into a condominium," to which she replied, "Oh, is this (therapist's first name)? Can I come live with you?" "No, this is Chuck." Ms. Q. then replied, "Oh, well then can I come live with *you?*" She reported this incident with laughter and obvious enjoyment. She told of how nervous she had been on the two occasions we had spoken on the telephone, but the exact meaning of this was unclear to both of us. She thought it was, "because it was not here," meaning the office. She expressed that she would like to redecorate and live here in the office. She talked about needing protection which could be provided by either her "fag" friends or women friends, some of whom are lesbians. I mentioned the protection provided in the office as well.

She said her boyfriend's therapist tells him how terrific she is for him. She said her boyfriend is concerned about her attraction to women, but lesbians turn her off. She asked if I were straight or gay and I explained again why I wouldn't answer that question, which she accepted and began to explore her fantasies. She said if I were straight she would be terrified and if I were gay, we could "have play time without sex causing difficulties . . . I mean it's hard to have a good time with somebody who wants to fuck you." (Meanwhile she is spreading her legs and lifting one or the other almost over head while talking like a little girl.)

Next she tells of how she hoped that the patient who follows her for the next appointment is really dull. She said that one Saturday when I was wearing blue jeans and a casual shirt I looked gay. Her gay friend agreed with her when she told him about it. But other times she knows I am not gay and she suddenly hesitated fearing she would hurt my feelings. I reassured her and then she said, "No fag would be caught dead in your baby blue suit, but you looked so cute in jeans. You're the only one who won't answer if you're straight or gay."

She told of seeing a man in a bank line this week who looked like me from the back. She moved up in line and tapped him on the shoulder, hoping he would go along with what she had in mind. She went to a motel with him, but he wouldn't play her game and insisted that she call him by his name and not her therapist's, whereby she immediately put on her clothes and left. She talked about, as a child, seeing her father fucking her sister, indicating how the tears were running from her sister's eyes and remembering how her sister looked at her, saying, "Help me." She spoke of wanting to book every one of my hours and how she felt the need to have someone (me) all to herself, adding she also thought that was silly. I reassured her that it seemed to be an important concern and she said she tries to get her boyfriend to pretend he is a virgin again so she can have something all her own.

She emphasized how she always meets others' needs but not her own. She told of being in a crowded elevator with a man who was looking at her legs and how turned on she felt, noting that if he had put his arm around her, "That would have been it!" (meaning frightening, the end). She "was climbing the walls" and couldn't wait to get out of the elevator.

She talked of how often she feels two contradictory ways; she calls it "the push-pulls." At other times she feels any one of a variety of ways. We spoke about her relationship to "barriers," as she calls them, and about how at times she appreciates them (e.g., "If you were only a fag") and other times wanting to have all of the barriers out of the way (e.g., the man in the bank).

With respect to her experiences of these many "needs," I agreed how important they must be to her and then she spoke of wanting the best of both worlds in a number of ways, one of which would be to be a fag and thus she could have all the beautiful men she wanted and at the same time people who she could have fun with. She ended the session speaking of her hope of "getting myself of one mind."

The Session: Developmental Points of View

The developmental points of view from the Listening Perspective of the Merger Object provide illumination of this woman's work. The perspective of symbiosis (I), with her movement toward rapprochement, has already been mentioned. Not necessarily evident in the material presented has been a slow differentiation of her affects from a good-bad split (II. affect differentiation) i.e., the "push-pulls," to a curious admixture of feelings nowhere better portrayed than in a recent essay she presented to her therapist prior to his vacation on "Why Therapists Need Vacations But Shouldn't Take Them"! A discussion of the mother-child adaptation (IV) and the role of father and sister would be fascinating but unfortunately run too far afield from the present material. Various aspects of the growth of the organizing processes the ego and self (V. organizing processes) are evident in the introduction to this hour.

Of particular interest in this material, however, is the visibility of a critical moment in the development of this woman's "private world," (III) that is, the movement from "incorporation" to "identification."

Prior human encounters have centered around "incorporation" experiences in which she "outrageously" and exhibitionistically merges boundaries with others, taking them "in" and feeling "safe and sane" in the process. Here she begins with the expression of the wish, "to make the inside look as good as the outside." She subsequently expresses an awareness that the establishment of a good, solid, inner identity is tied up with the establishment of firm interpersonal boundaries. She demonstrates how the issue of personal identity is confused with the development of sexual identity and how at least she can experience a rudimentary sense of her own "self" when she relates to people she isn't sexually interested in, i.e., gays and lesbians. Another way of stating this would be to remark that the symbiotic needs have become so confused with sexual needs in her mind that she can only be sure of who she is when sex is put aside. In the replication of the symbiosis (I), she has experienced her need for closeness to her therapist in highly sexualized, seductive modes. In this connection she recalls (or fantasizes) an incest scene to illustrate how parental and sexual closeness have remained blurred and frightening for her. It is interesting that in a similar context, on a different occasion, her associations produced a recall of "my father fucking me." The style and manner of these recollections has led the therapist to suppose that these "incest" reports are likely not veridical memories but mental constructions which certainly portray her lifelong confusion between the problems of personal identity and sexuality. The therapist also holds the opinion that she is neither overtly or latently "homosexual" in any important sense. Her sexual involvement with her somewhat older "boy-friend" is where her growing interest lies, despite the fact that the relationship has for several years been confounded with his role as a nurturing, identity-giving, father-mother. What seems eminently clear is that a rudimentary sense of personal identity (III. private world development) is slowly evolving out of the symbiotic matrix (I) of the therapeutic interaction, as a better sense of self-other differentiation occurs in the context of differentiating affects (II).

A SEPARATION-INDIVIDUATION DREAM SERIES (Michael)

Michael, now 18 and a music student in college, had been in therapy for about a year and a half. His subjective complaint was that he was experiencing inhibitions in his musical creativity. He is a talented musician and has aspirations of being a composer. Early sessions were devoted to a discussion of headaches, eye blurring and dizziness while practicing which were particularly perplexing to him since, "My music is just now to where I am taking off with it." This boy had enjoyed a deep and close relationship with his mother for many years. He experienced a number of school problems in earlier years as well as problems in motivation and withdrawing from peer contact during his teens, for which he had previously entered brief psychotherapy. About a year and a half prior to his reporting for treatment, his mother had begun her own analytically oriented therapy. The boy's commencement of treatment may have coincided with the mother's beginning efforts to individuate through her own therapy as reflected in her being able to tolerate greater independence and development on the part of her son. The dream series to be reported occurred after more than 15 months of once-a-week psychotherapy.

In early November, Michael asked me if I knew anything about dreams. I responded by telling him that I certainly knew some things, why had he asked? He called his first dream, "The Bounty Hunter." It was a long and convoluted dream with a composite of family members and houses. Both of his natural parents are divorced and remarried so that he lives with his mother and frequently visits his father. Only the end of the dream could he recall in which a deranged man, the bounty hunter, was going to "get" his family. He ran around to the back of the house, very frightened, in order to warn them or to save them, but it was too late. There was a bloody mess, and they were all slaughtered. Michael had studied some things about dreaming and was horrified at the thought that he had that much violence within him. In his discussion it would appear that the dream was a condensation of concerns about the psychotherapy process and the up-coming holiday season with his family. By this time he had graduated from high school and started college. He was very surprised (if not dismayed) at how well he was doing and at what good acclaim his music was bringing him. The blocks and headaches had lifted shortly after graduation and seemed related to the development of several new friendships outside his home. The interpretation of the dream we agreed at jointly was roughly that he did understand my role and the role of psychotherapy as being partially to help him move away from the over-close relationship which he has had with his mother and his family. With family reunion thoughts just around the corner at Thanksgiving and Christmas, the dream seemed to represent his fear that I, the bounty hunter, the deranged man, had already, in some way, destroyed his experience of his family, and it frightened him. It was further discussed that his own developing skills and enhanced identity (III. private world, and V. organizational processes) were responsible for his being able to partly make the break from such a close connection to his mother (I. symbiosis). It appeared that the deranged man and the violence represented split-off affects of unintegrated self and object representations (II. affect differentiation).

Immediately after the New Year, Michael reported this dream:

> Something was tapping in the room, like a piece of paper or a leaf in the wind. In the dream I was hearing both a melody and a rhythm. I was hearing it and composing the music and the melody to the rhythm. The melody was as if I were predicting the rhythm! You can't predict that. It was the wind. But it was perfect. The rhythm and the melody was a complete whole.

He then reported a second dream:

> All week I am immersed in music, so no wonder I have dreams about music. I was asleep. I am practicing classical music—Haydn. I was practicing or composing the music in my mind, and it began to get in too minor a key, and I got scared. I got up and looked around. This was scary. I was seeing it. The notes in my dream were all following a classical form with classical harmony. (Therapist: "What frightened you?") You know how some music frightens you? Like the "Rite of Spring" scares me. Well, it went into a minor key. It was *the sadness that scared me, the transition.*

Subsequent associations brought out that his teacher had been giving him considerable praise in front of the class. The other students were showing him tremendous respect and admiration. He was extremely pleased about this, if not a bit embarrassed. He said, "It's now much easier for me to learn things. I've gotten to a certain peak with all this praise. Also my step-dad gave me a good comment. He never does that." From his associations during the hour, we concluded an interpretation something like this: In the first dream he was aware of his creative capacity to be *totally in tune with an outside force* or rhythm. He had experienced pleasure in being able to be in perfect harmony. Only upon awakening was he puzzled and concerned about where the rhythm was coming from and reported having actually gotten up and looked around the room trying to find the source of the very faint noise.

In the second dream he seemed to highlight the importance of a sense of total immersion in the music. He said, "It was as though I *was* the notes, the music, the sound, the composer, the player and the instrument all at once." The dream remained comfortable so long as the composition retained a familiar classical style similar to that of Haydn. As his own originality in the composition began to depart from the established classical form, it moved toward a minor key, which suggested sadness at leaving the established pattern and going on his own. The "transition" frightened him!

The next dream occurred after a victorious semester at college and during the semester break. Michael arrived at the session commenting on how relieved he was to be visiting for several days at his father's home where it was peaceful and quiet without all the family making so much noise and without his mother constantly screaming at him to do one thing or another. He also added that even though it was loud at home, he was glad to be back. He had this dream while visiting his father's house:

A good friend or relative had a very nice Jaguar. It was very sporty—quite long with a short cab. He got killed somehow, it wasn't clear how. He wasn't murdered, and the car hadn't been in an accident because it was in perfect condition. In the front yard someone yelled, "Don't ride in that car. Remember what happened to ———," mentioning whoever's name it was (which I couldn't recall) that had gotten killed. I took it for a ride anyway. Suddenly a woman's face appeared on the windshield like it was a TV screen. From two other dreams I knew that I had to scream, "You're the devil!" or I'd be killed like in the other one. That's a weird dream. It stuck in my memory. I might have even been shouting in my sleep. It was a really attractive woman. She was acting real nice. I can't remember that face, but she was the same as in the other dreams. (Therapist: "Other dreams?") Last week at my dad's house three nights in a row. I can't remember the dreams but only that I had to yell in bloody terror "You're the devil!" or I would have gotten killed. (Therapist: "Do you have ideas about the dreams?") All of these dreams had something materially real nice. In this one the car, the Jaguar, and in one of the others, a really nice TV, something nice. I knew I wasn't supposed to have these things, but I had a tremendous sense of power. *Power to overcome her power.* The only way she could have power was if I ignored her.

(Therapist: "Who was that in the yard?") I have no idea—a relative of the guy who got killed, a woman also, but not the same one. She was young, about *my* age, maybe older. Funny the way things come about. They are so abstract. (Therapist: "Who was it that got killed?") Some tall guy with short hair, with a crew cut. Like someone you would find in the Midwest. So far [surprised] I've described my Dad. He used to have a Jaguar, and he also used to have a crew cut and was from the

Midwest. (Therapist: "He got killed?"). Only *I* knew how to overcome her mysterious forces; he didn't. I knew what would happen in the dream. I had total confidence in myself that I had the power to stop it. (Therapist: "What about the woman on the TV screen?") Well, she had brown hair, you know, but I can't remember if she was beautiful or ugly because of the face and her power. I can't remember how she looked, but when I was up against her I had fear; no, I had no fear but I had power. I knew I could yell and she would disappear on the screen, just like turning off or on a TV set. (Therapist: "What night was it you had the dream?") I had the dream Saturday at Dad's house and didn't remember the other two dreams from Thursday and Friday nights until I remembered this one. (Therapist: "It seems as though you have a very good sense about these dreams?") Yes, I felt good and powerful.

As we discussed the dream, I recalled previous dreams and our ongoing interest in his being able to strike out on his own, independent from his mother, to know that he had the power to do it. He responded by saying, "Dreams seem to bring me into balance. I think the conflict at home is resolved. In the past few days I feel quite different. Now I can accept living at home. Maybe the dream is a subconscious statement of that. Now I know I can avoid Mom if she starts getting on my case. Now, like when she starts bugging me if I'm practicing or something, I just say loudly and firmly 'No, not now. Bug off.' Just like with the person in the window of the car. Like 'God damn it, not now.'" He talked about his visit at his father's house and how his father and his father's wife consume so much food and alcohol that they are frequently grouchy and get into disagreements. He then asked, "What do you do for someone who doesn't want to admit that they are an alcoholic?" He indicated that he enjoys very much the respect that he gets there but how sad he is to see how his father has changed, how much under the control of his step-mother he has become. "I placed Dad in my shoes when I used to go with Barbara." This comment alluded to a very close, sticky and ultimately bizarre relationship that he had early in therapy. He had enjoyed the social prestige of having a pretty girlfriend but had selected one with intense symbiotic needs which he came to realize replicated in some ways his relationship with his mother. As he attempted to move out of the relationship, she became wild, dominant, and controlling, at one point even breaking into his house and stealing some of his music. He then said, "That dream could have been so many different things. It could have been my mother and her husband. It could have been me and my mother. It could have been my Dad and his wife. It could have been me and her. It could have been me and Barbara." (Therapist: "How did the dream end exactly?")

Well, I got back to my house. I remember driving back through my tract and not wanting to drive that car again, or at least not for a long time. (Therapist: "Why was that?") Just concern over what would happen. It was so terrifying to have to resort to such harsh authoritarianism in order to feel safe. At Dad's I was thinking of his wife's control over him and how much control Mom used to have over him. He never made it. I know I can, but I hate to have to resort to such an authoritarian approach in order to escape her power. Isn't it amazing how creative the mind is to symbolize all of those things. It's like watching a movie, your own, with you the writer, the producer, and the director and all the time just lying there in bed.

There must be many ways in which dreams such as these could be interpreted. They seem to be understandable within the context of a separation-individuation movement which this young man is making in his effort to grow up. It appears fortunate that his mother is in her own therapy so she can tolerate his psychological movement. He constantly reports her difficulties with compulsive eating and how much worse it has become in the last six months. He is vaguely aware that his mother's problems are related to his growth and at times has expressed a wish to be able to help her with her problems in one way or another. In the first dream he seemed to be expressing a fear of the therapy process (the deranged bounty hunter), as the threat of losing family ties emerged clearly. In the dream couplet, he portrays his perfect (symbiotic or selfobject) "in-tuneness" and becomes frightened when his own compositions move to a more difficult or advanced *minor* key from the tried and true classical mode. In the final dream reported, he sees he is making a separation-individuation attempt to get away from his beautiful and ugly (split affects: II) but powerful mother. He feels his father was not successful in making such a step but was killed in the process. He sees his father in the same situation with a new woman, being under her control. In the dream, he experiences a positive and pleasant sense of power which is nonetheless alarming. A power which he doesn't want to have to resort to at least for a long time, because it requires such intense effort. The positive note of the final dream and the positive note in the therapy is, of course, that the separation-individuation process is proceeding with both its positive and negative effects.

AN "INADVERTENT" REPLICATION (Robert)[4]
Introduction

The previous chapter distinguished between the concept of transference, used in listening to the more differentiated experiences of selfobjects and constant objects, and the concept of replication, useful in listening to experiences of merger objects. Empathic contact with persons arrested at or experiencing relatively undifferentiated, pre-rapprochement, and, usually, preverbal merger modes is achieved through the process of understanding

[4]The therapist is a woman. See note on contributors, p. xix.

replicated interactions. Mahler's (1968) developmental terms for the merger modes are "symbiosis," "differentiation," and "practicing." The distinguishing feature of the borderline personality organization is an insistence upon a style of dyadic relatedness in which the person holds to idiosyncratic mind-body boundaries. Through these developmental idiosyncrasies, the person persistently intrudes or provokes intrusions of various sorts. While mutual intrusiveness is an expectable quality in early, merged, symbiotic states, when the need for mutual intrusiveness persists, it often comes to look more like mutual abusiveness. It is inviting to imagine that the therapist can come to understand and to interpret accurately the exact nature of early merged states through inferences, cognitions, and transference analyses as in neurotic and narcissistic personality organizations. However, experience indicates the limited usefulness of transference analysis and transference interpretation in the usual sense when attempting empathic contact with merger experiences. Merger means two minds merging into a single "mutual cueing" process. Merger can only be understood when merger actually exists. Separation-individuation can only be accomplished from a merged state. In short, a therapist can only understand early merged states when *engaged* at the level of "primary undifferentiatedness" (Little 1980).[5]

According to this view of therapeutic contact with borderline personality organization, a considerable amount of time and mutual accommodation will be expected before a sense of psychological merger can be achieved and differentiating activities can begin. The next chapter will develop this approach within the context of various kinds of replicated interactions, or "scenarios," which can be expected during the course of therapy. Following that, the idea of countertransference as the "royal road" to understanding replicated scenarios will be developed. The present example serves to illustrate the concept of replication.

The first interaction to be described produced dismay and acute distress in the therapist as she felt unwittingly "dragged into" the merged state. The second interaction produced in the therapist elation and motherly pride in response to a differentiation achievement of the man with whom she was working.

The Therapist's Report

Robert has been seen once a week for three and a half years. During the first two years as the relationship developed changes were seemingly slow and minute. Robert's main mode of relating during that time was one of

---

[5]Little (1980) criticizes the term "symbiosis" because it is a "two body" concept. She maintains that therapeutic contact with early developmental states means experiencing togetherness in terms of "unity."

stating that he was feeling depressed about his lack of progress: "Nothing ever seems to change. It's always the same routine." Or he would recount in detail his work experiences. It seemed as though the therapist was not a separate person at all, but merely another part of himself to whom he was talking.

Robert repeatedly related a fantasy which he had had since early childhood. The fantasy consisted of viewing himself like a very small ant near a woman's foot. The thought of being crushed under her foot was "sexually" arousing to Robert. He would fantasize her walking and "unknowingly" crushing him under her foot. The woman was seen as large and looming over him. In this fantasy, it was important that the woman never noticed him. He reported that feeling her "substance" and weight fulfilled a need in him. As a child, he attempted to attain this contact by various means. He recalled hiding under some outside steps with his finger between the slats attempting to feel the weight of a woman as she stepped on the slats squeezing his finger. He had fantasies of burying himself in the snow in front of a driveway, so that he could experience a woman's weight as she drove the car out of the garage. He stated that he knew this would be foolish, but part of him felt that a woman could not really hurt him. He recounted another time, when the snow was quite deep. His neighbor had walked through the snow to her car. After she left, Robert picked up the footprint left in the snow and licked it, feeling, he said, contact with the woman. He wondered what it would be like if he buried himself in the snow where she would have to walk upon her return and step directly on his face, unknowingly. Another time, he licked the bottom of a woman's shoes, again, feeling a part of her. At times, he would be fascinated with the footprints left by his teacher as she walked in the snow, incredulous at her weight and "substance." He said that he knew she was "real" when he saw the indentations of her weight. He recalled a young friend of his being whipped with a belt and feeling envy at the contact with a woman that his friend was experiencing.

These fantasies continued throughout the years. He would watch waitresses as they walked, imagining that he was like an ant which could be inadvertently stepped on. For a long time, Robert stated that he never had such thoughts about the therapist. Only after three years of therapy was Robert able to tell the therapist that he did have such thoughts about her feet. He said that he often watched her walk down the hall and imagined what it would be like to be stepped on by her. An important session took place at the time Robert reported this. It will be partially recounted here. Prior to this particular session, Robert had needed to cancel one hour and the therapist had to leave town unexpectedly the following week. Robert stated that he had forgotten about the therapist's cancellation and had made the trip to her office.

Session Excerpts

Patient: Well, it's been a long time.

Therapist: Yes, it has. It's too bad about the mix-up last week.

Patient: It was no problem.

Therapist: You really had to go out of your way. Something like that is disappointing.

Patient: It's really been busy at work. A big job has come in, and I've asked to be put on swing shift. It is more challenging. I'm bored with the job I have now.

Therapist: What about the foreman's job?[6] (A higher position that the patient had spent a great deal of effort in applying for.)

Patient: That's kinda in limbo. It may be several months before that's decided. Anyway, if I get it, I'd come off swing shift and take it as it's a promotion. How are your hours earlier in the day?

Therapist: I have time. We can work something out.

Patient: Do you have any groups going now?

Therapist: I'm going to be starting a new one on Thursday nights, but if you're on swing shift, that wouldn't work. Is school not working out? [Patient had planned to take a business class that met four evenings a week, which affected our schedule. He had planned to take off early from work to come on some weeks and leave class early on other weeks.]

Patient: No, I'm too tired. I've been putting in 12-hour days at work. Besides, the teacher is coming right from teaching high school students. She insists on our using 8½″ × 11″ paper and making all of our headings with red pens. It's ridiculous. She treats us like children. I guess that's about enough reasons, maybe all rationalizations, I don't know. Also, class starts at six, and I need time to eat.

Therapist: Are you still going to restaurants?

Patient: Yes.

Therapist: Are you fantasizing during this time, as before?

Patient: Yes, that's the greatest pleasure. I don't suppose I should, but I don't feel especially guilty about it. There's this head waitress that busses the tables, and when she leans over, I see her breasts. I don't think there is anything wrong with looking at her breasts. I'm not a prude. I also watch her feet and imagine I'm the size of an ant, and she inadvertently steps on me. This is sexually stimulating.

---

[6]The therapist's interventions in this session represent a striking departure from the therapist's usual non-intrusive, non-directive style with this man.

Therapist: Is being at the restaurant the reason you're putting on weight?

Patient: No, that's from eating at home. I sit down and watch TV and eat. I think part of the reason is to make me unattractive to women.

Therapist: You don't want to be singled out by a woman?

Patient: No, if I think a woman is looking directly at me, I feel very uncomfortable. Also, if a woman deliberately kills something, like a bug, it's not as exciting as if she doesn't know she's killing something. These are reveries, not fantasies, that I have.

Therapist: Are these the reveries you have when you masturbate?

Patient: Yes, the climax is always as the woman inadvertently steps on me. My masturbation varies as to how often I do it. If I am staying with friends, I can go several months. If I'm idle and by myself, it may be every day or every other day.

Therapist: Have you had reveries about me?

Patient: Yes, I have. I imagine you crushing me under your foot. I sometimes watch you walk down the hall and imagine I'm under your foot. I know you're real when I see the indentation in the carpet. I have imagined myself the size of an ant under the Plexiglass in your secretary's office, and you step on it and inadvertently crush me. It's interesting; I don't feel embarrassed or guilty telling you this. You're not shocked. I feel pretty comfortable about it even though I've never told anyone before. [Patient appeared happy.]

Therapist's Afterthoughts

I was acutely aware this was a very important session, but I did not know exactly why. I knew my style was quite different during this session from any of the others. I was being blunt and intrusive with my questions, instead of the usual waiting for introduction of material by Robert. It had been a long time between sessions. But as I proceeded with my direct questions, I sensed a growing warmth in the patient. He seemed even to be glad I was intruding. Toward the close of the session, he did not want to leave. He seemed to feel content.

Driving home, I felt a need to really understand this important session and my unusual style. I kept thinking about the power of the patient's fantasy (reverie). I knew that it represented a symbiotic mode he was attempting to replicate in the therapy session, but how? I thought about the replication of the symbiosis. The merger with the woman must be *inadvertent*. Then I realized that during this session I had inadvertently crushed him with my intrusive questions. He had been "stepped on," and I didn't even know it! I had unwittingly participated in the replication of an important mode of interaction in an attempt to get back in contact with the patient after the separation. This explained his good feelings and his desire to stay. This post-analysis felt right.

Author's Comment

The session had caused acute distress in the therapist because the direct intrusions were not characteristic of her personal style. Momentarily she was even more appalled at herself when she realized what she had done to him. The hour stands as her empathic attempt to restore contact which had been lost—*contact of the kind she knew he could respond to.* She spontaneously "crushed him," replicating a pattern of contact from early childhood which gave him a feeling of contentment.

Therapist's Report Continues

Shortly after the last incident Robert reported fantasizing that he was lying on his bed very still and imagining himself quite small. A woman with large breasts was lying next to him and rolled over on him with her breasts enveloping him, but she did not know he was there.

Following that, Robert reported a dream. This was unusual since there was only one other time he had brought a dream. The content was that he had awakened during the night, feeling the urge to go to the bathroom. When he came back to his bedroom, he noticed that the ceiling of his room was covered with heavy spider webs and within the webs were spiders approximately the size of small dogs. The spiders were in cocoon-type holes in the webs, like they were laying their eggs. Robert (who has a mild phobia about spiders if they take him by surprise or are on him unknowingly) said he was quite surprised by his reaction since he did not feel the usual fear of the spiders. He felt they were safely laying eggs and would not hurt him.

A few weeks later, Robert reported another dream. He said that it was about the therapist. In the dream:

> The therapist was in charge of providing food for a large group of people. The people were all there, milling about, waiting to be fed. The therapist is looking for the bologna to put on the bread for the people. Robert and the therapist are away from the crowd. Robert comments that he prefers to be with the therapist rather than with all those people out there in limbo. The therapist is standing on a small stepladder, methodically looking through each drawer in a series of filing cabinets, for the food. Robert notes that the therapist has on a rust-colored jumper and white turtleneck top. Her shoes match the jumper and the soles are flat and wedged. He notices when she places her weight on the ladder, but he does not imagine himself an ant under her shoe. He is looking at her legs and feet and feeling a sense of enjoyment. He knows that the therapist is aware of him looking

at her legs, but she thinks that is alright. The therapist and Robert chat along, easily, while she is looking methodically for the bologna for the others. She finally finds it in the last drawer in the last filing cabinet.

Robert reported feeling very comfortable and relaxed while talking with the therapist. Robert seemed to feel good about relating the dream and appeared to feel close to the therapist.

After relating the dream, Robert's associations suggested that he had moved away from the "inadvertent crushing" mode of relatedness and for the first time viewed us as two people enjoying each other. The next session brought a re-enactment of the familiar (symbiotic) replication that had been experienced so often in the past. He seemed to want to "touch bases" with the old, familiar mode of relating after having moved away from it. He talked about his work, again seeming not to acknowledge or experience the therapist as being separate. He seemed to have been merged with the therapist again as he talked, almost non-stop, about various mundane activities. Few responses were allowed or wanted from the therapist. Toward the end of the hour, Robert said that he had been noticing her legs all evening and would have liked to look at her feet, but felt embarrassed to do so. This was the first time he had ever initiated this type of comment out of the context of a more general discussion. The therapist asked him how he felt when he looked at her legs and feet. He said that he felt like he would want to put his fingers under her shoe and have her step on them so he could feel the weight. He was asked what it would mean to him to feel the weight. At this point, there was a closeness between him and the therapist. He stated that if he felt the weight he would then be equal to the therapist in size, and they would be just two equal (therefore different) people. This was the first time during the three and a half years that Robert had stated that he could be equal to other people, especially equal to a woman. He said that he would no longer have to put the therapist on a pedestal. When he was ready to leave, the therapist said that she felt very close to him (one of the first I-Thou statements possible with him). He said he felt close to her (which here seemed to indicate that he had accepted her separateness).

At the next session, Robert came in discussing the old, familiar body concerns which constituted part of the "going nowhere" replication. The therapist began by entering into the "inadvertent" stepping on, which was a part of this replication. She had recently acquired some biofeedback equipment and when the patient complained of his symptoms, she mentioned that perhaps this new equipment would be helpful. Robert pulled back from the suggestion in a manner that was different from the past. This "stepping on" did not relieve him. He was asking for something different this time. The therapist felt he was asking for empathy (mirroring?) for his symptoms (a rapprochement mode?). When his plight was acknowledged and empathy was given, the tension dramatically subsided. This acceptance of mirroring empathy in this form, instead of the old replication, seemed to indicate another step had been made in effecting individuation. After the important realization that he could be equal (different from), Robert did not want an old replication but instead asked for a slight but important move away from it.

CONCLUSIONS

This chapter has served to indicate a direction for the systematic application of the five Developmental Points of View for diagnostic and therapeutic understanding. These viewpoints are (I) the replication of the symbiosis, (II) the differentiation of the affects, (III) private world development, (IV) mother-child adaptation, and (V) the organizing processes of ego and self. All represent viable ways of organizing one's thoughts in the very difficult task of listening to the changing nuances of the way persons with borderline personality organization experience the self merging with others, the experience of the merger object.

The general literature has been reviewed from which the five Developmental Points of View have been distilled, and preliminary applications have been made to several clinical vignettes. It is now possible to take a detailed look into the psychotherapy processes with persons who might be described as having borderline personality organization. The idea of treatment "Scenarios" will be introduced as a listening device for teasing out and responding therapeutically to the various ways in which borderline persons enact their own unique experiences of merger within the therapeutic situation. The theoretical analysis of enactments or "scenarios" will draw heavily upon Mahler's (1968) early developmental motifs. The concept of "scenarios" may be helpful in developing one's listening capabilities in understanding the merger objects of persons with borderline personality organization.

10 Borderline Treatment Scenarios

Suggestions regarding psychoanalytically oriented listening to persons with borderline developmental arrests have been diverse and often seemingly contradictory. Traditional writers tend to be cautious, guarded and frankly pessimistic. More modern writers optimistically advocate bold, modified, or confrontive treatment approaches. General agreement prevails on the lengthy course which reconstructive therapy requires, ranging from four to eight years or more. There is also widespread awareness that crisis, supportive and other short-term individual and group techniques can offer much to persons with borderline developmental arrests. These briefer treatment techniques aim at increasing self-awareness and strengthening various adaptive potentials. In justifying the lengthy reconstructive process, writers acknowledge that when it is known how to speed up human growth and development then it will also be known how to speed up treatment.

Traditional psychoanalytic treatment and its many derivatives conceptualize neurotic personality organization as manifesting various symptoms of internal conflict, the meanings and sources of which become interpreted during the course of therapy. Kohut's (1971, 1977) approach to the treatment of narcissistic personality organization focuses on the development of the mirror, twinship, and idealizing transferences to the therapist selfobject. Narcissistic trends improve as the therapist repeatedly acknowledges various disappointments which the patient experiences in relation to the therapist. Therapy is then seen as a process in which the patient develops the capacity to calm and reassure himself rather than constantly searching for mirroring, twinning, and idealizing selfobjects in the environment. Modern approaches to therapy with borderline personality organization depict various self or ego deficits which result from symbiotic and post-symbiotic experience in early childhood. The course of therapy consists of establishing an emotional tie or bond with the therapist. The original symbiotic or post-symbiotic qualities of relationship become emotionally *replicated* with the therapist.

Special appreciation goes to Hedda Bolgar, Susan Courtney, Charles Coverdale, Carolyn Crawford, Cecile Dillon, Arlene Dorius, Alice Evans, Lyda Hill, Barbara Kreedman, Linda Reed, Jeanna Riley, Terri Saleson, Linda Sanicola, Jerry Smith, Mariana Thomas, Robert Van Sweden, and Mary E. Walker for help with this chapter.

As replication of various emotional experiences occurs, a separation-individuation process is thought to begin in relation to the therapist. Thus many ego and self functions have a fresh opportunity to develop. In contrast, approaches to the more primitive or "organizing mental states" (the schizophrenias and the affective reactions) are thought to involve a range of experiences which permit the *formation* of a "therapeutic symbiosis" from which later development can proceed.

The line of psychological development which is capturing the attention of modern theorists and clinicians, is the special dimension of human relatedness referred to by Jacobson (1954) as "The Self and the Object World." Observation of childhood development has focused on the crucial transformations which typically occur between birth and the seventh year of life in the manner in which a child comes to experience self and important others in his or her life, i.e., the line which has been referred to by many as "object relations." Four major nodal points of personality organization have been noted in observations of young children and appear to correspond to the four major diagnostic categories long studied in adult psychopathology. The scientific approach which evolved out of the nineteenth century for the observation and modification of clinical syndromes is gradually giving way to an approach which highlights the therapist's task of *listening* to the self and other experience of persons who come to the consulting room presenting various levels of developmental arrest.

Regardless of the level of developmental arrest, the treatment process understood here remains basically the non-influencing free-association approach first advocated by Freud. The traditional approach is modified only by the adoption of the attitude, or Listening Perspective which is most appropriate to the personality issues experienced by persons with various types of developmental arrest. The scope of psychoanalytic interest remains, as always, the data of introspection and interaction grasped through vicarious introspection which has been termed empathy by Kohut (1959). As such, treatment is viewed more in the context of an "interpretive discipline" (Shafer 1976) than as a natural science or medically oriented technique. The psychoanalytic process is viewed as a systematic and progressive elaboration of meaning within the expanding fabric of personality. Regardless of the type of personality organization or the level of the developmental arrest, the process of therapy is thought to constitute certain kinds of personality growth. The kind of growth required by the individual will necessarily depend upon the type of personality organization he/she has been able to attain and the various implications in terms of ego and self functions which the level of organization has for the specific person. The feature of "growth" is nowhere more evident than in the discussion of treatment with persons having borderline personality organization.

Writers generally agree that more "personal involvement" tends to emerge in the treatment process of persons with preoedipal developmental arrests than is thought to be optimal in the treatment of the oedipal level neuroses. Kohut's (1971, 1977) Listening Perspective implies that the selfobject therapist be repeatedly available as a source of relief of various "psychoeconomic" tensions. In the Listening Perspective of the Merger Object, the therapist is often thought to resemble a "transitional object" (Winnicott 1953) serving various "holding" (Modell 1976) or "containing" functions (Bion 1962, 1963). While parameters of technique (Eissler 1953) are no longer widely advocated, Giovacchini (1979a) indicates that interventions or maneuvers *to preserve the ego integration of the therapist* are often necessary or appropriate.

The central problem with any attempt to elaborate specific treatment techniques is that one runs the danger of moving away from the essentially noninfluencing study of introspection and interaction toward a variety of manipulations and justifications which have seldom served well and which, in the long run, tend to maintain the arrest rather than to release forces which permit a continuance of growth. In Chapter 8, five Developmental Points of View were defined which have been evolving within psychoanalysis. The points of view permit more focused understanding of the personality issues likely to be encountered in the work of persons with borderline developmental arrests. Most of the so-called "character" formations seem to derive from similar kinds of arrests in the setting of borderline personality organization.

TREATMENT SCENARIOS

This chapter addresses the kinds of situations, dilemmas, binds, and, at times, even traumas which therapists encounter when working with these often very difficult patients. While there are many ways to observe and conceptualize dilemmas which arise in the course of therapy with borderline patients, it seems provisionally useful to speak of "Scenarios." *Scenarios are conceptualized as interpersonal exchanges which the patient arranges, manipulates, or insists upon setting up with the therapist and/or other persons during the course of therapy.* Scenarios are thought to represent either (1) a *replication* of idiosyncratic early experience *or* (2) *the creation of a new interpersonal situation* which is required to further elaborate and extend the domain of the personality.

Scenarios generally come to be experienced by the therapist as an engagement which is alien to the usual personal, professional and/or expressive style of the therapist. In a Scenario, the patient may come to be experienced as manipulative, demanding, frustrating, anger provoking, overstimulating, seductive, or otherwise elusive or puzzling. Therapists[1] have come to talk of "the helpless patient," "the hopeless patient," "the blissful patient," "the conforming patient," or even "the obnoxious patient" in order to come to

---

[1] Especially Giovacchini 1975, 1979b.

grips with the powerful effects which borderline patients generally produce in people close to them. Some Scenarios at first seem comfortable and harmonious with the therapy and the therapist. Only progressively do they come to be experienced as arranged or imposed. Occasionally a Scenario may be so compatible with the therapist's own nature or style of working that an outside consultant is required to help unravel the script of the drama unwittingly "foisted upon" the therapist. An effective Scenario (i.e., one which engages) often. provokes feelings such as shame or guilt in the therapist which, in turn, tend to produce worries about trusting one's own feelings or concerns about excessive "countertransference."

THE SEPARATION-INDIVIDUATION MOTIF IN PSYCHOTHERAPY

Margaret Mahler's (1968) theory of symbiosis, derived from her extensive studies of early childhood development, has provided a powerful metaphor for viewing the course of therapy with borderline developmental arrests. Mahler's phases and subphases have been discussed in a previous chapter and will not be reviewed here. The major use of her ideas in a therapeutic context will be to describe the "mode of relatedness" or "mode of experience" being expressed in a given Scenario. In what follows, patients will be described as relating "symbiotically" or "in a symbiotic mode." Actions and activities are spoken of as carried out in a "differentiating, hatching, practicing, rapprochement, separating, individuating, or object constancy mode." References will also be made to the other Developmental Points of View highlighting split affects, the development of identity, the mother-child adaptation and the evolving self and ego considered not only as functions but as organizing processes.

Psychotherapy with borderlines has often been discussed in terms such as "early, middle, and late" phases. It might be said generally that the early phase is characterized by the establishment of a symbiotic mode of relatedness, the mid phase being the separating mode and the late phase fosters individuation toward object constancy. However, clinical practice demonstrates that, even as in child development, movement is wide ranging and varied. Any and all modes can and do appear in and out of sequence. One way of speaking about this phenomenon would be to characterize rapprochement as a "pivotal" or "nodal" point of development (Blanck and Blanck 1979) when the ego and self serve to organize and integrate the personality on a new basis. Various functions may have reached advanced, independent states and may appear to have undergone individuation, but the overall personality organization referred to as borderline has not moved into a fully integrated consideration of narcissistic or oedipal emotional issues. *Working with* Scenarios (rather than working *through*) serves to permit growth into a more complex and structured personality. "Working through" in the Freudian and Kohutian approaches generally refers to the repeated experiencing of various transference manifestations in different contexts until whatever basic issue involved has been in some way resolved. Because of the level of self and other merger encountered in borderline arrests, a different attitude or approach is required. To say that a therapeutic atmosphere must be developed in which the patient has an opportunity to feel symbiotic relatedness to the therapist implies that the two must be *working together* in an almost symbiotic unison exploring the exact nature or quality of relatedness which is demanded, yearned for or automatically assumed in any given interpersonal interaction. As such, interactions or Scenarios are established in relation to the therapist. The patient requires a "working with" of the Scenario in order for the patient and the therapist to grasp the developmental and contemporary meanings of the Scenario.

Scenarios are thought to identify various (ego and self) processes which a young child experiences in the course of making a psychological attachment to and/or separation from mother. Further, they are thought to be useful ways of conceptualizing the processes which borderline patients must experience or go through in the course of long-term psychotherapy. As patient and therapist *work with* a given Scenario or set of Scenarios, the therapist's role is a double one. As an actor in the Scenario, or a participant, the therapist must engage in the scene being replicated and depicted by the patient. As an observer or a critic of the scene being depicted, the therapist must also be able to stand back so that he/she can see the scene for what it is and the way it operates in the psychological life of the patient. The traditional role of the psychoanalyst has been thought to be that of an "opaque mirror" which reflects the transference manifestations in such a way that they can be seen and interpreted. But in trying to learn about the nature of a patient's symbiotic experience of the world, the therapist *must participate* to a greater or lesser degree in that experience. It would be too simple to think that this participation is always and only at the level of shared feelings because patients often convey feelings through shared enactments.

A Scenario might take *any specific form* and is often so subtle in appearance that it takes months for a therapist to grasp what is happening. It may take months more to find something to "do" about it! Through empathy and time the therapist becomes included within the symbiotic "orbit" or "membrane" of the patient by more or less passively going along with the patient's expressive wishes. At some point the characteristic interchange may become so repetitive (and often frustrating or boring) the therapist senses something peculiar is happening. Some "unnecessary" or "unreasonable" accommodation is being requested by the patient. This uncanny sense can lead to an understanding of the way in which the original symbiotic world was structured for the patient who, given time, faithfully replicates the arrested area in both active and passive forms. Putting it another way, the patient is motivated toward re-establishing an early patterning or configuration of self and other experience within the therapeutic relationship. Needless to say, the less flexible the therapist is in nature or therapeutic style, the more difficult it is for the patient to express the symbiotic yearning in relationship form. When therapists discover a replicated feature, the *subjective* sense of the therapist is frequently one of having been "duped," "manipulated," or "set up." Subtle features of the replication almost always "creep up un-awares" on the therapist, leaving the impression the patient has found one's "Achilles heel"—often an unguarded unconscious or preconscious feature of the therapist's personality or technique. Since this aspect of the therapeutic replication is so regular in occurrence, many writers have come to advocate that the key to understanding and treating borderline patients ultimately is to be found in responding to "countertransference" features.

Another way of speaking of this set of phenomena would be to refer to the "permeability or fluidity of the mind-body boundaries" in persons arrested in some aspect of symbiotic relatedness. The therapist senses the influenceability or weak boundaries of the patient and/or soon begins to feel his/her own boundaries and space being "invaded" or "encroached upon."

The therapeutic approach to "handling" these difficult, interpersonal dilemmas or Scenarios regularly provided by borderline patients will be discussed after first a brief illustration of a Scenario.

EXAMPLE SCENARIO

A boy, almost 8 years old, with a history of severe abuse and abandonment by his mother before two years of age, was brought to therapy by his newly adoptive parents for wild, disorganized and disruptive behavior. During the initial sessions the child expressed destructiveness, anger, and an intense fear of retaliation, along with a wish to be rocked by the therapist. (See the diagnostic study of Bobbie in the previous chapter.) Soon he began darting from the therapy room, at first to go to the bathroom, then later to wander around and explore the building, a school where he is being seen after hours. As the connection to the (warm and accepting) woman therapist increases, the child demands (over her protests) to spend much of his hour outside the playroom. He, at last, succeeded in forcing the therapist to spend all of her time with him in the school yard and gymnasium. The child would not hear of returning to the play room as a sense of fear and urgency compels him to express his anger and destruction in a public place (perhaps so that he will not be harshly limited or punished and so that no one will be hurt).

The developing Scenario reveals that curiosity and investigation are believed by the child to elicit limits and punishment so that anger becomes merged with interest and curiosity expressed in various, wild, destructive attempts which keep the therapist on her toes every minute to limit and protect everything and everybody from harm. The mode of relating might be termed "symbiotic" in that two are required to play this replicated Scenario. When retaliation, which has been a part of the original Scenario, is only experienced in limit setting but not more direct abuse, the child plays out repeated games of pool in the gym, occasionally trusting the therapist with a pool cue and a "turn." She subsequently is instructed when and how to play for more than a year before he is willing to let her play on her own and to "bargain" for time back in the play room. Many forms of control over the therapist's wishes and person serve to recreate the original symbiotic atmosphere in both its active and passive respects. He instructs her to do the same things to him that he does to her. Only after the symbiotic mode is firmly established can the child venture to play a real game, to risk competing which represents his first "differentiating" or "hatching" attempt. Feeling secure within the symbiosis, the child gradually takes the play back to the play room, only occasionally venturing out to play pool when some problems erupt at school or at home. Once he experiences a sense of safety within the symbiotic orbit, he starts a separating course choosing many new games and activities which exercise new skills and move him toward a new mode of relatedness. He "practices" new skills and then rushes back to the old (more aggressive, frightening, and demanding) activities with the therapist (apparently to be sure that she, in her old symbiotic form, is still there). The rapprochement mode begins only slowly, in the third year of treatment, as Bobbie turns toward his therapist in excited anticipation of approval and mirroring for his new successes and his competitive strivings.

The Scenario most interesting and evident in this condensed example is the replication of early relationship experience, including the wish for closeness as well as the fear of injury and the aggressive fending-off of limitations. He guards against these dangers by meeting in a "public" place. The peculiar symbiotic mode needs to be re-established or re-enacted and then "confronted" by the therapist's refusal to injure and retaliate as many foster parents have done since his mother abandoned him many years ago for being "unmanageable." In order to follow the child in his developing expressions, the therapist *is forced to do things his way*, to accept *his* symbiotic mode. It becomes necessary for her to abandon her usual technique, to leave her room and provide all kinds of gentle and restraining "holding" (in both symbolic and literal senses) until the child is able to relinquish his wild and destructive symbiotic modes in favor of new options: the separating modes of differentiation, practicing, and rapprochement.

SYMBIOTIC SCENARIOS

Since the variety of ways in which mothers respond to and hold their children is virtually infinite, the kinds of Scenarios which might be re-enacted, re-established or replicated in treatment will take on highly idiosyncratic forms. It is interesting to observe the way a mother and her infant relate and the particular style of relatedness which each dyad develops together. The style or quality highlights various forms of merger, opposition, bliss, and constriction; qualities which serve to define and limit the ways in which the child is permitted and/or encouraged by his mother to experience the world *external* to his body. A given mother-child dyad also develops a stylized way of handling the oscillating *internal* states referred to as "affects" or "moods." Frantic, agitated, hypomanic states alternate with states of seeming helplessness, hopelessness, and depletion. They become responded to by mother in her own special way so that the symbiosis becomes a way of containing, partially containing, or failing to contain various affective states which originate or relate to events inside the child's body. The first group of Scenarios to be discussed relate to the way in which a child experiences or *thinks about the world* (which may later be described as reality appreciation or reality testing). The second group of Scenarios discussed will focus on the way in which a child experiences and comes *to regulate his internal affect states* (which may later be conceptualized as affective or mood regulation).

Merger Scenarios

Often, even from the first contact, the "assumption" of a state of symbiosis is evident. For example, the new patient who uncontrollably pours out highly personal or "deep unconscious" material before having realistically had time to assess who the therapist is and how this personal material is likely to be taken. This has often been considered indicative of "fluid mind-body boundaries" or "limitations in reality appreciation." As therapy develops, the merger or the assumption of symbiosis takes many forms. One child, for example, despite his obvious desires to the contrary, strictly limited himself to one cup of "my" hot chocolate from the waiting room during the early months of therapy. Only much later did the subject of food turn out to be a central focus. The exaggerated caution, it turns out, related to what he experienced as his mother's *coercions* as to when, where and what to eat or not to eat which appeared to vary according to mother's psychological and health needs rather than the child's. I later found myself feeling "coerced" to various eating activities even to the extent of conducting (against my wishes) many sessions in a nearby deli and later in several restaurants.

Children engage therapists in play and adults engage therapists in conversations which are often decidedly "one way." The rules of the game or the course of the conversation is pre-determined or controlled in such a way that independent or spontaneous moves, opinions or ideas offered by the therapist are simply ignored or go systematically unrewarded or even punished until the therapist conforms to the desired control (i.e., symbiotic) pattern of the patient. The patient then relaxes and tends to maintain comfort so long as the therapist conforms "properly."

One little girl played for months "This is mine? That's yours," thereby attempting to establish "ownership" over practically everything, including the therapist's name. One day she put down two sheets of paper and announced, "Today we are going to practice making A's" (a carryover from her classroom work). The therapist complied, acknowledging that she also needed to practice making "A's." The togetherness sense having thus been satisfied, the child relaxed and the therapist was able to pick up the child's silver barrette from the table and put it in her own hair, saying "Mine?" The child was at first confused and then delighted. The therapist was playing, "What's yours is mine, and mine is yours" with her. What had been previously expressed demandingly with serious intent of control could now be laughed about and played with so it was clear that the feelings were understood and properly respected by the therapist.

While many therapists are quite sensitive or intuitive in responding to such replication demands or yearnings, once they are in harmony with the symbiotic desires, they start to worry about such things as "going along with what should be confronted" or "reinforcing the pathology." They then attempt interpretations which either fall on deaf ears or at best are taken as unempathic intrusions. It soon becomes clear that this is the therapist's problem, not the patient's. The patient knows what is needed—symbiotic relatedness—before growth can proceed.

At the conclusion of this discussion of common kinds of Scenarios experienced in the treatment of persons with borderline personality organization, a detailed attempt will be made to distinguish between what has been traditionally thought of as interpretations (as a form of communication common in the treatment of neurotic and narcissistic personality organizations) from what are conceptualized as "differentiating actions, activities and interactions" (which are characteristic of the treatment of borderlines). As every therapist knows, interpreting and talking about various behaviors, social adaptations and therapeutic interactions in the traditional manner seem to be of limited use when treating borderline personality organization. Therapeutic progress appears to follow a different course. The patient strives to establish and to express various patterns of pre-verbal or non-verbal self and other relatedness which have remained active in the fabric of his/her personality. Since the arrest was so early, the borderline person *has no words* to describe or to tell the therapist about these modes of relatedness like the neurotic has of describing the way he/she experiences internal conflict. *The communication to the therapist comes in the form of various enactments and modes of relatedness.* True, the mode can be talked about; *but not until the dyadic or symbiotic mode is expressed by the patient in the therapeutic relationship and grasped empathically by the therapist, do any alternative self and other patterns become realistically viable to the patient.* Following the re-enactment of symbiotic relatedness, therapeutic progress is thought to occur as the therapist gradually begins to assert his or her ego and self boundaries in such a way as to block, confront or stifle the mode of relatedness being experienced or lived out by the patient. Another way of expressing this point would be to say that the therapist *must go along with* the symbiotic (or postsymbiotic) involvement until it is understood and then (and only then) is the therapist in a position to hold his or her own ego and self boundaries firmly against the particular mode of relatedness being expressed. An important differentiating interaction in the example Scenario cited above was the therapist's refusal to punish and abuse Bobbie. Abusive limit setting and punishment for curiosity had been a crucial part of the self-other patterning of his original symbiosis.

Giovacchini (1979a) indicates that the therapist makes many interventions not for any reason directly or obviously related to the patient's well being or immediate progress; but *so that the therapist can retain his or her own personal or professional boundaries, identity and integration.* In psychotherapy as in the early child rearing situation, it is only as the therapist (mother) spontaneously asserts firmly and clearly his or her boundaries that the (child) patient has something *to separate and individuate from!* Firm boundaries can be discerned and separated from. It is *not* the person or the patient or the behavior which is being confronted by the therapist; but rather the *mode of interpersonal relatedness* which the patient actively and passively lives and through replication has come to experience with the therapist. This distinction between interpretation and differentiating actions, activities and interactions will be further elaborated.

"Nothing Is Happening" Scenarios

Particularly in the first year or so of treatment after a symbiotic mode of relatedness has become possible, therapists report in frustration, "The therapy is stuck, at a standstill, nothing is happening, I'm bored." Often this sense of "going nowhere" continues for months with the child tirelessly playing the same games in the same way or the adult "obsessing about the same old things but making no progress, just going on and on." Closer examination usually reveals that something entirely different is happening. The borderline patient, in trying to express the problem which made therapy necessary, cannot possibly do so in words because *he/she is quite unaware of alternate ways of experiencing the world.* The patient can only recite symptoms, behaviors, and frustrations and point to external circumstances or to an internal sense of "fate." The only way his/her experience becomes fully known to the therapist is *through the replication activity itself* which takes many months to establish in all its various nuances and complexities. Since the borderline person has had so many unsatisfactory encounters with the world, he/she takes a long time with someone new before "finally getting down to the basics" of the particular way he/she experiences self and object merger. *So long as the therapist attempts to protest, disagree, or erroneously interpret, the sense of symbiotic relatedness is difficult for the patient to establish.* The often quite long prodromal period of symbiosis establishment can seem unchallenging, unstimulating and at times even downright boring to the therapist, but it need not be so. The highly special or idiosyncratic style which each patient presents in this process of "going nowhere" can be carefully studied. Such a study would include (1) the exact nature of the merger (i.e., symbiotic relatedness) which the person is seeking to re-establish and (2) an understanding of the *unique qualities* which that relatedness contains. As these gradually become understood and respected (as opposed to being challenged or interpreted), trust builds until *readiness for differentiation develops.* Sometimes periods of quiet are required; sometimes disagreements or a whole host of other seemingly odd, "untherapy-like" circumstances may develop as a part of the special expressions of symbiotic togetherness which replicate the early mother-child situation.

One little boy who lived in an extremely chaotic world regularly tore the playroom apart in the early hours of his therapy. His therapist continued to acknowledge "how severe the storm is today" or "how dangerous the tornado or hot lava is" and to reflect "how with all this going on, not even little children are safe." The child gradually settled in to brief periods of "quiet time," sitting on the couch next to the therapist, with her arm around him, reading together, and eating graham crackers until he could do this for almost the entire hour. One day, due to unfortunate circumstances, the toys were found in disarray, and the therapist had no time to straighten up before the child's session. The boy, upon seeing the disarray, was immediately stimulated again to wildness and destruction. In his eyes, the therapist had not been able to present herself and her toys in the usual ordered and calm manner and the boy was unable to retain the inner calm which he had begun to establish with her consistent availability. The boy became so agitated that he declared at the end of the hour that he was "never coming back." Then he asked the therapist's help in going to the bathroom!

In keeping with the general therapeutic approach advocated here, it seems best to prepare oneself for long periods of apparently "going nowhere." During these periods basic trust is being established through the therapist's consistent availability. A sense of firm relatedness slowly develops. The therapist does well to be alert to the nuances of relationship even to the tiniest and most subtle variation of themes. Interpretations and differentiating activities tend to be worse than useless during this period (or during such hours) as they simply slow down the process. When this period of calm is periodically disrupted by regressive swings, one can often discover in the therapeutic context or the living context of the patient, what circumstance led to the disruption. In later periods of therapy when new skills and affect controls are developing, regressive periods also occur. Frequently the patient comes for an hour which very much resembles the early style of rambling play or apparent disconnectedness which was established during the period of symbiotic relatedness. This seems to be a return to the tried and true symbiotically styled relationship when a sense of abandonment, loss or threat develops during the later rapprochement experiences. There are many times when the therapist may experience the therapy as "going nowhere" and feels that the patient is "not working." These periods may resemble the quiet, calm, smooth and comfortable relationship which prevails in a relaxed and trusting environment, and which can be observed when a young child simply plays with and enjoys his mother. Since this quality of connectedness is often related to other experiences which will unfold subsequently, the therapist might be well advised to simply sit back, like a mother and enjoy the play and communication in a warm and receptive manner until something in the mode of relatedness requires the therapist to assert his or her boundaries against the encroachment of the sense of symbiotic relatedness. The boundless experience of the symbiosis may be experienced by the therapist either as an intrusion into one's own boundaries or as a demand by the patient for some form of intrusion, manipulation or even abuse from the therapist.

Oppositional Scenarios

In natural development, a child cannot avoid some sense of separateness from mother as he/she is aware of mother's earliest comings and goings, of her periods of availability and unavailability. It is assumed that a child begins to make a natural differentiation in certain limited ways between the experiences which he/she has alone and the experiences that he/she has with mother. The child begins gradually in certain ways to oppose mother. The manner in which mother receives the opposition will be critical to later development. Many borderline persons develop a strong stubborn streak because they learned to stand against mother when their early needs for self-assertion and differentiation or exploration were not appreciated or were thwarted by her.

Clinicians are accustomed to encountering frequently in the treatment of borderline persons a streak of oppositionality or contrariness such that the therapist is somehow always being provoked into disagreement of one sort or another or into placing some kind of limitation. Normal symbiosis is accompanied and followed by a phase which mothers call "the terrible two's." "No" and opposition represent a child's normal attempts to define him/herself as separate from mother. Therefore, it is not difficult to understand why oppositionality is so frequently a necessary part of the establishment of a symbiotic-separation process. It seems as though the therapist has not much choice but to respond spontaneously to the provocations as best he/she can. The position is bound to be uncomfortable and puts the therapist immediately in contact with the dilemma faced by every mother of a two-year-old. The dilemma is how to welcome the "no" and to value the oppositionality and the aggressiveness while at the same time limiting and containing it. Mothers of two-year-olds frequently find themselves so frustrated that they begin yelling, fighting and feuding at a two-year-old level. This may represent a crucial form of empathic contact with two-year-olds and requires considerable flexibility on the part of the mother and, in replications, the therapist. There is no easy way out of the "terrible two's," either in child rearing or psychotherapy. The goal is to permit a sense of independence or separation while not creating a sense of abandonment. Not to struggle with some people would be not to care or not to be involved in the manner needed!

One child regularly pushed me into buying candy with caramel and peanuts whenever his life was disrupted at home or at school. He blamed his mother for his having to wear braces, and found that forbidden candies and nuts were an effective way of standing *against* mother. In time we found a variety of other snacks which were approved by his orthodontist, but anger and regression was regularly signaled by his wish for a Reggie bar!

This kind of Scenario is sometimes characterized by tense, ugly, and nasty oppositional scenes which certain patients insist on recreating with their therapists. Oppositional Scenarios exasperate the therapist through repeated provocation, abuse, as well as calls for rejection and abuse. Appropriate understanding and availability during these (sometimes seemingly endless) episodes are necessary for empathic contact which can permit the person to begin the process of separation from this stormy mode of contact. It is often only after the therapist has come to relax with and to appreciate (if not enjoy) the contrariness as necessary and appropriate to the separation process that the patient can begin to experience a differentiated self free of the constant need to oppose in one way or another. The acceptance and appreciation of the need to oppose within the context of firmly held, mind-body boundaries on the part of the therapist provides the atmosphere for various differentiating activities and interactions.

Conforming/Blissful Scenarios

In contrast to an oppositional or stubborn relationship with mother, a child may develop a conforming streak in his early attempts to separate from mother. While therapists are accustomed to speaking about the more raucous and obnoxious forms of borderline developmental arrests, clinicians are aware of persons whose borderline adjustment is quiet, peaceful, blissful and conforming. In schools, these children often go undetected and are thought of as shy, pleasant, but sometimes not too intelligent persons. Experienced teachers and family members often have some sense that a problem exists but have trouble putting their finger on exactly what the problem is. Such children come to the attention of child therapists when some specific learning disability has developed which cannot be worked with in regular or special education classrooms. In adult life, such persons tend to come to the attention of therapists when some crisis exposes their conforming adjustment pattern as a grossly inadequate one.

One diagnostician recently reported in a case conference her extreme distress over a 21-year-old man she was evaluating in a state hospital. The man was bright, sensitive, pleasant, ingratiating, gregarious, and liked by everyone. He was psychologically-minded enough so that the nurses, aides, and even the doctors had a hard time seeing anything wrong with him. There was a history of traumatic family experiences, several suicide attempts, and long morose depressive periods of poor functioning.

He was able to express how foolish the overdose had been which led to his hospitalization. The consulting diagnostician was alarmed lest this man be discharged without treatment. She called him "the likable patient" and in psychological tests found severe ego problems in a conforming, dependent, borderline personality. Many borderline children have this same pleasant, warm, affable nature and are slow to express any distress or anger at anyone. This is viewed as a symbiotic style worthy of understanding in detail and depth. The unknowing therapist might wish simply to foster more direct, assertive, confrontive or angry expression as though mere encouragement, behavior modification, or assertion training would alter the basic symbiotic mode of experiencing the world.

Constriction/Withholding Scenarios

While withholding or a "holding back" response has been studied in many contexts, the function of shy or withholding behavior may be to maintain some form of a dyadic mode of relatedness. This might be thought of as one way to restrict or constrict the functioning of the ego or the self. In a psychological testing situation, various ways in which people constrict or restrict personality functioning become readily available for observation. One feature apparent in psychological testing of many borderline patients is the use of ego constriction as a device for coping with the world. Ego constriction can be seen in many ways in the test battery and seems to serve the purpose of reducing or controlling the amount of complex stimulation which one takes in. Constriction limits the scope of (1) responsibility which one assumes, (2) what one perceives, and (3) the level of integration and synthesis which one can accomplish.

Constriction Scenarios in interpersonal terms represent an apparently superficial, restricted or abbreviated kind of relating. The full range of human emotional issues is simply not considered within the interpersonal relationship. Complex issues such as sexuality or identity may be considered but they are often dealt with in a stereotyped, undifferentiated, and pre-ambivalent manner. Such persons may seem shy, withdrawn or socially superficial and stereotyped, or simply limited or shallow. Many children present learning disorders based on or emanating from a general tendency for the ego to constrict and to control that which can be comfortably managed. Constriction Scenarios typically involve abbreviated or "carelessly" considered human relationships. The therapist, the therapist's role, and other important persons in the patient's life may all be considered from an intellectual, stereotyped or "role model" standpoint rather than from the rich context of interpersonal relatedness. The person may manage affairs relatively well but substance seems lacking in his/her life. There is often a strong sense of fate: "I can only be what I am," but in time one recognizes an implicit and habitual refusal to expand and grow.

Within the developmental schema of symbiosis to separation-individuation being considered here, various forms of personality constriction or restriction might be thought of as representing ways in which the ego and/or self functions have developed as related to the way the child experienced the early symbiosis. For whatever reasons mother's needs or encouragements were expressed in such a way that certain areas of functioning continued to develop while others did not, or became characteristically limited. Common clinical findings suggest that a certain behavior was "instrumental" in relating to mother's personality or conversely that certain kinds of behaviors or experiences were "forbidden" by mother. Masterson (1972, 1976, 1981) refers to the "rewarding" and "withdrawing" activities of mother and how these activities tend to encourage or discourage personality development. The child did not feel encouraged or felt actively discouraged in certain ways from separating psychologically from mother. The arrest in separation and individuation has served to limit the borderline person to predominantly symbiotic, dyadic modes of relatedness to which he returns in the course of therapy by way of a therapeutic replication. Such limitations may have various consequences for the development of many self and ego functions and processes.

Use of constriction is particularly noticeable in adolescents when, as a coping device, it falters or fails altogether. Developmentally, a child may have restricted or constricted the scope of his ego in order to continue certain forms of growing and to appear more or less normal. However, with the advent of physical puberty as well as its sociological complications and complexities, the stimulation becomes overwhelming, and the ego simply cannot integrate adequately. It is at this time that many adolescents appear in treatment centers. "Acting out" during adolescence frequently stems from a constricted ego trying to adapt to a social and cultural environment which is simply too complex. People of all ages may show up for psychotherapy when some new situation has become so complex that the constricted ego cannot cope. However, people may also feel a need for psychotherapy when there has been a self-initiated attempt to expand their personality beyond current capacity. As the expansion starts, there is insufficient flexibility of ego and/or self functions so the persons begin to experience themselves as deteriorating or decompensating. Furthermore, there are many times during the course of life or therapy in which, as a result of positive change marking an expansion of heretofore constricted or restricted function, the person may become frightened, confused or depressed. The fear or confusion stems from the loss of a stable, familiar organization of personality which is felt prior to the reliable establishment of a new level of integration. Particularly as a person begins to improve in therapy are these "states of confusion" to be expected. It is often helpful to the patient to have these periods acknowledged to be the natural result of change rather than to be heralded as some sort of a regressive or backward swing.

Agitated/Expansive Scenarios (Hypomanic)

The foregoing Scenarios represent some of the interpersonal interactions which a borderline patient may set up in an effort to communicate (replicate) the nature of his/her own symbiotic modes of relatedness. The symbiotic styles discussed thus far might be thought of as emanating from or relating to experiences which the child has with features *external* to his body, i.e., reality. Should there be a major adult decompensation in persons with these styles of symbiotic relatedness, it is to be anticipated that the decompensation would take the form of a *disturbance in the thoughts* one has about the nature of reality, the emergence of primary process thinking and confusions in the mind-body boundary experience. In situations of extreme stress and decompensation, these persons might exhibit what appears to be a thought disorder. The next two Scenarios or styles of symbiotic experience relate to the child's experience of his own body, specifically the elated and depleted affect states. One of the functions of human symbiosis is to provide a stabilizing or regulating influence on the innate or inborn affect potentials. Through symbiotic connectedness and empathic containing and holding, an infant gains a sense of regulation over moods and begins to develop a whole spectrum of affects which modulate between the "all good" elevated or hypomanic states and the "all bad" depleted states. If a child is chronically over-stimulated or under-stimulated or if empathic containing response is inadequate, the prominent features of symbiotic relatedness are likely to be excessive elation, excessive depletion or excessive and uncontrolled alternation of affect states. Later in life such persons under extreme stress would present exaggerated moods resembling the affective disorders. The ebb and flow of elevated and depleted states often can be seen clearly in connection with the person's loss of a sense of symbiotic relatedness. The recovery from exaggerated affect states can occur in a matter of seconds or sometimes requires a period of weeks. But when such a person has re-achieved a sense of symbiotic relatedness to a person, group or idea, the frenzy and agitation or helplessness and depletion subside. However, if there is a loss or another threatened disruption of the sense of connection, hyperactivity, frenzy, agitation, or depletion and depression again ensue.

Many so-called "hyperactive children" seem to fall into this category. Upon careful diagnostic examination, their personalities show the effects of borderline developmental arrests and, in particular, the failure to develop reliable controls over elation or depression. Such control is gained, like many other ego functions, through a harmonious symbiosis followed by a separating and individuating process. The person may search frantically for limits outside himself when inner controls are not available.

One such child in group therapy managed to arrange every week for what came to be known as the "everybody-attack-Freddy game." Formulated as a Scenario, it became evident that part of the hypomanic sense of relatedness which this boy required involved provoking other people into providing angry limitations and attacks. People experienced him as a "nuisance," but the function of being a nuisance turned out to be that the child became contained from all sides when he would otherwise be fragmenting or becoming hyperactive. It was astonishing to observe the power which this child exerted over group members as well as other peers and teachers. People were given no choice but to attack or attempt to control him. This kind of borderline wears people out "going nowhere!" Very many adults with borderline personality organization develop similar hypomanic life styles.

Helpless/Depleted Scenarios (Depressive)

These Scenarios present the other side of the previous one of a frantic, agitated nature. That is, the helpless, hopeless and despairing borderline person constantly attempts to elicit encouragement, support, and help from the environment. These persons are constantly expressing pain, fear, failure, helplessness, hopelessness and despair which coerces the other person into reassurances which, in themselves, seem not to help. What, however, does seem to help is a growing sense of symbiotic relatedness with the Other. In both the agitated/expansive Scenarios and the helpless/depleted Scenarios, the therapist frequently becomes frustrated and/or angry at the patient's constant attempts and demands for reassurance, calm, hope and so forth. The therapist can see that all of the responses which the patient demands are useless in the sense of providing immediate help.

A puzzling question arises in attempting to understand the relationship of elevated and depleted affects to the symbiosis. Affects must be considered activities and actions which, though related to physiology, represent definite modes of relating to others. This view is in keeping with Schafer's (1976) analysis of affects as activities and also with Sartre's (1956) idea that affects represent active attempts to engage or manipulate the Other. Many times when an affect has gone beyond moderation or might be said to be out of control in its pervasiveness and expressions, *the mere presence* of an interested empathic Other may permit the almost instantaneous (if not eventual) containment of the affect. One might infer that the exaggerated affect became controlled *as a result of* the establishment of a sense of symbiotic connectedness with the Other. This sudden and almost magical control of affects in the presence of the symbiotic Other should not strike one as surprising. Many ego functions—and *regulation* of affects is an ego function —follow this same principle. In the nascent form of development of all ego functions, there is a period in which the skill is present in the presence of the Other and is absent when the Other is absent. The control or regulation of affects should be no different. The central question becomes: Under what conditions and to what extent does the *loss* of control over affect activity represent the replication and to what extent does the *recovery* of regulation of affect activity represent the replication? All possible variations on this theme can be observed. The interesting aspect open for study with a given individual relates to when and under what conditions symbiotic relatedness is expressed by affect control and under what conditions symbiotic relatedness or replication is expressed in affects which are wildly out of control. Regulation of affect may be thought of as an ego function or as an activity of the developing self. However, the exact way in which such regulation participates in symbiotic connectedness with mother is a highly idiosyncratic matter. Extensive examples of these mood Scenarios are not deemed necessary in that everyone knows the experience of mood swings within oneself and how to observe mood activities in others. The therapeutic elaboration of moods is no different than the previous Scenarios which related more to thoughts or ideas about reality surrounding the problem of mind-body boundaries.

Many therapists are reluctant to go along with the various claims from the replication, feeling a "professional obligation" to interpret or to force the patient to claim responsibility and stop being helpless, hopeless or manic and "needlessly agitated." When viewed from the perspective of the need to establish a sense of symbiotic relatedness, these therapist responses represent misunderstanding. The patient cannot begin new growth until symbiotic relatedness is established *in whatever form it originally took*. Therapists, often against their own personality grain, must find some way of joining in so as to permit a sense of symbiotic relatedness and not attempt premature confrontations or interpretations which will only slow things down. How to withstand these constant demands and to receive them empathically without being dragged down and inundated by them is the difficult task which every therapist must face.[1a]

Conclusion: Other Symbiotic Scenarios

Reality appreciation and affect regulation are ego functions involved in interpersonal relatedness which are usually attained during the symbiotic and postsymbiotic (i.e., differentiating and practicing) periods of human development. Early thought and mood patterns become "entrenched" to such an extent that they seem indelibly imprinted on the character of the personality. Over the years attempts have been made to categorize the variety of styles of interpersonal relatedness which become established during the symbiotic period which tend to limit severely the ways in which a person can and will subsequently experience others. These patterns which have been observed and written about extensively are referred to as "character disorders," "personality disorders," or "trait disturbances." One of the most intriguing and exhaustive listings of characterological styles is to be found in Fenichel's *The Psychoanalytic Theory of Neurosis* (1946). At that point in the history of psychoanalytic investigation, Fenichel had at his disposal only the original, Freudian model of internal conflict to account for the formation of character. Within the context of a therapeutic study of internal conflict great pessimism was and still is expressed over the treatability of the "character disorders." It appears best to classify the character disorders as constellations emanating from the mother-child symbiosis and carrying the particular flavor of that dyadic exchange. Pessimism regarding treatment could then be classified along with general pessimism which has prevailed in traditional psychoanalytic studies regarding the treatment of all preoedipal conditions. However, modern psychoanalysts have developed the conceptual tools to form a viable treatment approach. Carl Jung, Melanie Klein, August Aichorn, Otto Rank and many other more recent contributors to the field of psychotherapy have maintained all along that character disorders and borderline states are treatable. The many treatment ideas put forth have not been without good empirical foundation but have tended to lack in theoretical clarity by means of which systematic observation and treatment could be reliably pursued. Thus the list of symbiotic Scenarios might be considerable, starting with paranoid states, schizoid adjustments, sado-masochistic and passive-aggressive exchanges as well as other adjustment patterns which have been deemed antisocial or dyssocial.

[1a]Christopher Bollas in an unpublished paper on moods is developing the thesis that moods in many forms function to preserve or conserve in the individual a special early relation to the love objects (what Bollas has come to call "the conservative object").

While loss of and separation from the symbiotic partner remains the key issue in borderline personality arrests, certain Scenarios become enacted or experienced specifically around the question of loss of connection, loss of support, loss of enthusiasm, loss of availability or a threatened loss of presence. Hypervitality, somatization, mental and physical disorganization as well as deterioration and "periodic collapses of functioning" all occur as a result of various kinds of loss.

SEPARATING SCENARIOS

General Comments

The second major type of Scenarios encountered in the treatment of persons with borderline personality organization might be classified as separating Scenarios. Separating Scenarios remain a constant companion to the symbiotic Scenarios and are often indistinguishable in a given instance. They are distinguished for conceptual clarity because many persons present developmental arrests not quite as early as the symbiosis proper but rather represent the ways the mother and child attempted to accomplish the separation process. Following Mahler's developmental theory (1968),[2] one might define Scenarios belonging to the differentiating or hatching mode and to distinguish those from the Scenarios enacted in the practicing mode and re-enactments which might even herald the appearance of rapprochement.

In therapy, once a sense of relatedness has been established through a series of Scenarios related to issues of togetherness, the issues change as the patient begins to separate and individuate from the therapist. It is at this point the term "ambitendency" is most relevant. In developmental terms the child is seen to be rushing toward mother with joy and then darting away from mother to explore and often to escape. Rapid movement by a borderline patient toward the therapist and then away from the therapist is often puzzling or disconcerting unless one understands the developmental achievement ambitendency represents.

Psychotherapists are accustomed to listening very closely to patients' reports of events outside the therapy hour. In the treatment of neurosis, Freud described the "acting out of the transference." By this Freud meant that infantile feelings being reactivated by the transference situation instead of being analyzed within the therapy context, were being acted upon outside therapy. "Acting out" in this narrow and technical sense has come to be viewed in a very negative light by many therapists. In psychotherapy with preoedipal conditions, *action and acting are often the only ways that a patient has of communicating the exact nature of the difficulty since the experiences to be expressed are largely pre- or non-verbal.* While the various Scenarios

[2]Outlined in the previous chapter.

being described here represent such action forms of expression and communication, it is also frequent that the person tries his/her new separating and individuating skills outside of therapy prior to or along with bringing that effort into the therapeutic relationship. Therapists come to listen very carefully for these "displaced Scenarios." One therapist observed her male patient separating emotionally from a girlfriend of a long time. He declared that he was not giving up the girlfriend but giving up his old ways of relying on her. At the same time, he was discussing cutting down the number of sessions per week with the therapist. The "displaced" Scenario with his girlfriend preceded his trying out his newfound sense of separateness from his therapist.

Another example would be with many children and adolescents as well as some adults who are dependent upon someone else to pay the therapy bill. While not ready to be "kicked out" of therapy by the therapist, they may behave in such a way to the third party so as to threaten the source of support for the therapy. An example of this was a man who managed to lose his job as part of a displaced Scenario. Since medical insurance from his employment was paying a major part of the therapy bill, the frequency of sessions had to be cut down until he could get a new job and reinstate insurance. An adolescent girl who was brought to therapy by her parents with complaints of "excessive drugs and sex" came to complain bitterly to her parents that the therapy was doing her no good. All she ever did with the therapist was to talk about drugs and sex. In context, this appeared to represent a way that the child could begin to achieve a sense of separation from her parents and the way in which she was doing it threatened a termination of the therapy. Displaced Scenarios can be responded to with empathy as a forerunner or prototype of the way the patient is likely to work out his/her separation-individuation with the therapist.

Disconnecting/Distancing Scenarios

An important part of the separating process is to move away from the close (symbiotic) connection with the therapist. Unless the therapist is prepared for this movement, the therapist may be personally upset or threatened by the withdrawal. One therapist recently reported in exasperation, "When I was there at the appointment time, I received a call indicating that the patient would not come. However, that evening when I was busy doing other things, an emergency call came, and again, another call on the weekend." Many patients need to withdraw or distance themselves psychologically or physically from the therapist often missing appointments, taking breaks, and creating various sorts of psychological and physical separations. The technical problem is again one of how to accept the distancing and withdrawing need without becoming threatened, frustrated or angry. One man located a "short term" consulting job in New York but then continued his weekly sessions by telephone to California for months! During this time he reported startling changes in his relationship with his mother and wife. He reported no longer feeling dependent on them for "confirmation."

During these separating Scenarios an awareness of "strange feelings" begins. Patients report "inner experiences" which they haven't had before and often a general aversion to the "feelings" which are starting to emerge. This may be understood as an important aspect of *beginning to feel separate.* Actually starting to be aware that one *has* bodily sensations and personal feelings *apart from symbiotic connectedness* is a novel experience and can provide considerable unrest. Heretofore, sensations and feelings have been experienced in a symbiotic sense, not in an individuating sense. Patients may even want to blame the therapist for these uncomfortable feelings and they are correct. The therapist and the therapeutic process are responsible for the beginning sense of personal awareness in the areas of body sensations and differentiated feeling states.

Alienating/Defiant Scenarios

Alienating and/or defiant attitudes and behaviors toward the therapist serve the purpose of separation though they are frequently difficult for the therapist to handle. The therapist's style or personality may come under harsh criticism. One patient said recently, "You aren't doing something right or I would be cured by now!" Therapists tend to become impatient or to feel devalued by this form of growth. Many premature terminations are suggested or permitted by the therapist as a result of this particular quality of Scenario which the patient needs to enact. The issue usually crystallizes as whether one "should let go" of the patient or not. One view is that with all this discontentment and unhappiness, the reasonable thing seems to be to let the person alienate him/herself and go on his/her way. But on the other hand, just as a young child needs support in developing a defiant, assertive attitude *in connection to* his parents, many borderline patients need this same support. It has been suggested that "loose holding" is the technique to be employed. A child overeager to walk may declare that he doesn't need help and then fall on his face without the protective, extended hand of his parent close by. Patients often want to take breaks in the therapy during these separating phases. Many such breaks are arranged using the rationale from Mahler's idea of the "practicing subphase." Mahler observed that many toddlers need to be able to leave mother to go into the other room to try new experiences; but these same children who so ruthlessly leave mother behind do so only with the knowledge that she is waiting there to greet them upon their return. Psychoanalytic literature on interruptions in therapy needs to be reviewed extensively in light of the practicing subphase metaphor. On the one hand it might be maintained that various breaks during the separating portion of the psychotherapy with borderline patients should be welcomed and fostered. How can one deal with separation unless one separates? On the other hand, the therapist's willingness to let the person leave therapy or take breaks from therapy may be experienced as a rejection or an abandonment. Worse is the person who wants to take a break, and feels encouraged to try out new skills. Then he "falls on his face," feeling quite disillusioned that the therapist would permit such a venture without insisting on some sort of loose connection or loose support ("checking back"). What considerations will govern this issue in the future are not clear. One cannot help the patient deal with issues of separating unless one is in contact; but conversely, separation can only be dealt with by some form of separating. Compromise techniques have been devised by therapists who allow the patient to cut down the frequency of visits during practicing periods or who suggest brief breaks with a very definite time and date for the next contact to resume. The important thing, of course, is the therapist's understanding of the patient's contradictory developmental needs.

Double-Bind Scenarios

Many times mothers place their children in double-bind situations. With one voice they express that the child must grow away from mother, while with another voice they pull the child back into symbiotic closeness. This may express the mother's own ambitendency! As the symbiosis is replicated in therapy, and the separation begins, double-binds may be experienced in both passive and active forms and are indicative of *the particular style of the early separation attempts.* An empathic therapist is frequently uncomfortable watching the beginning differentiating movements of the patient. One therapist recently said, "It's as though this were my son, and he's in some sort of trouble, and what can I do?" She further described the sensation of sitting on the edge of her chair, watching a young child foray into the world of obstacles and dangers with the impulse to reach out and protect the child while knowing one must restrain oneself so the child learns through experience, even if that experience is unpleasant.

Some of the double binds in borderline families are pronounced. In one instance, a mother complained that her daughter's new separation experiences resulting from several years of psychotherapy were "killing her." Tragically enough, shortly after the mother returned from abroad on her first separation experience from her child in 21 years, she found that the girl had handled it very well. The mother had a coronary and died.[3]

---

[3] In the last several years of consulting with therapists on borderline cases, I have observed seven deaths and three instances of possible terminal cancer in mothers of borderline adults who were experiencing forced separateness as a result of their son's or daughter's psychotherapy. Serious health problems of two fathers who were primary love objects are now being monitored as well. There are many more instances of turbulence, breakdown, and depression. Future thinking must consider more fully the implication of successful therapy for various family members.

In another instance of an adolescent boy's treatment, at every point of improvement his mother would become disorganized and call me to say that the boy was showing signs of severe, bizarre craziness. Then she rushed to her own psychiatrist to begin to put herself back together. The boy, who was just fine and stronger than ever before, threatened the mother's intactness with his separating movements. Another adolescent has to fight his parents in order to keep coming to see me. He lives under the threat of "If you improve, I'll become an alcoholic again." This same child, who comes by skateboard or has to transfer buses to get to my office in a very determined fashion, spends most of his hour dirtying my office and planning what he can either talk me out of or steal from me. He insists that I permit him to throw his candy wrappers and soda cans, as well as cigarette ashes, behind my couch. Once the janitors found this rather extensive collection of trash and removed it. A terrible hour of threats and punishment ensued. I had been charged with protecting his trash, with receiving and protecting his dirt like his mother. However, it was permissible and even to the point for me to constantly object and bitterly complain about the trash. The Scenario was being replicated through my simultaneously caring for and objecting to his trash. Masterson (1972, 1976, 1981) has described the problems of the rewarding and the withdrawing mother and how these experiences resurface in the course of psychotherapy with borderlines. The most difficult aspect for the therapist is when he or she finds him/herself in a replicated double-bind without an easy way out.

Tension Relief Scenarios

Kohut (1971, 1977) has described the selfobject transferences characteristic of narcissistic personality disorders. There is reason to assume that narcissistic personality disorders have their source in certain areas of faulty rapprochement experience. In the rapprochement phase, a child has made a preliminary distinction between self and other and returns to mother for mirroring, twinning, and idealizing. The selfobject mother or therapist serves a tension-reducing function by permitting mirroring, twinning, or idealization to occur. In the presence of an empathic selfobject, the sense of fragmentation of the self diminishes. Kohut has indicated that this model of fragmentation and cohesion of the self can be applied to the understanding but not necessarily the treatment of, many borderline persons. Therapists of patients with borderline personality organization frequently feel they are serving such a function to a greater or lesser degree with different patients and through different phases of therapy. However, as the therapy process moves toward rapprochement, it will be expected that mirroring, twinning, or idealizing functions described by Kohut will move toward center stage. As such, it may be interesting and important to begin listening also with the

Listening Perspective of the Selfobject. According to this perspective, tension arises when there is a breach in selfobject empathy. When empathy is restored, the tension diminishes. This kind of Scenario is thought to be more important and more relevant in advanced stages of therapy with borderlines, or with borderlines at higher levels of developmental arrest.

THERAPEUTIC RESPONSE TO SCENARIOS

Many therapists have difficulty with the increased involvement which borderline personalities require. Preoedipal patients make demands upon therapists which are often quite uncomfortable. Scenarios can be followed, like any other form of therapeutic material, through empathic understanding. The complexities and complications of such attempts are many and no easy way to avoid the problems seems available. The therapist feels very much like a parent and experiences many of the same difficulties with his/her patients as with his/her young children. While there are no rules for child rearing or psychotherapy with borderlines, several suggestions will be offered.

Following the Scenario

Scenarios are conceptualized as listening devices for grasping the exact and particular nature of *interpersonal experience* which is established within the therapeutic relationship by the patient and the patient's needs. Empathic following of the Scenario is essential to therapeutic technique. A Scenario represents an early mode of relatedness *which must be met where it is* in its full emotional impact before the normal course of development and differentiation can ensue. Interpretations in the usual sense or attempts to get the patient to change his techniques, tactics, or ways of expression, are done primarily for the protection of the therapist's personal and professional integrity and the therapeutic situation (Giovacchini 1979a). But intrusions of any type usually tend to slow the process down and represent an unempathic response to preverbal or nonverbal experience which is being systematically expressed in the relationship. Differentiating activities and interpretations will follow at a later time as separating and constant modes of relationship become available to the patient.

Not Mistaking the Extent of the Deficit

Many borderline people have extensively developed certain sectors of their personality and have acquired advanced personal and intellectual skills. The myth that borderlines always look "severely distrubed" or "nearly crazy" overlooks key developmental considerations. Many capacities and skills may have developed to a high level despite difficulties in self-other differentiation.[4] Consequently, therapists, in an attempt to rush therapy along, often thoughtlessly engage in social and intellectual discussions with the patient about his personality functions (or whatever) which are quite apart from *the basic need to establish a sense of relatedness.* Therapeutic interest is not so much in the content of the intellectualizations but in *the mood, the tone and the level and/or mode of relatedness.* The well developed sectors of the personality (such as intelligence or social adaptation) often are misleading in that the patient represents an inaccurate sense of well being or self-understanding. If the developmental diagnosis is correct, the failure to integrate at the selfobject and at the constant object level is a serious one even if not altogether obvious from a social or adaptational viewpoint. Efforts should be made to follow the symbiosis rather than to engage in intellectualizing, socializing or merely supportive therapy. If the patient presents such a tendency, it perhaps should be considered as *yet another Scenario* where the intellectualizing functions take precedence over emotional relatedness and prevent emotional relatedness from occurring. This tendency could be seen as having its historical roots in the symbiosis or the separation process. The technical difficulty is, of course, how to respond to the patient's needs to do or discuss whatever he/she feels is appropriate, while at the same time discerning and responding to the level or mode of relatedness. The trick is how to follow the content carefully and to participate in it while not getting caught up in it because the dimension or mode of relatedness is the crucial factor. The mistake most often made in listening too carefully and trying to decipher the content, is that one becomes lured by the intellectualizations while failing to recognize and respond to the mode of relatedness.

Differentiating Actions, Activities, and Interactions

Writers discussing psychotherapy with borderline personality organization, usually find it difficult simply to advocate a technique of following the patient's material. This difficulty arises from the interpersonal demands which the borderline patient makes upon the therapist. *More importantly, it is usually evident that the patient must eventually somehow be "led" or "pushed" out of the position of symbiotic relatedness.* These terms at first would appear to require an active, directive, influencing mode of interven-

---

[4]Striking discrepancies between sophisticated social adaptation and quite early arrests of integrations of self and other relatedness in the same person are much more widespread than has generally been realized. This has often been accounted for as a difference in "intellectual" vs. "emotional" development. Recently Giovacchini (1982) has accounted for such discrepancies in terms of a failure to develop a "bridging continuity" between the earlier amorphous layers of personality and the later developed, more differentiated functions and structures. He points out that in normal development each developmental layering is integrated with those which have gone before but that in many "primitive mental states" this sense of continuity has failed to develop.

tion. But active intervention modes are not in keeping with the spirit of psychoanalytic inquiry. Supportive interventions are not necessary, appropriate, or helpful in reconstructive psychoanalytic psychotherapy with borderline personality development.

The therapy process might be described somewhat differently. The therapist must be *available* for the patient to form a sense of symbiotic (or postsymbiotic) relatedness. Relatedness will be accomplished *naturally* by a patient in an empathic atmosphere, in which he/she can replicate the forms of relatedness available to or needed by the personality. The analogies of "holding" and "containing" apply to the therapist's stance of availability in receiving the patient's style or mode of relatedness. A series of Scenarios are likely to be enacted to express the patient's capacities for relatedness in various symbiotic and/or post-symbiotic terms. This general approach is *not* what some would call "gratifying the pathological symbiosis." Analogously, a parent's empathically accommodating the relatedness needs of a young child does not necessarily entail crippling "gratification" of those needs. In therapy as a specific Scenario becomes understood in its complexity and its entirety, opportunities arise for the therapist to spontaneously "block," or confront the symbiotic relatedness assumption. Once the therapist understands the kind of yearning or demand being expressed in its idiosyncratic specificity, the therapist is in a position to begin questioning or refusing to accept relatedness on that level any more. This questioning and refusing constitute a differentiating activity. Many times the therapist's holding firm or blocking of the symbiotic attitude is experienced as a frustration, while at other times it may be experienced as a relief. By initially accepting the yearning and responding empathically to it *as a yearning*, the therapist is then in a position to assert his or her own personal and individual boundaries against the symbiotic assumption. In different words, symbiotic relatedness serves the function of avoiding containment of the self. The therapist first holds and molds him or herself into a containing position in order to understand the specific nature of the containment need. Once that understanding is accomplished, the therapist is in a position to refuse to go along with the continued reliance upon the limiting symbiotic or separating mode. This therapeutic "push" or differentiating activity or interaction leads toward self-containment and makes possible another step in the separation-individuation process.

No matter how active, supportive, directive, or manipulative such a technique may sound, in practice it represents first and foremost a statement of the firmness of the therapist's own sense of boundaries. In refusing to continue accepting various symbiotic merger experiences, the therapist gently fosters the development of self and ego functions in a separating context. A parent reaches out and holds the child who is learning to walk. The empathic parent does not let go of the child until it is clear that the child is ready to walk and at that point frustrates the child's wish to be held in favor of the more important, self-initiated step. Parents repeatedly hold, support, and withdraw or back away so that the growth step can be made *by the child.* In the specific area of symbiotic relatedness brought to psychotherapy, the therapist does a similar thing. Mere support and mere containment are inadequate. *The therapist must withdraw or withhold symbiotic or postsymbiotic support at an optimal time when a separation step can be made.*

Differentiating interactions frequently produce immediate and striking results. Whole areas of ego functioning seem immediately available for activation. However, in other instances, the confrontation produces temporary, but massive, "regressive" episodes. When viewed carefully, what appears to have happened in these regressive instances when the empathy has been correct is that, as a result of the confrontation, a new sense of separateness and self is experienced. In experiencing the sense of a separate self, a tremendous loss of symbiotic connectedness is also experienced. Sometimes therapists fear the confrontations because of the potential regression. While empathic timing and wording are clearly important features, in an empathic context the regression represents a response to an important experience of a new sense of self and the loss of an "old self." Like other forms of mourning, when it passes, a new level of integration becomes available. During this period suicide fantasies or death fears may signal the loss of an old self. By the same token, this is the time for birth and regeneration fantasies and dreams.

Close Attention to Separations from the Therapist

The problem of missed hours, therapist's cancellations, and vacations has been discussed in many contexts elsewhere. The classical technique with neurosis has been to interpret various responses to the end of the analytic week and other separation experiences within the context of the psychoneurosis. The general rule of interpretation for the treatment of neurosis also prevails in separation situations: i.e., when in doubt, the therapist should not interpret but remain silent. To maintain this same position in the treatment of borderline personalities would be a grave error. Separation is the key issue involved in the treatment of borderline personalities. Often long months have gone into establishing a sense of symbiotic relatedness such that even a few days' vacation may have a dramatic effect on a borderline patient, depending, of course, upon many factors including the general developmental level of the patient at the time and the use of such mechanisms as massive denial. A rule of thumb here would be the opposite from that in the treatment of neurosis. "When in doubt, move firmly toward dealing with the separation." The sense of symbiotic relatedness is precarious and what seems like a metaphor of symbiosis is hardly a metaphor when the borderline patient is left in the lurch during a long vacation.

Following one therapist's vacation, the urgency for a patient to see his therapist prevailed over a series of minor heart attacks so that seeing his cardiologist was postponed until after the therapist could be seen! Many other instances equally as dramatic are available to indicate the extreme urgency of maintaining contact throughout the course of treatment (with the possible exception of "practicing subphase" issues). It would seem that if one is willing to take on the responsibility of treating a borderline patient, one needs to acknowledge that as the sense of symbiotic closeness is permitted, separations will be as intolerable to him or her as separations from mother are intolerable for a young child. During the course of treatment, many patients seem to feel a need to establish almost daily contact with their therapist. While therapists often feel abused by phone calls at all hours of the day, night, and weekends, the legitimate urgency for the sense of connection cannot be minimized. The suggestion is for the therapist to find some convenient way of meeting the need or yearning of the patient.

One highly experienced therapist tells about one of her patients who could not go a day without some form of contact, but could only afford two sessions per week. The phone calls were a burden. The patient's visits to her office to sit quietly in her waiting room on days when there was not a session also proved somewhat awkward for the therapist. At last the therapist understood the need and the subjective legitimacy of it in terms of this woman's therapy work. She asked the woman if she, the therapist, might call her every morning between 7:00 and 7:30 after she had had an opportunity to have her morning coffee and read the paper. The patient was grateful, and for some months the therapist called every morning, usually only for a conversation of a very few moments. Often they talked about nothing other than the weather, the front page news, or how the patient was feeling today. This sense of connectedness which the patient required could then be met through these phone calls at the therapist's convenience and provided a ready relief from the otherwise inconvenient nature of the woman's expressions.

When therapists imagine trying to arrange their lives or schedules such that convenient contact with borderline patients can be made, they express fears of "gratifying dependency needs" and "prolonging or reinforcing the pathology." These fears seem unfounded since clinical observation shows something quite different. In the case of the woman just cited above, the therapist waited a good many months until at last the woman said one day, "I don't believe it will be necessary for you to call tomorrow. I'm having a very good week, and I feel like I'll be able to do without it." The therapist offered to call her in two days, which she did. Soon the calls could be relinquished altogether. This illustrates the general tendency for patients to "wean" themselves from this dependency as they obtain a better sense of self through therapeutic relatedness. About a year later this same patient who had not been calling arrived on Monday to ask her therapist if the answering service had reported her call last Friday evening. When told "no" she said, "On my way to Santa Barbara I suddenly felt an urge to call you as I left the city. You were not available, but I knew you might worry so I asked them not to tell you I had called. I was okay in a few minutes and had a wonderful weekend." Such a shift over time from intense symbiotic relatedness to a gradual concern for the therapist's feelings (constancy) represents a reorganization into a new mode of relatedness.

Therapists who deal with borderline patients are now making it a point to remain in telephone contact with some of their patients, even when traveling abroad. One therapist reported that she first provided her patient with a full itinerary of where she would be and how she could be reached in the Bahamas. However, knowing this would not be enough for this particular patient, she also pre-set several telephone appointment times. These were times when the therapist felt relatively confident of being in a place and a mood to be able to handle a long-distance phone call. The calls were to be placed by the therapist person-to-person, collect at the appointed time. The patient was told that if she did not accept the calls, the therapist would know that everything was going fine and she didn't need to talk to her at that time. However, if she felt that she did want to talk, the therapist would be there and available. This technique managed to prevent a major regression during the vacation period. Ingenuity and planning around all interruptions and separations of the treatment process must be used in order to provide a solid sense of continuity for the patient. In addition, creativity is always required when dealing with borderline patients so that a sense of contact can be provided without undue inconvenience to the therapist. If one chooses to treat such patients, one needs to be prepared to alter one's schedule and personal arrangements so the contact in some way can be maintained.

The therapist is well advised to be somewhat assertive in handling separating situations because an error in technique is best made in the direction of connectedness rather than disconnectedness. Careful consideration of this issue is required in helping a patient through the practicing mode of relatedness when the patient wants to create various separations from the therapist. The therapist needs to be prepared to permit the separations but also prepared to bring or welcome the patient back. Simply letting the patient go is often insufficient and may be experienced as abandonment.

CONCLUSIONS

Mahler's (1968) observations of childhood development led to her theory of human symbiosis which can serve as an effective metaphor for conceptualizing treatment of borderline developmental arrests. The early period of therapy sometimes lasting for a year or so may be conceptualized as re-enacting, re-establishing or replicating an idiosyncratic style of relatedness which the person once enjoyed with an early symbiotic partner. Interactions which engage the therapist have been termed "Scenarios." A Scenario is a listening device for grasping the level or mode of relatedness the patient seeks to express through enactments. The need is to express and communicate to the therapist a range of preverbal or nonverbal experience. The most important therapy material comes in the form of interpersonal exchanges and enactments rather than words.

"Symbiotic Scenarios" highlight the yearning for or assumption of a merger. They often give the impression that "nothing is happening," and may take the form of either opposition or conformity. Marked ego and self-constriction are usually a part of symbiotic Scenarios. Agitated/expansive states and helpless/deflated states can be indicators of yet other types of symbiotic Scenarios. A wide range of character traits and character disorders are traceable to the idiosyncratic qualities present in the early symbiosis.

"Separating Scenarios" express the child's need for distancing, disconnecting, or alienating himself from symbiotic connectedness. Double-bind Scenarios reflect what Masterson (1972, 1976) describes as response to the rewarding and withdrawing aspects of mother.

"Tension relief Scenarios" follow a model suggested by Kohut (1971, 1977) as certain persons need to re-enact this aspect of rapprochement experience in their basically borderline personality organization.

Therapeutic response to borderline personality organization begins by following the Scenario in its interpersonal details while not mistaking the extent of the limitations of undifferentiated relatedness. Interpretations in the traditional sense are not helpful. First because they are verbal attempts to grasp preverbal modes of relatedness and, second, because they arise from the therapist's sense of "differentness" rather than the patient's need for a sense of "sameness" or "oneness." It gradually becomes possible for the therapist to "confront" the symbiotic, separating or tension-relieving mode of relatedness with his or her own expressions of boundary and integration as a separate person. Empathy in timing and language are the key to differentiating interactions. The image which is sometimes helpful, is a mother pushing a child away toward a new activity and engagement which she knows the child can manage. Someone suggested that differentiating activities are like a mother bird's timely pushing her fledglings out of the nest!

This approach to treatment of borderline persons is known to be lengthy and difficult. Countertransference reactions will be dealt with in the next chapter as central in understanding the exact nature of the Scenario being replicated. The treatment technique remains basically that of free association suggested by Freud but with the therapist using a different set of developmental conceptualizations in order to understand and follow empathically the preoedipal material relating to the symbiosis and to the separation-individuation process. Verbal interpretations in the traditional sense are not so important as the therapist's being prepared to block or confront the *mode of relatedness* which the patient has succeeded in establishing in the therapeutic interaction. Differentiating activities represent a refusal on the part of the therapist to confuse mind-body boundaries once he/she sees and understands the exact nature of the blurring of boundaries which the patient is compelled to replicate in the therapy as well as in outside relationships. It is this non-influential blocking or confrontation of patient's characteristic modes of relationship which fosters the separation-individuation experience.

11 Countertransference: The Royal Road to Understanding the Merger Experience

> The awareness of our sensitivities, usually referred to as countertransference reactions, can only lead to increased integration and forbearance for the analyst. In turn, the range of patients that we can treat is broadened and the benefits of analysis will become available to a larger number of persons who have, for the most part, known only suffering and misery.
>
> Peter L. Giovacchini (1979a, p. 264)

GENERAL CONSIDERATIONS

In conceptualizing how to listen to the kinds of experience which persons with very early developmental arrests bring to the psychoanalytic and the psychotherapeutic situation, writers in the field are moving increasingly toward the assertion that the study of the interactional or interpersonal component of the therapeutic situation is critical. "Countertransference" has become the rubric under which these interactions and transactions typically become discussed.

"Transference" and "countertransference" have their conceptual origin in the studies of Freud and originally referred to *unconscious* infantile patterns of strivings which become activated in the treatment situation by the patient or the therapist respectively. Thus narrowly defined, the concepts "transference" and "countertransference" attain their greatest relevance in a therapeutic situation in which the complex patterning and early responses to a (parricidal-incestuous) constant oedipal object or to a narcissistically experienced selfobject are being experienced within the therapeutic relationship. However, when these terms are used to discuss levels of emotional or psychic integration which might be considered "pre-rapprochement," the technical precision diminishes with "transference" and "countertransference" being used in the broadest sense to refer to all subjective emotional reactions (conscious or non-conscious) which patient and therapist have toward one another.[1] Some writers have suggested utilization of the terms "transference-like" and "countertransference-like" or "preconscious transference" and "preconscious countertransference" for these broad preoedipal, pre-rapprochement applications in order to distinguish these from the more structuralized reactions characteristic of introspective or retrospective investigation of later (selfobject and oedipal) developmental phases of self and other differentiation.

Since countertransference was originally defined as an *unconscious* reaction in which the therapist's infantile repressed strivings become activated in response to the treatment situation, there has tended to be a reluctance to study countertransference within the therapeutic setting. It has been thought that the study of unconscious infantile strivings is *not* properly taken up in relationship to the therapist's work but rather in the therapist's personal analysis. This point of view has generally prevailed when considering the psychoanalytic treatment of the neurotic personality organization.[2]

Kohut, in defining "selfobject" transferences has specified several expectable countertransference reactions which therapists frequently experience when attempting to follow the introspective material of narcissistic personality organization (Kohut 1971). Therapists frequently experience boredom, drowsiness, and a lack of interest in work with persons who have narcissistic personalities. Kohut says that at least in the analysis of neurosis the analyst is being experienced as an oedipal transference object, e.g., as a frightening or castrating father, or a depriving, neglectful mother. In contrast, the analyst is being experienced merely as an extension of the person's own self in the selfobject transferences. The therapist may well react to the listening experience with disinterest and withdrawal. Like the position generally taken in the classical analysis of neurosis, Kohut (1971) maintains that in the analysis of narcissistic personalities countertransference reactions may be helpful in alerting the therapist to developments of the selfobject transference; but that the only effective control of countertransference remains the analysis of one's own narcissistic configurations.

Thus, in the first two Listening Perspectives of psychoanalysis, countertransference has been conceptualized as unconscious and, therefore, unavailable for consistent, reliable use as an analytic tool. Countertransference has been seen in those instances as remediable only through personal analysis. Within the third and fourth Listening Perspectives dealing with

---

[1]The reader is referred to Kernberg's (1975) chapter on countertransference for a review of the literature and the usage of the term in both the narrow "classical" sense and the broad "developmental" sense.

[2]Langs (1976, 1978, 1980, 1981, 1982) and Searles (1980) have been notable challengers of this point of view.

earlier (pre-rapprochement) levels of psychic integration and developmental arrest, different attitudes and conceptualizations are evolving.

Problems arise in connection with the use of the explicitly *unconscious* terms "transference" and "countertransference" in pre-rapprochement, symbiotic and pre-symbiotic states of developmental arrest. In these states forms of splitting and not repression dominate. Ambivalence as well as the capacity for dynamically unconscious modes of functioning are presumably not yet fully developed or crystalized as in neurotic and narcissistic formations. Therefore, in constructing Listening Perspectives for studying the experiences of the merger object and the experiences of inconstant part-selves and part-objects, the narrowly defined terms "transference" and "countertransference" may prove to be misleading and have to give way to new terms. In responding to this problem, Blanck and Blanck (1979), have suggested the term "replication" to refer to the symbiotic-like state which is re-established by borderline personalities in an analytic setting. In a similar vein, Giovacchini (1979a) has suggested speaking of "the impact of the delusion," which is either *projected into* the therapist or *externalized onto* the ambiance of the therapeutic situation in "primitive mental states." Aware of the conceptual complexities in this area, Giovacchini openly states, "I do not wish to make any elaborate formulations about countertransference. I include all of the analyst's more or less primitive reactions which are related to his infantile environment in this concept" (1979a, p. 237). Although the definition of "countertransference" becomes blurred when other than unconscious attitudes are included, and although "countertransference-like" or "preconscious countertransference" may be more accurate but unwieldy terms, and since Giovacchini's term "the impact of the delusion" does not yet have general parlance; the current discussion must proceed with this broad developmental use of the term "countertransference" which Giovacchini retreats to.

THE ROYAL ROAD TO THE MERGER OBJECT

Countertransference reactions, as broadly defined, were an implicit part of the discussion on borderline treatment scenarios in the preceding chapter. The position was taken that the therapist must be able to meet the patient where he/she is in terms of modes of self and other relatedness. Persons arrested in the developmental phase referred to as the merger object, distinguish idiosyncratically between their own mind-body boundaries and those of others whom they experience more or less symbiotically. Since each mother-child symbiotic pattern of mutual cueing is unique, the therapist is not in a position to "second guess" the special style or idiosyncratic form the symbiotic mode will take with each person. Further, since the emotional arrest is at a *preverbal* level of development, abstract symbolic and verbal expression will not be effective in fully communicating the pattern to the therapist. Rather, interpersonal enactments (interactions) are the most common way of conveying specific self and other patternings. The patient must engage the analyst, *passively and/or actively*, in his/her world of experience. While many aspects of the nature of this engagement may become known to the analyst through observation and listening to outside experience, the specifically personal dimensions become fully known only through interpersonal relatedness, i.e., they become known *as experienced* through interactions and "countertransference" reactions.

Christopher Bollas on countertransference (1983) points out that the traditional treatment paradigm developed for working with neurosis assumed the patient's advanced (oedipal level) capacity for complex symbolic activity in a context of generative free association. The opaque mirror role of the therapist remains sufficient for the interpretive work necessary in psychotherapy with neurotics. Bollas maintains however, that in pre-neurotic states the traditional assumption about the patient's generative symbolic, free associative capacity is unwarranted. The patient simply relates or lives in the therapeutic relationship a personal idiom derived from his/her relationship with the early nurturing partner. Thus the locus of the free associative activity regarding the patient's various personal idioms of being is in the analyst or therapist, i.e., the countertransference rather than in the transference! Bollas' own approach to the therapeutic task includes first the therapist's becoming aware of the personal idiom which is being projected into the analyst and/or externalized onto the atmosphere, and interaction of the therapeutic situation. Only much later does it become possible to confront the patient with the personal style and meaning of the countertransference information. In Bollas' consultative work with therapists (personal observation), he tends to focus not so much on the ways in which the therapist naturally assumes the parenting role but rather he highlights the infantile aspects of the therapist's (countertransference) impressions and feelings vis à vis the parenting role which the patient has assumed toward the therapist. For example, a therapist feeling helpless, dominated, or abused at the hands of his or her patient is assumed to be registering in some countertransference form some aspects of the patient's early experience with his or her early caretakers. This form of countertransference information about the early interpersonal atmosphere experienced is referred to in the present book as the "active and passive" forms of the replication. The "passive replication" is thought to be the original form in which the patient assumes the child role and the "active replication" is its reverse in which the patient externalizes the child's role onto the therapist, thus expressing the experience of (or the identification with) the aggressive parenting processes.

More new ideas and conceptualizations are perhaps yet needed to expand and clarify these crucial dimensions of transference-countertransference interplay which characterize psychotherapy with early forms of personality organization.

PROJECTIVE IDENTIFICATION[3]

Closely allied to the concept of splitting which was developed in Fairbairn's observations (1954) and adopted by Klein (1957, 1975), Rosenfeld (1965), Bion (1967), and many others, is the notion of "projective identification." Kleinian concepts have encountered criticism because they often appear to be ascribing unwarranted (adultopomorphic) content or motivation to the infantile mind. Criticisms perhaps also arise because clinical usage of Klein's terms sometimes rings of magical thinking and fantasy formation on the part of the theorist-therapist. These criticisms have detracted from the possibility of more widespread consideration of a series of important developmental phenomena which can perhaps best be described under the rubric "projective identification."

Projective identification denotes many early developmental experiences which have been detailed in certain forms more recently by Kohut (1971, 1977). Formative experiences of self are thought to transcend the body and extend *into* many aspects of the nurturing environment as envisioned in Kohut's concept of the "selfobject." Freud maintained that the earliest body ego (the purified pleasure ego) was formed on the basis of the pleasure-pain principle and tended to exclude (negative) things such as itchy skin or an aching belly but conversely tended to include (positive) elements such as the nurturing breast or various other of mother's soothing aspects. The infant's increasing distinction between experiences within the body in contrast to aspects of the external environment is thought to be fostered by a number of attempts to expel unwanted "bad" experiences into others and to conscript various "good" experiences from others. Grotstein (personal communication) refers to these many attempts or experiments in infancy and later life as "imaginative conjury," a process which gives life to ideas and

---

[3]This book has not attempted to integrate contributions of the many branchings of psychoanalysis, including the "schools of thought" founded by Melanie Klein and Carl Jung. I believe any form of psychoanalytic thought to be complex so that extensive tutoring is required not merely to learn the concepts involved, but to master thoroughly the subtleties of clinical application. Lacking such tutoring, it has seemed advisable to limit my book to those ideas and applications with which I am thoroughly familiar. However, the concept of "projective identification" developed by Melanie Klein is too rich to go unmentioned. In struggling to find a place in the Self and Object schema to consider projective identification, I am indebted to James Grotstein for reading my manuscript and providing the tutoring from which ideas in this section emerged.

images, i.e., "If you can imagine it, it exists," and "One creates by extending an aspect of self into the object." According to Grotstein, projective identification lies at the root of psychoanalytic theories of psychic transformation. Bion (1962, 1963, 1967) was perhaps first to make explicit that the "containing" maternal environment is available to absorb the unwanted "bad" images and impulses. Through containment and absorption, projected images and experiences become continuously transformed through cyclical processes of (re-) introjection or re-identification and then re-projection. In a somewhat different light, Bollas (1978) points out that the first experience of the presence of the maternal idiom is through the early processes of transformation themselves. He speaks of the "transformational object." Grotstein (1981b) has defined in this early era a selfobject he calls the "Background Object of Primary Identification."

However one chooses to conceptualize these earliest experiences of or experiments with the nurturing, containing environment or maternal idiom, it is clear that sufficient parenting processes tend to pull or seduce the infant, through many (reinforcing) experiments or connections, into a state of being referred to as "symbiosis" (Mahler 1968) or "basic unity" (Little 1981). This dyadic state is characterized by complex processes of mutual cueing. Through symbiotic containment and connectedness, psychic controls over the internal (affect) world and the external (reality) world become slowly established in the course of normal development. Projective identification becomes understandable as a series of expectable developmental phenomena through which various images and impulses are first "projected into" (or are experienced as coming from) others and then re-incorporated to become experienced as aspects of self. To the extent that images and impulses experienced as troubling (or poisonous) have been successfully contained and absorbed by the maternal idiom, they tend to lose their troubling features (i.e., become "de-toxified"). But to the extent environmental containment may be insufficient, then "bad," "dangerous," or "persecutory" maternal images are not contained or absorbed but become reincorporated into the symbiotic exchange and consequently into the infant's version of the self.

Like so many other clinical phenomena which have first become clarified in highly disturbed individuals, projective identification can now be viewed as a series of normal developmental processes in which an infant experiences or creatively acts. The developmental consequences of his/her actions depend largely on the adequacy of the "containing" (Bion 1962) or "holding" (Modell 1976) qualities available in the environment.

An understanding of projective identification in different forms is important in all three preoedipal, pre-constancy Listening Perspectives but turns out to be crucial in listening to aspects of the borderline merger experience. The most important *clinical* formulation involving projective identification

(Klein 1952, 1957) is that bad or aggressive aspects of the self are projected *into* the therapist, thus turning the therapist into a dangerous, frightening, persecutory figure (in the same *style* as the person once experienced mother within the symbiosis). Unfortunate consequences of this tendency to project "envy and gratitude" can be that the person desperately flees or frantically attempts to control the therapist, who comes to be seen as dangerous and potentially overwhelming. Negative and positive countertransference feelings such as anger and hatred or unusual fondness toward the patient may be the therapist's first clues in understanding the exact nature of the containing and absorbing function which he or she is being required to perform. The commonly employed Kleinian formulation of projective identification is that the bad (aggressive) self is projected *into* the (body-) person of the therapist who then (through countertransference) *becomes* the persecutory object who must be feared and controlled.

A developmental formulation of projective identification would highlight the value of listening to such therapeutic exchanges as part of a replicated symbiotic or postsymbiotic Scenario—an arrest of the natural developmental processes of transformation. Projective identification seen in this light is understood as a common feature to all symbiotic or merger experience. Projective identification can be understood as an important listening dimension with borderline personality organization and can be seen to form part of the "royal road" to the merger experience, the countertransference.

The Listening Perspective of the Merger Object thus depends largely upon countertransference reactions for key information about the unique modes of interpersonal relatedness which characterize the patient's arrested patternings or configurations of self and other experience. It is thus that careful attention to countertransference becomes the "Royal Road" to understanding those persons arrested at the developmental phase of the merger object.

Many brief instances of countertransference reactions were provided in the previous chapter but they do not convey the painstaking difficulty with which one frequently has to unravel them. The next section will present a clinical hour in which the therapist felt "put on the line" by his patient. The therapist describes honestly and openly the emotional and physical reactions which led to his understanding of a crucial aspect of the young man's merger experiences. The section following will focus attention on a long and particularly stormy symbiotic replication through which a teenage girl provoked considerable countertransference in her therapist. The countertransference will be studied through the exasperating replication as well as through the extended metaphorical presentation in which the therapist herself searches for the hoped-for solution to the countertransference—The Wizard of Oz. The final report will focus on potential uses and misuses of countertransference information.

"OF COURSE YOU HAVE TO PAY ME
FOR THIS SESSION" (Kent)[4]
Introduction to the Session

In attempting to understand some of the interpersonal dimensions necessarily involved in the therapeutic realignment of internal patterns, the
concept "countertransference" continues to emerge to describe the therapist's own emotional (conscious, preconscious, and unconscious) reactions to
the patient. The therapeutic work of the following young man was brought
to my attention by his (male) therapist after they had been meeting once a
week for about a year. The patient had continued to come faithfully to his
sessions but remained totally aloof and elusive to the therapist. Quite
frustrated, his good intentioned therapist tried on numerous occasions to
offer gentle, helpful comments to the young man which seemed to be totally
unheard, if not unwelcome. His friends, his work, and his frenzied social life
depicted a similar pattern of loyal participation with a simultaneous almost
total withdrawal from personalized contact. His therapist and I began to
receive the thoughts and stories he had brought in light of an overriding
wish for a particular form of "symbiotic merger" (I).[5] There was also a
tendency toward severe splitting of his affects (V) a constricted sense of
identity (III) (based on popular music and an adherence to a stereotyped
version of the drug-disco youth culture). Despite isolated areas of good ego
development, there was an overall lack of development of ego and self as
organizing processes (V). As the therapist began to show appreciation of
this young man's need for acceptance in the symbiotic merger (replication)
(I), the patient's enthusiasm suddenly and dramatically perked up. For the
first time he began arriving early and "talking a blue streak throughout the
whole hour," making it manifestly clear that he was now getting what he
needed. More importantly, at some level he knew it. The most interesting
aspect of his material, as it then began to develop, was clarified by considering the adaptational perspective (IV). That is, while the alternating
withdrawal and (somewhat troubled) engagements with people clearly depicted problems with affect splitting (II), they more importantly seemed to
alert the therapist to some slowly emerging adaptational dynamics related
to alternating over-and-under involvement of his mother (IV). It seemed
that these tight and troubling dynamics had been historically transferred to
and acted out with his father, but that the oppositionality and negativistic
style of connecting was difficult to transfer to other people unless they
themselves had severe symbiotic disturbances. Thus, most of his friends and

---

[4]The therapist is a man. See note on contributors, p. xix.
[5]The Roman numerals in this chapter refer to the Developmental Points of View employed in
the formulations taken from Chapter 8.

activities had a "fringe" quality, and he himself had been viewed by the family as being either "retarded" or perhaps even having "minimal cerebral dysfunction." In the report which follows, the therapist at last is given a "full dose" of the impact of the young man's problems—via a "counter-transference" communication.

The Therapist's Report of the Session

Kent is in his late twenties, the son of a prominent lawyer and a narcissistically preoccupied mother. He was a first-born son and has been living at home (almost entirely) all of his life. He had seen a psychiatrist and also worked with a social worker at a rather well-known clinic, but only had short-term therapy there, dropping out because of "difficulties in establishing rapport."

I had been seeing Kent once a week for a year and was working to establish some kind of relationship with him, which I have felt very difficult to do. He was often quite late and then would leave the session early. The referring psychiatrist sent him to me for "supportive" treatment to deal with "damaged self-esteem and damaged self-object." After about a year of treatment, and just prior to this particular session, I had begun to understand much more clearly how Kent experienced many things in his life, and we had attained excellent rapport on one or two occasions. He was quite enthusiastic that I seemed to understand how his "mind and emotions worked." I was at this point "wide open," trying to understand the information that came my way and was experiencing myself more open than ever to experience empathic contact with a person who, up until now, had been very distant and frustrating to work with. We had even talked of getting together more often.

Kent, usually late, showed up seven minutes early today to talk about Bernie who had been his friend for five years. It seems Bernie had given Kent a check supposedly signed by Bernie's mother and had asked Kent to cash it because Bernie didn't have his ID. Bernie's mother discovered the missing check and called Kent's father. She hassled Bernie and kicked him out on the street. Bernie called Kent's father blaming the cashed check on Kent, saying he used it to buy drugs, party and drive the car while being "high." He spilled all of the private things Kent had told Bernie about in the past that the father did not approve of. Kent says now that Bernie is an "ex-friend." Kent talks about how his parents are on his case again. In the past Kent has cashed hundreds of dollars worth of his parents' forged checks (about two years ago). Then just two months ago, he had cashed his father's $1000 tax return check but had spent only $90 before father found out. Kent swears he "thought" it was his check, with his name, and that the computer made a mistake. [Unlikely.] Then Kent said that, on top of that, the computer where he works "fucked up" and that he didn't get paid and his parents think he blew it all on cocaine [which he probably did].

Up to this point in the session he was calm, relaxed, assured, and told me with pride that he now has told his parents that his money is *his*, and he will not be treated like a child; he will no longer be checked up on. He added to this, "They want to see my paycheck stubs again." I commented that just when he is getting some control over his life something happens and his parents strive for reinvolvement, like a hand that won't allow him enough distance. He said, "Yeah, I'm an individual, and I told them if I want to get high, I'll get high. [The declaration to his parents refusing to be checked up on and getting high if he wants are "firsts" for Kent, and he is proud to be able to make a stand.] I said that these things may be very difficult for them to understand. He said, "Yeah, they say that I am just as sick as Bernie for hanging around with him, and they would probably think that the people at the disco 'club' are all messed up too. They oughta go there!" Then there was some talk about the club and how the people there are "cool and relaxed," unlike at home. There nobody hassles anybody. I told him that I had been there on Tuesday, taking his suggestion to go [on a night when I knew he wouldn't be there]. He talked and talked about the sound system and the lights, and I told him how now I was able to understand how important the atmosphere is to him, and he seemed pleased with my understanding of his consciousness and of the consciousness there.

So far so good. Then he told me of wanting to take this chick to a rock and roll concert that night and how he needs money. I asked if he already had tickets and he looked sideways and said, "Uh, well, no, not yet." [I happened to know that the concert was sold out.] Then he tells me that he didn't tell his parents about the check situation we had arranged yet. I had offered to bill his parents rather than having him bring me the check each week because of the difficulty it had caused him having to go home and get a check before each session. He then pulled out a check from his parents to me to hand to me; but without handing it to me he starts fingering it, and asks if there is any way I can sign the check over to him. I said no and that I was sure that would only cause a hassle with his folks. No longer calm, he tells me this might work or that might work or if I could just do this or meet him after or whatever, and I start feeling totally overwhelmed and upset. I said I could see how money always seems to cause him trouble and that I was getting a feel for how difficult it must be for him. He tries again, and I explain my bind: that I wouldn't want in any way to cause his parents to be involved in our relationship, that I understood how money was a hassle and understand how dreadful it must be to deal with his parents regarding money. [At this point I had a number of symptoms myself! I felt dry mouthed, nervous, and unable to think clearly.] I reported the reaction I was having and asked him if he usually felt what I felt now. He replied that he did. I told him that I simply felt afraid to get involved with money and checks in that way with his parents and that now I knew what it felt like to be in his shoes. I understood how important it is for him. Then he said some other things about how he feels when his parents say no, and I said I was worried how he would feel toward me for saying no. He said, "Okay, even though I need the bread," and I voiced my concern on two hands. First of all, my fear that saying no would interfere with our relationship just at a time when I am starting to really feel like I am understanding what is happening with him. On the other hand, I realize the importance of his coming through with the money, of my being paid, and of protecting our relationship from the intrusion of his parents. I indicated I further understood how money had become a major connection to his parents and was beginning to understand just how important it was for him to be able to have a good time, and to "get lost" in the wonderful kinds of consciousness that money can buy him: experiences at the disco, drugs, and many other experiences with friends. Finally, and slowly, at the end of the hour, he handed the check over to me very reluctantly, so that in taking it I felt like a thief. [During the last twenty minutes of the session I really had trouble thinking, truly had a dry mouth and felt nervous. It was very upsetting. I was very relieved when the hour was over. I paced for a good ten minutes following that trying to shake off the awful feeling I had had!]

Comments on the Therapist's Notes

Kent opens his hour (more candidly than usual), making clear how he loses friends, and only later does it become evident how panicked he is over the potential threat of losing his therapist. That is, the ultimate management problem of the hour became reduced to how to "lovingly hold a bratty little child." If the therapist said no, the illusion of the good therapist (supported by the symbiotic need) would be shattered, running the risk that the now "good" therapist would suddenly be seen as "cold, rejecting and bad" (II). On the other hand, the dangers of colluding around the issue of checks and money and thus permitting parental intrusion into the relationship had been clearly spelled out in the episode of his "ex-friend," Bernie. At the time the therapist couldn't escape the impression that he was having done to him what had been done repeatedly to the patient.

Is this interaction then best regarded as an "identification with the aggressor" (A. Freud 1936) in which Kent turns a passive (masochistic, neglected) experience into an active (sadistic, neglectful, abusive) one? Or might this better be viewed as a "projective identification" (M. Klein 1952), that is, a wholesale disowning and projecting of negative experience into the therapist's body? Or to what extent might this event be regarded as stemming from countertransference in the strictest sense, i.e., from infantile intrapsychic conflicts of the therapist activated in the situation? Another possibility would be to simply view the therapist's reaction as a more or less appropriate response to a difficult and frustrating circumstance, i.e., a "reaction *to* the replication."

Within the ongoing context of this man's therapeutic work, this and other interactions may be most profitably viewed as instances in which the early symbiotic adaptational dynamics between mother and child (IV) are spelled out clearly in such terms that the therapist's holding functions will be of foremost importance. One might think here of the re-experiencing of the withdrawing and rewarding aspects of early "part object relations units" (Masterson 1972, 1976). This holding environment (Modell 1976) might be thought of as eventually providing a "corrective emotional experience" (Alexander 1961; Alexander and French 1946).

Another listening device which might prove helpful with this man is provided by Langs's (1976) conceptualization of maintaining the frame of the bipersonal field.[6] The patient loudly and clearly expressed his need for the firm maintenance of the frame which the therapist was able in many regards to provide. Since this material comes from a brief consultative encounter it is difficult to know which of the several listening possibilities will ultimately be of greater use.

As a follow-up note, it may be interesting to know that the next appointment was canceled an hour before on account of "not being able to afford enough fuel to get there." Following the reported session, a stormy set of scenes began occurring between the parents, and Father called the therapist to complain about the "boy's" therapy and to demand to be seen himself [declined], and Mother decided, for the first time ever, to take a trip on her own (a fling, it turns out), leaving father and son to fend for themselves. Those familiar with the treatment of borderline children will see in these events the distress and chaos which often ensue in the family when at last the therapy begins to take hold.[7] That is, Kent had been making the first strong steps to stand on his own and was able to determine effectively that his therapist would be with him. The long-standing and self-effacing symbiotic pattern had been blocked or broken at last. The ensuing turbulence in the family structure might be thought to mark the beginning or the resumption of Kent's separation-individuation process. The year following this critical incident found Kent declaring independence in many more ways from his parents and his therapist, while finding new ways at work and in his social life to relate to people without the withdrawn aloof style which had characterized his previous (symbiotically determined) life.

---

[6]To be discussed in more detail in Chapter 13.
[7]See my further comments on this alarming phenomenon in footnote 3 of Chapter 10 (p. 187).

"TOTO, WHAT A STRANGE PLACE!
I DON'T THINK WE ARE IN KANSAS":
THE YELLOW BRICK ROAD
TO COUNTERTRANSFERENCE (Ann)[8]

Author's Introduction

This section contains a summary of several years' turbulent work with a young borderline woman. The paper was prepared by her therapist originally as a class project and represents the therapist's own attempt to understand her many countertransference reactions in order to utilize them in helping her patient. Therapy with such wild, unpredictable, self destructive merger patternings can never be held up as model psychotherapy because the therapist is hardly ever allowed to function as a therapist. This paper is presented to portray an authentic struggle to understand a symbiotic pattern through countertransference. It also does a good job of bringing to bear what many authorities on the subject have to say.

The therapist's original idiom—the search for Oz—is retained because in it is conveyed brilliantly the countertransference struggle as well as the replication of an obstreperous symbiosis.

The Therapist's Report

Ann, plump, perpetual smile, came into my life three years ago. Ann was a 17-year-old high school junior, referred by her high school counselor. It was believed that Ann was a hypochondriac, missing weeks of school for a series of illnesses. She was in danger of not graduating with her class.[9] Ann had been hospitalized for six months at the age of 15 for a drug overdose with possible suicide tendencies. She was the youngest of four children and the only girl in a very athletic, competitive family. Ann expressed adoration for her older brothers, alienation from her father, and contempt for her mother.

The yellow brick road of therapy began—and suddenly twisted into one-way, no-exit turns. Ann, "an adjustment reaction," "a substance abuser," "a depressive neurosis," what road are we on? Ann was transferred to a special high school. Ann wrecked a car, sold drugs, cut school, was arrested for public drunkenness, and lied and lied. Along the bumpy road came a signal-alert: "Therapist should be prepared for slow progress and small results over long periods of time" (Masterson 1976, p. 186). We inched toward June and Ann's graduation. Therapy was dominated by Ann's wish for independence, her own car, her own apartment, her own life.

---

[8]The therapist is a woman. See note on contributors, p. xix.

[9]Graduation often poses problems for borderlines who have made a symbiotic transfer to the school situation in some way.

Ann did find a job with her father's large firm. Ann bought a used car and took on credit payments. Ann became increasingly depressed, sullen, and withdrawn. Giovacchini (1979b) noted that this type of patient may be so irritating that the therapist will experience a disproportionate amount of frustration. The frustration seems to be so great that it is felt for two, making up for the patient's inability to feel frustrated.

Ann came to session suicidal. She had begun mixing drugs and alcohol. There was no choice in treatment: Ann entered a short-term, acute care mental hospital. She was to stay four and one-half months. The psychiatrist diagnosed manic-depressive and began lithium treatments. Ann raged at me, the primary therapist. Temper tantrums ranged from setting off the fire alarm by holding a match under an overhead sprinkler (and emptying the entire hospital at two o'clock in the morning) to suicide attempts (always when hospital discharge was discussed). Toto, we are not in Kansas. Ann was a "borderline" patient.

Ann came out of the neuropsychological hospital in December. She was to return to a private hospital for possible ulcer treatment in January. In February she was hospitalized in a third hospital for alcohol addiction. The yellow brick road had become grey and worn. It was time to go inward, to consult, to know myself as a therapist and as a person. Countertransference: Freud (1910) first coined the word. As Giovacchini (1979a) noted, it was something that had to be done away with as quickly as possible and may in some instances require that the analyst seek further analysis for him/herself. Giovacchini (1979b) commented that today the therapist has acquired a greater respect for his unconscious. Masterson (1976) noted that the borderline patient projects so much and is so provocative and manipulative that he/she can place great emotional stress on the therapist. The therapist's task becomes not only to understand the patient's actions, but how these actions are affecting his/her own emotions. After all, Masterson (1976) points out, the patient is a professional provocateur and manipulator. The therapist is the amateur.

The major guidepost to this journey with borderline patients is provided by Hartocollis (1977, p. 351). The therapist's countertransference responses have meaning to the patient. Meanings that are subtle and intense, and "crucial to success or failure of the treatment." Searles (1979, p. 578) said, "My sense of identity has become . . . my most reliable source of data as to what is transpiring between the patient and myself, and within the patient." Clearly, I had not read the map to Emerald City with care. If the therapist knows his countertransference, Epstein (1979) declares, then therapeutically effective interventions and strategies can be developed.

By March, Ann was out of work, out of the hospitals, and back living at home. She complained of tension headaches. A long, trying session began with a "whine-list" of all her unhappinesses. Tearfully, she confronts me,

"You are going to kick me out. You're tired of this shit. You don't believe I'll ever get well." I had a tension headache; the road had no end. Inside, I knew that the supportive therapy was losing, that the focus had to be brought back to the here and now, to our relationship. I responded, "I anticipated your disappointment with me. Probably I'm like everyone else who doesn't take your pain seriously." The tears ebbed.

Epstein (1979) believed that countertransference reactions depend on the therapist's internal self and object relations. Success in treatment was dependent on the therapist having a good enough self, and a good enough internal parent. Epstein (1979) warned that if the residuals of a grandiose omnipotent child-self (that developed to respond to a persecutory internal parent) remain, then the therapist might retaliate viciously. In 1949, Winnicott (as quoted by Epstein 1979) spoke of the analyst's love and hate reactions to the actual personality and behavior of the patient. Borderline patients have experienced a maturational failure in childhood but run the danger of a second maturational failure in therapy. Winnicott believed that the therapist could precipitate this second failure by not responding in structurally corrective ways to the patient's internal (pathological) self and object relations.

Ann became an issue in my own therapy . . . I was overwhelmed and obsessed by the case. Masterson (1976) strongly supported the idea of therapists of borderline patients being in therapy in order to work out their own unconscious mechanisms that will otherwise distance them from difficult patients. It was another guidepost on the yellow brick road. Masterson (1976, p. 342) said that the single most difficult skill to acquire in psychotherapy with borderline patients is the ability to recognize and control one's own identification with their projections. The therapist neither "loves" nor "hates" the patient, but serves as a target upon which the patient can project a repetition of his early development struggles.

Ann had been drinking on Saturday. She reports in session returning to the neuropsychological hospital and looking for my car or the doctor's car. She settles for another car and smashes the side mirrors. "I wanted you to see how screwed up I am." Masterson (1976) had warned that the borderline patient would alternately cling, then distance self, unable to resolve separation-individuation. Ann was apparently working to distance herself by her acting out. In the next session she cried, "I realize I do crazy things . . . I have a problem. For God's sake, help me!" Kernberg (1975), in a classic study on borderlines, felt that the therapist's personality characteristics were the crucial prognostic variable in treatment. He felt that the ideal therapist would have the following characteristics: capacity for true object relationships, control of own hostility, clear moral values, and have overcome own narcissism. April: the phone call came at three o'clock in the morning. Ann feels like "something bad is about to happen to me . . . Just wondered what you are doing." Kernberg neglected to mention walking on water and the capacity to give up sleep in the symbiosis!

Masterson (1976) wrote about the dangers of either a compulsive or submissive therapist. Either the therapist will over-confront the patient's acting-out or never confront the acting-out. Masterson (1976) believes that the trap is in getting caught up in the patient's acting-out. If non-directive with the patient, the therapist will fail to provide two developmental necessities! A real object and a reality ego. If too directive, Masterson (1976) counsels, the therapist will take over the patient's life in a vain effort to make the patient feel he is loved and cared for. It was an easy trap with Ann to want to do "casework." She was not needful of direction. "Have you thought of a part-time job?" "Could you join A.A.?" "Perhaps it would help at home to be more a part of the family?" Ann would listen, then counter, "Why should I bother. Nobody thinks I can do it anyway!"

Further down the brick road, Glenda, the good witch, points out, "Utilize the bad moments in the patient's treatment for learning more about yourself" (Hartocollis 1977). Schwaber (1979) wrote with feeling about the paradox of empathy. We are called upon to place ourselves into the other's intrapsychic reality, to be used and responded to in the context of that reality. Schwaber (1979) continues that yet we, as the therapist, must be able to perform in therapy without the patient's experience either enhancing or threatening our own experiences. The paradox is that we offer ourselves as selfobjects, yet we don't take the patient in as a selfobject.

Late April: Ann sits in session scowling, refusing to talk. Suddenly she shouts, "Like hell you understand me! All I want to do is drink. I can't control it. I'm paying you to control me!" Later in the same session, Ann begins to mimic adults drinking. I smile, and quick as a flash, Ann responds, "How can you sit and work with me through all this shit and still smile?"

Toto, what is a borderline patient? Giovacchini (1979b) counsels to look for a patient who relates to the external world in an urgent, harassed manner, displaying tension apparently unrelated to any specific object or situation—a tension that is general, pervasive, and infectious. Kernberg (1975) states that a therapist should look for aggression in himself as an emotional reaction to the patients who always seem to bite the hand that feeds them. You give out something good and receive something bad in return. The result, writes Kernberg (1975), is a reactivating of the therapist's masochism, provoking paranoid fears or depressive guilt. The therapist will have disproportionate doubts in his own capacity and exaggerated fears of criticism by third parties. Supervision had become as tortuous a road as the yellow brick road of treatment. I felt in full retreat.

Epstein (1979) reminds the therapist that the persecuted child of the patient seeks vengeance and retaliates by frustrating the parent (therapist) by long periods of "strike," that is, a time of being passive and helpless. Masterson (1976) notes that the patient will act out in transference as the resistance to treatment, replaying original conflicts to relieve tension. Indeed, according to Epstein (1979), the borderline patient cannot tolerate a two-person situation. The patient is not internally organized as a full and separate person. The borderline's energy will go toward forcing the therapist into a role and function of some part of his self or of some internalized other. Epstein (1979) continues that the patient's unconscious fantasy is to infect the therapist with her "poisons" and to become a bad object. The patient expects the therapist to defend self, to counter-attack, to reject the patient, or to appease her. Hence, the patient is reassured of her power to dominate and control both the other person's insides and behavior. The result is that the patient's pathological organization of self and internal object is perpetuated. The clue: the therapist must continue to function as a separate person and to give evidence of survival in good health.

The sessions bogged down. "I'm waiting for you to give up on me," said Ann. She now "recites" the week's events for 35 minutes, then begins to "work" in the last part of the hour. She resists ending sessions on time, stalling in the waiting room. "I'm going to leave here and get drunk." Giovacchini (1979b) notes that sessions with borderline patients will have no beginning, no middle, no end. He continues that the borderline's needs seem impossible to meet, for their greatest need is to be needed and helpless. Giovacchini (1979b) continues that if the borderline stopped being helpless, the fear would be an unleashing of powerful, destructive forces that are terrifying.

Hartocollis (1977) draws on Winnicott's work in noting that with a borderline patient, the setting and the analyst do not represent the mother—they are the mother. Ann's mother, ill for years, able to make her first trip without Ann only weeks before, dies unexpectedly. Ann tearfully clings, insisting, "She didn't die. She couldn't leave me." The silences in treatment stretched into long periods of time. Giovacchini (1979b) notes that the borderline's silence means, "Take care of me; structure my needs."

Mother's Day dawned with frantic phone calls. Ann was lost, angry, grasping for reality. There was no spoken comfort. A note was left on my doorstep, "Happy Mother's Day. I hope you're having a good one . . . I've decided to try and join Mom . . . I'll be dead soon." Long hours follow, stretching into the next day. A month of detours followed. Ann was to regress to a constant smile. A clinging, pleasing little girl was to alternate with "Ann the Bitch" who swore and pounded on walls. Ann began to announce, "Therapy sucks; I'm going to quit!" An unavoidable shift in schedule forced me to move Ann's long-standing hour. Inadvertently, I put the hour in the slot needed to drive to supervision. I was late to supervision. Did I want to bring her to the supervisor . . . refer the case out . . . leave her behind?

Masterson (1976) states that the therapist of borderline patients experiences withdrawal. The therapist is late for appointments, has difficulty maintaining concentration in interviews, and in recalling the content of the interviews. Schwaber (1979) spoke of the negative countertransference of "seemingly demanding 'entitlement,' boredom or drowsiness, which can occur when we've simply not been responded to as separate and autonomous." Hedges (1980a) counsels patience with the borderline patient's timetable for therapeutic development, which is usually different from the therapist's timetable. Kernberg (1975) states that a good indicator of the therapist's concern is consultation about the case.

The road map was unfolded, two years into therapy with Ann. The yellow brick road did lead to Emerald City, and the wicked witch and the wizard were to be found in the therapist. Luckily, other travelers had been along this road too. Their advice was sought. Giovacchini (1979b) points to the borderline's clinging dependence, which frustrates the therapist by pushing difficult feelings to the forefront of the transference. The patient requests help, often pleading in insistent urgency . . . and it is fruitless. Masterson (1976) reminds the therapist that the borderline has not developed object constancy, hence the persistence of the fear of abandonment leads to separation stress. The patient's time of crisis cries for the stability of inner equilibrium. The therapist is called on to maintain contact to the point of daily conversations. By June, this became necessary for Ann. On one day, she sat in the waiting room, although I was with other patients, calmed by my close presence. No external separation could be tolerated without Ann feeling an overwhelming panic. This period was to last for eight days.

Ann began to unknowingly teach me how to help her. Ann was experiencing difficulty talking to her father. I began to use the sessions to interpret her thoughts and feelings. Each interpretation was met by questioning looks, confusion, denial, and, finally, ignoring. Searles (1979) states that with a borderline patient, no direct interpretation of the problem centrally in focus can be given. Epstein (1979) believes that the borderline receives interpretation of transference as a statement directed to his ego— an ego that is ready to be persecuted. Indeed, the communication is likely to be perceived as a deserved counterattack. The borderline patient defends against interpretation by nullification, hence the interpretation is ineffective. The negative end result is a more defensive ego and a higher level of paranoid anxiety. Of note, Epstein (1979) points out that the therapist's need to interpret as if he were working with a neurotic patient may come from the therapist's unconscious hostility. The result to the patient-therapist relationship is twice more noxious than if the therapist were open to his aggression. Epstein (1979) further explores the possibility that the borderline patient is responding to interpretation from envy of the therapist's competence. The patient perceives himself as already down, and the interpretation from the all-knowing, together therapist pushes him further down.

What is an analytically trained therapist to do with a borderline patient who cannot tolerate the major tool of a therapist? Epstein (1979, p. 391) suggests the following safe course: to contain projections, then restrict comments and questions to those which are directed away from the patient's ego and toward his own ego. The patient expresses the thought that the therapist is critical of him. Epstein (1979) suggests that the therapist respond, "You mean, I'm out to get you."

Ann bloomed with a variety of both short-term and long-term goals in June. She wanted college, she wanted to leave home, she wanted to buy another car . . . she obsessed that her father in his own grief would re-marry. Epstein (1979) counsels that all of the patient's ideas and perceptions are to be taken seriously in order to reduce the paranoid anxiety and reassure the patient that the therapist is unharmed against the projections and will understand. During this time, I was aware of my own agitation growing from her confusion of ideas and no plans to follow through. I confronted Ann with my confusion as how best to help her. Epstein (1979) counsels that the borderline patient can move with the therapist's "aggres-sion" in order to rebuild self-other boundaries. The borderline patient *can* tolerate confrontation of his actions, *not* interpretation of those actions. The borderline patient's psychological survival depends largely on the ego's use of primitive splitting and projective mechanisms. Hence, Epstein (1979) continues, the safe strategy for unconscious envy is to do interpretive work silently. Questions from the borderline patient are turned back to the patient with, "What are your thoughts about this?" The therapist's remarks are brief and reflective, aimed at getting the patient to produce his own under-standing and insight. Ann, speaking of "getting a plan ready," notes, "Mom always told me what to do." I respond, "Mom always backed you up." Ann, "Yeah, and now she's not here, Mom even made my doctor's appointments. . . . it's time I took charge."

The working alliance of Greenson's with a borderline patient is "pseudo," according to Kernberg (1975). Indeed, Epstein (1979) believes that to estab-lish a working alliance with the therapist becomes equal to submission. The therapist is cast in the role of the dangerous and powerful enemy. Hartocollis (1977) notes that the patient's rage will be directed full force at the therapist. The therapist may feel overwhelmed, helpless, exhausted and wish to ter-minate the case. Hartocollis (1977) continued that when the therapist's rejecting anger remains unconscious and unavailable to his scrutiny, the suicidal danger is greatest with the borderline patient. As June wore on, Ann's demands on my time had increased. I was exhausted from other pressures, and Ann added. I consulted a psychiatrist concerning taking Ann as a patient. Ann was unaware of the consultation. She now would hang onto the closing minutes of sessions. If I stood, attempting to close the session, Ann would respond, "You know, I can't make it through another week. I may just lose control of the car while I'm in the hills." A week later, she came to session on a Mo-ped, assuring me, "You know, it's a death trap. I'll probably get hit tonight."

Giovacchini (1979b) wrote at length about a borderline patient who spoke of suicide in session after session. "It finally dawned upon me that she just wanted me to be there and to keep my mouth shut . . . she just needed an audience, indicating that it was impossible to get others to listen to her without their becoming involved with the content of her attitudes and grievances. The analysis provides her with a setting where her right to feel as she does is not challenged. She needs this type of relationship to support her defenses" (p. 198).

Masterson (1976, p. 105) noted that the borderline patient is "exquisitely sensitive to the daily emotional state of the therapist." The patient listens to the tone of voice, watches the nonverbal gestures and body posture, and uses this information to seek out the therapist's personal Achilles' heel. Masterson (1976) felt that the borderline patient would provoke and manipulate the therapist in order to test his/her competence, to fulfill pathologic needs, and also to resist treatment. Indeed, the borderline patient wants personal information about the therapist, both for the emotional contact to act out the wish for reunion and as a resistance to therapy to provide ammunition for rage reactions. Ann's behavior around Mother's Day was an example of her need both to "be my child" and to destroy "my child's time" with me. Ann commented, "Must be nice to go to brunch with your kids . . . *My* Mom is dead!"

Masterson (1976) counsels that the therapist must be careful to maintain a consistent positive approach which is grounded in reality. To give ground to the patient is to reinforce the patient's projected emotions. The therapist maintains reality by cutting in, confronting and clarifying in order to prevent the therapy from stalemating. Masterson (1976) continues that the therapist must be flexible enough to switch from one therapeutic technique to another, almost instantly, as the patient's clinical state emerges and changes. Hence, the therapist will confront to set limits, but shift into working through when empathic responses are required. Since the borderline patient has poor object constancy, the therapist is careful to maintain consistency of environmental arrangements and hours in order to provide a framework for the patient's projections to be understood.

The end of June was coming and the time for my vacation. I would be out of the country two weeks. Masterson (1976) commented that the separation-individuation issue with borderline patients is paramount. In order "to feel good," the borderline patient has given up growth and development. Masterson noted, "The patient's feeling of infantile deprivation is so fundamental, so deep, and the feelings of abandonment so painful that he is willing in therapy, as he was as a child, to sacrifice *anything* to fulfill the fantasy of reunion while at the same time avoiding pain of abandonment" (1976, p. 109). The therapist is called upon to teach the patient "the appropriate attitude" by various limit-setting statements and by subjecting to investigations the patient's projections and wish for reunion fantasy.

Ann tried suicide threats, prolonging the hour and temper tantrums one week. The next session was followed by "Angel Ann" speaking of her mother's birthday, ". . . when you're at a beach somewhere" and her beginning college classes ". . . without your support." Sessions were added as the time for the break came nearer. I offered to call Ann collect at a predetermined time. I told her I would think of her during my absence. The last session before my vacation, Ann began the session, "It sucks, you know . . . your trip. I hate it! I hate you leaving me! But I know you need a break. Please, go and have fun . . . just send me a postcard, because I'm really going to miss you."

Will the yellow brick road lead to Emerald City for Ann . . . and will she ever find Kansas again? The wise writers of the guideposts predict that ultimately the borderline patient's destructiveness is drawn out by the therapist and deflected away from the patient's ego and diffused in process. Epstein (1979) stated that the therapist, by accepting the patient's view of her defective and imperfect self, gradually enables the patient's internal parent to become more tolerant of its child's deficiencies. The therapist's resistance to the patient's efforts to nullify her separate existence causes the patient's ego to come up against the therapist's ego boundaries repeatedly. In the process, the patient's boundaries of ego are strengthened. The ego is capable of tolerating frustration and of tolerating containing bad feelings without projecting them, or turning them against herself, or converting them into symptoms. Masterson (1976) states that if the therapist is a "real person" who is able to maintain a consistently positive supportive attitude, then the borderline patient will move toward individuation. For the borderline patient, it is the act of learning these insights himself that is as important as the insights.

Masterson (1976) was once asked why it took so long for therapy to show growth with a borderline. Ann is in her third year of therapy, including four and one half months of daily therapy in the hospital. Masterson answered, "Briefer forms of treatment do not work; when we find briefer forms of human development, then we will use briefer forms of therapy" (1976, p. 94). As the therapy continues, Masterson (1976) predicts that the individuation process will begin to flower. The borderline patient will bring to session new interests and will begin to practice styles of coping with reality. Epstein spoke of how this flowering occurs in analytical terms.

When the patient projects his or her bad self into the therapist, she provides him with an opportunity to break the internal vicious cycle. In this case, the therapist's interactions with the patient, which were shaped and sustained by her understanding of the countertransference data, ultimately subdued the hatred and suffering of the patient's internal parent and gained its acceptance of her deficient needy child, contributing thereby to the gradual growth of ego organization and strength. (1979, p. 385)

Postscript to the Case Study

Ann is a student at a local college. She has begun a vocational program. She proudly wears her work uniform to session. Ann's first tests in her college classes have been good scores. She tells me, "I showed them [tests] to Dad. . . . He didn't say anything. You know, I was hurt by his lack of response." Rapprochement has begun . . . tentatively.

HOMOSEXUALITY AND THE COUNTERTRANSFERENCE (Steve)[10]

Therapist's Report

Steve was 27 when I first started seeing him in psychoanalytically oriented psychotherapy one hour weekly. He is an intelligent, articulate, and well-motivated client. Steve identifies himself as "gay" and the focus of the sessions leading up to the events to be elaborated relate to the lack of empathy and understanding Steve had been subject to all his life, especially painful in his relationship with his father.

As our relationship progressed I was aware of an increasing discomfort I felt when I was with Steve. Since therapy had begun he had developed a love relationship with a man who by physical description (and perhaps also by sexual unavailability) strongly resembled both his father and myself. His (erotic and aggressive) descriptions and manner of relating to me had a mildly intrusive quality which I found myself backing away from.

I had been seeing Steve approximately nine months when I became aware of distancing feelings in myself which I worried were hindering my abilities to be helpful to Steve. During one of our sessions I became convinced that Steve was metaphorically communicating his awareness of my countertransference reactions (in an attempt to get me to resolve these feelings?). His communication consisted of talking about a friend who seemed intimidated by Steve and who appeared to have secrets that he could not share with Steve. Steve felt cut off and frustrated in his attempts to be close to this person.

In my belief that Steve was playing "therapist for the therapist," I interpreted Steve's material as relating to his relationship with me. I stated that he was feeling cut off and frustrated with me perhaps because he believed I was keeping a distance from him due to my discomfort with homosexuality. I apologized for the apparent empathic break, and indicated I would strive to ensure my feelings did not interfere with his therapy. I hoped in this manner to restore the therapeutic relationship.

This maneuver, however, had quite the opposite effect from that intended. Steve became self critical and wondered out loud how he had brought this

---

[10]The therapist is a man. See note on contributors, p. xix.

state of affairs in our relationship about. In this and the next few sessions his equilibrium seemed badly shaken. He related feeling immense anxiety, and he even reported difficulty functioning at his job. He became aware of murderous feelings toward me and worried that I might seek retribution for his rageful fantasies concerning me. He also worried that I was trying to punish him for some reason. It soon became evident that I, through my intervention, had repeated earlier insults. He recalled when he was in third grade his parents were called in for a conference with his teacher. The teacher expressed the opinion that Steve had a sexual identification confusion. Following this conference, Steve remembers his father becoming emotionally cold and even sadistic toward him. While there was much rage about his father's distancing, Steve wondered how he had caused his father to withdraw, experiencing this as punishment at the hands of his father. Further, Steve had been similarly unfortunate in later relationships with other men and felt similarly victimized yet somehow to blame for driving them (and me) away.

Reliving these memories caused Steve immense emotional turmoil. His anxiety was so overwhelming, and his feelings of disconnectedness from me so painful, that he brought up the question of terminating therapy. I empathized with the pain and agitation Steve was experiencing. I shared my own uncertainty about our relationship but told Steve that any talk of termination must be postponed at least until we worked through the present emotional crisis together. I pointed out that the current feelings were not new. Since they were recurring, however, we now had the opportunity to see and understand them better in the context of our relationship as he had been unable to do in previous relationships.

The change in Steve was startling. He reported feeling "connected" with me again. His intense emotions had subsided. He began feeling more in control of himself. Steve felt relieved when I postponed any discussion of termination until after our crisis was resolved. He also reported feeling appreciative that I had shared my own confusion about what was happening in our relationship. With the confidence that *together, we two* would find some way of working it through, Steve felt assured that I would not desert him and felt optimistic concerning being able to work through the painful memories that had been stirred up.

Author's Comments

Countertransference here proved the listening key as the therapist became aware of Steve's alienating intrusiveness. While the material on the surface appears to relate to an erotic encroachment from past yearning and rage at being rejected by his father, the patient's enactments in therapy do stem from a borderline personality organization and there is every indication that this replicated Scenario will ultimately be traced back to a symbiotic mode of relatedness with his mother. It is frequent in borderline male homosexuals to see this shift from symbiotic involvement with mother to father. It has been suggested in these instances mother's "seduction" mode (in this case also with rejection) may have been so strong the young child turned to father to escape engulfment but nonetheless carried the already established pattern into a quest for male (symbiotic) closeness which may not be so threatening. Another variation of a more general nature is that the child, lacking growth opportunities due to mother's intense symbiotic needs, turns his/her affection to the next available figure for support. In therapy the experiences and memories of later figures usually covers from immediate view the deepest traumatic circumstance which occurred with the primary caretaker.

Another issue which this vignette brings up is the frequency with which borderline patients (of whatever sex or sexual preference) eroticize the therapeutic relationship, usually to the distress of the therapist. The solution to this puzzle lies in the fact that the quest for merger experiences established in earliest childhood dominates mental functioning. The biological advent of sexuality in its two forms at ages 5 to 7 and again at puberty cannot be easily integrated by borderlines into more differentiated object relations. Rather, arousal can and does occur regularly in the context of any relationship which replicates the original symbiosis. That is, sexuality and symbiotic intimacy often come to mean the same thing except when "false self" formations inhibiting various forms of sexualization are strong. True psychological gender identity appears to develop later, in the context of differentiating object relations. This view accounts for why so many borderlines appear "confused" in either their own gender identity or their sexual preference.

The most important therapeutic feature illustrated in this vignette is "how to" and "how not to" employ information from the countertransference when working with borderline personality organization. Countertransference is bound to be evoked or provoked in therapy with borderlines. That is, the personal Symbiotic Scenario must have its hearing in the relationship so the therapist must be continually on the lookout for countertransference clues as to the nature of the mode of relatedness being expressed. Every empathic communication of countertransference information can pose formidable problems, especially since the patient has likely been "accused" all his/her life of just what the therapist has noticed. The critical variable in the use of countertransference findings is that they *be communicated from within the shared symbiotic relatedness mode.* "I-thou" statements usually constitute breaches in empathic contact, whereas "we," "us" and "togetherness" statements resonate with the merger experience. In this instance extreme agitation and murderous fantasies were produced by the therapist's mere mention of *his* discomfort in the relationship—an "I-thou" form of communication. When the therapist shifted to "*we* have something trouble-some which somehow *together, we* must solve," the patient's distress dramatically subsided. To the therapist, "symbiosis" may be a theoretical concept, but to the borderline patient psychological merger is the only known form of meaningful emotional existence. "Merger" means that the therapist must be prepared for emotional merger. In the process, countertransference reactions leading to therapist discomfort will naturally appear. Use of countertransference information must remain within the context of the merger experience, i.e., "*We* have something to study and work through together."

CONCLUSION: THE LISTENING PERSPECTIVE OF THE MERGER OBJECT

Many brief illustrations of countertransference reactions were contained in the previous chapter on "Scenarios." The present chapter has defined the crucial importance of Countertransference reactions as the "Royal Road" to an understanding of symbiotic merger experiences. Three examples have been provided of difficult moments in psychotherapy reported by colleagues in consultation. The interactions were marked by intense countertransference struggles which resulted in increased understanding of the complex engagements which the patients had continued to live out with the world around them.

The Listening Perspective of the Merger Object has been characterized as having five developmental perspectives: I. Human Symbiosis, II. Differentiation of Affects, III. Private World Development, IV. Mother-Child Adaptations and V. Ego and Self as Organizing Processes.

Commonly encountered treatment "Scenarios" have been defined which may serve as listening devices in attempting to grasp the unique aspects of the patternings of Self and Other experience. The necessary interactions or enactments with the therapist can be expected to result in countertransference reactions which can serve as ways of listening to persons who come to the consulting room with borderline personality organization.

These chapters stand as threshold conceptualizations as the door slowly opens which leads to systematic and reliable treatment technique with borderlines which can be submitted to widespread clinical validation.

V

Inconstancy: The Listening Perspective of the Part-Self and the Part-Object

12

The Organizing Personality

As one approaches the task of listening to the earliest levels of psychological development, the sense of tentativeness and uncertainty increases. This is partly because relatively little can be ascertained with confidence regarding the phenomenological experience of an infant in the first half year of life and also because in the history of psychoanalysis the later periods of childhood received the earliest attention by Freud and the Ego Psychologists. Recognizing the inadequacies of Freud's oedipal-incestuous listening stance for early developmental arrests, Melanie Klein became a pioneer in extending the psychoanalytic focus to the earliest eras of human development.

It is not within the scope of interest here to review the historical sequencing of thought of Klein, Segal, Guntrip, Balint, Fairbairn, and, more recently Bion, Grotstein, and Rosenfeld. But Klein and the so-called English School have paved the way for contemporary thinking in this most difficult area of psychoanalytic investigation. Kernberg in his recent book (1980a) reviews extensively from his point of view the contributions of the Kleinians in an area of inquiry which he refers to as *The Internal World and External Reality.*

Remaining within the context of this survey of psychoanalytic thought, the interest of this chapter will focus on listening in the broadest sense to free associations whether they be pursued in an introspective or interactive mode. The earliest experiences presumed available for psychoanalytic listening tend to involve body parts, organizational aspects and the more or less mechanical or unpredictable temporal-spatial relations of part aspects of self and others. Somatic delusions and sensory hallucinations are believed to form an important part of the earliest realities. "Part-Self" and "Part-Object" are terms which indicate that the dominant aspects of psychic life at the earliest period revolve around issues other than the psychological recognition of or establishment of complete or whole love objects. Traditional

Special thanks for help with this chapter go to Christopher Bollas, Carolyn Crawford, Cecile Dillon, Dee Fryling, James Grostein, Denise Ibsen, Timothy Maas, Dolly Platt, Linda Reed, and Mary E. Walker.

diagnostic categories here are, of course, the "schizophrenias" and the "affective (mood) reactions."

In the previously discussed "Listening Perspective of the Merger Object" it was maintained that five Developmental Points of View could enhance listening and responding to the introspective processes of persons who had attained a more or less satisfactory, special or exclusive relationship with a symbiotic partner. In those instances the symbiotic relationship is thought to protect the child from traumatic overstimulation emanating either from the inside (the affects predominantly) or from the outside (external reality factors). It was acknowledged that in most persons commonly referred to as "borderline," a sufficient organization of symbiotic experience prevailed to prevent *massive* flooding of affect or *massive* breakdown of reality appreciation. However, it was also noted that in many borderline individuals periodic collapses of functioning are observed in which either a major flooding of affect or faulty reality testing temporarily appears. Such episodes were seen predominantly as a response to some break or breach in a tie or bond experienced as symbiotically organizing. Borderline "breaks" with reality or "breakdowns" in affect control are typically shortlived, dissipating in the face of the reestablishment of some form of symbiotic contact. "The Listening Perspective of the Part-Self and Part-Object," in addition to being relevant to understanding introspective and interactive efforts of people with major arrests in the development of reality controls (schizophrenics) or affect controls (manics and depressives), is also helpful in listening to borderline individuals *during periods of collapsed or "psychotic-like" functioning.*

In formulating an idea of the most helpful attitude or Listening Perspective for this earliest period of psychological development, one is struck with the wide diversity of ideas and approaches as well as an array of somewhat radical treatment techniques. Persons with developmental arrests in the earliest months of life have historically been thought of as prophets, seers, mystics, witches, and, in more modern times, regarded as demented, insane, or highly creative. It would be a fascinating anthropological study in itself to note how cultures throughout time have responded to these early forms of psychic arrest. In the era of modern psychiatry various forms of physical stimulation, neurosurgery, electroshock, and chemotherapy have been utilized. Volumes have been written attempting to discern or to define the origin of "psychotic" manifestations. An attitude of maximum experimentation has characterized modern treatment efforts, which have been largely aimed at reducing the disturbing effects which these individuals periodically or regularly have on persons around them. Stated differently, the goal of most psychiatric therapies has been to reduce the "symptomatology" of the schizophrenias and the affective disorders. Various forms of "supportive" psychotherapy have been aimed at helping these persons adjust to a social environment which defines them as odd, peculiar, eccentric or downright crazy.

Freud very early in his studies believed psychoanalytic technique, as he had developed it, was limited in the treatment of these, what he called, "narcissistic neuroses." The mainstream of the psychoanalytic tradition has continued Freud's bias in this regard choosing generally to believe that psychotic reactions have a hereditary, biological, or physiological basis. The "psychoses" are responded to with strong (or radical) treatment approaches based on somatic therapies, socialization techniques and behavior modification. The general belief in the classical analytic community until quite recently has remained that the introspective or retrospective process which characterizes psychoanalysis is appropriate only for the treatment of psychoneuroses. This idea was challenged long ago by the Jungians, the Kleinians, and many others who have attempted a broader application of psychoanalytic principles than those envisioned by Freud and largely retained in the "classical school" of psychoanalysis.

Recently many psychoanalysts with more or less traditional outlooks have begun in their work to challenge the assumption that the psychoses do not represent psychological problems and therefore are not amenable to psychological treatment. In this country Harry Stack Sullivan, Freida Fromm-Reichmann, and others at Chestnut Lodge, as well as pioneering studies at the Menninger Foundation and the Reiss-Davis Child Study Center, to mention only a few, have made systematic attempts to apply psychoanalytic principles and thought to a study of these early developmental arrests commonly referred to as psychosis.

The present chapter cannot review the many studies in this area but rather will address the problem of formulating a viable Listening Perspective for present and future psychoanalytic work in this area. Most of the available formulations suffer from the same flaws that have plagued so many areas of psychoanalytic investigation: the continued use of scientific mechanistic language of the 19th century; the Hegelian and Newtonian outlooks; and a bias toward employing the structural concepts of Freud which serve well in the study of psychoneurosis. Most of these pioneering studies, as penetrating as their insights and as important as their findings and contributions have been, continue to make use of an outmoded philosophy of science and have continued to use terms and concepts taken from one universe of discourse somewhat uncritically in another. These comments are not indicated in a critical vein, but rather as a commentary on the historical development of the field of psychoanalysis. This chapter purports to demonstrate that enough studies, ideas, and formulations have now been provided so that a basic framework or Listening Perspective is beginning to be defined, even if its definition is presently in a nascent or outlined form.

INCONSTANCY: EARLY ORGANIZATIONAL
ASPECTS OF PERSONALITY

In constructing a Listening Perspective for the comprehension of earliest mental phenomena, it is difficult to refrain from applying concepts derived from observing later developmental experience. Notions such as "unconscious processes," "internal conflicts," "tension regulation," and "unification Scenarios" may be useful in considering definite consolidations of self and other experience. But prior to the basic unification of experience into a stable (borderline) personality organization, described variously by Mahler (1968) as Symbiosis, Little (1980) as Primary Unity, or Lichtenstein (1964) as Primary Identity, other possibilities must be considered.

There are many ways of considering earliest mental processes as well as questions about how far back into the biological origins of a human being "mind" can or might be traced. The dimension of self-other relatedness at its most rudimentary level can provide a viable basis for clinical listening. Kernberg (1976), extending Glover's (1932) classic formulation of "ego nuclei," defines the basic building blocks of personality as early "ego states" comprised of a representation (image or memory) of Self and a representation (image or memory) of an Other with an accompanying (linking) affect. While this formulation does not increase the clarity of what "ego states" might mean experientially, the term "ego states" serves to describe a pattern, memory or image which results when the psychic system encounters some aspect of the nurturing environment in a pleasurable or painful manner. Many prefer here to speak of "part-self" and "part-object" experiences. Laing (1960) speaks of many "partial systems" activated at different moments in time which "do not show a mutual awareness of each other." Kernberg (1976) characterizes these unintegrated partial systems as "nonmetabolized" ego states. Gedo (1979a) refers to the "self system" as the central psychic process running throughout development. At the lower end of epigenetic development he refers to sensorimotor processes which are in constant danger of overstimulation (traumatization). Organization of sensorimotor experience is accomplished through the environmental processes referred to as "pacification" (Goldberg and Gedo, 1971).

Attentive parents of infants can be seen waiting patiently for some bodily aspect of the child to be oriented in such a way that contact (brief recognition, connection or interaction) is possible. The early months of infant care can be exhausting since the parent has to do practically all the work in maintaining equilibrium through contact (pacification) which provides protection from traumatic overstimulation. The intense parental strain of constant vigilance gradually subsides as the process of mutual cueing develops which permits delays and serves to modulate extremes of overstimulation in intensity as well as frequency. During this period, Winnicott (1952) refers to the early development of a basic sense of self as needs become integrated in connection with the nurturant other. He describes the development of the "false self" as the infant *conforms* to the demands of the nurturing other. The false self is based on accommodation to the other's needs as well as renunciation (or non expression within the relationship) of genuine needs of the infant. Children without an adequately accommodating other attempt to achieve a sense of continuity and organization of the early self system through any means available, producing striking behavior patterns of self mutilation, hallucinatory creations, hypochondriacal complaints and exaggerated affect states.

Regardless of the way one chooses to conceptualize early mental life, it is clear that the infant is constantly *extending* his/her domain and in the process is organizing and transforming. Indeed, the earliest experience of others is in processes of early transformation (Bollas 1979). To the extent a person may not have been able to negotiate a self-other symbiotic connection (unification), he/she may remain in a relatively unorganized state or develop an extensive false self system which may or may not serve well in subsequent adaptations to environmental demands.

These developmental considerations define the basic listening task with (presymbiotic) "organizing personalities." The therapist, like the parent, must patiently wait *until the person is momentarily oriented for contact.* Contact is usually fleeting and, *in essence non-verbal* (though words and sounds may constitute the medium of contact). The parent waits until the eyes (or other parts) become available for contact. Then comes the smile, laugh or warm squeeze which forces attention on (and reinforces?) the organizing or transformational contact. The infant begins a sucking motion and soon a breast is properly placed. The infant shows wonderment or surprise when his hand disappears from his field of vision. The alert parent makes contact in restoring the lost hand with warm caresses and understanding words. The wise mother, just as the wise therapist, is alert and attentive but saves her energy for the moment that counts—the moment of orientation when the infant/patient *can be met in his/her own extension.*

The term "psychotic," so often applied to this level of psychic organization, has been conspicuously missing from discussions in this book. Aside from the stigma attached to the word, it seems a term best reserved to describe an active state of bizarre confusion or pervasive affective disturbance. The "Organizing Personality" or "Personality in Organization" being described here may or may not be subject to psychotic episodes of either brief or prolonged duration. Conversely, not all psychotic episodes emanate from this level of development. Persons with Borderline Personality Organization may well have psychotic episodes characterized by faulty reality appreciation and/or defective affect regulation. Such episodes can generally be traced to some loss of a sense of (symbiotic) connectedness and usually pass away shortly when a sense of connection or relatedness in some form can be re-established. It is also well known that under special circumstances persons with Narcissistic and Neurotic Personality Organization may also display psychotic manifestations. More importantly, terms such as "psychotic," "schizophrenic," and "manic-depressive" are omitted from current consideration because they do not focus or describe critical aspects of the listening situation. The traditional "symptom constellations" describe well known clinical pictures which at this point in time are not always so clear cut or florid due to modern chemical and somatic therapies. The traditional clinical pictures are primarily descriptive. The dynamics usually described are formulated in terms and concepts largely borrowed from an understanding of more complex levels of psychic organization and applied to these phenomena of an essentially different (less well developed) order. From a listening standpoint, for example, the crucial aspects of "paranoid schizophrenia" cannot be understood simply through the analysis of the symbolic content of the delusional system, the so-called "defenses" such as denial and projection, or various vicissitudes of the "instincts." The listener would do better to study points of possible contact with the person, that is, to begin *to listen for moments in which the person can be met (contacted).* The traditionally defined symptoms and syndromes of psychosis can be conceptualized as faulty or abortive attempts to organize basic experience. The "good" social adaptations of these same persons usually represent elaborate development of the false self. As such, neither the psychotic syndrome *per se* nor the false self represent points of potential contact. Both are "red herrings." Likewise, the rich and fascinating content with extensive affective processes of the psychoses do not represent potential points of exchange or transformational experience. The value of studying these for "symbolic meaning" as one might in a neurosis is extremely limited and likely to be misleading. For example, the study of the "influencing machine" (Tausk 1919) may acquaint one with available fantasies and verbalizations and is even likely to show how the patient experiences various aspects of body and self. But a symbolic analysis of the influencing machine alone cannot be expected to lead to further psychic development. In more developed states, established psychic patterns need to be broken down (i.e., analyzed). But in pre-symbiotic states, the road to growth is through *building up experiences of connection* and, through new connection, new organizations of various "ego nuclei," "ego states," or "partial self systems."

Empathy with early processes and states is still seen as the central observational tool of the psychoanalyst—but empathy with what? A developmental listening approach to understanding "Organizing Personalities" would focus attention on the central needs of earliest infancy (protection and pacification in the sensory and motor spheres) while neglecting or setting aside from consideration many false self developments as well as many disturbing "symptoms."

The sections which follow bring together ideas from several sources which serve as orienting beacons to guide the listening process. These ideas may help the listener maintain an attitude of patient availability, while studying clinical content for clues about potential points of contact. The study of the earliest organizing aspects of personality remains the great frontier of psychoanalysis.

KAFKA: SPOKESMAN FOR
THE ORGANIZING PERSONALITY

The literary genius of Franz Kafka lies in his capacity to portray what he himself called "my dreamlike inner life" (Kafka 1914 in 1979, p. xi). One becomes aware in reading Kafka that his characters and situations are forever changing and elusive in their essence. Attempts are constantly renewed to organize perceptions and intentions and to maintain a sensible hold on reality. In psychological terms, one might refer to these repeated mini-organizations of people and situations as "ego nuclei" or "islands of mental organization" which are creatively developed throughout his work. A clinician wishing to grasp the subjective position of people developmentally arrested at a pre-symbiotic level of organizing processes of personality will find a study of Kafka enlightening.

While there are constant, fleeting manic-depressive and paranoid references in the development of character, Kafka's descriptions basically portray the purest forms of organizing experience without the presence of psychotic elaboration. The exception to this is "The Burrow," a short story written only months before his death at age forty, following a six year struggle with tuberculosis. This story, a first person narrative told by a large burrowing animal, depicts with clarity the frantic attempt to find safety in his "Castle Keep," the heart of his enormous burrow which he has laden with huge stores of food. Through time, as his fears of various possible but imagined enemies mount, his defensive efforts at constructing an even more invincible secret burrow succumb to a persistent whistling in his ears. He systematically searches for the noise, thinking at first it is only air rushing through his many chambers. Explanation after explanation is sought as he nearly destroys his burrow searching. The evidence points toward the noise as not coming from without. He even at one time acknowledges the likelihood that the whistling originates from the blood rushing in his inner ear. But the furry narrator then confesses the silent belief that he has held all along: the noise is coming from a monstrous beast burrowing near and perhaps toward him. In his fear he cannot eat; but when he thinks the noise has stopped he eats voraciously, only to spit up when the noise resumes. In the end he is reduced to a frantic, ineffective helplessness, and is unable to discern any change in what he has concluded to be an encompassing ominous presence. While one might understand this story as a symbolic representation of encroaching tuberculosis or as manic-depressive reaction to his approaching death, Kafka never engaged in symbolic expression of that sort, explicitly striving to *project* inner realities into external circumstances and characters.

There are sufficient references to auditory hallucinations, out-of-the-body experience, visual hallucinations, food hoarding, anorexia, bulimia and finally to the crystallization of a paranoid object to warrant calling this story a clearcut expression of psychotic experience. While fleeting mention of these kinds of experiences abound in Kafka's earlier works—especially many puzzling auditory images—only here does he describe in clear, vivid detail the construction of paranoia. "The Burrow" stands as a most interesting account which should be of interest to those wishing to understand the formations of paranoia.

A central theme running throughout Kafka's work is guilt—not "oedipal" guilt in which one feels bad for competitive, hurtful wishes or deeds toward someone that one loves—but basic, primal guilt. Kafka's guilt is for *simply being alive*, for having needs that must be met by someone, for wanting more than is in one's own resources, more than one's parents had to offer. And guilt for not being able to help one's fragmenting parents be better parents. In *The Trial* (1914 in 1937) he searches fruitlessly for what he is guilty of, and in the end accepts the knife without protest—his crime is being alive. In Kafka's last major work, *The Castle* (1922 in 1926), he is guilty for desiring recognition and pushing for individual identity. The Castle, to which it appears he was summoned, "hidden, veiled in mist and darkness," is unapproachable and elusive to the Land Surveyor. The desperate search for recognition and a rightful role in the world can be read variously as a search for organizing experiences with mother, father, or other frustrating aspects of the outer world. But more importantly, it seems to stand as a persistent personal search for successful negotiation with one's own personality organization and the frustrations provided by a series of maternal and paternal figures whom he believes can help him but who ultimately fail him.

The appeal of Kafka's work, though disturbing to many, may be his treatment of the universal experience of repeated organizational attempts native to the process of early personality building. In rawest developmental form, this process consists of attempts to organize the sensorimotor systems around various experiences with available and empathic parental figures. Kafka dwells on basic infantile guilt for having needs of parents who are limited in what they can give and the frustrating search for a core identity through symbiotic connection (i.e., being accepted by the Castle) and definition of personal identity boundaries (i.e., "land surveying").

Kafka's harsh indictment in "Letter to his Father" (1919 in 1979), accuses his father of self preoccupation such that the growing needs of a young boy for understanding and connection could not be attended to properly. But in the imagined rejoinder from his father, blame is shifted back on the boy for being an unreceptive child, "overly clever and overly affectionate," unwilling (or unable) to assume his share of the responsibility for the faulty relationship.

Kafka's deathbed story, "Josephine the Singer, or the Mouse Folk" (1924 in 1979) appears to represent simultaneously a final, compassionate understanding (forgiveness?) of his mother's preoccupation with herself as well as an insightful comprehension of himself and his relation to literary art. Mice folk do not sing nor even enjoy music, but nonetheless Josephine set herself up as a dramatic prima donna who, despite danger to the mouse folk, from time to time would arise and demand a large attentive audience as she sang. True, the folk were captivated by her, but, the narrator asks, "Was it really singing she did, and how could one explain the devoted crowds at her command?" Josephine sought "unconditional devotion" and was permitted by the people latitude even beyond the established laws in her many demands. The furry narrator conjectures that the people see her as a small, frail creature needing protection and that they feel obligated because she is entrusted to their care. The people look after Josephine "much as a father takes into his care" a child whose "little hand is stretched out to him." But Josephine believes it is *she* who protects the people. When in political or economic trouble or whenever there is bad news she rises up at once to sing, stretching her neck "to see over the heads of her flock like a shepherd before a thunderstorm." Through her singing, the people are permitted withdrawal into dreaming, momentarily to regain something of the lost happiness of earliest childhood which "can never be found again." The people "marvel helplessly at her art" and "feel themselves unworthy of it."

The tragic flaw which develops in the relationship between Josephine and the mouse people is that Josephine feels she occupies a special place and should not be obliged to participate in the ordinary sustaining work of the community! But though the mouse people are devoted to her, they here show "their cold, judicious aspect" in refusing her request. The narrator says it is as though a man had been giving in to her steadily while all the time nursing the wild desire to someday end all his submissiveness. A natural end to his sacrifices for her would come, and with it the inevitably curt refusal. Josephine began deliberately flawing her performances in hopes of gaining acquiescence to her petitions. First she cut her grace notes short. Then she claimed to have injured her foot while working. Then she pleaded fatigue, that she was not in the mood for singing, or that she was feeling faint. She would be glad to oblige but she simply could not. Finally, Josephine is carried by her supporters to the selected spot where she is to sing—only to burst into tears. She attempts to rise and sing but cannot. She "breaks down" in front of "everyone's eyes." She does at last sing, indeed with unusual feeling. As she leaves, she refuses all help from supporters, measuring the crowd with cold eyes. Shortly Josephine disappears—just at the time when she is supposed to sing. Many devote themselves to the search; but she has vanished, driven on by her "sad destiny." Of her own accord she abandoned her position and the power which she had attained over the crowd. The narrator asks how she ever managed to have such power since, after all, "she knows so little about these hearts of ours." In the crucial twist of Kafka's ending, the people *"who can only bestow gifts and not receive them"* continue on their way. Josephine's singing becomes a memory lost in the numberless throng of folk heroes. Ironically, Kafka concludes with Josephine rising "to the height of redemption" through being forgotten.

Franz Kafka's work stands not only as a phenomenological statement of the basic organizing activities and processes of personality but extends to an explication of the crucial role of the empathic, connecting, nurturing other in making possible (or not possible) an interpersonal organization and solidification of early sensorimotor experience. The so-called ego nuclei or islands of early development can be thought of as organizing under the influence of an available, empathic, connecting parental caretaker. Through fostering a mutual cueing process, the caretaker can pull the infant's mental processes into symbiotic organization; thus avoiding false, abortive, or secret organizations represented by such constellations as mania, depression, and paranoia. Since Kafka maintained there was not a dividing line between his personal experience and the literature he created, much of what he wrote may stand as an indictment of his own parents for being so preoccupied with their personality needs that they could not help him further to organize his own personality.

But whether Kafka himself was arrested at the earliest stages of mental organization and was able to avoid frank psychotic manifestation through extensive literary efforts or whether he simply had unusual access to these most basic formations of personality, his work stands as an unparalleled penetration into the deepest recesses of the human mind. An appreciation of Kafka's obsessive reworking of sensorimotor experience with many parental figures in such elusive, mysterious, contradictory, disparate and dissociated images, contributes richly and profoundly to the establishment of a Listening Perspective for understanding personalities arrested in the basic organizing processes.

FREUD'S FIRST MODEL OF THE MIND

As a general backdrop for the Listening Perspective of the Part-Self and Part-Object, it seems useful to review several of Freud's earliest ideas. Parallel to Breuer and Freud's *Studies on Hysteria* (1895), Freud was attempting to formulate a theory on dreams, which crystallized as a result of his dream of "Irma's injection" on July 24, 1895. By September of that year Freud wrote the first part of his "Project For a Scientific Psychology" which represented his earliest attempt to come to grips with problems raised by his study of dreams and dreaming. "The Project" gave a clear indication of one of Freud's most momentous creations; the distinction between two different modes of mental functioning, "primary" and "secondary" process. During the following year (1896) Freud wrote what he considered to be the most important contribution of his lifetime, *The Interpretation of Dreams* (1900), which he set aside and temporarily refrained from publishing because he felt it contained a major gap in the psychological theory. By May 1899, Freud began writing on the book again, adding the first chapter, which was a review of the literature. Toward the end of the summer he completed the last psychological chapter, the now well known Chapter 7, Freud's first major theoretical treatise.

In discussing "psychical locality" and the "mental apparatus" Freud states, ". . . I shall carefully avoid the temptation to determine psychical locality in any anatomical fashion" (p. 574). In a firm determination to keep his theory on psychological ground, Freud continued:

> I propose simply to follow the suggestion that we should picture the instrument which carries out our mental functions as resembling a compound microscope or a photographic apparatus or something of the kind. On that basis, psychical locality will correspond to a point inside the apparatus at which one of the preliminary stages of an image comes into being. In the microscope and telescope, as we know, these occur in part at ideal points, regions in which no tangible component of the apparatus is situated. I see no necessity to apologize for the imperfections of this or any similar imagery. Analogies of this kind are only intended to assist us in our attempt to make the complications of mental functioning intelligible by dissecting the function and assigning it different constituents to different component parts of the apparatus. (p. 575)

Continuing, Freud stated, "We are justified, in my view, in giving free rein to our speculations so long as we retain the coolness of our judgment and do not mistake the scaffolding for the building" (p. 575).

> Accordingly we will picture the mental apparatus as a compound instrument, to the components of which we will give the name of "agencies," or (for the sake of greater clarity) "systems." It is to be anticipated, in the next place, that these systems may perhaps stand in a regular spatial relation to one another, in the same kind of way in which the various systems of lenses of a telescope are arranged behind one another. (p. 575)

After stating that these psychical agencies or systems need not literally be arranged in a spatial order according to the telescopic metaphor but perhaps according to other orders *such as a particular temporal sequence,* Freud goes on to speak of components of the apparatus as "ψ-systems." Freud continues, "The first thing that strikes us is that this apparatus, compounded of the ψ-system, has a sense of direction. All our psychical activity starts from stimuli (whether internal or external) and ends in innervations" (p. 576). (Freud uses "innervation" generally to mean the transmission of energy to an efferent system to indicate a process tending toward discharge.) (See Fig. 3.)

> Accordingly, we shall ascribe a sensory and a motor end to the apparatus. At the sensory end there lies a system which receives perceptions; at the motor end there lies another, which opens the gateway to motor activity. Psychical processes advance in general from the perceptual end to the motor end. (p. 576)

As Freud developed the idea of perceptions entering the system, he followed with the notion of various memory traces leading to the development of a "Mnemic system" (p. 577) as shown in Figure 4.

The basic image of a reflex arc has been modified to include the effects of the permanent acquisition of memory traces. The impact from incoming perceptions to outgoing motor activity becomes affected by memory traces in much the same way as the telescope analogy would have incoming images affected by means of lenses. In continuing his discussion drawing upon evidence from dreaming, Freud ventures:

> . . . the hypothesis of there being two psychical agencies, one of which submitted the activity of the other to a criticism which involved its (the activity) exclusion from consciousness. The critical agency, we concluded, stands in a closer relation to consciousness than the agency criticized: it stands like a screen between the latter and consciousness. (p. 579)

Freud then locates this psychical system at the motor end of the apparatus and labels it "the preconscious . . . to indicate that the excitatory processes occurring in it can enter consciousness without further impediment pro-

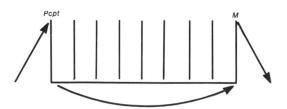

Figure 3 / Schematic Picture of the Psychical Apparatus

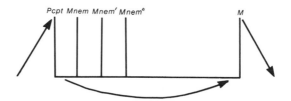

Figure 4 / Freud's Mnemic System

vided that certain other conditions are fulfilled" (p. 579). Freud then describes the system which lies behind the preconscious as "the unconscious . . . because it has no access to consciousness *except via the preconscious*, in passing through which its excitatory process is obliged to submit to modifications" (p. 580). (See Fig. 5.)

If Freud's metaphor of the psychic apparatus as reflex arc had been developed only this far, it would still be of interest in that it gives an image of a beginning point of mental development, a middle, and an end. Earliest psychological development might be characterized as an undifferentiated reflex arc leading more or less directly from perception to motor discharge. An intermediate stage would seem to involve the filtering of psychic life through a series of memories or memory traces. And finally the end point of psychic development is conceived in which the reflex arc is considerably modified by the existence of preconscious and, later, unconscious modes of thought.

In using this reflex arc model of the mental apparatus, Freud explained dream formation and the censorship which exists between the two systems, unconscious and preconscious. In a curious twist Freud explained hallucinatory dreams by saying that:

The excitation moves in a *backward* direction. Instead of being transmitted towards the *motor* end of the apparatus it moves towards the *sensory* end and finally reaches the perceptual system. If we describe as "progressive" the direction

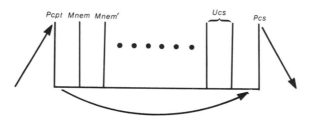

Figure 5 / Progressive Development of the Reflex Arc Model

taken by psychical processes arising from the unconscious during waking life, then we may speak of dreams as having a "regressive character." (p. 581)[1]

Freud further develops his idea of dreams being a "regressive" process in which complex ideational acts or thoughts move "backwards" toward the raw material of memory traces underlying them. It is in this way that the dream thoughts become comprehensible. He further develops this "regressive" idea to account for a variety of delusions and hallucinations, mental processes in which *the systems unconscious and preconscious cannot be seen as monitoring, censoring, or forming more complex mental activities in deference to images, hallucinations, and delusions which* arise from the perceptual system!

The importance of this reflex arc metaphor for present purposes is to indicate that Freud conceptualized mental growth as a series of developmental phases toward the increasing differentiation of the mental apparatus until the formation of the systems preconscious and unconscious can sensibly be inferred. This topographic conceptualization of psychic organization (the concepts of conscious, preconscious and unconscious) has been thought of as characterizing the *advanced* psychological development characteristic of neurosis. In the Listening Perspective pertaining to the "oedipal or constant object," the ideas of unconscious and preconscious remain viable. However, as has already been seen, in earlier developmental phases the Listening Perspectives are based on processes of dissociation or so-called "vertical splitting" of mental content without the concepts of preconscious or unconscious (horizontal splitting) being seen as crucial in the systematic observation of introspective efforts. Freud's earliest intermediate models (Figures 3 and 4) might best be thought of as characterizing the status of the mental apparatus during preoedipal developmental periods.[2] Thus, presumably without the interference of the dynamic unconscious (which is only developed or crystalized later), earliest psychic development can be thought of more concretely as a series of "reflexive" processes which may pass progressively or regressively into and out of the psychic apparatus freely. This model of the early apparatus provides the basis for conceptualizing the Listening Perspective of the Part-Self and Part-Object. Phenomenologically, the world of the infant might be thought of as vascillating more or less freely ("oceanically") from perceptions to consciousness (attention) and regressively from consciousness toward sensory-hallucinatory experiences.

---

[1] In these passages describing the reflex arc model, the word "regressive" is used simply to mean backward direction and must not be confused with Freud's later use of "regression" in describing psychodynamics.

[2] The exception to this would be the beginnings of dynamic unconsciousness in the shame-filled disavowal of narcissistic selfobject needs, i.e., what Kohut (1971) calls resistances to the narcissistic transferences which he sees as walled off (vertical split) rather than repressed.

Thus, within this free ebb and flow of the reflex arc metaphor, an infant would be presumed to experience a wide range of stimulation, attention, and hallucinatory images with limited development of memory traces or mnemic system. Phenomenological experiences of whole love objects would *not* seem necessary to postulate in the formulation of a Listening Perspective for observing presymbiotic organizing personalities.

In returning to Freud's original conceptualizations, it seems clear that all formulations regarding the systems preconscious and unconscious refer to relatively later developmental phases. Alternating states of consciousness in early psychic development were conceptualized by Freud as reversible (i.e., "progressive" and "regressive") *reflexive* processes. In attempting to build a Listening Perspective for the earliest developmental phases the *available introspective material would be expected to be comprised of passing reflexive processes*. Gearing up to listen to relatively reflexive states of consciousness has the advantage of not entailing making "irrefutable assumptions" about the earliest mental states (Schafer 1976). For example, one might frequently hear of experiences of "influencing machines" (Tausk 1919) but would recognize this as *content* by which the person seeks to express his ongoing mental experiences. Expressions of the earliest experiences of part-selves and part-objects could be expected to reflect an almost kaleidoscopic set of inner and outer realities passing reflexively in a subjective (often delusional and hallucinatory) manner that comes to the attention of the therapist.

SEARLES' NONHUMAN ENVIRONMENT

Searles, in his remarkable monograph, *The Nonhuman Environment* (1960), points out that most of the effort in psychiatry and psychoanalysis to date has been directed at understanding the individual's relationship to intrapsychic processes and to the interpersonal, sociological-anthropological aspects of functioning. Searles says that relatively little has been done within the field to broaden the appreciation of man's relationships with his nonhuman environment (pp. 22–23). He dwells extensively on the infant's subjective oneness with his nonhuman environment (pp. 29ff.), citing many examples from the developmental psychology of Heinz Werner (1940, 1948) in which the nonhuman has been shown to permeate the imagery of humans. Searles points out anxiety which dates back to infancy when the world seemed comprised largely or wholly of "chaotically uncontrollable nonhuman elements" (p. 39). He feels anxiety about loss of human contact may also relate to "unconscious memory traces of our experience with losing a non-human environment which had been sensed, heretofore, as a harmonious extension of our world-embracing self" (p. 39). Primitive mental states are characterized by a pervasive sense of the nonhuman. The classic paper of Tausk (1919) focused on the experience of the external world as "the influencing machine." Other papers by Hanns Sachs (1933), Lizabeth Sachs (1957), Ekstein (1954), Bornstein (1949), and Rank and MacNaughton (1950) describe patients who:

> (a) either delusionally experience fantasied machines by which they are influenced or which the patients themselves can wield in a subjectively grandiose way; (b) or who identify with various machines in their environment. In each instance, the machine in question, whether real or fantasy, is described by the writer as serving—by reason of the symbolic meaning with which it is invested—a defensive function in the patient's ego functioning. (Searles, 1960, p. 73)

The experience of influence coming from without additionally has its precedent in historical and anthropological data.

In attempting to understand some of these observations, Searles pointed out that the nonhuman environment makes important contributions to normal childhood development. The nonhuman environment provides a significant contribution to the child's "emotional security, his sense of stability and continuity of experience, and his developing sense of personal identity" (p. 80). The nonhuman environment is also "in general more simple and stable and manipulable than the human environment, [and] provides him with a kind of practice ground in which he can develop capacities which will be useful to him in his interpersonal relationships" (p. 85). The nonhuman environment further:

> . . . offers release from the tensions, and satisfaction for the hungers which arise in this life among other human beings. He (the child) is often able to find in it peace, stability and companionship at times when his interpersonal relationships are filled with anxiety and loneliness; and he can often vent on it various feelings which he cannot release toward a human being in his environment. (p. 87)

Searles further points out that in the nonhuman environment "the child can become aware of his own capabilities (referring here to the physical strength and dexterity, ingenuity and various intellectual abilities) and of the limitations upon those capabilities" (p. 88). In adolescence, the mature person can become "committed to his status as a human being" (p. 89).

Searles holds that the mature person's attitude toward his nonhuman environment can be expressed in one word: "relatedness." By relatedness he means:

> . . . a sense of intimate kinship, a psychological concomitant to the structural kinship which . . . exists between man and the various ingredients of his nonhuman environment . . . as well as kinship with respect to the evolutionary history of mankind and the biological fate of the individual human being. (p. 101)

Searles feels that:

> Although the mature person does not shield himself from experiencing a sense of real and immediate kinship to, for example, a dog or a tree or an inanimate object, he does not shield himself either from the awareness that he is inescapably human. He does not relinquish his ego boundaries, he is not deluded into the conviction that he can be in union with nonhuman elements of Nature or with any other ingredients of the nonhuman environment. He knows that he is irrevocably, irreversibly a member of the human species, and can rejoice as well as despair in this knowledge of his unique humanness. In this regard then, the sense of relatedness which the mature person experiences toward the nonhuman environment is qualitatively different from mystical experience. (p. 102)

In discussing difficulties which certain people (particularly schizophrenics) experience with the nonhuman environment, Searles points out the *confusion* which is frequently felt between the self and the nonhuman environment.

> This confusion in the chronologically adult patient may be regarded as a testimony both to (a) some degree of failure to achieve at the normal time, in infancy, as clear-cut and profound differentiation of the self from the total environment as is achieved by the healthy infant; and (b) the depth of present-day regression, coming as a result of the impact of very intense anxiety and involving the reactivation of this mode of experiencing one's existence as being chaotically undifferentiated, this mode which is presumably characteristic of all infants, even normal infants, at a very early phase of development. (pp. 143–144)

In a thorough discussion of the subject, Searles develops the ideas of (a) anxiety lest one become, or be revealed as, nonhuman; (b) the experiencing of parts of oneself as being nonhuman; (c) the desire to be nonhuman as a defense against various feeling states; (d) the desire to become nonhuman as a function of the striving toward maturity via "phylogenetic regression"; and (e) reacting to other persons as being nonhuman.

Searles takes the view that psychotherapy and psychoanalytic work with primitive mental states permit the patient a "regression" to the level of experiencing the nonhuman environment and its potential influence so that development may proceed. Furthermore, his monograph makes clear that to simply consider the psychotic's experience in terms of psychiatric symptomatology or mental content is inadequate for establishing empathic contact with these individuals. He believes *the entire world of experience in which the nonhuman plays a large part must be grasped empathically by the therapist before growth resumes its course.*

Ekstein in a paper entitled "The Space Child's Time Machine" (1954), recounts an experience with a disturbed boy over a three-year period prior to his turning 12 years of age. The boy's progress is discussed in terms of a series of fantasies about a time machine. In the early phases the time machine was experienced as a weird contraption quite different from ordinary human experience. Later, there was a transformation to a lovely little house with colorful doors and windows. The child asked, "Does that mean I'm getting better now that I'm building things that look like houses even if they are not?" As the therapy progressed, the time machine no longer took this child millions of years back but only a few years. "He did not speak about the past in archeological and historical terms, but the past had now assumed a personal significance. It was the past in his own life."

Ekstein's books and papers (1954, 1980) concerning his work with schizophrenic children are full of fascinating examples in which various mechanical nonhuman experiences slowly evolve in time and space toward the world of human engagement.

It is difficult to imagine that psychotherapy or psychoanalysis can be conducted with individuals having such early developmental arrests without the therapist having a full appreciation of the various roles and influences of the nonhuman. Searles, in many of his later papers (see his collection, *Countertransference*, 1979) demonstrates the variety of ways patients with early developmental arrests come to experience him and his influence in the psychotherapeutic situation. He furthermore describes extensively many of his own countertransference reactions to being experienced as nonhuman.

Searles outlines several considerations in his theoretical approach to the treatment of schizophrenic patients (1979).

1. The therapist's own early modes of experience are not permanently done away with in his own analysis but simply become more accessible.

2. There is always a reality basis for the patient's delusions.

3. The patient can only reindividuate following the establishment of a therapeutic symbiosis in which the analyst must participate to a feeling degree.

4. The patient's strivings toward the analyst, including guilt and grief about having failed his fragmented mother so that she could be a whole and fulfilled mother to him are fundamental to the symbiotic phase.

5. The therapeutic symbiosis functions to humanize the patient who has failed to develop a full human identity.

Searles continues:

. . . my approach focuses . . . upon the countertransference realm, in the broadest sense of that term, as being of the greatest and most reliable research and therapeutic value. This focus is not intended as a means of providing narcissistic gratification to the analyst-researcher; quite to the contrary, his personality and especially his sense of identity is found, in one practitioner after another, to be a most sensitive and reliably informative scientific instrument providing data as to what is transpiring, often in areas not verbally articulable by the patient in the treatment situation. (pp. 375–376)

In another paper on "Transitional Phenomena and the Therapeutic Symbiosis" (1979), Searles elaborates his 1958 term "therapeutic symbiosis." This mode of patient-analyst relatedness makes possible new growth.

The individuation which he undergoes more successfully this time in the context of the transference relationship is in a real sense mutual, in that the analyst, too, having participated with the patient in the therapeutic symbiosis, emerges with a renewed individuality which has been enriched and deepened by this experience. (p. 504)

Thus Searles focuses on the increased ego integration not only of the patient but also of the analyst. He comments on how frequently the analyst relates to the patient's symptoms as the therapist's "allies" and instances in which symptoms are experienced as "transitional objects." He points out how difficult it is for the therapist to endure various "nonhuman" transference roles. In discussing Modell's (1970) elaboration of Winnicott's (1953) concept of transitional object, Searles feels that his own concept of "therapeutic symbiosis" is fully consonant with what has been described as the transitional object form of transference relationship with the analyst. He indicates that during the "therapeutic symbiosis" phase of the work, it is also true that the analyst manifests a transitional object relatedness with the patient. Searles concludes:

I believe that in order for any effective transference analysis to occur . . . the analyst must have come to accept at least a transitional-object degree—if not more deeply symbiotic degree—of relatedness with the particular transference image or precept, which is holding sway presently in the analysis. (p. 576)

Summary

While these brief comments hardly do justice to the richness of Searles's ideas, they serve to illustrate that in the more primitive levels of developmental arrest two features are important to recognize. One, that the images, percepts, and experiences of presymbiotically arrested persons are likely to contain a preponderance of nonhuman, impersonal, or mechanical imagery which must be responded to empathically in order to effect contact. Two, that although the therapist brings a certain perspective on reality and the patient brings another perspective on reality, before the therapy can progress the therapist must be able to engage deeply in a therapeutic relationship in which the patient's images can be understood. Searles conceptualizes this exchange as a "therapeutic symbiosis" and likens it to a transitional object (Winnicott 1953) experience on both sides in which *the symptomatology* becomes a transitional object for both patient and therapist. This deep personal involvement on the part of the analyst appears required before the appropriate regression to nonhuman experiences can take place, the regression from which growth will develop later. These two points, i.e., the preponderance of nonhuman imagery and the requirement of a therapeutic symbiosis, are the hallmark of Searles's approach to understanding psychotic states and therapeutic growth.[3]

GIOVACCHINI'S "PRIMITIVE MENTAL STATES"

While Searles focuses on aspects of the interactional exchange in terms of experiences of the nonhuman environment and the necessity for forming a therapeutic symbiosis, Peter Giovacchini remains more traditional in his terminology. Nevertheless, he must respond to the same problem outlined by Searles, namely: in the treatment of "primitive mental states" interactional or interpersonal dimensions take center stage rather than the intrapsychic repetitions which characterize more advanced psychic development. Giovacchini, in a series of important books and papers (1964, 1972, 1975, 1979a, and 1979b) represents a style of thinking and conceptualizing which many analysts have adopted in attempting to describe their work with borderline, schizophrenic and affective states. Giovacchini's (1979a) basic position is that most analysts do feel uncomfortable when dealing with psychotic states. Along with Bettleheim (1974), Giovacchini acknowledges that the therapeutic productions of pre-symbiotic psychic organizations stimulate the emergence of disruptive impulses in the therapist which, if nondefensively experienced, can serve to lead the therapist to higher states of personality integration and thus to more effective work.

Giovacchini (1979a) is aware he introduces a paradox. One begins treatment of a person who has previously been thought of as untreatable (a schizophrenic or affective reaction), then the patient, by provoking countertransference responses, teaches the therapist how to treat him. One treats the untreatable in order to receive treatment so that the "therapeutic armamentarium" and knowledge of developmental failures are enriched sufficiently to diminish the list of conditions one considers to be contraindications to treatment. While Searles speaks of the "pathology" of the therapist and the "patient treating the pathology of the therapist," Giovacchini asserts

---

[3] In the processes leading to the formation of what Searles has called the "therapeutic symbiosis" it may be important to consider the Kleinian notion of projective identification elaborated in the chapter on countertransference.

that the nature of primitive mental states is bound to be disruptive to the smooth functioning identity of the therapist. The disruptions give rise to a variety of kinds of "countertransference" reactions which then often become the key to understanding the nature of the introspective experience which the patient brings to the therapist.

Giovacchini emphasizes that, just as the patient brings a special perspective on "reality," so likewise does the analyst. A term which Giovacchini (1979a) introduces which may become an important one is "the impact of the delusion," which refers to the effects (both positive and negative) which the patient's experience of reality produces on the level of comfort and on the personal and professional identity of the analyst. He further suggests the term "counter-impact of delusion" to refer to the effects which the analyst's slant on his own identity, the analytic situation, and "reality" produces on the patient.

Giovacchini (1979a) describes cases in which patients attempt to bring the analysis into congruence with the delusional outer world which the patient has constructed, and other instances in which the patient brings "the delusional outer world into the analysis." He courageously describes his own "countertransference" reactions to the impact of these attempts. Giovacchini states that he usually feels forced to "confess" his adverse reactions to the patient. In his review of the literature on the subject (1979a), Giovacchini concludes:

> In all of these articles, the authors directly or indirectly refer to maneuvers the analyst has to resort to in order to feel comfortable and be able to function from an analytic perspective. The discomforts emphasized here represent potentially disruptive countertransference reactions that are the outcome of the loss of the analytic stance. These patients threatened my analytic identity and I felt uncomfortable. To threaten one's identity or to make the functional aspects of the identity sense inoperative must lead to an existential crisis. It may not exactly reach crisis-like proportions but to some extent, one must feel confused and impotent. (Giovacchini 1979a, p. 250)

Giovacchini speaks extensively of the problems involved in maintaining, losing, and regaining the analytic stance. He illustrates efforts on the part of the patient to confront the analyst in such a fashion that the analyst is unable to maintain a calm, analytic attitude. He also cites actions on the part of the analyst which indicate that demands are being made on the patient *so that the analyst can continue functioning as an analyst!* Giovacchini holds that either type of maneuver differs considerably from Eissler's (1953) "parameters." The purpose of a parameter is to relate to the patient in a nonanalytic fashion so that analysis can proceed later. In contrast, the interventions or maneuvers which Giovacchini says occur in response to Primitive Mental States have the purpose of *preserving* the analysis and:

. . . are instituted so that *the analyst rather than the patient achieves some degree of ego integration that he needs to function analytically.* . . . The parameter, on the other hand, is designed so that the patient can feel sufficient security so that he can become engaged in an analytic relationship. (Giovacchini 1979a, p. 254)

In taking this point of view, Giovacchini holds "that the interaction between therapist and patient is the crucial factor which determines whether psychoanalytic treatment is possible, not the psychopathology per se" (1979a, p. 255). Giovacchini (1975, 1979a) distinguishes carefully between *projection* of infantile feelings, internal objects, and other parts of the psyche *into the analyst* and *externalization* in which the patient constructs an environment surrounding the analyst who has become the receptacle of the projections. This environment or ambience represents a reconstruction in the outside world of the traumatic infantile environment in which the feelings and introjects were originally formed.

The patient attempts to externalize the background infantile ambience and make it part of the analytic relationship. He needs to surround the analyst, who has become the target of his projections, with such an atmosphere. The analyst's task is to make himself available for the patient's projections, but not to become part of the infantile ambience. *The patient may try to externalize, but his externalizations and the analytic atmosphere are not compatible.* (1979a, p. 262)

Giovacchini further adds,

In many instances it is impossible to distinguish between transference projections and externalization *because the boundaries between the self and the outer world are so poorly structured, the projections of parts of the psyche and the externalization of the infantile environment are no longer separate and discreet processes.* The analytic setting becomes submerged by the ambience the patient creates, and the analyst becomes part of that ambience. The analyst finds himself immersed in the patient's delusional world and, as discussed, this causes problems as he struggles to remain an analyst. (1979a, p. 263)

Despite the conceptual limitations which the continued use of the terms "transference" and "countertransference" provide, Giovacchini's systematic discussion of countertransference reactions to "primitive mental states" is one of the most thorough and penetrating to date. He recognizes the interactional aspect of transference and countertransference maneuvers, and feels that a non-defensive study of "countertransference" reactions yields critical information which aids in "the construction of an observational frame of reference for analyst and patient to cooperate in creatively exploring how the patient's mind works" (1979a, p. 238).

THE KLEINIAN CONTRIBUTION TO LISTENING:
FROM GREED AND ENVY TO GRATITUDE AND LOVE

Melanie Klein's remarkable contributions to psychoanalytic theory (1952, 1957, 1975) have traditionally been considered a separate line of thought competing for attention with Freud's classical theory and Anna Freud's ego-psychological approaches. Klein's experience with children and profoundly disturbed individuals focused her attention on earliest infantile experience and led her to postulate a series of developmental processes involved in the first three months of life. Uncritical use of Klein's extended metaphors and overgeneralization of her ideas to account for all levels of psychological development has obscured the profundity of her contribution toward understanding the foundations of personality and perhaps unwittingly left the door open for careless or "wild" analysis (Greenson 1978).

Klein's fundamental contribution to listening is her study of the earliest organizing processes of the personality. Her metaphoric descriptions are rich in detail and implication but limited in several important ways. First, her formulations reflect an unswerving commitment to the Freudian paradigms of instinct and defense which were derived primarily from a study of subjective experiences encountered in neurosis. Second, Klein's data was drawn from an understanding of children and adults who had suffered significant disturbances in the early organizing processes so that her statement of theory is often skewed in favor of disturbed or distorted developmental sequences rather than balanced or normal developmental experience. Third, Klein's theory as stated, confounds different levels of clinical and theoretical abstraction so as to invite confusion, misinterpretation and criticism. The basics of her terms and relational postulates will be summarized and then subjected to critical scrutiny in an effort to grasp the key features which may enrich clinical listening possibilities.

Klein's "paranoid-schizoid position" describes the earliest (autistic or presymbiotic) organizing attempts, while "working through the depressive position" might be thought of as referring to events from symbiosis through separation-individuation. The infant's hungry search for boundless nurturing stimulation is termed "greed," while the infant's various reactions to frustration with nurturing sources is referred to as "envy" or "hatred." Metaphorically, the infant desires limitless sucking privileges at mother's breast and reacts with distress, rage and attack when the breast is withdrawn. The capacity for sucking as well as the propensity toward rageful attack when the breast is withdrawn are considered instinctual. Bion (1967) cites ethological research demonstrating that humans are not the only species born into the world with instinctive dependency needs as well as an angry, accusatory cry which serves to bring the nurturing mother back.

"Good" and "bad" feelings are thought to arise in connection with various nurturing and frustrating experiences. Metaphorically this is expressed as experiences of the "good" and "bad" breast. Kernberg (1976, 1980) believes inborn predispositions toward positive and negative affect states become activated in connection with early images or memory traces of self and other (object) experience. Biologically determined bifurcated affective response is referred to as "split affects," and the persistent phenomenon of nonintegrated, contradictory affect states is called "splitting."[4]

"Projective identification"[5] refers to developmental processes occurring at a time or in a state of mind in which distinctions between self and others are not reliably maintained. An object is perceived in such a manner that inner experience is thought to become (creatively) projected onto or into the external object. In subsequent contact with that not yet experienced as fully separate object, the (projected) experience may become taken back into, introjected, claimed or owned by the developing sense of self. Metaphorically, a frustrating breast produces anger and attack response. The attacked (bad) breast required for further growth is likely then to become experienced through introjection as a "bad" aspect of self. "Persecutory anxiety" is said to arise from annihilation fears regarding failures of a frustrating or enviously perceived breast. "Guilt" is used to describe the infant's sense of responsibility for the depriving, withdrawing or frustrating activities of the breast. With "good enough mothering," the breast-mother may absorb and survive envious and hateful attacks (Winnicott 1952).[6] However, a repeatedly frustrating breast-mother who becomes introjected as a bad part-self is said to create unpleasant persecutory anxiety within and subsequently to stimulate various efforts to "expel or evacuate" the "bad."

An ongoing optimal *balance* (split) between greed (instinctual pleasure) and envy (rage or instinctual unpleasure) leads toward unification experience (Little 1981) with a "whole" mother, that is, one who can be both loved for giving and tolerated for frustrating.[7] Repeated "working through" of this balance leads to, and developmentally through, the "depressive position." Favorable circumstances eventually permit an integration of self and object representations (memory traces) and a differentiation of split (bifurcated) affects into an entire range or spectrum of affect potential (Kernberg 1976). The movement from inconstant experiences of objects toward object constancy is marked by the gradual appearance of the capacities for "love" and "gratitude." Whether through innate factors in the child or limitations of environmental response, overstimulation (excessive traumatic experience)

[4]For a fuller description of Kernberg's position on split affects see Chapter 8.
[5]Discussed in detail in Chapter 11.
[6]See discussion of Winnicott in Chapter 8.
[7]Neither Little nor Winnicott have been a part of the Kleinian group in London but their contributions are related to her work as summarized here.

of either greed or envy interferes with the establishment of a mutual cueing experience (basic unity or symbiosis). Excessive greed experience stimulates the infant toward perpetual manic searching (for all manner of environmental nutrients), while excessive frustration leads toward a state of chronic rage and/or depression often accompanied by various bodily preoccupations. In either extreme the relation to the external world (reality) becomes permanently colored by exaggerated affect states (i.e., manic and/or depressive dispositions).

The infant's developing capacity to *relate* to the comings and goings of the breast without extreme comfort or discomfort is thought to determine the extent to which he/she is able to establish an affectively balanced sense of togetherness (unification, symbiosis) which is predictable or controllable through a set of signals (mutual cueing). Winnicott (1971) stresses the importance of the infant's sense of "possessing" the breast so that, paradoxically, the infant simultaneously calls for the breast to come while believing it is his/her own creation. The earliest experiences of "not-me" have been referred to by Winnicott as "transitional phenomena" (1953, reprinted in 1971). Winnicott refers to the "space between" infant and breast in which the "good enough" mother permits a sense of free play—creative involvement with objects which can sometimes be experienced as "me" and at other times as transitions to the "not-me." Creative play permits gradual development of distinctions and links between body parts and products recognized as aspects of self and body parts and products attributed to (m)other. Kernberg (1976, 1980) points out that such self and object distinctions and links (memory traces) are formed within the context of the biologically based affective state active at the moment (i.e., pleasure-unpleasure, good or bad).[8]

The vicissitudes of experience in this "play space" (Winnicott 1971) absorbed Klein's primary attention. She was able to formulate a series of complex dynamics which appear as a result of a disturbed early mother-child relationship. Kleinian oriented theoretical and clinical contributions abound, so a delineation of dynamics and their clinical applications will not be attempted here.[9] For many, serious reading of the Kleinian contributions requires a "willful suspension of disbelief" as one journeys into a theoretical world populated by good and bad breasts giving or withholding good or poisonous milk. Superimposed on this basic motif are faeces, urine, eggs, sperm, penises, uteruses and wombs—attitudes toward which carry the basic legacy of the individual's early experiences of greed and envy at the

---

[8]Kernberg further ties these affect states to instinctual pleasure and unpleasure located in various body zones (oral, anal, urethral, phallic and genital).

[9]A recent review of the literature was done by Kernberg (1980a). Others are: Klein (1952, 1957, 1975), Rosenfeld (1965, 1971, 1972), Bion (1962, 1963, 1967), Balint (1952, 1968, 1969), Grotstein (1981a, 1981b), Guntrip (1968, 1971), Kernberg (1975, 1976, 1980a) and Segal (1962, 1973).

breast. The vicissitudes of the infant's attempts to identify and thereby to distinguish or link part-selves and part-objects are studied as various aspects of "projection" and "introjection." Complicated versions of these two basic organizing processes involved in various merger and separation experiences are discussed as "projective identification"[10] and "introjective identification." Limited or faulty distinctions and/or links between experiences of self and experiences of others are taken as the basis for a faulty appreciation of the outer world in general, i.e., "reality." Persistent reality deficient functioning in fragmented and/or withdrawn modes constitutes the clinical picture of schizophrenia and various schizoid states. Such persons are caught in an ineffective but incessant search for connections through which basic organizing self-other distinctions and links can be achieved.[11] Such people's organizing attempts are perpetually stifled by their own overuse of "schizoid mechanisms" (splitting and projective identification) which Klein has described so well.

While this cursory summary hardly does justice to the richness of Kleinian writings, it is sufficient to make possible an appreciation of the Kleinian contributions toward understanding the earliest organizing processes and to lead toward a statement of several technical problems inherent in her theoretical formulations.

A TECHNICAL APPRAISAL
OF THE KLEINIAN APPROACH

From the present point in the history of the development of psychoanalytic thought it is possible to re-appraise Klein's work and to honor the valuable contribution which is uniquely hers while at the same time shedding light on the linguistic, conceptual and theoretical difficulties which she encountered in her studies of individuals whose functioning in the world is arrested at or limited to the earliest organizing processes of personality.

1. Klein's Scientific, Philosophic and Linguistic Outlook

The first problem with Kleinian theorizing is one which runs throughout psychoanalysis and has repeatedly been pointed out in this book. The investigative outlook is basically Newtonian in spirit, i.e., a search for the "nature" of envy and greed and for a "definitive understanding" of the psychic processes of projection and introjection. Disputes arise about whether there "really are such things" as Life and Death instincts (the presumed basis for greed and envy) or if it wouldn't be "more accurate" to study "sexual and aggressive drives." Is there "really" an Oedipus complex in

---

[10]Discussed further in Chapter 11.
[11]Kafka's writing vividly portrays this endless search.

early life or are there only precursors? Addressing theoretical issues in this mode of early scientific inquiry introduces serious bias into an open listening situation.[12] Further, Schafer (1976) points out conceptual and linguistic problems which arise in psychological theories which rely on internalization metaphors. For example, if one wishes to say "the angry, retaliatory breast has become internalized" one should be clear about what "inside" is spoken of and exactly how angry, retaliatory breast came to be "in there."[13]

These scientific, philosophical and linguistic attitudes have led toward heated controversy in the field with the disadvantage that many contributions end up being rhetorical presentations of theory or polemical case studies as if to justify or "prove the validity" of theoretical propositions. A listening approach to psychoanalytic inquiry has no place for polemics or arguments about what "really is" but rather seeks to value any and all propositions and applications which enrich listening possibilities. Klein's fundamental ideas clearly constitute such an enrichment.

2. Klein's Use of Extended Metaphor

All attempts to describe psychological events of earliest infancy are bound to entail assumptions inextricably bound up in the very terms selected. Take as examples: "breast," "greed," and "envy." While such terms are taken from a more differentiated world view than is possible for an infant, they are descriptive, evocative, and in themselves not necessarily loaded with untenable or irrefutable assumptions. Other Kleinian terms and relations discussed in the preceding sections are also not objectionable in themselves, especially when employed to aid in grasping personal modes of experience of someone coming to the consulting room. The objection to Kleinian terminology and formulation is rather to the overuse of early metaphor to account for all of psychic life as well as the superimposition of an adultomorphic point of view on early events such that primal envy, greed, guilt, splitting and projective identification are often spoken of as operating in a highly complex, organized manner resembling adult logic or advanced repressive activities.

3. Issues in Kleinian Levels of Abstraction

Any theorist seeks abstractions which account for the phenomena under investigation. Klein began her studies with the basic Freudian notions of the primacy of instincts, the regulation of functioning by ego and superego processes, the conflicts involved in emotional triangulations of the Oedipus complex, and the influence of the dynamic (repressed) unconscious. Freud developed these concepts over a lifetime in an effort to account for the

---

[12]See discussion on these points in Chapter 2.
[13]For discussion of Schafer's ideas refer to Chapter 13.

conflictual free association data arising in the analytic study of psycho-neurosis. While Klein's study of earliest mental states ultimately evolved highly original conceptual tools quite different from Freud's, her approach never became divested of the pervasive influence of topographic, structural, genetic, or dynamic frameworks. To take one example, Freud's early (1900, Chapter VII) model of the dynamic unconscious identifies the capacity for repression as a comparatively late and complex psychic development. However, Klein and others speak as though dynamic unconscious processes were operating almost from birth. Such an approach fails to distinguish between Freud's idea of active repression of unacceptable mental content which characterizes the conflicts of the later oedipal period from earlier preoedipal forms of non-consciousness such as inattention, unheedfulness, non-reflectiveness, avoidance and negligent, inaccurate, faulty or uninformed perceptions and cognitions.[14] The implications of what and how Klein considers "unconscious" are far reaching since Klein's formulations regarding early experiences of body parts and products are modeled on *relational* concepts borrowed from Freud's study of the structural oedipal neuroses. In the neurotic transference, Freud's unconscious instincts (often referred to as drives) are thought to emerge with phenomenological clarity as complex sexual and aggressive oedipal constellations long held in repression. In contrast, Klein's greed (sucking instinct) and envy (instinctual rage over feeding frustrations) are closer to biologically based threats of annihilation and hardly qualify for the label "unconscious" in the repressed Freudian sense.[15]

Also following the Freudian model for neurotic conflict, Klein spoke of (unconscious, ego) defenses against the instincts envy and greed. Klein (1957, p. 216) lists as defenses: omnipotence, denial, splitting, idealization, confusion, identification, flight, devaluation of self or object, dispersal of feelings, greedy internalization to counteract envy, stirring up envy in others so as to reverse the envious situation, stifling love or intensifying hate to ward off the pain or guilt arising from envy, withdrawal of contact, and "acting out" the split to avoid integration of envious part-selves. As can

---

[14]Kernberg (1976) addresses the issue of the development of the unconscious in his comments to the effect that the id has a definite organization because it can be said to form only late as a result of the repression of oedipal concerns. He further treats this topic (1975) in noting that the "split" content of borderlines (and psychotics) is present or absent from consciousness but *not held unconscious* (repressed). Kohut (1971, 1977) makes a similar case for the dissociation (vertical splitting) of narcissistic investments, stating clearly that narcissism is *not* unconscious in the usual dynamic repressed sense but rather habitually not permitted entry into full consciousness, i.e., it is walled off, suppressed or dissociated. In addressing the same point, Stolorow and Atwood (1981) refer to nonconscious mental contents in preoedipal periods as the "pre-reflective unconscious."

[15]Cellular processes of anabolism (building up) and catabolism (breaking down) are more likely to have their corollary in infancy in what Klein has termed the Life and Death instincts than in anything which Freud ever discussed. It is not to be forgotten than an infant who is unsuccessful at summoning the mother figure for more than routine custodial care in fact does die of marasmus.

readily be seen, these are *not* defenses in the strictly classical Freudian sense. They rather can be thought of as ego mechanisms (prestages of defense) or modes of dealing with envy and greed by various forms of avoidance, inattention, neglect, unheedfulness or turning away. The many problems of conceptualizing non-repressive preoedipal activities as "defensive" are spelled out by Stolorow and Lachman (1980).[16] The term "defense" would seem best reserved to describe a process through which unacceptable impulses or contents have been relegated to unconsciousness through active repression in consequence of the advanced capacity for ambivalent (oedipal level) relationships as seen in psychoneurosis. In early life good and bad affect states are best considered separate (split) or mutually exclusive (ambitendent rather than ambivalent). What Klein regards as unconscious defenses are perhaps best understood as attempts of the early ego to avoid or ward off experiences of overstimulation by the instinctual forces of envy and greed. These discrepancies between the Kleinian and Freudian conceptualizations of instinct and defense arise as a function of differing levels of abstract formulation. Differing levels of abstract consideration suggest distinctly different listening situations in which the capacity for dynamic unconscious processing through repression is held to be either absent or present. Likewise, differences on the early or late attributes of such constellations as the Oedipus complex or the superego constitute very different levels of abstraction implying radically different developmental stages of integration and the necessity for developing different conceptual vantage points for use in clinical listening. To generalize an established observational stance to different observational situations may indeed be helpful at times. But conceptualizing different levels of psychic development is to consider different possible integrative focal points for the organization of personality and to acknowledge that different conceptual tools are likely to be differentially effective in the correspondingly different listening tasks. Terms derived from one universe of discourse do not necessarily generalize well to another. One helpful way of viewing a certain style of personality organization may not be so helpful when viewing personalities organized according to different developmental trends and motivational priorities.[17]

---

[16]See Chapter 13 for their argument and their ideas regarding the prestages of defense.

[17]Klein is not alone in her tendency to overgeneralize her theoretical propositions. Before her, Freud attempted to extend his ideas (developed in studying neurotic personality organization) to all of life as well as to a study of history and culture. Kohut (in press) likewise uses self psychological concepts (developed in his work with narcissistic personality organization) to account for psychosis, borderline conditions and finally neuroses in his re-analysis of Freud's "rat man" case study. Indeed, Kohut's final work defined mental health as "self to selfobject resonance from birth to death." Such attempts at overgeneralization need not be seen as detracting from the fundamental contribution but do need to be considered judiciously lest any single set of organizing dynamics bias unduly the listening situation.

In conclusion, Klein's basic theoretical dimensions involving infantile self and object vicissitudes of projection and introjection affectively colored by envy and greed, contribute significantly to the Listening Perspective of the part-self and part-object for the psychotherapeutic study of organizing personalities. Additionally, the many dynamic possibilities which Klein and her followers have delineated often come to represent stable styles of symbiotic relationship fostered by processes of mother-child mutual cueing. As such, many of the dynamic patternings defined by the Kleinians would be expected to emerge in therapy with clarity as replicated "scenarios" in borderline personality organization. Just as manic, depressive, schizoid and schizophrenic states can be understood as abortive or faulty attempts to organize the personality in the absence of sufficient environmental response,[18] so many borderline scenarios are likely to bear the distinguishing earmark of traumatic overstimulation through greed or envy resulting in the establishment within the symbiosis of a mutual cueing situation based on dynamics carried over from the earlier period which Klein's work so aptly studies.[19]

It is furthermore to be expected that interpretations of the "deepest" dynamics of narcissistic and neurotic personality organization will also in some way touch on the foundation of personality formation laid down in the first three months of life. After all, the broadest statement of early Kleinian defined dynamics is simply that people have intense needs and yearnings which are frequently thwarted in one way or another eliciting many responses. Likewise, the essence of all creativity is the projection into the parameters of the world a vision or belief which is then taken back into the self as reality. The Kleinian fallacy is to overgeneralize the subjective significance of early personality dynamics to the exclusion or neglect of those which develop later. As psychological development proceeds, emergent nodal points of personality integration can be defined which become increasingly central as differentiation evolves toward the advanced psychic achievements of ambivalence, repression and object constancy.

Summary

Freudian conceptual tools have been of limited value in the study of earliest infantile development whereas Klein's basic metaphoric dimensions excel. Theoretical and clinical considerations provided by Melanie Klein contribute significantly to the set of listening possibilities available for empathic contact with persons limited to incessant strivings toward more

---

[18]This statement does not rule out biological predispositions for which the best mothering may not constitute sufficient response.
[19]For example, see the discussion of "agitated" and "depleted" scenarios in Chapter 10.

complex and cohesive forms of personality organization. Klein's scientific and philosophical outlook, her use of conceptual and relational abstractions as well as the historical controversy surrounding her theoretical and clinical approach has unfortunately served to detract from the clinical value of her basic insights and fundamental formulations.

No attempt will be made to utilize Kleinian theoretical ideas in the case material which follows as her approach has been amply illustrated elsewhere (see Rosenfeld, 1975 and Segal, 1962). Furthermore, a Kleinian approach was not employed by the particular therapist who submitted the following hour and to attempt a Kleinian *post hoc* analysis seems inappropriate.

JOSH: A PERSONALITY ORGANIZING[20]

The following notes were recorded verbatim by the therapist during a session in the fifth year of treatment with a 13-year-old boy. The work is conducted twice weekly in a playroom at a therapeutic school. During the first four years, the therapist had difficulty simply enduring the hours because the child so infrequently related to her. She managed patiently to contain her own frustrations while being perceived sometimes as only a part of or appendage to his activities and at other times representing merely some basic maternal function, providing him with something asked for or giving some recognition of his activities as he talked and played. The year prior to the session to be reported, Josh began to address her more directly and to show a recognition that she is there, waiting and available. He began talking often about his "girlfriend," a girl formerly in his class but recently moved to another class. She is not rude to him but does see him as "weird," and she, like the other children, does her best to stay away from him. In the sessions preceding the one to be reported, Josh often talked obsessively about her. He also spoke frequently of "hard" things, "dirty and messy things," and would stand with crossed legs while playing a small organ in the playroom. The therapist cautiously began exploring this material until he was able to let her know how confused he was about his penis getting hard when he thinks of his girlfriend. The sand-tray play which led up to that clarification had centered around rockets taking off from brains. He has heard at school of right- and left-brain function. The following hour illustrates a significant organizing connection with the therapist.

Therapist's Report

Josh entered the room asking if I had seen Lisa his girlfriend. He went to the round damp sand tray and molded two breast-like mounds and began to caress them. The two mounds became "a monster." He showed me how to

[20]The therapist is a woman. See note on contributors, p. xix.

"pull the ears off," then to "take a tool" [a clothes pin]. "They take an eye out like this—the ears are pulled off with bare hands—they take brain out—monster's head—here it is—bury it in sand—this is magic—what kind of tool do we have to remove monster?" (I produced a case knife.) "Now cut his mind out—his brain inside of here—we cut the monster's head and this is gross." (The monster's brain was carried to the bucket which was half full of water.) He walked with crossed legs as he carried the large lump of sand from tray to bucket; it made a splash as he dropped it. Then he went back to the tray. "This is gross." (Another handful of brain was carried to the bucket.) "This is soaking." (He did a "magic twirl" using his whole body, and carried more sand to the bucket of water, then stood with eyes squeezed shut.) "It's melting; look at this." (He kicked the bucket—returned to the sand tray.) "We got it all," as he carefully gathered up spilled sand from the floor. "Monster's brain in half—this is my work to do—the other half-brain—got killed by evil robots—it's mush—it's gross brain—it's like liquid—like mud—like gross stuff—look at that mud—this is real mud—a monster's brain mixed with soap." (The sand made bubbles, a soapy look.) He gave a funny laugh as he stood looking into the bucket with legs tightly crossed. He did another "magic twirl." "Here's the monster's eye—cutting up the monster's head—here's eyes" (put it into bucket) "outer space." "Do you have a monster's eye to throw in?—I'll make one up—here's a gross eye—a out eye—here's the other eye—have to soak the monster's head in a bucket of water—gets so deep—gets so liquid—his is huge—the monster's nose" "Ugh oh." "It gets overloaded." (The bucket overflowed onto the floor.) "That's the whole monster's head—here's the nose—the last thing to put in—this is becoming a mess—a big, big mess—if anyone drinks this solution —will turn into a monster—anyone who touches it with their mouth—they are in trouble—turn into a monster—act like a bad guy—steal—cheat—a person who acts like a monster—an evil monster—anyone who touches this with bare feet will turn into monster—Where's the gun?" (Therapist: "In the white cupboard.") "Danger" (as he walks backward to cupboard with legs crossed). "It's on 'safe,' but it still fired." (A dart flew across the room; he returned to the bucket.) "Fire one," as he shot into the bucket. "Fire two—fire three—a gas bomb." (As water splashed on me, I told him I would move.) "Oxygen destroyer," as he repeatedly shot into the bucket of water and sand. By holding the gun close to the surface of the water he controlled the splash so he got little on him. "Last bullet," he sang out. "Now it's become a big mess—now we have to put bugs in—insects—every single insect" (he got two trays of these from the shelves). "Now we have to put death in—first it had to be killed—I hope this will be here Thursday [his next hour] so I can go on." (Therapist: "Oh, no it won't be. My job is to clean up and put things where you can find them.") We had both looked at the clock and knew the hour was over. He started to leave but stopped at the door and looked back. "You can take the bugs out," he said as he closed the door. Only then did I discover I had failed to move my purse out of his way. It got spattered with the brain-dart work.

Author's Comments

The onset of puberty is clearly creating new body concerns which Josh is able to express to his therapist. While in the past he has only related to her from a position of inconstancy—part-selves and part-objects—in this hour he expresses a connection which has been slowly developing. He shows his (brain) confusion and gives her permission to "take the bugs out." Various islands or nuclei have been developing around his good and bad experiences of her (e.g., the breast mounds in sand). He has for months equated good and bad body parts with machines, monsters and magic (identity with the non-human). Now he reports his brain-penis is responsive to people, his first recognition of person-to-person relatedness. "Pacification" (Gedo and Goldberg, 1971) has provided the main forms of contact with this child, though recent developments point toward "unification" experience through a therapeutic symbiosis. The child's need to organize and connect his sensorimotor experiences *through his relationship* with her has led the therapist to adopt a tolerant, permissive, "connecting stance." One might conjecture that it was her empathy with his need to connect his brain-penis "mess" directly with her person in some way that caused her to "forget" to remove her purse from the range of his activities (i.e., countertransference or the "impact of the delusion").

Work with this child has illustrated the usefulness of listening with Freud's reflexive model of the mind as subject and object, passive and active, and both primitive as well as developed aspects of personality emerge repeatedly in timeless, spaceless organizing attempts, much as one works and reworks problems in dreams. Inconstant part-self and part-object images and experiences abound in his talk and play much as they do in Kafka's organizing attempts. "Pacification" moving toward "Unification" modes characterize the slow movement in therapy with the "delusional" state having its inevitable effect on the therapist. A Listening Perspective geared to respond in a connecting way to these kinds of reflexive, nonhuman organizing experiences holds fresh possibilities for understanding this great frontier of the mind.

SOME IMPLICATIONS OF THE LISTENING PERSPECTIVE APPROACH WITH ORGANIZING PERSONALITIES

The Listening Perspective approach advocated in this book has several crucial implications for the study of the early organizing processes of personality. At this point in time these can only be enumerated. Detailed elaboration must await further experience.

1. The Abandonment of Symbolic and Symptomatic Analysis

Eliminating from systematic *theoretical* consideration an analysis of "symbolic content" and/or "symptom formation" in Organizing Personalities has the advantage of doing away with many irrefutable assumptions which have continued to cloud investigations in this area. Attempts to describe "the psychotic process" or "the nature of primitive mental states" have tended to introduce conceptual and linguistic limitations into this difficult area of study. Discussions of how things "really are for the psychotic" or efforts to describe "merging with the psychosis" have led to conversations and contributions which seem as "crazy" as some of the persons being studied! Clarity in conceptualization and discourse seems to lie in some other direction. The careful elaboration of a perspective from which to listen to the organizing processes of personality offers one possibility.

2. The Avoidance of Excessive Developmental Metaphor

The study of organizing processes is *not* open to developmentally based thinking as with borderline personality organization in particular and as with narcissistic and neurotic personality organization to a lesser extent. Since reliable mutual cueing processes between infant and environmental others which might have left a definite organizational imprint on the personality have essentially failed, attempts by the therapist to form a sense of relatedness with some specific arrested mode of experiencing such as symbiosis or rapprochement will also fail. It is easy to say that organizational attempts in temporal extension must be met in an empathic way by the therapist as in usual childhood nurturing and soothing situations. It is also easy to say that the therapeutic task is to be responsive to basic (reflexive) sensory and motor processes in order to provide protection from overstimulation (traumatization) through processes of pacification as parents do for an infant. But in clinical practice simple use of developmental metaphor in an attempt to form a treatment approach for unorganized, searching or abortively organized persons is insufficient. An Organizing Personality cannot be considered, so to speak, a *tabular rasa* in the same sense that an infant often can be. In such persons the original organizational strivings and extensions are presumed to have gone awry either through faulty environmental response or through some (organic?) inability of the infant to make use of ordinary soothing and nurturing. Conventional forms of empathic contact are likely to be fraught with difficulties for such persons. For example, based on a symbolic or symptomatic analysis of a patient's verbal and interactional expressions, a therapist may attempt an empathic response which in most instances could reasonably be expected to produce tension relief or provide some form of nurturing understanding. The Organizing Personality, however, based on a history of faulty or traumatic interpersonal contacts may well withdraw, fragment or decompensate in minor or major ways. Contact which might lead toward the establishment of a reliable mutual cueing process would *not* be through "introspection" (Kohut, 1959) *nor* even through "interactional" (Hedges, 1980b) but rather through "interception." (See point 4 below.)

3. The Avoidance of Extensive Countertransference Analysis

The study of organizational processes of personality is *not* open to systematic analysis of countertransference as are the more definite forms of personality organization referred to as borderline. Countertransference may constitute the "royal road" to merger experiences in that certain very definite patternings of early self and other experience persist in the personality structure and functioning and become known to the therapist through the therapist's noticing how his or her experience of the relationship is developing. Countertransference reactions such as boredom, drowsiness, consternation, and helplessness as well as somatic or mental preoccupations or representations may be appropriate responses to certain personalities in organization. Such reactions might also represent ideosyncratic responses the therapist brings to a situation in which he/she is regarded as a bizarre fantasy figure, a mechanical object, a good or bad breast or some other part aspect of the patient's amorphus and unstable mental states and representations. Such countertransference reactions may make a therapist feel in need of more supervision and/or more personal analysis, but systematic study of countertransference alone cannot reasonably be expected to yield reliable information about the patient's vacillating (internal) states or about the therapist's unconscious perceptions or spontaneous interactions with persons in such states. Therapists with great skill in reaching Organizing Personalities often appear not even to be listening to their patients or reacting at all to what would otherwise be upsetting or bizarre enactments or verbalizations. These same therapists may even report paying very little attention to most of the things their patients do or say as if the therapist is engaged in observing and responding through an almost trance-like free floating or hovering attention to events beyond words, discrete enactments and even the moment to moment interactions or transactions of the therapeutic situation. This altered frame of reference (or altered state of consciousness?) does not represent an "empathic immersion in the psychosis." Such therapists are not wrapped up in either the content or the process of the interpersonal chatter but can better be considered as being in a state of fine attunement to whatever opportunities or cues may arise for momentary interpersonal contact.

4. Interception as a Mode of Observation

Kohut (1959) pointed out that any field of science is limited by the modes of observation at its disposal. He postulated that introspection and vicarious introspection (empathy) form the limits of psychoanalysis. Ryle (1949) has shown the "divided mind" assumption inherent in the concept of introspection (That is, one part of one's mind looking "inside" at another part.) and has suggested use of the less popular but philosophically less objectionable term "retrospection." The concept of retrospection includes looking at events in the instantaneous past as well as the more remote past. Conceptualizing retrospection and vicarious retrospection (empathy) as the limiting modes of psychoanalytic observation broadens Kohut's notion to include the interaction processes and countertransference studies so vital to studying borderline personality organization. Retrospection would also encompass the essentially "interceptive" modes of observation which characterize study of Organizing Personalities and have been discussed throughout this chapter. That is, the focus for therapeutic observation would *not* be the generative, verbal, symbolic content thought to characterize the introspective processes *nor* the mutual enactments or generative countertransference phenomena thought to characterize interactional processes but rather the ways through which and the moments during which the individual presents or can be urged to present him or herself for environmental contact which limits, expands, nurtures or soothes. *Contact intercepts organizational attempts at specific moments in time and leads toward the establishment of a reliable mutual cueing process* akin to that established in an ordinary mother-child symbiosis. The skill is in learning how and when each individual can be empathically intercepted (contacted). This particular and highly refined skill when carefully and slowly exercized *is neither supportive nor manipulative but simply a different form of retrospective observation* in which both patient and therapist are active. Interceptive observation can be considered a listening tool for extending the broadening scope of psychoanalysis beyond the already established (retrospective) modes of introspection and interaction.

CONCLUSIONS

Attempts to listen to the introspective elaborations of persons with arrests *prior to* what Mahler (1968) has termed the symbiotic and separation-individuation phases, have provided psychoanalysts and psychotherapists with a most formidable task. The disruptive and often defeating reactions which these persons provide for their therapists have been studied in many ways.

Freud's original metaphor of the mental apparatus (1900, Chapter 7) was a telescope in which additional lenses (analogous to psychic development, i.e., memory traces) make the usefulness of the instrument one directional. Making no apology for this metaphor, Freud felt that the oedipal level achievement of (preconscious and) unconscious barriers more or less limited the regressive or backward tendencies in persons who had achieved advanced development. Whereas, in less developed persons psychic events might "flow" forward and backward reflexively, producing a variety of hallucinatory and projected exprinces. Freud's early model indicates that he viewed preconscious and unconscious processes developing relatively late but definitely available in the study of the oedipal transference neuroses. In considering earlier developments, "unconscious" concepts such as resistance, transference and countertransference are seen as less than optimally useful. Concepts highlighting a more or less mechanical (Tausk 1919) or nonhuman experience of the world (Searles 1960) become increasingly interesting.

Using the term "countertransference" loosely to refer to all (conscious, preconscious, and unconscious) reactions which the therapist has to "projected and externalized maneuvers" (Giovacchini 1979a), represents one way of understanding the world in which the patient lives and suggests a method of listening to the way a patient experiences his/her realities.

Of particular interest in forming a Listening Perspective for grasping experiences of early development are the ideas of Glover (1932) regarding "ego nuclei" and the way in which these early islands of development are in a perpetual state of organizing. Kafka (1914, 1922) is taken as spokesman for this early quality of experience. His characters and situations depict tireless, obsessive searching for parental images and relationships which fit with his early needs to be empathically received and to develop individual identity.

People with very early developmental arrests are becoming increasingly thought of as "treatable." The development of a Listening Perspective for studying the interceptions, interactions and introspections of persons with early developmental arrests which leave their personalities in a perpetually organizing state has developed very slowly. However, extensive countertransference analysis does *not* represent the key listening tool with presymbiotic states as it does in later developments.

METAPSYCHOLOGICAL CONSIDERATIONS

Freud's *general metapsychology* (the pleasure principle, the reality principle, the homeostasis principle, the principle of repetition compulsion and the principle of overdetermination) has served satisfactorily in the previous three Listening Perspectives and also provides the metapsychological assumptions for the Listening Perspective of the Part-Self and Part-Object. However, Freud's *specific metapsychology* requires modification here.

The topographic point of view, highlighting the distinctions between conscious and unconscious functioning, is a less than optimal set of ideas for listening to early mental states. Instead, mental contents may be heard as passing into and out of consciousness reflexively but are not held "unconscious" by repression. *The structural point of view*, whether including the concepts of id, ego, and superego or the concept of the self remains of questionable value since these structures develop mostly during later periods. *The dynamic point of view*, in which an interplay of forces is seen to be operating in time, still holds sway but the forces are seen to be much more primitive as well as reversible (reflexive) and perceived by the person often as mechanical, mystical or chaotic. *The economic point of view*, highlighting the distribution, transformation, and expenditure of psychic energy also seems largely inapplicable here because of the lack of advanced psychic structure. The historically defined trends in the *genetic development* of libido, the self, or self and object representations seem also largely irrelevant in the study of "psychotic" phenomena since the usually discussed aspects develop much later. None of these lines of thought is seen as consistently useful in developing a Listening Perspective for early psychic arrest since advanced functions are presumed largely undeveloped, and only various ego and self functions have continued to develop in relative isolation.

The main metapsychological bent inherent in the Listening Perspective of the Part-Self and Part-Object is that *very little psychic or emotional integration has occurred and that whatever slant on reality has developed is likely to be projected into or externalized onto the therapy situation or the therapist.* In psychotherapy, persons arrested at these early levels can best be thought of as Organizing Personalities working toward the formation of a reliable symbiotic experience from which to differentiate emotionally.

The idiosyncratic experiences of "primitive mental states" can perhaps best be studied at this point in time by simply paying attention to *interactional* and organizational components without further metapsychological assumptions. Therapeutic technique would involve searching for potential points of contact and waiting for a moment in which the person is oriented (mentally and/or physically) and can recognize that contact briefly. The gradual establishment of a mutual cueing process leading to the unification experiences of therapeutic symbiosis, can be fostered by the alert and patient therapist. Other ideas may emerge with clarity which take into account the undeveloped or unintegrated aspects of schizophrenic and manic-depressive states and do not uncritically generalize downward from later nodal points of psychic development.

PART **VI**
Conclusions

13 The New Wave of Psychoanalysis

GENERAL COMMENTS

This book has underlined the assertion that the focus for psychoanalytic or psychotherapeutic investigation is essentially the study of introspective (or interactive) experience via vicarious introspection (empathy) (Kohut 1959).[1] The position has also been taken that systematic study of complex phenomena requires the development of specific points of view or conceptual lenses: in the case of psychoanalysis, Listening Perspectives. This book has presented a review of four major Listening Perspectives which have been developing within the field of psychoanalysis. The first perspective was defined by Freud as he pushed his studies back to the infantile period of the Oedipus complex (the parricidal and incestuous object) in his understanding of introspective data presented by persons with various psychoneuroses. The second perspective has been provided by Kohut in his innovative definitions of the mirroring, twinning and idealizing trends involved in the study of "selfobject transferences." The third perspective of psychoanalytic investigation focuses on early experiences of merger objects. Based on studies of the differentiation of self and object experiences, the separation-individuation processes, and a differentiation of the affects within the context of object relations; an effort is being made to understand patients with "borderline" developmental arrests. The fourth perspective, useful in studying the earliest levels of psychic organization, focuses on the organizing processes of part-selves and part-objects. Based on Freud's original model of reflexive mental processes in conjunction with an understanding of the experience of the nonhuman environment, the interpersonal "impact of delusion" experiences, and the developmental sequence from envy and greed to love and gratitude, this perspective seeks to understand or to establish empathic contact with personalities in organization.

While four major Listening Perspectives have been defined thus far in psychoanalysis, other perspectives may also prove useful. The Listening Perspectives derive their conceptual clarity from a study of early childhood

---

[1]Ryle (1949) suggests the term "retrospection" be used in place of the philosophically more complex notion of "introspection." For elaboration of his argument see footnote 3 on p. 51.

development. The basic assertion of the developmental approach is that one must understand the nodal point of psychic integration of any particular person before empathic contact (which is known to promote therapeutic growth) can be attained. This particular set of perspectives is based upon the metapsychological assumption that other people come to be experienced as "love objects" and that a developmental line can be defined in which experiences of "self" become gradually differentiated from experiences of "objects." Psychotherapy and psychoanalysis of preoedipal developmental arrests have been viewed as processes in which a resumption of natural growth may occur. Therapeutic progression has been presumed to be related to the therapist's ability (or flexibility) in listening to the ideas, imagery, enactments and engagements of persons presenting various developmental levels of self and object differentiation.

This final chapter will be devoted to several general issues in modern psychoanalytic thinking which have overall implications for the Listening Perspective approach.

KOHUT VERSUS KERNBERG ON NARCISSISM

A lively controversy centering around two apparently conflicting approaches to narcissism has been felt by professionals everywhere. At first it appeared that the average clinician would "side" with Kernberg because Kernberg spoke the familiar languages of Ego Psychology and Object Relations. Furthermore, he seemed to represent a bringing together of these two historically divergent trends of thought. At first, Kohut's formulations were so maverick in conceptualization as well as language that it appeared only clinicians willing to devote themselves to careful study would be able to hear what Kohut had to say. As the controversy raged, several things became apparent. A Kohut "cult" began to spring up. Kohut's emphasis on the soothing effects of empathic understanding had a mesmerizing effect on a large sector of the therapeutic community. How was one to account for these vastly different points of view?

The first possibility is that narcissism formulated from a traditional Freudian-Hartmann approach (Kohut) is simply going to sound very different from formulations with a Klein-Mahler slant (Kernberg).

The second possibility is that due to subtle factors of selection these two men were looking at very different patient populations, and, as a result, talking about very different things. Kohut had been a training analyst in Chicago, presumably seeing mostly psychiatrists in training who had developed quite strong internal structures but continued to present analyzable selfobject fixations. In contrast, Kernberg had been deeply involved in the long-term psychotherapy research project at the Menninger Foundation and was encountering many deeply disturbed (and often hospitalized) borderline narcissistic patients. This possibility suggested that perhaps each can be considered "right" in his own regard. That is, Kohut was observing one population of basically intact people capable of forming narcissistic (selfobject) transferences, while Kernberg was observing another entirely different population of essentially borderline people who would be properly classified "on the upper border." Kernberg would then be justified in modifying slightly and extending ideas which were developed in his borderline studies to the study of narcissistic patients. In papers delivered at a conference on The Narcissistic Personality, Kernberg systematically surveyed and critiqued the positions of Rosenfeld and Kohut on the narcissistic personality and contrasted them with his own (Kernberg, 1980b).

The possibility began to emerge that the differences between Kernberg and Kohut were *not* to be found in their different theoretical underpinnings, for each is very creative and original in his own approach. Likewise the idea of their formulations being derived from and applied to wholly different patient populations is insufficient to account for the differences. A careful comparison of case studies offered by both men reveals a striking similarity of developmental level in contrast to descriptions of neurotic patients on the one hand and more clearly borderline patients on the other. The patients reported by both men might be characterized as being fixated in one crucial aspect or another of what has been called the "rapprochement subphase" (Mahler 1968) or "rapprochement crisis" (Blanck and Blanck 1979).

It then seemed plausible that each theorist had grasped *a different aspect of inadequate rapprochement experience* and formulated a way of listening to persons fixated with that experience and appropriately responding to it. No one doubts, for example, that Kohut has contributed greatly to what has been called the "transference lexicon" (Oremland 1980) with his emphasis on the mirroring, twinning and idealizing needs which become activated in preoedipal analytic work. On the other hand, no one doubts that intense rage potential exists with these same patients (a Kernberg emphasis). Perhaps with each different patient and even with changing therapeutic phases of any single patient, creative listening (empathy) skills are challenged, and therapists have to switch Listening Perspectives.

To use a hypothetical and quite limited example, it would seem clear that different empathic responses would be appropriate at different times when a very young child, feeling insulted and rejected by mother, runs to father for help. Many times the child merely wants acceptance and mirroring from the idealized father (Kohut perspective). The main soothing effect is derived simply from empathic contact: the child needs self acknowledgment or confirmation of his/her own feeling states in order to restore self-esteem. An important Other can perform this soothing, tension-relieving function in the style of Kohut's selfobject. On the other hand, there are times when the same child runs to father (or some important Other) feeling hurt, angry, conflicted, sad, or inhibited because of neglect or rejection by mother (or someone). In such instances, the child may well need help in experiencing the intensity of the envy and the hatred toward mother within the context of a firm or steady "holding environment" (Modell 1976). Such episodes may demonstrate clearly the operation of "splitting" of the affects and the objects. The parental and the therapeutic responses are much the same in that "interpretation" and analysis of the source of the envy or the hateful attitude within the context of empathic containment appears to be the critical factor which ultimately provides for a differentiation of affect and an integration of good and bad representations of self and other. This latter experience is essentially what Kernberg describes.

In short, the "grandiose self" a term which Kernberg uses and credits Kohut with, may need to be listened to in various veins in different persons or at different times with the same person. However, in any particular patient, the needed response will likely be peculiar to that person and characteristically consistent. It seems that some narcissistic personalities require primarily selfobject reassurances (Kohut's listening perspective) while others seem to require an analysis of defenses against the emergence of primitive affect states so that the split affects can differentiate and so that self and object representations can integrate (Kernberg's listening perspective).

It would seem at this point in time that the differences between Kohut and Kernberg may not be so much in terms of theoretical preference nor in terms of population selection factors, but in terms of a focus on *different aspects of developmental experience during the crucial rapprochement era.* The developmental arrest is presumably to be accounted for in terms of either too much (over-gratification) or too little (over-frustration) parental response. In either extreme, the original parental response would not have been optimal, and one might say that persons with narcissistic personality organization[2] suffer from "inadequate subphase experience during the rapprochement crisis." In either case (Kernberg's or Kohut's perspective), the basic therapeutic process remains the same. Creative and empathic listening serve to recreate the original separation-individuation atmosphere within the therapeutic context such that the rapprochement experience has an opportunity to be expanded and elaborated within the organizing fabric of the personality. Both theorists hold an optimistic attitude with regard to psychoanalytic psychotherapy with persons having a narcissistic personality organization. Both men describe a long-term, slowly evolving process which resembles in many ways a sort of "non-influencing re-parenting." The goal of psychoanalytically oriented psychotherapy or psychoanalysis with narcissistic personalities is to permit a resumption of growth toward a fuller

[2]A term suggested by Jerome Oremland (1980) in a discussion of Kernberg's (1980b) paper.

or more differentiated and mature appreciation of others as "separate centers of initiative" (Kohut 1971) which permits the development of mental structure, structural conflict, and repression as well as the capacity for the establishment of self and object constancy with ambivalent, triangular relationships.

Kernberg's Criticisms of Kohut

While Kernberg (1980b) acknowledges Kohut's contributions in the areas of elaborating narcissistic transferences and narcissistic resistances, he raises the following objections to Kohut's approach:

1. Kernberg believes that Kohut has failed to note the differences between idealization activated in the narcissistic transferences and idealization reflecting defensive operations under the impact of the integration of object relations. He charges that Kohut thus collapses: (1) idealization as a defense against aggression (thus splitting idealization from devaluation); (2) idealization as a defense against oedipal guilt; and (3) idealization as a projection of the grandiose self. By *accepting* idealization rather than *analyzing* it in the transference, the differences between various levels of defensive operation are missed.

2. Kernberg also feels that Kohut tends to confuse patients' subjective *statements* of experience with the actual nature and degree of their regression. He cites as an example the concept of the merger transference, stating that the patients which Kohut and his colleagues present in no way approach actual merger experience.

3. Kohut neglects the interpretation of negative transference as if there were only a buildup of grandiose and idealizing images and no buildup of the image of a bad self or a bad mother. In deciding to ignore the transferential implications of regressive states and to consider only the fragmentation of the self Kohut has deprived himself of learning about the deepest, most primitive layers of the psychic apparatus. Kohut acknowledges that his approach brings about improvement in the narcissistic sector of the personality but not necessarily in the object related sector. In contrast, Kernberg holds that systematic interpretation of the pathological, grandiose self and primitive id-ego states which emerge, permits a simultaneous resolution of narcissistic pathology *and* of related pathology of internalized object relations.

4. Kohut's treatment approach artificially fosters idealization in the transference, developing a supportive, "re-education" approach by helping patients rationalize their aggressive reactions as a natural consequence of the failure of people in their past as well as failures of the analyst.

5. Kohut's restriction of the use of "empathy" to the analyst's emotional awareness of the patient's central subjective state neglects the broader issue of psychoanalytic empathy in the analyst's simultaneous awareness of what

is dissociated, repressed or projected. It is easy to consider as empathic an intervention which fits both the analyst's theory and the patient's conscious expectations. Fundamental truths which are being avoided often bring about pain and suffering. Also, Kohut never illustrates empathy with the patient's excited, lustful, joyful aggression. "That cruelty and sadism can be fun" is obscured by references to the frustrating conditions which the analyst sees as motivating them.

6. In failing to distinguish between the pathological, grandiose self and normal self formation, Kohut's approach attempts to preserve the grandiose self and to make it more adaptive which results in a lack of resolution of the pathology of internal object relations resulting in a crucial limitation in the treatment of his patients.

7. In indicating that narcissism represents an independent line of development from object relations, Kohut's treatment approach attempts to preserve, protect, and reinforce the grandiose self while only implicitly attempting to tone down its disruptive effects on others. Kernberg favors a systematic analysis of both positive and negative transference which leads to the uncovering of the defensive function of the grandiose self and its eventual replacement by a normal self formation.

8. Kernberg feels that Kohut's direction of abandoning drive theory will force him to abandon Freudian metapsychology entirely in favor of a total psychology of the self. In this task, Kernberg feels that Kohut must formulate an alternative motivational system for the self. Is he going to have to postulate a "growth drive"?

While Kernberg's points are well stated, they are derived from his own point of view of internalized object relations and do not represent an impartial assessment. As such, the very terms of his questions and the way that his points are framed introduce bias which at times seems to lead to misunderstanding. It is clear that many issues are not yet settled. The differing formulations suggest the possibility that Kohut and Kernberg are describing the operation of somewhat different developmental phenomena.

THE CHALLENGE OF STOLOROW AND LACHMAN: DEFENSE RECONSIDERED

A book remarkably consistent with the views articulated here, *Psychoanalysis of Developmental Arrests* (Stolorow and Lachman 1980), extends developmental thinking into the areas of narcissism, masochism, sadism, and defense. Placing importance upon "the evolution of the representational world of self and others" (Sandler and Rosenblatt 1962 and Stolorow and Atwood 1979), the authors maintain that "severe characterological, narcissistic, borderline, and psychotic disorders are now treatable within the framework of the more encompassing theory" (p. 3). Revisions, refinements, and elaborations of psychoanalytic developmental psychology have placed the analyst in a better situation to understand these "difficult-to-treat patients." The book focuses on major differences between the traditional psychoanalytic point of view and more recent developmental views.

Stolorow and Lachman propose that there is a:

> . . . developmental line for each defensive process with precursors or *prestages* of the defenses occurring prior to the consolidation of self and object representations. Furthermore, we demonstrate that it is of utmost importance clinically to distinguish between mental activity that functions principly as a defense, warding off components of intrapsychic conflict and superficially similar mental activity that is more accurately understood as a remnant of an arrest at a prestage of defensive development characterized by deficiencies in the structuralization of the representational world. (pp. 45ff)

They take the same position offered in this book; i.c., that "defense" may be an appropriate concept in the study of neurosis, but activity which resembles defense may stem from arrests at earlier developmental phases.

The example that Stolorow and Lachman (1980) cite in making their case is a young child who loses his parents to death. They maintain there is a difference between conceptualizing the child's inability to accept the loss of a parent as defensive (neurotic) and considering that "the young child had not yet developed the prerequisite psychological structures for *acknowledging* the loss and adapting to it" (p. 48). They resolve the contradictory views of denial as a defensive process versus the developmentally determined inability to register or to affirm an event, by the conceptualization of a "prestage of denial." They suggest that the concept of denial, and the concepts of psychological defense in general, be reserved for those:

> . . . situations in which the child's representational world may be expected to have matured sufficiently for him to acknowledge a reality—for example, the differences between the sexes—but he cannot do so because of the conflictual meanings, associations, or implications involved in that perception. (p. 48)

Other forms of failure to register or affirm events are not properly conceptualized as denial. While the example is taken from child development, the implications are many. In terms of the Listening Perspectives presented in this book, the notion of defense would be used properly in the Freudian Listening Perspective when neurosis (based on internal conflict and defense) is present, and to a limited extent in the selfobject Listening Perspective in which there may be a tendency to ward off conscious recognition of narcissistic trends. In pre-rapprochement phases of development, the concept of defense *would be deemed inappropriate* because neither structural conflict nor walling off of narcissistic investments is involved. This position presupposes repression to be the basic model for "defense" and would suggest that "splitting" and other early mental mechanisms are usually *not* defensive in nature but represent developmental processes.

Stolorow and Lachman (1980) extend their argument to grandiosity and idealization (pp. 63ff). In a comparison of case studies they demonstrate that with one patient grandiosity and idealization were predominantly manifestations of a developmental arrest at a prestage of defense while for another patient they were predominantly defenses against intrapsychic conflict. The differences in the *function* of grandiosity and idealization in the two patients cited were related to the degree of intrapsychic separation obtained. In terms used in this book, the distinction would be between a neurotic patient using idealization and grandiosity in the service of defending against structural conflict and another (preneurotic) patient using idealization and grandiosity in service of various developmental needs.

In considering projection, incorporation, and splitting (pp. 88f), Stolorow and Lachman (1980) maintain that these operate primarily through the lack of clarification and *distortion* of self and object representations. *As defenses* they operate to ward off from awareness aspects of the representational world associated with painful affects and intrapsychic conflict. However, *the developmental prestages* of projection and incorporation can be found in symbiotic states of earliest infancy, in which self and object representations are undifferentiated. They cite as examples toddlers who believe their mothers know their thoughts or have put thoughts into their heads, which would be the normal developmental equivalent of the "influencing machine" (Tausk 1919).

The distinction which Stolorow and Lachman (1980) draw between defenses against intrapsychic conflict (neurosis) and prestages of defense (preneurotic) has crucial implications for therapeutic approach. Whether one views the self and object confusion necessarily involved in projection, incorporation and splitting as defenses warding off intrapsychic conflict or whether one views them as rooted in developmental arrest is important. They make a strong point for careful diagnostic work, particularly so that the early phases of therapy can proceed with empathic intervention.

> When the analyst interprets as resistive what the patient accurately senses to be a developmental necessity, the patient often experiences the interpretation as a failure of empathy, a breach of trust, a narcissistic injury. It recreates for the patient a trauma similar to those which originally resulted in the developmental arrest (Balint 1969; Kohut 1971). To interpret a defense as a developmental arrest may make the analyst appear at least too benign, at most Pollyannish, but generally this can be corrected when a more accurate understanding of the patient's psychic reality is achieved. (pp. 112f.)

The interpretive approach to a defense is clearly to locate what the patient needs to ward off whereas the approach to a developmental deficit is to focus empathically on the state which the developmentally arrested patient needs to maintain or achieve.

Stolorow and Lachman (1980) hold that:

> . . . in the treatment of patients with developmental arrests at prestages of defense, the analyst's aim is to promote sufficient structuralization of the representational world to make possible a subsequent, more classical analysis of the defenses against intrapsychic conflicts. (p. 116)

This last quotation documents a difficulty in their formulation. Stolorow and Lachman take the position that developmental arrests must be responded to for exactly what they are. They realize that growth will then proceed but at that point in their thinking repeatedly talk about making "classical psychoanalysis of intrapsychic conflict possible." Perhaps more accurately stated would be to say that the growth derived from an appreciation of the developmental arrest *makes possible the developmental emergence of intrapsychic, structural conflict.* Because of the developmental arrest a level of intrapsychic structural conflict has simply not been attained. Therapeutic growth makes structure and conflict possible. Kohut (1977) makes reference to the same point when he indicates that at the end of the analysis of the selfobject transferences, his patients seem to pass through a brief period of what he calls "oedipal development." Kohut's implication is that these persons *have not ever had* an oedipal period and that only as the narcissistic or selfobject fixation is cleared up does it become *possible* to fully experience emotional triangulations. Kohut indicates that the brief-lived oedipal investment toward the close of therapy often involves curiosity about the analyst and the analyst's personal life. The classical notion about how therapy works with neurosis is that the intrapsychic conflict (instinct versus defense) has an opportunity to attain full emotional relevance *within* the transference situation. That is, the intrapsychic conflict experienced in childhood has an opportunity to be experienced in the transference neurosis by the mind of an adult. This is basically the definition of "cure" in neurosis and Stolorow and Lachman's idea of "making a more classical analysis of defenses against intrapsychic conflict" possible seems unnecessary since the level of development which makes such conflicts possible has presumably not been attained in any full or integrated sense.

Carrying their thesis further, Stolorow and Lachman (1980) show that death anxiety, hypochondriasis and depersonalization may occur in developmentally arrested patients as "symptoms" of deficiencies in the consolidation of a structurally cohesive and temporally stable self-representation. Death anxiety, hypochondriasis and depersonalization are conceptualized as closely related along a continuum of narcissistic decompensation. All three are evoked by the specter of a fragmenting or disintegrating self-representation.

> Death anxiety occurs as a signal when self-fragmentation is merely anticipated as a threatening possibility. Hypochondriasis sounds the alarm when the regressive self-disintegration has actually begun and the preoccupation with bodily organs or mental functions already contains a concretizing effort at self-stabilization and self-restitution. In depersonalization, the process of self dissolution has proceeded even further and is directly represented in the uncanny feeling that the self has become unreal or estranged. (p. 141)

In these phenomena, they maintain the importance of determining the "motivational priority" or urgency of the different functions which these symptoms may be serving for a particular patient at a particular point in the treatment. It is:

> . . . important to assess whether the symptom is primarily serving the purposes of defense or whether it is more accurately understood as reflecting deficiencies in the structuralization of self-representation as a remnant of developmental arrest at a prestage of defense. (p. 142)

In summarizing their theoretical position, Stolorow and Lachman (1980) draw four general conclusions:

> First, the developmental lines leading to differentiation, integration, and consolidation of self and object representations are of critical importance in conceptualizing the more severe forms of psychopathology and their treatment.
>
> Second, in order to be able to understand and treat structurally deficient, developmentally arrested patients, the principle of multiple function (Waelder, 1936) must be expanded to include a consideration of the ways in which the psychopathology functions to restore or maintain precarious or imperiled self and object representations which, in the course of development, have not been adequately consolidated.
>
> Third, the concept of defense must be reformulated within a developmental framework. There is a developmental line for each defensive process with precursors or prestages of defense occurring prior to the structuralization of self and object representations. Hence, a defense in the usual sense of the term represents the end point of a series of developmental achievements.
>
> Fourth, it is of utmost theoretical and therapeutic importance to distinguish between mental activity that functions principally as a defense warding off components of intrapsychic conflict, and superficially similar mental activity that is more accurately understood as a remnant of an arrest at a prestage of defensive development characterized by deficiencies in the consolidation of self and object representations. This distinction . . . makes possible the recognition of the ways

in which a variety of psychological products may not only express psycho-pathology, *but also signal the attainment of developmental steps in the structurali-zation of the representational world.* (italics added) (pp. 172ff)

Stolorow and Lachman offer an extensive elaboration of the difficulties entailed in interpreting at a faulty level based on a faulty diagnosis of developmental need. Faulty interpretation accounts for many premature endings of therapy.

We suggest that many therapeutic impasses and disasters are the product of a specific failure in empathy, wherein the analyst misunderstands and misinter-prets the meaning of the patient's archaic states by amalgamating them into his own much more differentiated and integrated world of self and object represen-tation. Such misunderstandings typically take the form of erroneously interpret-ing remnants of developmental arrests as if they were expressions of resistances defending against intrapsychic conflicts. . . . The patient will experience such a misinterpretation as a gross failure of empathy, a severe breach of trust. (p. 190)

In this regard, the authors harshly criticize Kernberg's (1975) approach to the systematic interpretation of the patient's transference resistances. They feel interpretation of transference resistances is appropriate "only for those patients who have achieved a prerequisite degree of differentiation and integration of self and object representations" (p. 191).

The seminal contribution of this very important book is to point out that behavior heretofore considered defensive may stem from a variety of arrests in the development of self and object differentiation. In addition, their formulations regarding continua of defensive processes liberates current thinking from strict Freudian metapsychology and adds the metapsycho-logical dimension of "self and object representations." The general approach taken by Stolorow and Lachman (1980) is consistent with the approach this book has taken. In studying the problem of defense they have concluded that defense is an important aspect in structural conflict in psychoneuroses. However, in preoedipal, prestructural mental states, the concept "defense" is no longer appropriate. They give numerous illustrations of what they call "prestages" of defense. While their book only discusses oedipal level defense vs. preoedipal levels of prestages, the current book has broken down the preoedipal experience into three nodal points of psychic development such that four Listening Perspectives have been envisioned.

THE CHALLENGE OF ROBERT LANGS: THE ADAPTIVE CONTEXT

One of the few psychoanalytic writers to address directly the listening process is Robert Langs (1976, 1978, 1980, 1981). His evolving approach focuses on the spiraling communicative network involved in the adaptive context of psychotherapy. According to this view, both patient and therapist are faced with an adaptive task. The precise manner in which each party experiences the prevailing adaptive context may be seen as "encoded in derivative communications." According to Langs, the systematic study of encoded derivative communications can lead to "mutative interpretations" (Strachey 1934) which validate the listening process. Langs's ideas will be briefly summarized in order to show their relevance to the development of Listening Perspectives.

Drawing upon the long tradition of classical psychoanalysis and the rich awareness of interpersonal interaction of the Kleinian school of psychoanalysis, Langs (1976) conceptualizes a "bipersonal field" as a "frame" or "framework" with specific limits, controls, safeguards, and boundaries which serve to "contain" (Bion 1962, 1963) or "hold" (Modell 1976) both the patient and the therapist. According to Langs, it is within the frame or framework that the transference can ultimately be "secured as analyzable and illusory" (Langs 1976, p. 252). The patient's "first order adaptive task" is to recognize and respond to the therapeutic frame.

Modifications of the frame (or the basic psychoanalytic ground rules) constitute a "therapeutic misalliance" (1976, p. 70) or a "vicious circle" (Baranger and Baranger 1966) in which the reality of the therapeutic situation, "the outer world," cannot be meaningfully distinguished from the patient's "inner world." Thus the "therapeutic differential" becomes blocked from view. According to Langs, the only proper course for therapeutic action in the case of a modification of the frame (by either patient or therapist) is a "rectification" of the modification such that boundaries, controls, and safeguards are once again restored. When a therapeutic misalliance is active, interpretation is not possible, and any therapeutic progress can only be labeled "modification cure."

Langs's concept of the bipersonal field is essentially a metaphor involving two poles (the therapist and the patient) and "vectors of pathology" between the two.[3] This conceptualization implies that the "pathology" of the therapist remains realistically active within the frame of the bipersonal field as does the "pathology" of the patient. Conceptualization of the therapeutic situation as a bipersonal field places a special emphasis on the interpersonal interaction and "the reality of the pathology of the therapist" with its expectable influence on the patient. Familiar and traditional aspects of the frame or the framework of the bipersonal field are such things as maintaining total confidentiality, fostering an exclusive one-to-one relationship, confining the therapeutic interaction to the space of the consulting room, the

---

[3]The reader is referred to Langs's *The Listening Process* (1978) for a detailed account of these ideas, particularly Appendix B. Further elaboration of his ideas is contained in *Psychotherapy: A Basic Text* (1982).

therapist's retaining a position of relative anonymity and the therapist's limiting interventions to a position of relative neutrality.

Langs repeatedly makes the point that it is *the patient* via derivative communications who insistently expresses a need for the special frame of the bipersonal field. He further indicates a hierarchy of therapeutic tasks. "First, the therapist must deal with interactional resistances" (1976, p. 217). Either the patient or the therapist may introduce modifications of the frame. The first order of attention is the resistance to rectifying these modifications and to the re-establishment and maintenance of the frame. The second area of priority of therapeutic intervention:

> . . . relates to the interpretation of interactional mechanisms and interactional contents as well as to containing functions. This brings our attention to both the container and the contained, and the importance of dealing with—by both modifying and interpreting—alterations in the framework and the interactional pathology related to both the therapist's and the patient's containing functions. (p. 218)

Here Langs includes a reference to needs on the part of the therapist to introject and contain "the patient's sickness in a non-therapeutic manner." He also refers to "inappropriate needs on the part of the patient to accept into (him or) herself the pathology of the therapist who has a complementary need to use the patient as a pathological container."

The basic maxim has always been to deal with resistances before content. Langs adds dealing with the interactional sphere before the intrapsychic sphere and, as part of that, taking up the intrapsychic contributions to interactional resistances and contents before dealing with the primarily intrapsychic. In defining the priority of therapeutic intervention, Langs says, "It is only when the interactional dimension is under control that we are in a position to get around to the focus on the patient's intrapsychic conflicts and pathological introjects" (p. 218). Langs does not think that the therapeutic work with the interactional dimension is a "second order job," but that such work offers:

> . . . the patient crucial cognitive insights and positive introjective identifications with the therapist. In working on this third level—the intrapsychic—in which the focus is on the patient's inner world, we again deal with defenses and resistances, before content—core unconscious fantasies and introjects. In all of this work we shift from the present to the past and generally we will tend to go back and forth from the interactional to the intrapsychic realms, stressing one or the other, depending on the bipersonal field and the two participants. (p. 218)

Langs's recent work (1978, 1980, 1982) deals mainly with an elaboration of the "spiraling communication network" which develops in the psychotherapeutic situation. He places special emphasis upon listening for encoded derivative communications which reveal the patient's experience of the adaptive or interactional context of the therapeutic situation. Langs's studies aim at piercing that area of "mutative interpretations" which Strachey as early as 1934 noted analysts and therapists (defensively) avoid. The patient's material, according to Langs, may be organized on three levels: manifest content (the surface of association and behavior); Type I derivatives (inferences drawn from the material based on theory, symbolism, knowledge of the patient, etc.); and Type II derivatives (crucial meanings and functions arising from the prevailing adaptive context of the interpersonal situation). Communications relating to the adaptive context are seen to have highest relevance to the treatment process (Type A communications). Communications characterized by a need for action discharge, projective identification and merged identities (Type B) are of less importance while communications based on broken or ruptured interpersonal links (Type C) are thought to disrupt or destroy meanings and to seal off inner and interactional chaos.

Langs only considers interventions validated when (Type II) adaptive context meanings become organized into new configurations via what Bion (1962) calls the "selected fact"—a new formulation which introduces order and new meaning into previously disparate experiences. Such validated interventions Langs believes merit the designation "mutative interpretations."

Langs's formulations regarding the listening process involved in understanding the communicative network of the adaptive context are intended to be applied broadly to all psychotherapeutic and psychoanalytic situations. However, the precise implications of Langs's approach have not yet been studied with regard to listening to various developmental phases of differentiation of Self and Other experience. A problem with attempting to extend Langs's thinking in this regard is a quasi-moralistic *tone* which pervades his writings. His formulations are stated in such a way as to point toward a specific therapeutic approach or technique, i.e., the way "good" psychotherapy "should" be conducted. This tone does not appear fundamental to Langs's ideas but rather seems to stem from his general background in Classical psychoanalysis. As has been previously pointed out, the Classical position owes its derivation mainly to a study of the psychoneuroses, the relatively advanced (oedipal) levels of Self and Other differentiation. Langs's "ideal therapeutic environment" with a secure frame leading ultimately to the analysis of encoded (Type II) derivatives of the adaptive context describes the *developmental capabilities* of persons who have achieved the advanced capacity for repression of oedipal incestuous-parricidal strivings. Langs's "ideal therapeutic environment" also effectively describes a level of development in Self and Other differentiation *which may eventually become a possibility* for persons arrested at earlier phases of "part-object," "merger-object," and "selfobject" experience.

While the establishment of a secure therapeutic frame may be an eventual *goal* in work with preoedipal developmental arrests, Langs has not yet specified other approaches to "holding" (Modell 1976) and "containing" (Bion 1962) which may be appropriate for the earlier phases of therapy with such persons. Whether one thinks in terms of introducing (supportive) parameters (Eissler 1953) so that the patient can engage in later analytic work, or whether the therapist introduces various maneuvers to preserve his/her own personal or professional identity (Giovacchini 1979a), "modifications in the frame" can hardly be avoided if empathic therapeutic contact with less than differentiated Self and Other experience is to be accomplished.

Countertransference factors become a prominent feature in all modifications of the frame. As a result, extensive studies of countertransference have come to characterize thinking about preoedipal analytic work. By way of analogy, it might be said that for an adult to expect a two-year-old child to relate on the basis of advanced (mutual) levels of Self and Other differentiations is to misunderstand the way the child experiences the world. Such a striking lack of empathy on the part of the adult could only stem from a lack of experience or understanding in how to relate to childhood (merger) experiences or else reveals that the adult had himself not attained a mature enough level of Self-Other differentiation to be able to respond to the child as a separate center of initiative with independent and different Self-Other motivational experiences. For a psychotherapist to remain preoccupied with maintaining the frame and promoting the ideal therapeutic environment when attempting to relate to persons with early developmental arrests runs the same dangers as parents who attempt to rear their children "by the rule book." The effect—gross empathic failure—may be the same *even if* moving to a level where the frame does represent mutually empathic respect for two independent and separate selves is the ultimate goal. Langs's understanding of this general point is implicit in his ideas on interpretive priority in which he states that the interactional aspects of the adaptive context must be addressed before the intrapsychic. Translated into developmental terms, Langs appears to be saying that the patient's experiences of merger and selfobject needs require attention before the realm of intrapsychic conflict (oedipal and constant objects) can be meaningfully addressed.

Developmental considerations regarding the gradual differentiation of Self and Other experience call for a slight alteration in the tone or the vocabulary of Langs's formulations to include the recognition that the "ideal therapeutic environment" is a situation which implies advanced experiences in Self-Other differentiation. A cautious willingness to permit or engage in various modifications in the frame may represent the therapist's awareness and responsiveness to the earlier developmental experiences of selfobjects, merger objects, and part-objects. In a similar vein it may be possible to understand the natural and expectable quality of Type B and C communications in the treatment of early developmental arrests. Rather than to assume these forms of communication represent the erection of barriers to communication, they may come to be viewed as evidence of developmentally determined inabilities to form consistent communications on more differentiated levels.

Perhaps the most important aspects of Langs's work for the present purposes of establishing Listening Perspectives is the general backdrop his formulations provide. Just as Freud's topographic model of the mind (conscious, preconscious, and unconscious aspects of mental functioning) provides an end point in the basic conceptualizing of mental development, a goal generally attainable through favorable developmental opportunities; so a person's ability to adapt to Langs's "ideal therapeutic environment" might be thought of as an end point in conceptualizing early Self-Other differentiation. Psychotherapy addressed to earlier developmental phases might be expected to entail various phase-appropriate adaptations. Langs has indicated an interest in extending his ideas on the listening process to a study of the representational world of Self and Others (1980), so clarifications on these issues will likely be forthcoming.

The capacity to adapt favorably to the therapeutic frame seems to imply a measure of self and object constancy. A securely held frame can provide the backdrop for the gradual unfolding of the neurotic transferences based on intrapsychic conflicts regarding oedipal (parricidal and incestual) strivings. Persons seeking psychotherapy for preoedipal developmental arrests lack the necessary experience of self and object constancy required for this classical treatment technique. Modifications in the frame or holding environment will be expected as the therapist seeks to fully understand the particular style or idiosyncratic quality of Self and Other experience which dominates each preoedipal personality. In therapy with preoedipal arrests the therapist must first permit him or herself to be molded (interactionally) to the particular style or mode of Self and Object experiences which the patient lives. Only then is the therapist in a position to understand fully and gradually to block the merger or assert his/her boundaries empathically *against* the patient's infantile relationship demands, i.e., rectification of the frame. As in early mothering, it will be the therapist's gradual (frustrating) assertion of self boundaries within the atmosphere created by the patient's needs for repeating part- merger or selfobject patterns, which will permit and foster the separation-individuation experience. This interactional process can be expected to dominate the therapy until self and object constancy begins to appear along with (parricidal and incestual) intrapsychic conflicts. Such conflict will usually appear in direct relation to the therapist who for these persons in fact comes to serve as the oedipal object. Only in the latter phases of therapy can the frame be secured and intrapsychic conflict analyzed according to classical technique. Langs's focus on the frame and the adaptive context serves as a constant reminder of what the person cannot yet attain and serves to clarify the direction of the therapeutic growth process of Self and Other differentiations. Growth requires that the therapist shift Listening Perspectives as the therapeutic process evolves.

THE CHALLENGE OF ROY SCHAFER:
ACTION LANGUAGE

A voice calling out against uncritical use of Freud's metapsychological principles is Roy Schafer in his 1976 book, *A New Language for Psychoanalysis*.[4] From the point of view of epistemology and linguistic analysis, Schafer directs attention to a number of problems in psychoanalytic theory stemming from the traditional language of psychoanalysis. Schafer felt Freud's need to cast psychoanalytic theory in a biological framework was based on Freud's personal interest in a Newtonian model of science and the philosophical framework of the Hegelian dialectic. It was Heinz Hartmann who "attempted to develop to its highest possible point, Freud's natural science model of mind" (p. 99). Hartmann's basic contribution was to establish another general theory of psychoanalysis (Ego Psychology) just as Freud established his general theory of psychoanalysis based on the concept of the unconscious. Hartmann's weakness, according to Schafer, was his continued adherence to the natural science model. Schafer views psychoanalysis as an *interpretive discipline* and proposes another approach to psychoanalysis based on what he terms "action language."

The "fundamental rule" of action language is that each psychological process, event, experience, or behavior be regarded as some kind of activity. Each activity or action should be designated by use of an active verb stating its nature. Schafer also honors the use of adverbs for stating the *mode* of activity or action.

"Action" or "activity" is understood by Schafer to include all private psychological activity that can be made public through gesture and speech, such as dreaming and the unspoken thinking of everyday life, as well as all public activity such as ordinary speech and motoric behavior which has some goal directed or symbolic properties. Whether initially private or public, the activity may be pursued consciously or unconsciously.

The use of action verbs and adverbs precludes the use of nouns and adjectives. Nouns and adjectives are appealing in psychoanalysis because of their congruence with the archaic body language of infancy. Statements such as "she is all heart" or "it comes straight from the heart" or "he has a

---

[4]In this section I am quoting and paraphrasing Schafer's book extensively and liberally. I make no claim to these ideas and only hope that this review does justice to Schafer's thinking as put forward in his remarkable collection of papers.

strong ego" are examples which Schafer uses to illustrate how nouns or adjectives have a permanent place in everyday language.

Schafer points out several consequences of adopting such a fundamental rule of language. The first consequence results in being unable to refer to a location, movement, or direction because the "inside" of a person is only imaginary. It is also impossible to speak of a "depth" of a motion or a cathexis because such references also refer to a spatialization metaphor. The second consequence is the elimination of the verb "to have," because it is not an action verb. The linking verbs "to be" or "to become" must also be used cautiously. A third consequence of the fundamental rule of action language is that propositions can be stated only in the active voice, and the linguistic constructions must be limited to those which clarify *activity* and *modes of activity*. The fourth consequence is that the idea of special classes of processes that prepare or propel mental activity (such as instincts and motives) be abandoned. Action language admits no special processes which propel or prepare mental activity. Action language simply states "preliminary actions" that make possible "final actions."

Persons act, not minds, instincts, egos or unconscious processes. Traditional psychoanalytic theorizing offers personifications and anthropomorphic modes of thought which then lead to these "entities" being able to act and interact as people might! "The ego interacts with the id," "the superego governs the ego," etc. *The central problem with using action language is how one can view the person as a whole and describe his activities in action terms without becoming simplistic or behavioristic.* Schafer holds that action language:

> . . . is not a behavioristic language in any usual sense of that designation; for it includes everything that psychoanalytic propositions have included from the beginning. Rather the difference lies in this; that in certain respects we shall speak about people more plainly and, while continuing to emphasize the action in the unconscious mode, we shall neither engage in speculation about what is ultimately unutterable in any form nor build elaborate theories on the basis of unfalsifiable propositions concerning mental activity at the beginning of infancy. Attributions of meaning and thus of action reach a vanishing point as one moves back toward that period of life. (Schafer 1976, p. 10)

Schafer describes Freudian metapsychology as utilizing a language with a set of rules for saying things of the sort that constitute or communicate a particular version of "reality." It is the mechanistic version of reality communicated through the language of metapsychology that Schafer finds particularly problematic and concretistic. Psychoanalysis has stringently modeled itself after the natural sciences and has concomitantly developed a physiochemical and biological language which corresponds. Freudian metapsychology conceptualizes human beings as biological entities who are, for example, subjected to or invaded by forces, driven by desires, and over-wrought by impulses. In this manner, reasons come to be spoken of as forces, emphases as energy, activities as functions, thoughts as representations, affects as discharges. Particular ways of struggling with the inevitable diversity of intentions, feelings, and situations become spoken of in terms of structures, mechanisms, and adaptations. Furthermore, the human being comes to be spoken of as a more or less mechanical and mindless object or as a being that must be made into an object of observation and scrutiny. In short, Freudian metapsychology removes the purposive agent, the experiencing human being, the active self, the "I," and reduces that personal "I" to an unintentional "thing," organism, and apparatus (Schafer 1976).

Schafer proposes to replace the established Freudian metapsychology with a language of action where each individual becomes an agent of his/her own actions. In this way, the central agent is viewed as *the person* who does things for reasons and creates his/her own experiences. Action language is conceptualized by Schafer as a technical language which uses plain, English locutions. It seeks to specify psychological facts and relations plainly, lucidly, and consistently. It is designed for the purpose of systematic discourse about human beings and human lives. According to Schafer, *psychoanalysis is best conceptualized as an interpretive discipline, not a natural science,* which goes along with the emphasis and logic of action language. In essence, action language refutes the biological metapsychology originally conceptualized by Freud and offers itself as the "new language of psychoanalysis." Schafer anticipates that one of the major difficulties in replacing metapsychology language with action language will be the analyst's resistance in shifting from the familiar language to the utilization of something new.

Schafer follows Wittgenstein's conception of language as a set of rules for saying things of the sort that constitute or communicate a version of reality or a world which includes psychic reality.

> It is only by means of sets of language rules that we are ever able to achieve a systematic approach to knowing anything, including knowing anything psychoanalytic. By adopting these rules we establish what we shall count as fact, factual coherence, and ascriptive limits; thereby we also establish criteria of consistency and relevance in our psychological discussions. (Schafer 1976)

Schafer sees the need to replace the established metapsychology with another language to render that "sense of being" of the people of our civilization that is based on both their personal and communal history. He proposes this alternate language consist of words which, through common use, are already endowed with significant, extensive, and personal constitutions. He maintains that for purposes of psychological describing and explaining it will become necessary to codify certain usages that are "familiar, direct, evocative, and plastic; additionally the language must be personal and must provide a basis for some kind of eloquence." Choice of language is important in order to avoid misunderstanding and other criticisms which have been directed against Freudian metapsychology. Schafer believes action language can satisfy the criteria of developmental, historical, and cultural relevance together with actual and potential communicative richness.

Action Language Interpretation

According to Schafer's action language approach, the *strategy of interpretation* would be to:

> . . . identify a network of intelligible actions where none was thought to exist, thereby expanding the range of acknowledged activity in the analysand's experience of his own life, and to develop a history of his own life as intelligible activity.

Instances of *masked activity* are referred to as "disclaimed actions." A "slip of the tongue" is thought of as an action, something the analysand has done, something that is intelligible in terms of actions one wishes to perform and the conflicts one experiences in this regard. Rather than locutions referring to the mind as a place or thing, the action model of interpretation would hold that *"the mind is something that we do*; it is neither something we have or something we are not related to or in possession of." *Conflict* may be conceptualized as a psychological event which involves a minimum of three constituent actions. "As agent, one engages in two actions, which in a third one believes to be incompatible with one another." Schafer defines *impulse* as an action a person would do were he not effectively refraining from doing it. *Thought* is silent or silenced speech. In Schafer's sense, *"action is human behavior that has a point, it is meaningful human activity, it is intentional or goal directed performances by people, it is doing things for a reason"* (italics added). There is no limit of vantage points from which an action may be regarded and therefore no limit to the ways that it may be defined or described. The issue of *free will* does not arise for an action language. *Disclaimers* may be verbalized or non-verbalized. *Verbalized disclaimers* tend to be drawn from expressions in everyday life. Disclaimers have typically been classified in terms of "mechanisms of defense," such as isolation, splitting, introjection, and projection. Disclaimers help avoid a feeling of being held responsible, and contribute to a wish to "get off the hook." They are frequently used to protect relationships. It is in keeping with the action model of interpretation to subsume all notions of "resistance" under the heading of "disclaimed action" just as it is to subsume "insights" under the heading "claimed and reclaimed action." Schafer believes the fundamental rule of psychoanalysis (free association) encourages the analysand to disclaim responsibility for action, promotes the assumption of a passive position, and supports intellectualization.

Self and Identity

Schafer holds that concepts such as "self" and "identity" represent a transitional phase of a conceptual revolution that is replacing natural science language with terms and explanatory propositions better suited to the methods and data of the psychoanalytic study of human beings. In making clear what he is referring to, Schafer cites Mahler's concept of "separation-individuation," as referring to changes in the degree and stability of the child's differentiation of its self representations from object representations and changes in the degree and flexibility of the child's independent activity in the social and physical world. Representational differentiation Schafer sees as the core of the separation-individuation concept. "Self" and "identity" serve as supraordinate concepts for the self representations, which the child sorts out (separates, individuates) from its internally undifferentiated subjective experiences of the mother-infant matrix. In adolescence "representational cohesion" seems to be an important connotation of the "self" and "identity" as representational differentiations from "others." Self and identity according to Schafer are not facts about people but technical ways of thinking about people.

They have become ways in which many people think about themselves. Each is merely one type of representation or one way of representing. Self and identity as terms may be interchangeable based upon the observer's changeable purposes in using these terms. They are classes of representation that exist in the vocabulary of the observer and are quite varied in scope, time of origin, and objectivity; many are maintained unconsciously, and many remain forever uncoordinated, if not contradictory.

Action Language as Operationism*

While there must be many ways to receive Schafer's penetrating critique and definitive action language proposals, one way would be to view his ideas as steps toward introducing an operational slant into psychoanalysis. In the history of physics, it will be recalled that the Newtonian model of inquiry generally sought to discover the "immutable laws of nature." The "laws" were once viewed as "discovered principles" and seen as great and permanent contributions, the observations from which were but stepping stones to the plane of "Eternal Verities." Einstein not only replaced the principles of Newton, but he also destroyed completely the underlying

*Thanks to Charles Margach for the ideas as contained in this section.

concept of laws. Today's physicists no longer delude themselves that they are "discovering permanent principles." Instead, they pay homage to the God Utility. "What concepts," modern physicists ask, "are the most useful at this moment in time? Whatever they may be, use them to best advantage today for tomorrow they will have been replaced by other concepts destined to flourish briefly and then too, in turn, be replaced by fresh ideas." An obvious question then is: Is this an endless chain, or is there some end point where and when there shall have been formulated the definitive "eternal verities" of the universe? P. W. Bridgman, in *The Logic of Modern Physics* (1927), made two crucial points in this regard. First, he stressed the importance of differentiating clearly between the observations and the inferences (conceptual schemes) in any discipline. Such differentiation involves not only the initial identification of various propositions into the appropriate category, but also establishing the utilization of each category. His second point emphasized the importance of realizing that fundamentally, regardless of subsequent elaborations and extensions, any inference (concept) is defined by the operations utilized in identifying it (i.e., the operational definition). Thus Bridgman's answer to the question, "Will it ever be possible to formulate one or more of the eternal verities?" would be, "If there are ultimate concepts, then we must be able in advance to specify how we are to identify them, i.e., we must be able to specify what the operations are that will enable us to know when we have achieved such an end." Thus, within the confines of the operations which are considered authentic and credible by the natural sciences, there can be no way of knowing when or if one has formulated an eternal verity and such truths can be known *a priori* to be unattainable. While mystics disagree with this line of thought, physicists (and other scientists) are limited in a post-Einsteinian world to operational definitions and a search for useful, not true, conceptual schemes.

The operationism of Bridgman served a similar role for physics that the behaviorism of Watson peformed for psychology. What is *observedly* happening? What items in systematic discourse exceed that input? Sophistication has gradually been attained in differentiating between observation and inference. At the same time physicists, linguists, psychologists, and others with a scientific bent began to realize that operationism in its purist form totally lacked heuristic implications. Operationism only indicates what has happened and makes no suggestions as to where to turn next. The "What next?" question draws only operational blanks. The answer to the question, "Is operationism dead today, a victim of its own sterility?" depends to a considerable extent upon the solution to the dilemma of whether it is conceivable that a person may be simultaneously operational and heuristic. That is, can a worker advance a theory in full recognition of its tentative nature and still be prepared to retreat when sufficiently challenged to a fully operational position?

Schafer, although there was no mention of Bridgman in his text, was surely aware of operationism in physics and early psychology. If one were to assign Freud a role in psychoanalysis equivalent to that of Newton in physics, it would be clear that as yet anyhow, no "Einstein" of psychoanalysis has appeared. Despite major contributions to the field of psychoanalysis no one seems to have shared Freud's permanence as a figure in this field let alone to have displaced him as Einstein displaced Newton. However, as Bridgman (1927) points out, the Einsteinian theory of relativity which replaced Newton's three laws of motion is less important in itself than its methodological implications subsumed under the doctrine of operationism. Theories of relativity are relevant primarily to physics. Operationism is of universal applicability across the total spectrum of human inquiry. Psychoanalysis does not need to await its Einstein before it can benefit from the application of operationism to its content and to its procedures. Schafer's "Action Language" suggestions go along with this general line of thought and fall clearly into two categories:

1. The importance of differentiating between observations of human behavior ("actions") and the inferential labels applied to these observations.
2. The problem of accomplishing this differentiation with regard to some of the more complex areas of human activity, i.e., practicing operationism with respect to various verbal, nonverbal, and unconscious activities studied by psychoanalysis.

Differentiating clearly between observations of activity and inferences about those activities seems in many ways more difficult in psychoanalysis than in physics. Newton saw the apple fall, and he inferred "gravity." When the patient says "two plus two is four," can one realize that "memory" or "mental calculation" are only inferences? When one hears the patient say "shit!" how easy is it to realize that one only infers such things as "the id breaking through the censorship of the superego"?

Practicing clinicians have spent years translating actual observations of human behavior into metapsychological terminology. As the translation became easier through practice, so simultaneously has it become more difficult to realize that one makes the translation and also to be able to report the observation free of the translation. Schafer's monumental contribution to the field highlights this difficulty. One might consider that Schafer has taken up where strict Watsonian behaviorism stopped. Watson undoubtedly recognized that speech and silent speech were action, yet he chose to ignore it in his system, perhaps because he found it so difficult to separate inference from observation. The brilliance of Schafer's ideas lies in his step-by-step analysis of the present day morass of psychoanalytic linguistics. He points out how laboriously people in the field translate naive observation into a framework of supposedly "eternal verities." He further points out shrewd use of inferential categories to "shift the blame" (or responsibility) to some convenient non-protesting construct such as "the mind" or "the unconscious."

In considering that Schafer is introducing an operational perspective into psychoanalysis, it needs be said that strict operationism in psychoanalysis, as in physics, is untenable. Operationism in its pure sense spawns only eclecticism without guiding or integrating conceptual frameworks. The question arises as to which inferential framework one wishes to use. It might be maintained that the psychoanalytic clinician (just as the researcher in physics) who believes that he "has truth by the tail" and is steadily pulling closer and closer to "ultimate reality" is likely to be imbued with a fervor and gusto that his eclectic colleague lacks. If the "truth holder" is on a non-fruitful trail he, of course, reaps disaster; but if perchance he has chosen a fruitful alternative he is likely to reach his destination well ahead of his less committed eclectic colleague. In this regard it is interesting to note that Einstein himself, for all his iconoclastic shattering of the laws of Newton and the consequent establishment of the tentative nature of all hypotheses, in his later years abandoned laboratory work and concentrated solely on theoretical development. He is reputed to have adopted the belief that physics is a logical system of thought in a state of evolution. "Its basics cannot be obtained merely by experimentation and experience. Its progress depends on free invention. . . . I haven't the faintest doubt but that I am right."

One might say the overall "Gestalt" of an inferential system may offer to the investigator much more than the sum of its components. A psychoanalytic investigator imbued with a theoretical perspective may indeed encounter the problem of confusing observations with inference. But so long as he/she recognizes the tentative nature of the theoretical formulations, he/she remains able to retreat to an operational position such as the one provided by Schafer's action language. However, Schafer's (1976) advocacy of wholesale utilization of action language, like Klein's (1970, 1973) advocacy of wholesale abandonment of metapsychology, tends to neglect the historical truism that creative thought has always been caught in a vacillating tension between reference to operationally defined facts and intuitively defined schemas. The notion advocated in the present book of developing a series of overlapping, maturationally defined Listening Perspectives has the advantage of simultaneously recognizing (1) the importance of operational facts (actions) which the analyst observes and (2) the necessity of utilizing and developing to their fullest various conceptual or schematic frames of reference (Listening Perspectives), for the continuous purpose of classifying and organizing ideas *about* actions.

Summary

Three general approaches to scientific inquiry have thus emerged. The earliest was Newton's approach based upon the assumption that there are "eternal verities" which are knowable. The job of scientific man is to "discover" the laws of the universe. Einstein introduced the relativist approach which generally relies on the assumption that reality is unknown and unknowable. According to this second approach scientific man busies himself developing concepts, constructing theories and building models. These approximations of reality will be cast aside when their "usefulness" is outlived in favor of more "useful" theories and models. The third approach to scientific inquiry was adopted by Einstein in his later years and holds that man has a variety of ways of interacting with reality. Scientific man thus applies his ingenuity and creativity to the task of organizing his ideas about reality and toward expanding his means of observing and interacting with reality. *By developing new perspectives, the scientist is in a continuous process of creating new realities.*

This book follows Einstein's later approach in asserting that modern psychoanalysis has developed four basic Listening Perspectives or ways of following the introspective and interactive experience of persons who come to the consulting room. These perspectives are organized along a developmental axis which places importance upon *the experience of* intrapsychic representations of self and other. The four Listening Perspectives discussed correspond roughly to the traditional diagnostic conceptualizations of psychotic, borderline, narcissistic and neurotic personality organizations.

Schafer's key ideas on language in psychoanalysis have been reviewed extensively in order to illustrate the profound effect which the way one talks has on the way one listens, thinks and creates. While the present book is not wholly successful in applying Schafer's new language ideas to modern psychoanalysis, every attempt has been made to benefit from Schafer's penetrating analysis and to avoid wherever possible the pitfalls he has so carefully delineated.

THE CHALLENGE OF LACAN:
A RETURN TO FREUD

The influential and controversial work of the French psychoanalyst, Jacques Lacan, has only recently become available to English readers in *Écrits: A Selection* (1977).[5] Lacan takes the view that the practice of psychoanalysis, particularly object relations and ego psychology, has moved away from Freud's basic insights regarding unconscious processes as outlined in

[5]The nine lectures date from 1936 to 1960.

The Interpretation of Dreams (1900), *The Psychopathology of Everyday Life* (1901), and *Jokes and Their Relation to the Unconscious* (1905).

In a startlingly fresh reading of Freud, Lacan has declared that the locus of Freud's unconscious is to be found in the symbolic order of the structure of language which can be referred to as "the Other," or to use Freud's own term "the other scene."[6] Following the Lévi-Strauss (1949, 1951) elucidation of the "universal laws of man" which regulate unconscious mental activities and the structural linguistic work of Saussure (1916) as well as Jakobson and Halle (1956), Lacan holds that it was only through a quirk of history that the conceptual tools of modern anthropology and structural linguistics were unavailable to Freud in his formulation of ideas about unconscious mental processes. Nevertheless, Lacan demonstrates that the essence of the so-called "structuralist" approach did not escape Freud, but rather, permeates his writings. Freud's successive attempts at establishing a topography for understanding the manifestations of unconscious activities have been used by his followers, claims Lacan, to ossify the mere outline of Freud's early discoveries and to betray or evade entirely Freud's revolutionary insights. Lacan's most often cited example is Freud's famous dictum translated, "Where Id was, there shall Ego be" (1923).[7] Through extensive argument and careful analysis of the surrounding German text Lacan shifts the translation to, "There where it was, I must come to pass" (1977, p. 171). A more elaborate translation reads, "There where it was just now, there where it was for a while, between an extinction that is still glowing and a birth that is retarded, 'I' can come into being and disappear from what I say." "It" is supposed to mean the symbolic order. Lacan's lifetime project of scrutinizing the Freudian text would be impossible to summarize here, but the radical difference in Lacan's reading of Freud and the available English translations has enormous implications, several of which are crucial in the clinical listening task.[8]

The linguistic example just cited is one of many instances through which Lacan maintains Freud attempted to describe man's consciousness and its relation to the symbolic order, "the other scene," the unconscious. As his point of departure for a systematic study of the subject's experience in analysis, Lacan cites as prototypical of human development the well-known anecdote from "Beyond the Pleasure Principle" (Freud, 1920, pp. 14-15).

---

[6]Lacan also uses the terms: *Logos*, the Word, the Law, the Phallus and the Name-of-the-Father as synonyms for "the Other" and "the Other Scene."

[7]In German, *Wo es war, soll Ich werden.*

[8]Kernberg (personal communication) states a basic agreement with Bruno Bettleheim's recent *New Yorker* articles criticizing the English *Standard Edition* translation of the works of Freud. Kernberg feels that in the near future translations based less on Ego Psychology interpretations of the Freudian text will become available and that some of Lacan's points will be easier to consider and evaluate.

Freud's grandson engaged in the solitary game of throwing a wooden reel with a piece of string tied around it over the edge of his curtained cot when dealing with separations from his mother. As the reel disappeared he uttered an expressive "o-o-o-o" (for *"fort,"* i.e., "gone") and as he pulled it out he hailed its reappearance with a joyous *"da"* ("here"). The *"Fort-da"* game according to Lacan represents a pairing of phonemes in an effort to make the mother present in her absence. This child's speech thus represents his first pair (of twelve possible binary pairs) of phonemes available to each language (Jakobson and Halle, 1956). As such, these words represent his initiation into "the world of meaning . . . in which the world of things will come to be arranged" (1977, p. 65). "It is the world of words that creates the world of things . . . by giving its concrete being to their essence . . ." (ibid.)

As early as 1936[9] Lacan studied mirroring phenomena of early childhood. The illustrative paradigm is a child's mirror play as he/she studies the relation between the complex movements assumed (identified with) in the reflected image (and likewise in the reflected environment) and the reality of his or her own body and feeling states. Infantile motoric incapacity, turbulent movement and sensations of bodily fragmentation are first experienced as unity in the human infant through some form of (external) reflection of itself. A transformation marks the "jubilant assumption" of his/her specular image into the child's developing symbolic matrix. ". . . The *I* is precipitated in a primordial form, before it is objectified in the dialectic of identification with the other, and before language restores to it, in the universal, its function as subject" (1977, p. 2). The stability of the external image contrasts with the instability of early experiences of bodily fragmentation such that the external (visual) form assumes a lure of its own. Lacan views this process of the assumption of the externalized reflected image as "an alienating identity," which will mark the child's subsequent mental development However, not only is the mirror image reversed but early on it is easily fused or confused with images of others in a series of developments Lacan refers to as "transitivism."

> The child who strikes another says that he has been struck; the child who sees another fall, cries. Similarly, it is by means of an identification with the other that he sees the whole gamut of reactions of bearing and display, whose structural ambivalence is clearly revealed in his behavior, the slave being identified with the despot, the actor with the spectator, the seduced with the seducer. (1977, p.19)

In the fixation of the human individual upon an externally based image of self, Lacan formulates that the ego progressively becomes objectified, i.e.,

[9]"The Mirror Stage as Formative of the Function of the I as Revealed in Psychoanalytic Experience" first delivered at the Fourteenth International Psycho-Analytical Congress at Marienbad, (1936, translated in Lacan 1977).

(permanently) alienated from the "I" in the earlier specular (mirror) images as well as from the fused/confused images of others. The phase of transitivism marks the beginning of a long (merged) dual unity with a symbiotic partner. The biological "needs" which characterized earlier phases erupt into "desires" when the symbiotic tie is ruptured through the child's "birth" into the symbolic order represented by language (the "*fort*-da" game). The experienced lack-of-being gives rise to endless desire for "paradise lost" and a dialectic with mother in which the subject's ultimate desire is to be desired (recognized) by the desired.[10] Traditionally the Phallus has come to be known as the universal signifier for desire for perfect union with the Other ("the other scene"). Thus, for Lacan the "birth into symbolic language" when "desire becomes human" constitutes what comes to be considered a primordial castration experience.[11] The "I" is relinquished in favor of desire for the desire of the Other in order to recapture the lost plentitude through experiences of having or being or seeming to have the symbolic Phallus.[12] It is The Word (*Logos*) or the authority of the symbolic order (The Name-of-the-Father) which manifests in the structure of language and makes it possible for things to be present in their absence through the spoken word. Lacan says, in the development of the psychoanalytic discourse the "subject becomes realized" as he passes from "empty speech" to "full speech." In empty speech the subject speaks of himself as if he were another—an ego alienated from the deeper subjectivity of his desire. In contrast, full speech constitutes an articulation of the past which renders it present in the analysis, conferring also a sense of necessities to come. Psychoanalytic full speech is addressed *to* another in such a way that "intersubjective continuity" of discourse becomes established.

Intersubjective continuity implies contact with the Other, the unconscious, "that part of the concrete discourse, in so far as it is transindividual, that is, not at the disposal of the subject in re-establishing the continuity of his conscious discourse" (1977, p. 49). The unconscious chapter of one's history is marked by a blank, a falsehood, or censorship. But Lacan says the truth can be rediscovered because it has been written down in: (1) monuments of one's body, (2) archival documents of childhood memories, (3) the semantic evolution of one's language, life style and character, (4) tradition and legends of personal heroic history and (5) traces of distortions necessitated by linking an adulterated chapter to those surrounding it.

[10]The influence of Hegel and Heidegger on Lacan's thought here are acknowledged. Kohut's selfobject concept would fit here.

[11]The law itself, the Name-of-the-Father, the Other that demands subversion of the "I" requires symbolic "castration."

[12]This formulation holds true for both sexes since the Other becomes the symbolic order itself, not the real or imagined father or penis.

Lacan holds that the unconscious is structured in the same way as language, a fact which Freud's discoveries clearly confirm. Condensation, for example, is a form of linguistic substitution and therefore can be located along the linguistic axis of selection constituting metaphor. Displacement is a form of contiguity to be located along the linguistic axis of combination constituting metonymy. It therefore becomes meaningless to consider the workings of a "personal unconscious" apart from the effects of transindividual unconscious linguistic structure.

In light of the foregoing considerations it becomes clear to Lacan that Freud's emphasis remained on the centrality of the Oedipus Complex because inherent in its structure is the basic symbolic order of language and society, the Phallus, the Symbolic Father and therefore the Law. The Phallus is the universal cultural symbol for the structural order itself, the Other which intrudes into the primary symbiotic unity of mother and child. The assumption of mirrored images leads toward an alienated ego enunciating words which mark the initiation of the individual into the symbolic order and the simultaneous castration of the "I". Biological needs become demands out of which develop human desires, chief among which is to be desired by the one desired. Thus the subversion of the subject (the 'I') becomes accomplished through the dialectic of desire. The power of the oedipal myth derives from its symbolization of the dialectic of desire with its self-mutilating effects.

In the foregoing summary it has been possible only to gloss the highlights of the Lacanian contribution. Major omissions are:

1. The linquistic distinction between signifier and signified which made possible the entire Lacan reading.
2. The implications of structuralistic consideration for the imaginary[13] and realistic realms of life.
3. Mathematical analysis and analogies.
4. Substantiation of theory through myth.
5. Detailed linguistic consideration of metaphor, metonymy and the pairing of phonemes and.
6. Last but not least, Lacan's fascinating reconsideration of well known Freudian texts within a broadened cultural and linguistic framework.

Lacan has dealt harsh criticisms toward those he believes have attempted to solidify, codify and thereby to deny a full hearing to the essential contribution of Freud in understanding the nature of unconscious processes in their broadest transindividual implications. His message is radical and, in many

---

[13] Studied extensively by Carl Jung.

circles, unpopular. But it is now clear that his arguments are penetrating and full of implication which must be reckoned with.

Listening Implications in the Register of Lacan

Most of Lacan's ideas are perhaps best suited for the analytic understanding of relatively well developed persons who have successfully negotiated the rapprochement crisis. In these individuals the loss of the symbiotic unity with mother has been mastered with words. The study of neurosis *par excellence* is a study of the dialectic of desire. Lacan's broader reading of Freud can serve as a fresh register in which to hear the time honored workings of Oedipus, castration and the vicissitudes of sexuality and aggression in light of the Phallus as the governing (castrating) symbolic order, the "other scene".

Lacan at the time of the original *Écrits* (1936–1960) generally saw attempts to speak of preoedipal problems as evasive betrayals of the centrality of the Freudian discovery with its emphasis on the human domain of the unconscious order and the Oedipus complex. However, in one paper, "On a question preliminary to any possible treatment of psychosis" (1958 in 1977), he addresses the preoedipal problem clearly and directly in a reconsideration of Freud's Schreber case study. In contrast to the usual repressive forces operating in neurosis, Lacan designates the central mechanism of Schreber as "foreclosure" or "repudiation" of the fundamental signifier (i.e., the Phallus, the Other). In a detailed linguistic analysis of Schreber's hallucinatory text Lacan describes an "inadequacy of the signifier," a fundamental default that he calls "foreclosure of the Name-of-the-Father in the place of the Other" (1977, p. 215). The "fort-da!" experience normally develops in accord with logical links operating through the signifier as metaphor and metonymy. The *symbolic* Father and the Law must be accorded prestige by the child and by the child's mother in order to prevent "primordial foreclosure." Otherwise the signifier of the Other in which consist order and the social law develops a "hole" or "bankruptcy." In other words, Lacan acknowledges the importance of the development of the unconscious in neurosis, and with it the gradual relinquishment of the symbiotic tie through the intervention of (Paternal) Law and Order and the consequent castration of the individual "I" through the governing structure of language. But this state of affairs is clearly an end product of early development which does *not* prevail in the various preoedipal conditions where the symbolic order has been repudiated or foreclosed rather than adopted and identified with.

Nowhere in the available English texts does Lacan make reference to borderline or narcissistic personality organization in the sense currently being studied. One could only conjecture that in terms of the failure of the full assumption of identity within the structural symbolic order, Lacan would also describe various preoedipal "repudiations" and "foreclosures" in what are currently being referred to as narcissistic, borderline, and organizing personalities.

The listening implications of this frame of reference are intriguing. What factors, forces or processes, for example, in a given individual prevent his/her "birth" into the full ramifications of the symbolic order? At what price and in what manner is the early "I" partially retained and why has the human dialectic of desire not flourished? If "empty speech" is characterized by objectification of the ego and "full speech" is characterized by temporal (past, present, future) contiguity alive in a transindividual dialectic of desire, how might speech be considered at the various nodal points of personality organization currently being studied? How does the individual's relationship to the symbolic order manifest itself in preoedipal object relations and in the development of the organizing centers called ego and self? And most importantly, if the governing symbolic order manifest in the Oedipus complex is to be restored to a place of centrality in modern psychoanalytic thought, i.e., Lacan's plea for a "Return to Freud," how are the various processes and phases of the epigenetic development of its assumption in a human individual to be understood? Many of these questions are alluded to in *Écrits* and others are no doubt addressed in Lacan's many yet unpublished and untranslated seminars and lectures. Lacan's cultural and linguistic research provides another register for psychoanalytic listening, the full impact of which has yet to be realized.

THE CHALLENGE OF SARTRE:
THE SEARCH FOR ONE'S "ORIGINAL PROJECT"

Psychoanalytic and psychotherapeutic studies tend to alternate between an interest in understanding personal intents, purposes, and meanings (Klein 1970, 1973) and an interest in organizing and justifying one's thoughts *about* meanings in terms of the nature of man (Rubenstein 1976). All forms of therapeutic inquiry are based upon an assumption of the possibility of personality growth or expansion. Careful and interested listening holds forth the possibility of promoting or fostering such growth, primarily through encouraging the progressive elaboration, expansion, and clarification of personal meanings implicit in the way one lives. A key dimension of human growth which has provided the theme for this book, is the progressive differentiation and organization of meaningful experiences of Self and Other.

That there is a range of possible meanings which cannot be clarified except in the presence of an Other is not altogether self-evident. Freud called upon the notion of the unconscious mind in order to account for why one cannot by oneself intuitively grasp certain sets of meanings which can become available through psychoanalysis. Sartre (1956), for wholly different considerations, concluded that the "original project" of our lives is, in principle, not discoverable by introspective and reflective efforts of one's solitary consciousness. By "original project," Sartre means the choice or set of choices which people are or represent actively in the way they live and relate to the world and, in particular, to the Other.

For many, "choices" may appear a euphemism. For example, a person living what an observer might term a "borderline development arrest," presumably established his/her "original project," or way of relating to the world and to the Other as a result of life experiences so early that it seems a far reach to call the persistent mode of experience a "choice." Furthermore, to apply Sartre's advanced concept of "bad faith" (otherwise translated "self-deception") to such persons also seems a far reach. Their "choice of being" or "original project" has served to systematically limit their range of perceptions and conceptions to such an extent that "self-deception" can hardly be said to be occurring in quite the same complicated sense which Sartre suggests. Sartre's conceptions seem more aptly applied to persons having achieved a level of human reality or human development commonly seen in the life of a six- or seven-year-old child. At that developmental level what Freud has described as the defense mechanisms of repression are thought to be in operation. The variety of choices made during that epoch constitute what Freud labeled the Oedipus complex. One might think of a nodal or pivotal point in the development of human reality occurring in the sixth or seventh year when a series of choices are confirmed which might be called a "complex" (Freud) or a "project" (Sartre) which one lives. Such a project embarked on or such a complex crystalized is done in light of the human possibilities available at that late age for self-deception (Sartre) or repression (Freud). This nodal point is characterized by the development of "unconscious meanings" (Freud) or meanings thought to be "non-reflectively conscious" (Sartre).

Both Freud and Sartre have attempted to extend their insights to an understanding of all human reality, including that which existed prior to the development of the capacities just mentioned—with only partial success. Each insight (i.e., Freud's and Sartre's) is based upon understanding a *final achievement* of human existence, i.e., the Oedipus complex or a capacity for self-deception. Both Freudian psychoanalysis and existential psychoanalysis study, hint at, and allude to various human processes which lead up to these capacities but remain limited in the amount of light they can shed on the "pre-oedipal" or "pre-self-deception" aspects of evolving human reality.

This book has sought to extend the search for "original projects" to pre-oedipal and pre-self-deception phases of human development through the concept of Listening Perspectives, a study of the perceptual stances or styles of the analyst (Freud) or the Other (Sartre). Focus on these earlier phases does not necessitate a basic alteration in observational technique but rather requires the elaboration of conceptual tools to be applied to the process of analytic listening. Self and Other Psychoanalysis necessitates an experiential (existential or phenomenological) base with observations and concepts geared to foster the elaboration of early developmental aspects of self-other differentiation. This book cannot, therefore, conclude without turning to Sartre for a brief review of his ideas on how existential analysis seeks to focus on the "original project" of one's life, regardless of the developmental level of its origin.

Sartre maintains that in psychoanalysis it is not enough merely to decipher behavior patterns, drives or inclinations. *It is necessary to know how to question them* (1956, p. 726).[14] The principle of psychoanalysis is ". . . that man is a totality and not a collection . . . there is not a taste, a mannerism or human act which is not revealing" (p. 726). The goal of psychoanalysis is to decipher activities, thus bringing out into the open the revelations "which each of them contains and to fix them conceptually" (p. 726). Sartre indicates the point of departure for psychoanalytic study is *experience* and that:

> . . . the essential task is an hermeneutic; that is, a deciphering, a determination, and a conceptualization. . . . Both kinds of psychoanalysis [Freud's and Sartre's] consider all objectively discernible manifestations of "psychic life" as symbols maintaining symbolic relations to the fundamental, total structures which constitute the individual person. . . . Both consider the human being as a perpetual, searching, historization. Rather than uncovering static, constant givens, they discover the meaning, orientation and adventures of this history. Due to this fact both consider man in the world and do not imagine that one can question the being of a man without taking into account all of his *situation* (p. 727). . . . Empirical psychoanalysis [Freudian] and existential psychoanalysis both search within an existing situation for a fundamental attitude which cannot be expressed by simple, logical definitions. . . . Empirical psychoanalysis seeks to determine the *complex*, the very name of which indicates the polyvalence of all the meanings which are referred back to it. Existential psychoanalysis seeks to determine the *original choice*. (p. 728)

The result is that the complexes uprooted from the depths of the unconscious, like projects revealed by existential psychoanalysis, will be apprehended *from the point of view of the Other*. . . . (p. 729) What always escapes these methods of

---

[14]In light of this Sartrian approach, the listening devices and techniques suggested in this book for work with preoedipal developmental arrests can be considered relational *ways of questioning* persons when the mode of expression is preverbal (interactional) rather than verbal.

investigation is the project as it is for itself, the complex in its own being. This project-for-itself can be experienced only as a living possession; . . . the subject's knowledge of it can in addition contribute to *clarify* reflection, and that reflection can then become a possession which will be quasi-knowing. (pp. 729–730)

In contrasting Freud's deterministic and materialistic approach with his own phenomenological approach, Sartre indicates that:

Our goal could not be to establish empirical laws of succession, nor could we constitute a universal symbolism. Rather the psychoanalyst will have to redis- cover at each step a symbol functioning in the particular case which he is considering. . . . Furthermore, the psychoanalyst will never lose sight of the fact that the choice is living and consequently can be *revoked* by the subject who is being studied. . . . Thus existential psychoanalysis will have to be completely flexible and adapt itself to the slightest observable changes in the subject. Our concern here is to understand what is *individual* and often even instantaneous. The method which has served for one subject will not necessarily be suitable to use for another subject or for the same subject at a later period. (p. 733)

Sartre points out the limitations inherent in the Freudian idea of inter- pretation. It represents the *analyst*'s hypothesis and not the subject's.

In this case as we have seen, the traditional psychoanalytic interpretation does not cause him to attain *consciousness* of what he is; it causes him to attain *knowledge* of what he is. It is existential psychoanalysis then which claims the final intuition of the subject as decisive. . . . It is a method destined to bring to light, in a strictly objective form, the subjective choice by which each living person makes himself a person; that is, makes known to himself what he is. Since what the method seeks is a *choice of being* at the same time as a *being*, it must reduce particular behavior patterns to fundamental relations—not of sexuality or of the will to power, but *of being*—which are expressed in this behavior. It is then guided from the start toward a comprehension of being and must not assign itself any other goal than to discover being and the mode of being. . . . Its criterion of success will be the number of facts which its hypothesis permits it to explain and to unify as well as the self-evident intuition of the irreducibility of the end attained. To this criterion will be added in all cases where it is possible, the decisive testimony of the subject. The results thus achieved—that is, the ultimate ends of the individual—can then become the object of a classification, and it is by the comparison of these results that we will be able to establish general con- siderations about human reality as an empirical choice of its own ends. . . . This psychoanalysis has not yet found its Freud. (pp. 733–734)

The reader will recognize that the psychoanalytic method of Freud coupled with the phenomenological approach of Sartre form the structure and classification pointed to in *Listening Perspectives*.

CONCLUSIONS

Freud's theories represent his pioneering effort to conceptualize the introspective experience he had the opportunity to observe in himself and others. His conceptualizations, chiefly the topographical and structural theories of the mind, still provide a viable listening approach for treating persons who have attained self and object constancy of the oedipal level neurotic personality organization. Kohut (1971, 1977) has contributed a fundamentally different set of concepts which aid in listening to the introspective experience of narcissistic personality organization. Developmental schema afforded by Jacobson (1954, 1964), Sandler and Rosenblatt (1962), Mahler (1968), Kernberg (1975, 1976, 1980), Little (1981), Masterson (1972, 1976, 1981), Rinsley (1968) and many others have provided conceptualizations for listening to persons who experience merger objects as part of a borderline personality organization. Kafka's literary statements (1914, 1922, 1924), Freud's earliest conceptions of the mind (1900, Ch. 7), Searles's "nonhuman environment" (1960), and Giovacchini's (1979a) "impact of the delusion" provide crucial direction when listening to persons attempting to organize a world of inconstant part-selves and part-objects.

The four Listening Perspectives defined in this book are conceptualized as overlapping *modes of psychoanalytic and psychotherapeutic inquiry.* While they may be roughly parallel or analogous to phases or stages in human development, a central thrust of this book is to move away from the naive 19th-century scientific attitude of attempting to define "what's really out there" or "how it really is" and to acknowledge that it is mainly our own perceptual and conceptual devices and lenses which we as therapists (others) can confidently hope to develop. With four quite distinct perspectives we can open our ears and thoughts to many different styles and complexities of human experience. These perspectives are organized along a dimension of self and other differentiation and integration. Depending on how a given person has come to experience this dimension of relatedness it is helpful to look and listen in differing modes. Furthermore, experience with prolonged therapeutic inquiry suggests that persons tend to shift toward more differentiatedness in their mode of self-other experience as a consequence of exposure to what Sartre has called "apprehension of one's freedom by the Other."

Each listening mode defines a "type" of personality organization along the self-other relatedness experiential dimension:

Neurotic Personality Organization—Self and Object Constancy experience

Narcissistic Personality Organization—Selfobject experience

Borderline Personality Organization—Merger Object experience
Organizing Personality—Inconstancy: Part-self and Part-object experience.

Implicit in this developmental listening approach is the idea that each more differentiated "layer" or nodal point of personality organization is marked by a more complex style of self-other relatedness. Each "layer" is conceptualized as being built firmly upon fundamental prior experience of a less differentiated nature which determines to a greater or lesser degree the qualities of which are to follow. None of the previous modes of experiencing is ever lost but rather *becomes incorporated or embedded in* the more complex later patterning of personality organization. The therapeutic *listening* implications of this statement are immense; for it means that one must always be prepared on a moment's notice to focus inquiry upon earlier more basic or pervasive modes of experience. For example, in analysis of every neurosis a selfobject, merger object or part-self and part-object experience may appear with clarity either (1) to illustrate that one of the fundamental patterns underlying the oedipal concern is from an earlier era, (2) to serve as a resistance to experiencing a more differentiated oedipal transference paradigm, (3) to mark a regression from a dreaded emergence of an oedipal incestuous or parricidal wish or fantasy, or (4) to demonstrate that the progress of the analysis has made earlier more undifferentiated modes of experience less dreaded, thus providing the person with more accessibility to the personal varieties of inner modes available for the purposes of enhanced or more joyous spontaneity and creativity in work, play and love.

One crucial diagnostic implication focuses on the importance of an accurate assessment of the central mode of self-other relatedness potential *characteristically* available to the person. While variations can and do appear in the course of a single hour or tend toward differentiation over a much longer period of time, most variations early in therapy will be expected to be "downward" rather than "upward" until much later when therapeutically determined shifts "upward" begin to appear. For example, if the therapist has determined the primary usefulness of a Listening Perspective which holds the central mode of experience to be that of symbiotic merger in one form or another, then occasional "regressive" swings to less differentiated or more basic modes will not be surprising. On the other hand, most references to what might appear to be selfobject or triangular constant object experience are likely to be misleading in such a person and in most instances should be listened to as variations of or complicated symbolic portrayals of still very basic merger experiences.

The most frequent pitfall stems from therapists' extensive exposure to traditional (Freudian based) thinking using ideas and techniques which were derived from an understanding of complex, differentiated, structured oedipal level personality organization. For example, to continue to listen and interpret as though a borderline or narcissistic personality had achieved a level where unconscious motivation, resistance and defense are operating would be an error in listening and many times would represent a grave error in empathy which would produce naturally what many have called a "negative therapeutic reaction." On the other hand, as Stolorow and Lachman (1980) have pointed out, to respond at a "lower" level of understanding is relatively harmless, being perceived as inaccurate or, at worst, pollyannish by the patient. When "upward" shifts do begin, they are rarely missed since both patient and therapist have been long waiting for more differentiated possibilities to appear and both readily greet changes with enthusiasm and relief. The chronic error of most therapists is to mistake every attempt to be reassured as the appearance of "higher" selfobject tension or every three-way relationship as an oedipal triangle when both may stem from much less differentiated experience relating primarily to the need for unification or pacification therapeutic experience.[15]

The implicit thesis of this book can now be stated explicitly. People, like all living beings can be seen to grow. People develop physically as well as psychologically. Various environmental conditions are required to foster and stimulate optimal development.

In the growth of "human reality" or human consciousness, Sartre (1956) has delineated a series of complex processes through which various "projects" come to be apprehended in relationship to the Other. His thinking depicts the ontological evolution of the human capacity for self-deception and points toward the growth potential inherent in ultimately achieving "undeceived knowledge" about the way one lives. His penetrating analysis of growth can be extended to the many new conceptions regarding the earliest phases of human experience which evolve prior to the oedipal attainment of a full capacity for self-deception (repression).

In psychoanalytic studies we find ourselves tensed on one hand by our wish to establish conceptions and schema through which to stabilize and concretize our understanding; while on the other hand we are caught with the moment-by-moment realization that listening and responding to the subjective reflections of a particular human consciousness in a particular situation is our ultimate pursuit. This book is offered in the spirit of this

---

[15]This "level" approach as stated remains unrefined since most people exhibit qualities which might be considered from several levels. In this book I remain committed to the idea of it being possible to define a core or characteristic level in each person which might be said to constitute a style or type of personality organization. However on the basis of intellectualizations or false self socializations a person might display much "higher" or at least apparently higher level functioning. Giovacchini (1982) also notes that multiple layerings are definable. He holds that what failed to develop was a sense of "bridging continuity" between more primitive amorphous levels and later developed more differentiated structures and functions. He ties this to short-comings in the early "nurturing matrix."

essentially Sartrian paradox. We search to objectify and classify for the purpose of knowing consciousness and the projects contained therein; while at the same time we live with the counter-realization that it is consciousness (for-itself) rather than our reflections about it which constitutes the distinctive quality called human reality. Explicitly focusing alternately on (1) our own perceptual (listening) processes and (2) the experiences of self and other conveyed by patients within the adaptive context of psychotherapy, constitutes a new wave in modern psychoanalysis.

I have reviewed only some of the many innovative conceptions evolving today. I have presented them in a spirit which hopefully conveys that I take conceptualizations to be crucial aspects of human understanding but in themselves limited to the extent that they provide the analyst simply Listening Perspectives or *modes* of psychoanalytic and psychotherapeutic inquiry. The analyst as the Other assumes the fascinating position of being able to apprehend the state of freedom or limitation which potentially exists for each of his or her patients. As Sartre so aptly declares, it is only in turning to the Other that we can "apprehend who we are," and I might add, who we wish to become.

14 Listening Perspectives and the Therapeutic Action of Psychoanalysis

> [Psychoanalysis] is then guided from the start toward a comprehension of being and must not assign itself any other goal than to discover being and the mode of being. . . .
>
> Jean Paul Sartre
> *Being and Nothingness*, p. 734

Freud spoke of "cure" in both contexts of expanding awareness ("making the unconscious conscious") and increasing dominance of cognitive structure ("Where Id was, there Ego shall be."). Kohut (in press) spoke of "cure" in relational terms—the "opening up of lifelong channels for self to selfobject resonance." In a different vein, Sartre saw the goal of psychoanalysis as the attainment of an expanded sense of one's being and one's mode of being in the world.

Perennial interest in what constitutes the goal or cure in psychoanalysis revolves around the central therapeutic function of interpretation. Strachey's (1934) pivotal paper, as alive with issues today as when it was written, explicitly defines "mutative interpretation" as *a process* rather than a discrete action or event. The *process* of mutative interpretation was conceptualized by Strachey in two phases: (1) the patient's gradually becoming conscious of a particular "id-energy" being directed at the analyst and (2) the patient's becoming aware that this energy is in fact being directed at an archaic fantasy object, not the real analyst. Strachey acknowledges that extra-transference interpretations and various other para-analytic activities (abreaction, suggestion, etcetera) may "prepare the battlefield," but the "capture of a key position" is reserved for the process of mutative interpretation which possesses a crucial *immediacy in the analytic relationship and a specificity direct and concrete enough to win the day*!

Strachey mentions a personal communication from Melanie Klein suggesting that there must be some quite special internal difficulty to be overcome by the analyst in giving interpretations since they are so widely avoided. Strachey agrees with Klein in noting the temptation analysts feel to do anything but engage in the mutative interpretation process. He concludes that mutative interpretation is crucial "for the analyst as well as

for the patient . . . he is exposing himself to some great danger . . ."
(p. 291). Strachey came to believe that during the interpretive process:

> . . . the analyst is in fact deliberately evoking a quantity of the patient's id-energy
> while it is alive and actual and unambiguous and aimed directly at himself. Such a
> moment must above all others put to the test his relations with his own uncon-
> scious impulses. (p. 291)

Later additions to Strachey's two phase process of mutative interpretation have come from Segal (1962) as well as Sandler, Dare and Holder (1973)
who have contributed ideas on the subsequent working through process (i.e.,
a phase 3 of mutative interpretation). Rosenfeld (1972), in basic agreement with Strachey's hallmark contributions, updates the formulations to
specify that "good and bad introjects" as well as "good and bad parts of the
self" are also projected onto the analyst and must be subjected to the
interpretive process. Strachey had spoken of the patient's "superego," with
the analyst acting as "auxiliary superego." He was using Freud's early
(1923) meaning of superego to include what many (e.g., Sandler and Rosenblatt 1962) have later come to call "self and object representations."

The metaphoric image which Strachey used to describe the mutative
process in psychoanalysis was derived from Rado's (1925) concept of a
"parasitic superego"—one which draws off the energy and takes over the
functions of the subject's original superego in hypnosis. In contrast to the
hypnotist, Strachey feels the analyst serves the function of a parasitic
superego in "aiming . . . at something much more far-reaching and permanent—namely, at the internal change in the nature of the patient's
superego itself" (p. 279). This statement in context can be updated (following
Rosenfeld 1972) to read "aiming at changes in the nature of the self and
object representations." In the language of the current book, the mutative
process can be seen as a developmental step in the further differentiation
and consolidation of the experiential or representational world of Self and
Others.

Running through most discussions of interpretation and the mutative
process is a general awareness seldom addressed directly but expressed
clearly, if not unwittingly, in Strachey's battleground metaphor. Therapists
understand that the mutative process involves, or is experienced as involving, a meeting or confrontation at some basic level of interpersonal boundary.
Strachey points out that no matter how well the necessary and beneficial
aspects of interpretation are rationalized (by analyst and patient as well),
interpretations are often felt to be either magical tools which are experienced as welcome, gratifying and rewarding or as magical weapons which
are dreaded, frightening, and dangerous.

The present conceptualization of the psychoanalytic process focuses on
the progressive differentiation and consolidation of modes of experiencing

Self and Other leading toward the experience of others as separate centers of initiative. The bifurcated affective response to interpretations (i.e., good magical tools or bad dreaded weapons) which Strachey mentions would, in the *usual* developmental outcome, lead toward the experience of ambivalence. Object Constancy as the natural outcome of human growth represents a balance between the wish for sameness and blissful merger and the equally intense desire for the experience of separateness and independent selfhood (Kaplan 1978). Differentiated balance of these ambivalent (positive and negative) opposing trends (i.e., merging and individuating) characterizes the current understanding of the outcome of the separation-individuation process in child development as well as the developmental achievements made in psychoanalysis. The less than optimal integration of these affective trends in preoedipal personality organizations is often referred to as "affect" or "object splitting" (e.g., Kernberg 1975, 1976).

Kaplan's (1978) definition of the attainment of object constancy as the expectable outcome of human growth is not inconsistent with Kohut's idea of maturity as an increased capacity to enjoy freely "self to selfobject resonance." Nor do either of these fresh formulations refute or replace prevailing notions of therapeutic outcome. Rather, they supplement traditional ideas of "curative" or "growth" processes by including reference to the contemporary focus of psychoanalytic inquiry, differential modes of Self and Other experience or relatedness.

Sartre's investigations into the philosophical basis for self knowledge are particularly helpful in articulating the continuity between that which has been said in the past regarding cure and the new overarching developmental conceptualizations which are arising in consequence of intense study of preoedipal personality organizations. Sartre (1956) held that one's "choice of being" or "original project" (for itself) can become known (to consciousness) only through being "apprehended" by an Other. The fear and dread of one's potential freedom being apprehended by an Other (the analyst) works against the wish for increased self knowledge which one expresses when engaging in the analytic process. It is only through being apprehended by the Other that one solitary human consciousness apprehends the possibility of being or experiencing *in any way other than* that constituted in one's developmentally determined "original project." The person brings certain living modes of Self and Other experience and relatedness to analytic inquiry. The very act of being apprehended by the analyst, an Other, provides the possibility of confirming or revoking one's "original choice of being," one's characteristic modes of experiencing Self and Others.

As one confronts an "apprehension" of oneself through the gradual process referred to as mutative interpretation, one may feel pleased and gratified or threatened, wounded and angry. Through mutative interpretation, one's original project or choice of being comes to be known for just what it is: actively chosen modes of experience with limiting consequences.

One's original project thus *becomes altered* by the mere fact of increased knowledge of one's "being in the world." Sartre holds that one's original project and choices can be revoked only when they are known. They can only become known through their apprehension by an Other.

Kohut (in press) alluded to a developmental line of empathy indicating that the process of understanding (apprehending) is accomplished variously at different maturational levels. The concrete holding, touching, smelling modes of understanding infants slowly give way to abstract, verbal, and gestural forms of empathy possible with older children and adults. Kohut's formulations and treatment technique rely heavily upon verbal introspection and vicarious introspection and can be seen as adequate for developmental arrests of emotional issues stemming from verbal childhood eras. Different empathic modes for understanding arrests in preverbal aspects of personality development have been suggested by many including Winnicott (1971), Modell (1976), Bollas (1979), and Little (1981). Defining idiosyncratic treatment Scenarios and careful attention to countertransference information have been suggested in the present book as possible listening devices for establishing empathy with preverbal, interactive aspects of arrest.

The developmental approach to psychoanalysis and psychotherapy also suggests that *communication* of empathy—explanations, interpretations, differentiating activities—must be considered *with respect to the developmentally determined capacities to feel apprehended by the Other*. Human reality and consciousness expand in consequence of being apprehended by an Other. In preoedipal arrests apprehension depends not only upon the Other's capacity to understand early (and often preverbal) emotional issues but, more importantly, upon the Other's capacity for *communicating* understanding of early issues in clear, simple and often nonverbal manners.[1] Therapeutic "holding response" and "differentiating actions, activities, and interactions" spoken of in this book provide avenues for communicating the analyst's understanding of many preverbal issues. The complex task of providing empathy and explanatory response—Kohut's (in press) "basic therapeutic unit"—at different levels of developmental achievement gives rise to the need for establishing various *Listening Perspectives*—a series of ways of receiving and communicating understanding of basic emotional experiences.

The possibilities for achieving self knowledge which Sartre puts forth rely on the critical notion of "being apprehended by an Other." In the verbal and symbolic world experienced by the person with neurotic personality organization, Freud's Listening Perspective, including unconscious motiva-

---

[1]Kernberg (1980) addresses the importance of preverbal and nonverbal communication with early developmental phenomena.

tion and defense as well as the experience of conflicts between an enduring sense of drivenness (id instincts) and the more reality and socially oriented moderating trends (ego and superego), continues to offer guiding landmarks to the analyst.

Kohut's focus on the developmental era of the selfobject provides a crucial Listening Perspective with persons having achieved the level of narcissistic personality organization. Kohut (in press) has also shown how Self Psychology augments and, to a certain extent, may alter the time honored ideas of Freud regarding oedipal neuroses.

Studies of Winnicott, Jacobson, Mahler, Little, Kernberg, Masterson, Bollas, Blanck and Blanck, as well as many others, have contributed to forming a Listening Perspective for attending to many heretofore undefined features of the experience of (symbiotic and postsymbiotic) emotional merger which is expectable in borderline personality organization.

In developing a Listening Perspective for work with "organizing personalities" experiencing part-Selves and part-Objects as well as breaks in reality testing and breakdowns in affect regulation; the phenomenological experiences of Kafka, Freud's model of reflexive mental processes, Searles' "non-human environment," Giovacchini's "impact of delusion" and Melanie Klein's studies of greed and envy provide avenues of apprehension through various kinds of connecting and pacifying responses.

THE THERAPEUTIC ACTION

The concept of therapeutic action in psychoanalysis remains much the same today as it was for Strachey in 1934. The patient brings to the analytic setting his/her experiential world comprised variously of good and bad self and object representations. The effect when the:

> . . . patient comes into contact with a new object *in analysis* is from the first moment to create a different situation. . . . Owing to the peculiarities of the analytic circumstances and of the analyst's behavior, the introjected image of the analyst tends to be rather definitely separated from the rest of the patient's [representational world.[2]] (p. 281)

The natural disparity between the patient's ongoing experience—expectations based on his/her representational world, and actual encounters with the novel person of the analyst creates the setting in which the process known as "mutative interpretation" becomes possible.

---

[2]Strachey's word here was "superego" which he used at that time to refer to what are now called the good and bad representations of self and other comprising the "representational world."

Loewald (1960) states these same ideas somewhat differently.

> . . . ego development is resumed in the therapeutic process of analysis, and this resumption of ego development is contingent on the relationship with a new object, the analyst. . . . New spurts of self-development may be intimately connected with such "regressive" rediscoveries of oneself as may occur through the establishment of new object relationships, and this means new discovery of "objects." I say new discovery of objects, and not discovery of new objects, because the essence of such new object-relationships is the opportunity they offer for rediscovery of the early paths of the development of object-relations, lending to a new way of relating to objects as well as of being and relating to oneself. (pp. 16, 18)

Each person coming to the consulting room has achieved a certain maturational level in the progressive differentiation of experiences of Self from experiences of Other. Idiosyncratic modes of relatedness constitute one's "original project" and, as such, one's "choice of being." Apprehension by the analyst (Other) through empathy and explanatory response (verbal and nonverbal interpretation) creates the possibility for increased self knowledge.

The mutative interpretation *process* can be considered now in three phases:

1. The progressive elaboration of the bondage of representational expectations or commitments which in therapy become directed toward oneself and toward the analyst.

2. The apprehension of different (more differentiated) representational possibilities in consequence of the relational freedom experienced through apprehension of oneself by the analyst.

3. A gradual elevation of consciousness and/or relatedness by repeated working with and working through the disparity between one's representational commitments (original project) and one's relational freedom as apprehended by the analyst (the Other).

With the advent of new developmental concepts, psychoanalysis is no longer bound to the exploration and treatment of neurotics. Developmentally sophisticated forms of listening and responding now make possible the opening of new lines of empathy and interpretation for work with persons having achieved various levels of preoedipal personality organization. Ongoing creative elaboration of developmentally based *Listening Perspectives* makes possible the extension of the therapeutic action of psychoanalysis to a study of all variations of Self and Other experience.

References

Abelin, Ernest L. (1980). "Triangulation, the Role of the Father and the Origins of Core Gender Identity During the Rapprochement Subphase." In Ruth F. Lax, Sheldon Back, and J. Alexis Burland. *Rapprochement: the Critical Subphase of Separation-Individuation.* New York: Jason Aronson, pp. 151–169.

Alexander, Franz (1925). "A Metapsychological Description of the Process of Cure." *International Journal of Psychoanalysis.* 6:13–34.

—— (1961). *The Scope of Psychoanalysis.* New York: Basic Books.

—— and French, Thomas M. (1946). *Psychoanalytic Therapy.* New York: Ronald Press.

Balint, M. (1952). *Primary Love and Psycho-Analytic Technique.* London: Hogarth Press.

—— (1968). *The Basic Fault.* London: Tavistock Publications.

—— (1969). "Trauma and Object Relations." *International Journal of Psycho-analysis.* 50:429–435.

Barten, S. S. and Franklin, M. B. (1978) (eds.). *Developmental Processes: Heinz Werner's Selected Writings* (2 Vols.). New York: International Universities Press.

Bergman, Gustav (1957). *Philosophy of Science.* Madison: The University of Wisconsin Press.

—— (1959). *Meaning and Existence.* Madison: The University of Wisconsin Press.

—— (1964). *Logic and Reality.* Madison: The University of Wisconsin Press.

Bettleheim, Bruno (1974). "Countertransference Problems in Workers in a Residential Treatment Center." In *Tactics and Techniques in Psychoanalytic Treatment,* Vol. II. *Countertransference,* ed. P. Giovacchini. New York: Jason Aronson.

Bion, W. R. (1962). *Learning from Experience.* New York: Basic Books.

—— (1963). *Elements of Psycho-Analysis.* New York: Basic Books.

—— (1977). *Second Thoughts.* New York: Jason Aronson.

Blanck, Gertrude and Blanck, Rubin (1974). *Ego Psychology: Theory and Practice.* New York: Columbia University Press.

—— (1979). *Ego Psychology II: Psychoanalytic Developmental Psychology.* New York: Columbia University Press.

Bollas, Christopher (1979). "The Transformational Object." *The International Journal of Psycho-Analysis.* 59:97–107.

—— (1981). "On the Relation to the Self as an Object." Unpublished paper delivered to the International Congress of Psychoanalysis, Helsinki, August 1981.

—— (1983). "Expressive Uses of the Countertransference: Notes to the Patient from Oneself." *Contemporary Psychoanalysis*. January, 1983.

—— (1983). "Moods and the Conservative Object." A paper read at the Newport Center for Psychoanalytic Studies January 7, 1983 (cassette recording available, Box 8100, Newport Beach, CA 92660).

Bornstein, B. (1949). "The Analysis of a Phobic Child." *The Psychoanalytic Study of the Child*. 3/4:181–227. New York: International Universities Press.

Boyer, Bryce (1979). "Countertransference with Severely Regressed Patients." In L. Epstein and A. Feiner (eds.). *Countertransference*. New York: Jason Aronson.

Breuer, J., and Freud, S. (1893–1895). "Studies on hysteria." *Standard Edition 2*.

Bridgman, P. W. (1927). *The Logic of Modern Physics*. New York: The Macmillan Co.

Brody, S. and Axelrod, S. (1966). "Anxiety, Socialization and Ego-Formation in Infancy." *International Journal of Psychoanalysis*. 47:218–229.

Chertok, L. (1968). "The Discovery of the Transference: Towards an Epistemological Interpretation." *International Journal of Psychoanalysis*. 49:560–577.

Chessick, Richard D. (1977). *Intensive Psychotherapy of the Borderline Patient*. New York: Jason Aronson.

Deutsch, Helen (1938). "Folie à Deux." In *The Psychoanalytic Quarterly*. Vol. 7 (1938), pp. 307–318.

Eissler, K. R. (1953). "The Effect of the Structure of the Ego on Psychoanalytic Technique." *Journal of the American Psychoanalytic Association*. 1:104–143.

Ekstein, Rudolph (1954). "The Space Child's Time Machine: On 'Reconstruction' in the Psychotherapeutic Treatment of a Schizophrenoid Child." *American Journal of Orthopsychiatry*. 24:492–506.

—— (1978). "Further Thoughts Concerning the Nature of the Interpretive Process." In S. Smith (ed.). *The Human Mind Revisited: Essays in Honor of Karl A. Menninger*. New York: International Universities Press.

—— (1980a). "Borderline States and Ego Disturbances." In G. Prooz Sholevar, Ronald M. Benson, and Barton J. Blinder (eds.). *Treatment of Emotional Disorders in Children and Adolescents*. Jamaica, New York: Spectrum Publications Inc.

—— (1980b). "Residual Trauma-Variations On and About a Theme." *Family and Child Mental Health Journal*. 6:1 Spring/Summer 1980, pp. 34–62.

Epstein, Lawrence and Feiner, Arthur H. (1979) (eds.). *Countertransference*. New York: Jason Aronson.

Erikson, Erik (1950). "Growth and Crises of the Healthy Personality." In "Identity and the Life Cycle." New York: International Universities Press.

—— (1954). "On the Sense of Inner Identity." In Robert P. Knight and Cyrus R. Friedman (eds.). *Psychoanalytic Psychiatry and Psychology*. New York: International Universities Press, pp. 351–364.

—— (1959). "Identity and the Life Cycle." *Psychological Issues*. Monograph No. 1. New York: International Universities Press.

Fairbairn, W. R. D. (1954). *An Object Relations Theory of the Personality*. New York: Basic Books.

Fingarette, Herbert (1969). *Self Deception*. New York: Humanities Press.

Freud, A. (1936). *The Ego and the Mechanisms of Defense*. New York: International Universities Press.

—— (1963). "The Concept of Developmental Lines." *The Psychoanalytic Study of the Child*. 18:245-265. New York: International Universities Press.

—— (1965). *Normality and Pathology in Childhood*. New York: International Universities Press.

Freud, S. (1895). "Project for a Scientific Psychology." *Standard Edition* 1:283-388.

—— (1900). *The Interpretation of Dreams*. New York: Avon Books.

—— (1901). "The Psychopathology of Everyday Life." *Standard Edition* 6.

—— (1904). "Psychoanalytic Procedure." *Standard Edition* 1:283-388.

—— (1905a). "Fragment of an Analysis of a Case of Hysteria" (Dora). *Standard Edition* 7:3-124.

—— (1905b). "Jokes and Their Relation to the Unconscious. *Standard Edition* 8.

—— (1912a). "Papers on Technique. The Dynamics of Transference." *Standard Edition*. 12:97-108.

—— (1912b). "Papers on Technique. Recommendations to Physicians Practicing Psychoanalysis." *Standard Edition* 12:109-120.

—— (1914). "On Narcissism." *Standard Edition* 14:141-158.

—— (1916-1917). "Introductory Lectures on Psycho-Analysis." *Standard Edition* 15 and 16.

—— (1920). "Beyond the Pleasure Principle." *Standard Edition* 18:7-64.

—— (1923). "The Ego and the Id." *Standard Edition* 19:3-68.

—— (1924). "The Dissolution of the Oedipus Complex." *Standard Edition* 19:172-179.

—— (1940). "Splitting of the Ego in the Process of Defence." *Standard Edition* 23:271-278.

Frijling-Schreuder, E. C. M. (1969). "Borderline States in Children." *Psychoanalytic Study of the Child*. 24:307-327. New York: International Universities Press.

Gedo, John (1979a). *Beyond Interpretation: Toward a Revised Theory for Psychoanalysis*. New York: International Universities Press.

—— (1979b). "Theories of Object Relations: A Metapsychological Assessment." *American Psychoanalytic Association Journal*. 27:361-373.

—— (1981). *Advances in Clinical Psychoanalysis*. New York: International Universities Press.

——, and Goldberg, Arnold (1973). *Models of the Mind*. Chicago: University of Chicago Press.

Gill, M. M. (1963). *Topography and Systems in Psychoanalytic Theory*. New York: International Universities Press.

—— (1979). "The Analysis of the Transference." *Journal of the American Psychoanalytic Association Supplement*. 27:263-288.

—— and Holzmon, P. (1976) (eds.). "Psychology Versus Metapsychology: Psycho-analytic Essays in Memory of George S. Klein." *Psychological Issues.* Monograph No. 36. New York: International Universities Press.

—— and Muslin, H. (1976). "Early Interpretation of Transference." *Journal of the American Psychoanalytic Association.* 24:779–794.

Giovacchini, P. L. (1963). "Integrative Aspects of Object Relationships." *Psycho-analytic Quarterly.* 32:393–407.

—— (1975). *Psychoanalysis of Character Disorders.* New York: Jason Aronson.

—— (1975). *Tactics and Techniques in Psychoanalytic Therapy.* New York: Jason Aronson.

—— (1979a). "Countertransference with Primitive Mental States." In L. Epstein and A. H. Feiner (eds.). *Countertransference.* New York: Jason Aronson.

—— (1979b). *Treatment of Primitive Mental States.* New York: Jason Aronson.

—— (1981). "The Unreasonable Patient." UCLA Conference on the Borderline Syndrome, March 14, 1981.

—— (1982). "Structural Progression and Vicissitudes in the Treatment of Severely Disturbed Patients." P. L. Giovacchini and L. B. Boyer (eds.) *Technical Factors in the Treatment of the Severely Disturbed Patient.* New York: Jason Aronson.

—— and Boyer, L. Bryce (1982). *Technical Factors in the Treatment of the Severely Disturbed Patient.* New York: Jason Aronson.

Glover, E. (1932). "A Psycho-Analytical Approach to the Classification of Mental Disorders." In *On the Early Development of the Mind,* Chapter 11. New York: International Universities Press.

—— (1943). "The Concept of Dissociation." In *On the Early Development of the Mind,* Chapter 20. New York: International Universities Press.

—— (1956). *On the Early Development of the Mind.* New York: International Universities Press.

Goldberg, Arnold (1978) (ed.). *The Psychology of the Self: A Casebook.* New York: International Universities Press.

—— (1980) (ed.). *Advances in Self Psychology.* New York: International Universities Press.

Greenson, Ralph (1967). *The Technique and Practice of Psychoanalysis.* New York: International Universities Press.

—— (1978). *Explorations in Psychoanalysis.* New York: International Universities Press.

Grinberg, Léon (1975). "An Approach to Understanding Borderline Disorders." In Hartocollis (1975), p. 123.

Grinker, Roy (1968). *The Borderline Syndrome: A Behavioral Study of Ego Functions.* New York: Basic Books.

—— and Werble, Beatrice (1977). *The Borderline Patient.* New York: Jason Aronson.

Grotstein, James (1981a) (ed.). *Dare I Disturb the Universe?* Beverly Hills, California: Caesura Press.

―――― (1981b). *Splitting and Projective Identification*. New York: Jason Aronson.

Guntrip, H. (1968). *Schizoid Phenomena, Object Relations and the Self*. New York: International Universities Press.

―――― (1971). *Psychoanalytic Theory, Therapy and the Self*. New York: Basic Books.

Hartmann, Heinz (1939-1958). *Ego Psychology and the Problem of Adaptation*. New York: International Universities Press.

―――― (1950). "Comments on the Psychoanalytic Theory of the Ego." *The Psychoanalytic Study of the Child*. 5:74-96. New York: International Universities Press.

Hartocollis, Peter (1975) (ed.). *Borderline Personality Disorders: The Concept, The Syndrome, The Patient*. New York: International Universities Press.

―――― (1977). *Borderline Personality Disorders*. New York: International Universities Press.

Hedges, Lawrence E. (1971). "Whose Little Boy Are You?" *Reiss-Davis Bulletin*. 8:2, pp. 133-139.

―――― (1980a). "Psychoanalytic Developmental Psychology: A Paradigm for the Diagnosis and Treatment of Borderline Personality Development." Lecture presented at the California Graduate Institute, April 25, 1980 (cassette recording available, Box 8100, Newport Beach, CA 92660).

―――― (1980b). "Narcissism in the Clinical Encounter." Lecture given at the Newport Center for Psychoanalytic Studies, November 1, 1980 (cassette recording available, Box 8100, Newport Beach, CA 92660).

―――― (1981). "Borderline Treatment Scenarios." Lecture presented at Kaiser Permanente, April 2, 1981 (cassette recording available, Box 8100, Newport Beach, CA 92660).

―――― (1982). "Kohut: A Retrospective." Lecture presented at the Newport Center for Psychoanalytic Studies, January 15, 1982 (cassette recording available, Box 8100, Newport Beach, CA 92660).

Hegel, G. W. F. (1807). *The Phenomenology of the Mind*, Rev. 2nd Ed. London: Allen and Unwin (1949).

Holt, Robert R. (1965). "A Review of Some of Freud's Biological Assumptions and Their Influence on His Theories." In Norman S. Green and William C. Lewis (eds.) *Psychoanalysis and Current Biological Thought*. Madison and Milwaukee: The University of Wisconsin Press, 1965, pp. 93-124.

―――― (1967). "Beyond Vitalism and Mechanism: Freud's Concept of Psychic Energy." In Jules H. Masserman, M.D. (ed.). *The Ego, Science and Psychoanalysis: Vol. XI*. New York, London: Grune and Stratton 1967, pp. 1-44.

Horner, Althea J. (1979). *Object Relations and the Developing Ego in Therapy*. New York: Jason Aronson.

Jacobson, Edith (1954). "The Self and Object World: Vicissitudes of Their Infantile Cathexis and Their Influence of Ideational and Affective Development." *The Psychoanalytic Study of the Child*. 9:75-127. New York: International Universities Press.

―――― (1964). *The Self and Object World*. New York: International Universities Press.

—— (1966). *Depression.* New York: International Universities Press.

Jakobson, R. and Halle, M. (1956). *Fundamentals of Language.* The Hague: Mouton.

Joffee, W. G. and Sandler, J. (1965). "Notes On Pain, Depression and Individuation." *Psychoanalytic Study of the Child.* 20:394-424. New York: International Universities Press.

Jones, E. (1953). *The Life and Work of Sigmund Freud* (3 vols.). New York: Basic Books.

Kafka, Franz (1926). *The Castle.* New York: Schocken Books.

—— (1937). *The Trial.* New York: Vintage Books.

—— (1979). *The Basic Kafka.* New York: Pocket Books.

Kaplan, Louise (1978). *Oneness and Separateness.* New York: Simon and Schuster.

Kernberg, Otto F. (1975). *Borderline Conditions and Pathological Narcissism.* New York: Jason Aronson.

—— (1976). *Object-Relations Theory and Clinical Psychoanalysis.* New York: Jason Aronson.

—— (1980a). *Internal World and External Reality.* New York: Jason Aronson.

—— (1980b). Lecture given at the conference on "The Narcissistic Personality." Los Angeles, October 1980, sponsored by the Los Angeles Psychoanalytic Society and Institute.

Klein, George S. (1965). "Peremptory Ideation: Structure and Force in Motivated Ideas." In R. Holt (ed.). "Motives and Thought, Psychoanalytic Essays in Honor of David Rappaport." *Psychological Issues.* Monograph No. 18/19. New York: International Universities Press.

—— (1970). "Two Theories or One?" *Bulletin of the Menninger Clinic.* Vol. 37 (1973), pp. 102-132.

—— (1973). "Is Psychoanalysis Relevant?" *Psychoanalysis and Contemporary Science.* 2:3-21. New York: Macmillan.

—— (1976). *Psychoanalytic Theory: An Exploration of Essentials.* New York: International Universities Press.

Klein, Melanie (1952). "Some Theoretical Conclusions Regarding the Emotional Life of the Infant." *Developments in Psycho-Analysis.* London: Hogarth Press.

—— (1957). *Envy and Gratitude.* New York: Basic Books.

—— (1975). *Love, Guilt and Reparation and Other World.* New York: Delta Books.

Kohut, Heinz (1957). "'Death in Venice'" by Thomas Mann: A story about the disintegration of artistic sublimation." *The Psychoanalytic Quarterly.* 26:206-228. (In Kohut 1978).

—— (1959). "Introspection, Empathy and Psychoanalysis: An examination of the Relationship Between Mode of Observation and Theory." *Journal of the American Psychoanalytic Association.* 7:459-483. (In Kohut 1978).

—— (1960). "Beyond the Bounds of the Basic Rule: Some Recent Contributions to Applied Psychoanalysis." *Journal of the American Psychoanalytic Association.* 8:567-586. (In Kohut 1978).

—— (1971). *The Analysis of the Self.* New York: International Universities Press.

—— (1977a). *The Restoration of the Self.* New York: International Universities Press.

—— (1977b). Preface to "Psychodynamics of Drug Dependence." National Institute on Drug Abuse Research, Monograph No. 12, U.S. Department of Health Education and Welfare, May 1977.

—— (1978). *The Search for the Self.* 2 Vols. Paul Ornstein, ed. New York: International Universities Press.

—— (1981). Summarizing Reflections at UCLA Conference on "Progress in Self Psychology," October 5, 1981.

—— (unpublished). *How Does Analysis Cure?*

—— (unpublished). "Four Basic Concepts of Self Psychology."

—— and Levarie, Siegmund (1950). "On the Enjoyment of Listening to Music." *The Psychoanalytic Quarterly.* 19:64-87. (In Kohut 1978).

—— and Wolfe, E. (1978). "The Disorders of the Self and their Treatment: An Outline." *International Journal of Psychoanalysis.* 59:413-426.

Lacan, Jacques (1977). *Écrits: A Selection.* New York: W. W. Norton.

Laing, R. D. (1960). *The Divided Self.* London: Tavistock Publications.

Langs, Robert (1976). *The Bipersonal Field.* New York: Jason Aronson.

—— (1978). *The Listening Process.* New York: Jason Aronson.

—— (1982). *Psychotherapy: A Basic Text.* New York: Jason Aronson.

—— and Searles, Harold F. (1980). *Intrapsychic and Interpersonal Dimensions of Treatment.* New York: Jason Aronson.

Lax, Ruth F., Bach, Sheldon and Burland, J. Alexis (1980). *Rapprochement.* New York: Jason Aronson.

LeBoit, Joseph and Capponi, Attilio (1970). *Advances in Psychotherapy of the Borderline Patient.* New York: Jason Aronson.

Lévi-Strauss, Claude (1949). "The Effectiveness of Symbols." In: *Structural Anthropology.* New York: Basic Books, 1963, pp. 186-205.

—— (1951). "Language and the Analysis of Social Laws." In: *Structural Anthropology.* New York: Basic Books, 1963, pp. 55-66.

Lichtenstein, Heinz (1961). "Identity and Sexuality: A Study of Their Interrelationship in Man." *Journal American Psychoanalytic Association.* 9:179-260.

—— (1964). "The Role of Narcissism in the Emergence and Maintenance of Primary Identity." *International Journal of Psychoanalysis.* 45:49-55.

—— (1965). "Towards a Metapsychological Definition of the Concept of Self." *International Journal of Psychoanalysis.* 46:117-128.

Lipton, Samuel D. (1977a). "The Advantages of Freud's Technique as Shown by His Analysis of the Rat Man." *International Journal of Psychoanalysis.* 58:255-274.

—— (1977b). "Clinical Observations on Resistance to the Transference." *International Journal of Psychoanalysis.* 58:463-472.

Little, Margaret (1981). *Transference Neurosis: Transference Psychosis.* New York: Jason Aronson.

Loewald, Hans W. (1960). "On the Therapeutic Action of Psychoanalysis." *International Journal of Psychoanalysis.* 41:16-33.

—— (1979). "The Waning of the Oedipal Complex." *Journal of American Psychoanalytic Association.* 27:(4) 751-776.

—— (1980). *Papers on Psychoanalysis.* New Haven: Yale University Press.

Mahler, Margaret (1968). *On Human Symbiosis and the Vicissitudes of Individuation,* Vol. I, *Infantile Psychosis.* New York: International Universities Press.

—— Pine, Fred and Bergman, Anni (1975). *The Psychological Birth of the Human Infant: Symbiosis and Individuation.* New York: Basic Books.

Masterson, James F. (1972). *Treatment of the Borderline Adolescent: A Developmental Approach.* New York: John Wiley and Sons.

—— (1976). *Psychotherapy of the Borderline Adult: A Developmental Approach.* New York: Brunner/Mazel Publishers.

—— (1978). *New Perspectives of the Borderline Adult.* (Contributions by Masterson, Searles, Kernberg, and Giovacchini). New York: International Universities Press.

—— (1981). *The Narcissistic and Borderline Disorders: An Integrated Developmental Approach.* New York: Brunner/Mazel Publishers.

Meissner, W. W. (1980). "The Problem of Internalization and Structure Formation." *International Journal of Psychoanalysis.* 61:237-247.

Meissner, W. W. (1981). *Internalization in Psychoanalysis.* New York: International Universities Press.

Modell, Arnold H. (1970). "The Transitional Object and the Creative Act." *Psychoanalytic Quarterly.* 39:240-250.

—— (1976). "'The Holding Environment' and the Therapeutic Action of Psychoanalysis." *Journal of the American Psychoanalytic Association.* 24:285-308.

Nelson, Marie Coleman (1977) (ed.). *The Narcissistic Condition: A Fact of Our Lives and Times.* New York: Human Sciences Press.

Oliker, Ditta (1978). *Klein, Balint, Winnicott.* Unpublished manuscript.

Oremland, Jerome (1980, unpublished) A discussion of Kernberg's 1980b lecture.

Ornstein, Paul (1981). "A New Perspective on the Curative Process in Psychoanalysis: A Summary of Kohut's Recent Views." Delivered at the Progress in Self Psychology Conference, U.C. Berkeley, October 5, 1981.

Pearce, Joseph C. (1974). *The Crack in the Cosmic Egg.* New York: Julian Press.

Peterfreund, E. (1971). "Information Systems and Psychoanalysis: An Evolutionary Biological Approach to Psychoanalytic Theory." *Psychological Issues.* Monograph No. 25/26. New York: International Universities Press.

—— and Franceschini, E. (1973). "On Information, Motivation and Meaning." *Psychoanalysis and Contemporary Science.* 2:220-262. New York: Macmillan.

Piaget, Jean (1937). *The Construction of Reality in the Child.* New York: Basic Books (1954).

—— (1962). *Play, Dreams and Imitation in Childhood.* New York: Norton.

Pine, Fred (1974). "On the Concept 'Borderline' in Children." *Psychoanalytic Study of the Child.* 29:341-368. New York: International Universities Press.

—— (1979). "On the Pathology of the Separation-Individuation Process as Manifested in Later Clinical Work: An Attempt at Delineation. *International Journal of Psychoanalysis.* 60:225–242.

Poe, Edgar Allan (1850). "The Poetic Principle." In Leon Edel, et al. *Masters of American Literature* (Vol. 1). Boston: Houghton Mifflin, 1959, pp. 256–262.

Rado, S. (1925). "The Economic Principle in Psychoanalytic Technique." *International Journal of Psychoanalysis.* 6:35–44.

Rank, B. and MacNaughton, D. (1950). "A Clinical Contribution to Early Ego Development." *The Psychoanalytic Study of the Child.* 5:53–65. New York: International Universities Press.

Rapaport, David (1950). "The Autonomy of the Ego." In *The Collected Papers.* ed. M. M. Gill. New York: Basic Books, 1967, pp. 356–367.

—— (1967). *The Collected Papers* of David Rapaport, ed. M. M. Gill. New York: Basic Books.

Rinsley, Donald (1968). "Economic Aspects of Object Relations." *International Journal of Psycho-Analysis.* 49:38–48.

Rosenfeld, H. (1965). *Psychotic States: A Psychoanalytic Approach.* New York: International Universities Press.

—— (1971). "A Clinical Approach to the Psychoanalytic Theory of the Life and Death Instincts: An Investigation into the Aggressive Aspects of Narcissism." *International Journal of Psychoanalysis.* 52:169–178.

—— (1972). "A Critical Appreciation of James Strachey's Paper on the Nature of the Therapeutic Action of Psychoanalysis." *International Journal of Psychoanalysis.* 53:455–462.

Rubenstein, Benjamin (1974). "On the Role of Classificatory Processes in Mental Functioning: Aspects of a Psychoanalytic Theoretical Model." *Psychoanalysis and Contemporary Science.* 3:101–185. New York: Macmillan.

—— (1976). "On the Possibility of a Strictly Clinical Psychoanalytic Theory: An Essay in the Philosophy of Psychoanalysis." In M. Gill and P. Holzman (eds.). *Psychology Versus Metapsychology: Psychoanalytic Essays in Memory of George S. Klein.* Monograph No. 36. New York: International Universities Press.

Russell, J. Michael (1978a). "Sartre, Therapy, and Expanding the Concept of Responsibility." *The American Journal of Psychoanalysis.* 38:259–269.

—— (1978b). "Saying, Feeling and Self-Deception." *Behaviorism.* 6(1):27–43.

—— (1979). "Sartre's Theory of Sexuality." *Journal of Humanistic Psychology.* 19(2): 35–45.

—— (1980). "How to Think about Thinking." *Journal of Mind and Behavior.* 1(1).

—— (in press). "Reflection and Self Deception" to appear in *Research and Phenomenology.*

Ryle, G. (1949). *The Concept of Mind.* New York: Barnes and Noble.

Sachs, Hanns (1933). "The Delay of the Machine Age." *Psychoanalytic Quarterly.* 2:404–424.

Sachs, Lisbeth (1957). "On Changes in Identification from Machine to Cripple." *The Psychoanalytic Study of the Child.* 12:356–375. New York: International Universities Press.

Sandler, Joseph (1960). "On the Concept of the Superego." *The Psychoanalytic Study of the Child.* 15:128–162. New York: International Universities Press.

—— (1976). "Countertransferences and Role Responsiveness." *The International Review of Psychoanalysis.* 3:34–47.

—— and Rosenblatt, Bernard (1962). "The Concept of the Representational World." *The Psychoanalytic Study of the Child.* 17:128–145. New York: International Universities Press.

—— Dare, and Holder (1973). *The Patient and the Analyst: The Basis of the Psychoanalytic Process.* New York: International Universities Press.

—— and Sandler, A. (1978). "On the Development of Object Relationship and Affects." *International Journal of Psychoanalysis.* 59:285–295.

Sartre, Jean-Paul (1956). (Tr. Hazel E. Barnes). *Being and Nothingness.* New York: Washington Square Press.

Saussure, F. de (1916). *Course in General Linguistics.* C. Bally and A. Sechehage (eds.) New York: McGraw Hill (1966).

Schafer, Roy (1976). *A New Language for Psychoanalysis.* New Haven: Yale University Press.

—— (1980). An Address "On Empathy and Psychoanalysis" presented to the Los Angeles Society for Psychoanalytic Psychology, March 7, 1980.

Schwaber, Evelyne, A., M.D. (1979). "Narcissism, Self Psychology and the Listening Perspective." Pre-presentation reading for lecture given at the University of California, Los Angeles Conference on The Psychology of the Self-Narcissism, October 5–7, 1979.

Searles, Harold F. (1960). *The Nonhuman Environment.* New York: International Universities Press.

—— (1965). *Collected Papers on Schizophrenia and Related Subjects.* New York: International Universities Press.

—— (1979). *Countertransference and Related Subjects. Selected Papers.* New York: International Universities Press.

Segal, Hanna (1962). "Symposium on Curative Factors in Psychoanalysis: III." *International Journal of Psychoanalysis.* 43:212–217.

—— (1973). *Introduction to the Work of Melanie Klein.* New York: Basic Books.

Spiegel, L. A. (1959). "The Self, the Sense of Self, and Perception." *The Psychoanalytic Study of the Child.* 14:81–109. New York: International Universities Press.

Spitz, R. A. (1959). *A Genetic Field Theory of Ego Formation.* New York: International Universities Press.

—— (1965). *The First Year of Life: A Psychoanalytic Study of Normal and Deviant Development of Object Relations.* New York: International Universities Press.

Spotnitz, Human (1976). *Psychotherapy of Preoedipal Conditions: Schizophrenia and Severe Character Disorders.* New York: Jason Aronson.

Stolorow, Robert D. and Atwood, George E. (1979). *Faces in a Cloud: Subjectivity in Personality Theory*. New York: Jason Aronson.

―――― and Lachman, Frank J. (1980). *Psychoanalysis of Developmental Arrests*. New York: International Universities Press.

―――― and Atwood, George E. (1981b). "Psychoanalytic Phenomenology of the Dream." Delivered as the William Menaker Memorial Lecture, New York University, New York, May 16, 1981. Also presented at the UCLA Conference on The Dream after 80 Years, Los Angeles, June 6–7, 1981.

Stone, Michael H. (1980). *The Borderline Syndromes*. New York: McGraw-Hill.

Strachey, J. (1934). "The Nature of the Therapeutic Action of Psychoanalysis." *International Journal of Psychoanalysis*. 50:275–292.

Sullivan, Harry Stack (1953). *The Interpersonal Theory of Psychiatry, the Collected Works* (2 Vols.). New York: W. W. Norton & Co.

Szasz, T. S. (1963). "The Concept of Transference." *International Journal of Psychoanalysis*. 44:432–443.

Tausk, Victor (1919). "On the Origin of the Influencing Machine in Schizophrenia." *The Psychoanalytic Quarterly*. 2:519–556.

Tolpin, Marian (1971). "On the Beginnings of a Cohesive Self: An Application of the Concept of Transmuting Internalization to the Study of the Transitional Object and Signal Anxiety." *The Psychoanalytic Study of the Child*. 26:316–352.

―――― (1978). "Self-Objects and Oedipal Objects: A Crucial Developmental Distinction." *Psychoanalytic Study of the Child*. 33:167–186. New York: International Universities Press.

Volkan, Vamik D. (1976). *Primitive Object Relations: A Clinical Study of Schizophrenia, Borderline and Narcissistic Patients*. New York: International Universities Press.

Waelder, R. (1936). "The Principle of Multiple Function: Observations on Over-Determination." In S. A. Guttman (ed.). *Psychoanalysis: Observations, Theory and Application*. New York: International Universities Press. 1976, pp. 68–83.

Werner, Heinz (1940, revised ed. 1957). *Comparative Psychology of Mental Development*. New York: International Universities Press.

Winnicott, D. W. (1949). "Hate in the Countertransference." *International Journal of Psychoanalysis*. 30:69–75.

―――― (1952). "Psychoses and Child Care." In *Through Paediatrics to Psycho-Analysis*. New York: Basic Books.

―――― (1953). "Transitional Objects and Transitional Phenomena: A Study of the First Not-Me Possession." *International Journal of Psychoanalysis*. 34:89–97.

―――― (1958, revised 1975). *Through Paediatrics to Psycho-Analysis*. New York: Basic Books.

―――― (1960). "The Theory of the Parent-Infant Relationship." In *The Maturational Process and the Facilitating Environment*. New York: International Universities Press, 1965, pp. 37–55.

―――― (1965). *The Maturational Processes and the Facilitating Environment*. New York: International Universities Press.

――― (1971). *Playing and Reality.* London: Tavistock.

Wittgenstein, Ludwig (1953). *Philosophical Investigations.* (G. E. M. Anscombe, tr.) New York: Macmillan Publishing Co., Inc.

Wolberg, Arlene Robbins (1973). *The Borderline Patient.* New York: Intercontinental Medical Book Corporation.

Zetzel, E. R. (1965). "The Theory of Therapy in Relation to a Developmental Model of the Psychic Apparatus." *International Journal of Psychoanalysis.* 46:39–52.

Index